E · n

D1796228

Lesbian, Gay and Queer Parenting

Palgrave Macmillan Studies in Family and Intimate Life

Titles include:

Graham Allan, Graham Crow and Sheila Hawker
STEPFAMILIES

Harriet Becher
FAMILY PRACTICES IN SOUTH ASIAN MUSLIM FAMILIES
Parenting in a Multi-Faith Britain

Elisa Rose Birch, Anh T. Le and Paul W. Miller
HOUSEHOLD DIVISIONS OF LABOUR
Teamwork, Gender and Time

Jacqui Gabb
RESEARCHING INTIMACY IN FAMILIES

Stephen Hicks
LESBIAN, GAY AND QUEER PARENTING
Families, Intimacies, Genealogies

Peter Jackson (*editor*)
CHANGING FAMILIES, CHANGING FOOD

Riitta Jallinoja and Eric Widmer (*editors*)
FAMILIES AND KINSHIP IN CONTEMPORARY EUROPE
Rules and Practices of Relatedness

Lynn Jamieson, Ruth Lewis and Roona Simpson (*editors*)
RESEARCHING FAMILIES AND RELATIONSHIPS
Reflections on Process

David Morgan
RETHINKING FAMILY PRACTICES

Eriikka Oinonen
FAMILIES IN CONVERGING EUROPE
A Comparison of Forms, Structures and Ideals

Róisín Ryan-Flood
LESBIAN MOTHERHOOD
Gender, Families and Sexual Citizenship

Tam Sanger
TRANS PEOPLE'S PARTNERSHIPS
Towards an Ethics of Intimacy

Elizabeth B. Silva
TECHNOLOGY, CULTURE, FAMILY
Influences on Home Life

Palgrave Macmillan Studies in Family and Intimate Life
Series Standing Order ISBN 978–0–230–51748–6 hardback 978–0–230–24924–0 paperback
(*outside North America only*)

You can receive future titles in this series as they are published by placing a standing order. Please contact your bookseller or, in case of difficulty, write to us at the address below with your name and address, the title of the series and one of the ISBNs quoted above.

Customer Services Department, Macmillan Distribution Ltd, Houndmills, Basingstoke, Hampshire RG21 6XS, England

---

Lesbian, Gay and Queer Parenting

Families, Intimacies, Genealogies

Stephen Hicks
University of Salford, UK

palgrave
macmillan

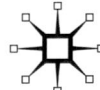

First published 2011 by
PALGRAVE MACMILLAN

Palgrave Macmillan in the UK is an imprint of Macmillan Publishers Limited, registered in England, company number 785998, of Houndmills, Basingstoke, Hampshire RG21 6XS.

Palgrave Macmillan in the US is a division of St Martin's Press LLC, 175 Fifth Avenue, New York, NY 10010.

Palgrave Macmillan is the global academic imprint of the above companies and has companies and representatives throughout the world.

Palgrave® and Macmillan® are registered trademarks in the United States, the United Kingdom, Europe and other countries.

ISBN: 978–0–230–59445–6

This book is printed on paper suitable for recycling and made from fully managed and sustained forest sources. Logging, pulping and manufacturing processes are expected to conform to the environmental regulations of the country of origin.

A catalogue record for this book is available from the British Library.

Library of Congress Cataloging-in-Publication Data

Hicks, Stephen, 1966–
    Lesbian, gay, and queer parenting : families, intimacies, genealogies / Stephen Hicks.
        p. cm.—(Palgrave Macmillan studies in family and intimate life)
    Includes index.
    ISBN 978–0–230–59445–6 (hardback)
    1. Gay parents—Great Britain. 2. Parenting—Great Britain.
3. Homosexuality—Great Britain. 4. Gays—Family relationships—Great Britain. 5. Lesbian—Family relationships—Great Britain. I. Title. II. Series
HQ75.28.G7H53 2011
306.874086'64—dc23   2011024169

10 9 8 7 6 5 4 3 2 1
20 19 18 17 16 15 14 13 12 11

Printed and bound in Great Britain by
CPI Antony Rowe, Chippenham and Eastbourne

Contents

Acknowledgements

I am very grateful to Helen Cosis Brown, Lynne Fanthome, Peggy Gillespie, Dharman Jeyasingham, Gigi Kaeser, Janet McDermott, Julianne Pidduck, Damien Riggs and Madeleine Walton for their generous comments on my book. My thanks also go to Phillipa Grand, Andrew James and Olivia Middleton at Palgrave Macmillan, to the members of the Northern Support Group for gay and lesbian foster carers and adopters (1994–2010), and to members of the Positive Parenting Campaign in Manchester (UK).

The author and publishers wish to thank the following for permission to reproduce copyright material: Gigi Kaeser and the University of Massachusetts Press for photographs and front cover from the *Love Makes a Family* book and exhibition (Family Diversity Projects, 2004–8; Kaeser and Gillespie, 1999).

Every effort has been made to contact all the copyright-holders but, if any have been inadvertently overlooked, the publishers would be pleased to make the necessary arrangements at the first opportunity.

Series Editors' Preface

The remit of the *Palgrave Macmillan Studies in Family and Intimate Life* series is to publish major texts, monographs and edited collections focusing broadly on the sociological exploration of intimate relationships and family organization. As editors, we think such a series is timely. Expectations, commitments and practices have changed significantly in intimate relationship and family life in recent decades. This is very apparent in patterns of family formation and dissolution, demonstrated by trends in cohabitation, marriage and divorce. Changes in household living patterns over the last 20 years have also been marked, with more people living alone, adult children living longer in the parental home, and more 'non-family' households being formed. Furthermore, there have been important shifts in the ways people construct intimate relationships. There are few comfortable certainties about the best ways of being a family man or woman, with once conventional gender roles no longer being widely accepted. The normative connection between sexual relationships and marriage or marriage-like relationships is also less powerful than it once was. Not only is greater sexual experimentation accepted, but it is now accepted at an earlier age. Moreover, heterosexuality is no longer the only mode of sexual relationship given legitimacy. In Britain, as elsewhere, gay male and lesbian partnerships are now socially and legally endorsed to a degree hardly imaginable in the mid-twentieth century. Increases in lone-parent families, the rapid growth of different types of stepfamily, the de-stigmatization of births outside marriage, and the rise in couples 'living-apart-together' (LATs) all provide further examples of the ways that 'being a couple', 'being a parent' and 'being a family' have diversified in recent years.

The fact that change in family life and intimate relationships has been so pervasive has resulted in renewed research interest from sociologists and other scholars. Increasing amounts of public funding have been directed to family research in recent years, in terms of both individual projects and the creation of family research centres of different hues. This research activity has been accompanied by the publication of some very important and influential books exploring different aspects of shifting family experience, in Britain and elsewhere. The *Palgrave Macmillan Studies in Family and Intimate Life* series hopes to add to this list of influential research-based texts, thereby contributing to existing knowledge and informing current debates. Our main audience consists of academics and advanced students, though we intend that the books in the series will be accessible to a more general readership who wish to understand better the changing nature of contemporary family life and personal relationships.

We see the remit of the series as wide. The concept of 'family and intimate life' will be interpreted in a broad fashion. While the focus of the series will clearly be sociological, we take family and intimacy as being inclusive rather than exclusive. The series will cover a range of topics concerned with family practices and experiences, including, for example, partnership; marriage; parenting; domestic arrangements; kinship; demographic change; intergenerational ties; life course transitions; stepfamilies; gay and lesbian relationships; lone-parent households; and also non-familial intimate relationships, such as friendships. We also wish to foster comparative research, as well as research on under-studied populations. The series will include different forms of book. Most will be theoretical or empirical monographs on particular substantive topics, though some may also have a strong methodological focus. In addition, we see edited collections as also falling within the series' remit, as well as translations of significant publications in other languages. Finally, we intend that the series has an international appeal, in terms of both topics covered and authorship. Our goal is for the series to provide a forum for family sociologists conducting research in various societies, and not solely in Britain.

GRAHAM ALLAN, LYNN JAMIESON AND DAVID MORGAN

1
Genealogy

Helen: And what's your part in this little Victorian melodrama? Nursemaid?
Jo: Serves you right for bringing her here, Geof.
Helen: It's a funny-looking set-up to me.
Jo: It's our business. (Delaney, 2000: 61)

A Taste of Honey

Jo, pregnant by her former lover Jimmie, sets up home with Geoffrey, a gay art student, in Shelagh Delaney's 1958 play, *A Taste of Honey*, filmed in 1961 by Tony Richardson. Geof asks Jo to marry him, she refuses, but they carry on with their own version of family life for a while. When compared with other relationships in Jo's life – her brief affair with Jimmie, her constant bickering with her mother and her mother's string of useless boyfriends – Geof offers Jo a sense of intimacy and constancy. Although she tells him that theirs is 'not marrying love', Jo also quips that she and Geof have 'been married for a thousand years' (Delaney, 2000: 76). They set up home together, and prepare for the baby. But, to Jo's mother, Helen, 'It's a funny-looking set-up' (Delaney, 2000: 61).

It is important to remember that, at the time both play and film were produced, homosexuality was illegal in the UK. According to Nicholas de Jongh, the Lord Chamberlain's Examiner required that the homosexual elements of Delaney's original script be reduced (de Jongh, 1992). Indeed, the word 'homosexual' is not mentioned in *A Taste of Honey* at all. Instead, Jo tells Geof she has always wanted to know about 'people like you' (Delaney, 2000: 48). In addition, the idea that a young woman with an 'illegitimate', mixed race child might set up home with a gay man was probably a lot more 'funny-looking' then than it might be today. Or maybe not? For the things that provoke Helen's response – male effeminacy and homosexuality, the idea of a heterosexual woman and a gay man setting up home together, a gay man offering to help bring up a child – elicit serious questions, then and now, about an appropriate way of living.

Much of this has to do with Geof and what he represents – homosexuality within a family setting. He is frequently referred to in terms that suggest effeminacy or a lack of proper manliness: he is 'a big sister' to Jo (Delaney, 2000: 54), she teases that he will 'make somebody a wonderful wife' (Delaney, 2000: 55), and – later – that he's 'just like an old woman' (Delaney, 2000: 72). Helen and her boyfriend, Peter, reject Geof's caring domesticity as unmanly. Helen's jibe, 'Nursemaid', feminizes Geof, and this is echoed in Peter's 'What's this, the father? Oh Christ, no!' Later, Peter calls Geof 'Lana,' 'Mary' and 'Cuddles' (Delaney, 2000: 65–6). Jo, on the other hand, teases Geof but, nevertheless, appreciates the intimacy she shares with him. Although she casts him in something of a 'surrogate mother' role (de Jongh, 1992: 92), at the same time she asks him if he'd like to be the 'father' of her child, to which he replies, 'Yes, I would' (Delaney, 2000: 57).

Still, this 'set-up' provokes concern. Philip Kemp's DVD liner notes, for example, describe Jo and Geof as 'like two children playing house, for a while finding an innocent and fragile happiness' (Kemp, 1998), and the spoken commentary by Murray Melvin (who played Geof in both the original stage play and film) suggests that, although today Jo and Geof might make a go of it, back in the 1960s this just wasn't possible (Melvin, 1998). The ending of the play and film also see Geof banished from the flat by Helen. This seems to put a stop to the relationship, although Jo's thoughts are with Geof at the close, and the audience is left with the possibility that he may return. Nevertheless, however fragile Jo and Geof's relationship might appear, Delaney contrasts this with a markedly pessimistic view of conventional heterosexuality through the character of Helen and her boyfriends. So, one question at the centre of *A Taste of Honey* is what place homosexuality has, or might have, within the context of intimacy, the family, and caring for children. But another might be how it could change those very forms.

Queer genealogies

This book begins to answer these questions through investigation of images and narratives by or about lesbian and gay parents, with a particular – but not exclusive – focus on those who foster or adopt children. It analyzes questions of kinship, family, everyday life, gender, race, state welfare and intimacy as concepts socially, rather than psychologically, produced and used. Whereas a lot of research on lesbian/gay parents is concerned with the interior self and identity, this book treats such concepts as powerful forms of knowledge, used to construct versions of gay parenting, family, kinship, and so on. I bring stories about lesbian/gay parents into contact with various sociological theories; especially those derived from interactionist, feminist, discursive and queer theories. My focus is on stories and images of everyday life, since I am interested to know how ideas about gender, race or sexuality are made relevant in quotidian situations and because I am interested to ask how the extraordinary is lived in ordinary circumstances. Being a *lesbian* or *gay* parent is currently a highly marked category since the terms 'lesbian' and 'gay' are not usually associated with those to do with family, children or parenting. Social categories have to do with the 'relations of inequality in which they are interwoven' (D. Smith, 2009: 79), and there are exclusionary practices that work to displace lesbians and gay men from imagined realms of lives involving family and parenting.

This book spends considerable time analyzing the everyday lives of lesbian and gay parents in order to present a complex and contradictory picture, one in which *essential*, *either/or* type arguments – gay parents are *essentially either* radical *or* assimilative – are rejected. And this is, in part, because I agree with Les Back that 'we have to allow the people about whom we write to be complex, frail, ethically ambiguous, contradictory and damaged' (Back, 2007: 157). But also, it is because research ought to grapple with complexity and engage theoretical perspectives with the messy world of everyday lives, as they are practised and accounted for. Try telling any lesbian or gay parent that they are *essentially* conservative or radical and you will be given a much more nuanced and contradictory account of life. And to represent gay parents' lives as somehow less queer, more queer, less radical, more radical, less conservative, more conservative than those of any other bisexual, lesbian, trans, gay or queer person is itself an exclusionary and hierarchical discursive move. To treat lesbian or gay families as essentially *anything*, is to 'thingify' them, a situation in which research would be 'reinforcing and *creating* in them – rather than "discovering" – the very thingified condition we have defined as "natural" ...' (Gouldner, 1975: 426).

It is possible, however, to find examples where this happens. Gay and lesbian parents are often represented as radical and different (in both negative and positive versions) or conservative and assimilative (negative and positive). The Christian right, for example, argues that gay families are negatively different to the standard family and, therefore, radically threatening. It designates the heterosexual, married couple a 'basic social institution' (Wardle, 1997: 898), a 'moral norm' (Morgan, 1995: 84), 'the quintessential network of bonding' (Almond, 2006: 206) and the 'gold standard' (Cameron, 1999: 282; Morgan, 2002: 44). Gay families are represented as a threat to the family and to children via assertions about confused gender roles; unstable relationships; poor social, sexual and psychological outcomes. However, a positive version of the radical/different theory also exists, and it is one in which gay families are made to stand for new, experimental and even postmodern ways of life. Judith Stacey, for example, says that 'queer families serve on the pioneer outpost of the postmodern family condition' (Stacey, 1996: 143), echoed in Anthony Giddens' work on intimacy (Giddens, 1991, 1992), and in Maureen Sullivan or Fiona Nelson's work on lesbian mothers (Nelson, 1996; Sullivan, 2004).

In the negative version of a conservative/assimilative account, *some* queer and feminist theorists suggest all gay parents are essentially aping heterosexuality, reinforcing the oppression of women or even contributing to what Michael Warner calls 'heteronormativity' (Warner, 1993: xxi). Claudia Card has suggested that 'many lesbian and gay couples do their best anyway to emulate heterosexual models, which usually means assuming the responsibilities without the privileges' (Card, 1996: 17), although it is largely the institution of motherhood, in its standard version, that she defines as oppressive to women. David Bell and Jon Binnie suggest that 'the struggle to define "families we choose" bears the mark of [a] privatization impulse, as if the retreat into family-space is a necessary strategy for claiming citizen status' (Bell and Binnie, 2000: 5). However, in the positive version of conservative/assimilative accounts, equally problematic claims are made (including by some gay and lesbian parents) that gay families are essentially the same as, akin to, heterosexuals and that questions about love, parenting and the labours of childcare – rather than sexuality – are all that matters (see some contributions to Gigi Kaeser and Peggy Gillespie's *Love Makes a Family*, 1999). This final version is present in many neo-liberal accounts of gay parenting, which emphasize universal family tropes over those to do with sexuality and questions about the heteronormative.

These versions of the gay family appear to opt for one or other side of an extraordinary/ordinary divide. The extraordinary is invoked in both conservative, anti-gay and radical, challenging accounts, while the ordinary sits at the heart of both assimilative and sameness models. This book, however, rejects such *either/or* models in favour of an approach that asks how and why gay parents might make use of both conformity and rebellion claims in everyday contexts. Either/or models have been rejected by others (Agigian, 2004; Clarke, 2002; Goldberg, 2010a; Hayden, 1995; Lewin, 2009; Riggs, 2007a; Ryan-Flood, 2009; Thompson, 2002; Weeks et al., 2001; Woodford et al., 2010), since, as Amy Hequembourg argues, the assimilative/resistance framework seems to fix people into 'subject positions that [reflect] only a rigid and limited understanding of their narrated experiences...lesbian mothers' subjectivities are not *completely* constituted by normalizing discourses, nor are they radical examples of resistance' (Hequembourg, 2007: 5 and 51).

This is not to dismiss the very interesting questions about how and why gay parents may challenge or subvert heteronormative ideas about, and practices of, family life, relationships and parenting. To say that gay families are not inherently subversive is not to say that they do not engage in some subversive or alternative claims and ways of life. This book asks how lesbian and gay parents challenge heteronormativity and why they deliberately assert 'difference' at times, but it also asks why there are occasions when blending into the background is necessary and how dominant discourses about family, sexuality, race and so on constrain creative forces.

My book analyzes interviews with about 15 lesbian or gay parents, mainly but not exclusively foster carers and adopters, carried out between 1992 and 2010. In some cases, I have re-interviewed people that I first spoke to many years ago. I also refer to interviews with about 30 foster care and adoption social workers and managers carried out for previous research (Hicks, 1998). In addition, I consider data generated through a case study, and materials taken from auto/biographical narratives, photographs, films, a formal inquiry into sexual abuse, and policy debates on gay and lesbian parents. The book asks questions about whether lesbian/gay parents create new kinship forms, whether a queer kinship is possible, and whether 'kinship' itself is a good way to think about social relations. I also ask whether lesbian/gay parents represent new forms of the family, why and how family claims are made in narrative and photographic forms, whether the chosen family is a helpful idea and what some of the problems with a 'love defines family' position might be. The book considers the everyday lives of gay/lesbian parents to ask how and why sexuality is made to matter in mundane contexts, how it is negotiated in relation to institutions and others, and how quotidian homophobia works. I spend two chapters looking at questions of gender and race, in order to ask how those categories are put to work in relation to lesbian/gay parenting and what work it is that they are made to do. I ask why concerns about gender role models, about gender identities, about racial 'types' and cultural forms are used, and how lesbian/gay parents negotiate those forms of knowing and doing. My book also considers the boundary between gay/lesbian parenting and state social welfare – particularly the fields of foster care and adoption – in order to ask how ideas about sexuality, and about sexual types, are produced and used within the ruling relations of institutional and state practices.

The problem with 'difference'

Judith Stacey and Timothy Biblarz's 2001 article, '(How) Does the Sexual Orientation of Parents Matter?', makes the point that much of the existing research on lesbian and gay parents 'almost uniformly ... reports findings of no notable differences between children reared by heterosexual parents and those reared by lesbian and gay parents.' Stacey and Biblarz argue there is an 'implicit hetero-normative presumption governing the terms of the discourse – that healthy child development depends upon parenting by a married heterosexual couple ... Because anti-gay scholars seek evidence of harm, sympathetic researchers defensively stress its absence (Stacey and Biblarz, 2001: 160). Much of the early research into lesbian and gay parenting was a direct response to such institutional and legal discrimination, in part written to challenge cases in which lesbians lost legal 'custody' of their children on the basis of their sexuality (Hanscombe and Forster, 1982; Martin and Lyon, 1972). Nan Hunter and Nancy Polikoff's work identified courts' 'assumptions that lesbianism is equivalent to, or tantamount to, unfit-ness' (Hunter and Polikoff, 1976: 714), and Donna Hitchens and Barbara Price advocated lessening 'the impact on the court of the mother's lesbi-anism, thus creating a situation where the mother may be judged on her own individualized merits' (Hitchens and Price, 1978/79: 479). This kind of legal discrimination was also repeated in prohibitions against gay or les-bian foster care and adoption; in denial of assisted fertilization/reproductive technologies to lesbian mothers; in the UK's Section 28 (1988–2000/03), which prohibited the teaching in any state school of 'the acceptability of homosexuality as a pretended family relationship' (Smith, 1994: 183); and in arguments that the children of lesbians or gay men would be likely to suffer abuse, distorted psychosexual development, mental health and peer-group problems or gender role confusion. For these reasons, early research set out to refute these suggestions and to challenge legal and institutional discrimination against gay and lesbian parents.

In the UK, Susan Golombok and Fiona Tasker's longitudinal study of lesbian families (1976/7–91) argued that the children of lesbian mothers showed no differences in peer-group relations (including being teased or bullied), sexual orientation or mental health. They were more likely to think about their sexuality and to try a same-sex experience, have better relation-ships with their mother's partner, and to recall teasing about homosexuality at school, even though this was not statistically significant in the study's terms (Golombok and Tasker, 1994, 1996; Golombok et al., 1983, 1997, 2003; Mooney-Somers and Golombok, 2000; Tasker, 2002, 2005; Tasker and Golombok, 1991, 1995, 1997). The authors argued boys were no less 'mascu-line', but that single and lesbian mothers might be 'explicitly encouraging their sons to have more sensitive and caring attitudes than the stereotypical male' (MacCallum and Golombok, 2004: 1416). Co-mothers 'in lesbian-led families played a more active role in daily caregiving than did most fathers in heterosexual families' (Tasker, 1999: 162). In further work with Helen Barrett, Tasker suggested that children of gay fathers knew about their par-ent's sexuality, with daughters being slightly more positive about this than sons (Barrett and Tasker, 2001: 71). Gay fathers were concerned about their children having to keep 'a family secret', about teasing or children being made to feel different (Barrett and Tasker, 2001: 73), but most felt able to deal with these challenges.

In the USA, the National Longitudinal Lesbian Family Study stated that lesbian mothers who had children through donor insemination were concerned about the effects of homophobia, but also that having a child resulted in their being more open about their lesbianism (Gartrell et al., 1996, 1999). Their children were healthy and well-adjusted (Gartrell et al., 2000, 2011; Van Gelderen et al., 2009), with similar social and psychologi-cal development to those in heterosexual families (Gartrell et al., 2005). The children did not report any physical or sexual abuse (Gartrell et al., 2010), and were resilient to any experienced homophobia (Bos et al., 2008b; Gartrell et al., 2006). The authors argued that 'an affirmative gay or lesbian social environment counter[s] the negative effects of homophobia on the psychological well-being of these children' (Bos et al., 2008a: 468). Interviews with adolescent children in the study indicated that they 'demonstrated higher levels of social, school/academic, and total competence than gender-matched normative samples of American teenagers' (Gartrell and Bos, 2010: 6).

Charlotte Patterson suggested that lesbian parents demonstrated 'egalitarian divisions of family labor' (Patterson, 1995: 118), although biological mothers reported doing more childcare. She argued that the children of lesbian mothers and gay fathers showed no problems in the development of 'normal' gender identity, sex role, sexual orientation, mental health, personal development, peer-group relations or intelligence, and concluded that 'not a single study has found children of gay or lesbian parents to be disadvantaged in any significant respect relative to children of heterosexual parents' (Patterson, 1992: 1036; and see Patterson, 2009). Richard Green's work on gay and transsexual parents also argued that children showed 'normal' gender and sexual identity development (Green, 1978, 1982) and a 'reasonable understanding' of trans parents' gender identities (Green, 1998: 3/5). These findings are repeated in many other studies and meta-analyses (Allen and Burrell, 1996; Anderssen et al., 2002; Bailey et al., 1995; Ball and Pea, 1998; Bozett, 1987; Brewaeys et al., 1993, 1997; Chan et al., 1998; Crowl et al., 2008; Fedewa and Clark, 2009; Flaks et al., 1995; Green and Bozett, 1991; Howard, 2006; Howard and Freundlich, 2008; King, 1991, 1995; Kirkpatrick, 1987; Kirkpatrick et al., 1981; Kweskin and Cook, 1982; McNeill et al., 1998; Millbank, 2003; Parks, 1998; Patterson and Wainwright, 2011; Pertman and Howard, 2011; Ryan and Brown, 2011; Steckel, 1987).

It is important to recognize the work that these studies have done in challenging notions of gay/lesbian parents as dangerous or damaging to their children, but this has also resulted in what Stacey and Biblarz refer to as defensive research (Stacey and Biblarz, 2001: 160) and claims that gay/lesbian families are no different than others. As Clarke et al. state, 'lesbian and gay parents are defensively and apologetically normalized, their sameness maximized, and their difference (including their sexual difference) minimized' (Clarke et al., 2004: 546). More nuanced studies are beginning to emerge that ask different questions; that is, rather than asking how gay/lesbian parents are 'just like' heterosexuals, studies are now asking about the specific and possibly different experiences of gay/lesbian families, and questioning the reinforcement of 'normality' in earlier studies (Agigian, 2004; Almack, 2007, 2008a, 2008b; Brodzinsky et al., 2011; Clarke, 2000, 2001; Gabb, 2001a, 2001b, 2005a, 2005b, 2008; Goldberg, 2010a; Hequembourg, 2007; Lev, 2010; Lewin, 2009; Perlesz et al., 2006a, 2006c; Riggs, 2006a, 2007a, 2010; Ryan-Flood, 2009; Taylor, 2009; Thompson, 2002). That is not to say that the Golombok/Tasker research or the National Longitudinal Lesbian Family Study do not consider questions of difference, since they do, and other studies have also reported on the differences of growing up with gay or lesbian parents and dealing with societal homophobic attitudes and values (Fairclough, 2008; Gartrell et al., 2010; Goldberg, 2007; Goldberg et al., 2008; Golombok et al., 2003).

Nevertheless, it is important to avoid simplistic 'gay/lesbian families *are different/are not different*' dichotomies, since these repeat and reinforce either/ or-type arguments, maintain the heterosexual as the norm, and fix lesbian/ gay families into essentialized positions. This is also about the avoidance of what I would term the ontologization of difference in relation to gay and lesbian parents/families, since questions of difference have to do with claims about, and reactions to, gay families within different (sometimes overtly homophobic) contexts, rather than essential qualities, 'variables' or 'outcomes'. This point may be illustrated by some of my concerns about the Stacey and Biblarz article (2001). Their review of research on gay parenting (up to 1998) leads them to suggest that 'on some dimensions – particularly those related to gender and sexuality – the sexual orientation of these parents matter somewhat more for their children than the researchers claimed' (Stacey and Biblarz, 2001: 167). That is, although they view such differences in a positive light, Stacey and Biblarz attribute particular gender identity and sexual orientation outcomes to the children of lesbians and gay men. They find no such differences in the areas of psychological well-being, cognitive function, social adjustment or quality of relationships, but they do say:

> Children with lesbigay parents appear less traditionally gender-typed and more likely to be open to homoerotic relationships. [The evidence] hints that parental sexual orientation is positively associated with the possibility that children will be more likely to attain a similar orientation – and theory and common sense also support such a view … This may be partly due to genetic and family socialization processes, but what sociologists refer to as 'contextual effects' not yet investigated by psychologists may also be important. (Stacey and Biblarz, 2001: 176 and 178)

This is a highly problematic set of claims for a number of reasons. First, existing research does not support the view that the children of gay and lesbian parents will be 'likely to attain a similar orientation'. I can find no evidence of this, but there are studies which argue that children of lesbian or gay parents are more likely to consider and try out a same-sex experience or relationship (Gartrell et al., 2010; Tasker and Golombok, 1997). Of course, it is important to support Stacey and Biblarz's anti-heteronormative stance, part of which is to ask why it would be a problem if the children of lesbians and gay men were to become gay, but that is not the same thing as saying that there is an existing association of gay parents with gay children in the research. Indeed, Golombok et al., in reply to Stacey and Biblarz, have said:

> classifying studies as showing a difference even in cases where this difference was true for only a small number of variables out of many and by failing to consider the spurious differences that result from chance effects when large numbers of individual variables are studied, Stacey and Biblarz (2001) have overemphasized the differences that have been reported between children with lesbian and heterosexual parents. (Golombok et al., 2003: 21)

Second, to suggest that this association is supported by 'theory and common sense' is dangerous since there is a 'common sense' assertion that children of gay/lesbian parents will 'turn out gay'; one that is also claimed by right wing, Christian and other opponents of all gay parenting. Some of the press reporting of the Stacey and Biblarz piece did, indeed, read it as evidence that 'gay parents create gay kids' (Bronski, 2001). More importantly, however, my objection to this is epistemological. Any 'difference' that is claimed, imputed or even experienced in relation to lesbian or gay families and their children is just that – an effect of discourses and practices that locate, define and maintain the idea of that 'difference' – but it is not a result of essential characteristics.

Stacey and Biblarz's version of difference does talk about the possibility of social/contextual 'effects', but still their work sees gender and sexual identity as discernable and transmittable variables. In addition, they take up what I would see as a naïve position in which 'a difference *really is* just a difference' (Stacey and Biblarz, 2001: 164), a point that ignores the fact that difference is rarely, if ever, imputed to the heterosexual family/parent since heterosexuality is taken as the norm from which others are said to deviate. In my view, this actually contributes to heteronormative values. Reliance upon gender and sexuality as variables or measurable outcomes in children, as things acquired and affected by 'parental genes, practices, environment, or beliefs' (Stacey and Biblarz, 2001: 163), is not a view of gender/sexuality that this book supports. In Chapter 5 on gender, for example, I challenge another piece by Biblarz and Stacey (2010) for its reliance upon the 'thingification' of gender. Gender and sexuality are not things acquired through genetics or family socialization, and this book spends considerable time challenging such views.

Assessment for adoption: whose perspective?

In 1998, Corinne Aves, a child psychotherapist, published an article 'Assessment for adoption: the child's perspective' in the *Journal of Social Work Practice*, the journal of the Group for the Advancement of Psychodynamics and Psychotherapy in Social Work (Aves, 1998). This article talks about a nine-year-old, Asian girl called Mina and her subsequent placement for adoption with a lesbian couple, Marisa and Judy:

> We [that is, Aves and her social work colleague] wondered how Mina would cope with the intensity of life as an only child with two intensely devoted parents. It was something she had not experienced. Since losing her mother she had, on the contrary expended a great deal of mental energy in remaining separate and unclaimed. From Mina's point of view there might be dangers in close relationships with mother figures.
>
> My colleague and I were also concerned for her emotional and sexual development, especially during adolescence. Mina had very little experience of good paternal figures ... and this taken with the fact that she had been placed with a lesbian couple could well be a recipe for confusion around a developing sexual identity. (Aves, 1998: 36)

This is a fascinating narrative since, although Aves is not opposed to the adoptive placement (she describes Marisa and Judy as 'sensitive ... realistic and thoughtful'), she ascribes a negative 'intensity' to lesbian adopters. This use of 'intensity/intensely' along with the 'dangers' that Aves ascribes to 'close relationships with mother figures' attributes some kind of threat to the situation. Rather than seeing Marisa and Judy as committed adopters likely to share the care of Mina, Aves sees this as intense and dangerous. Her use of 'mother figures' is also interesting as she clearly sees Marisa and Judy as potentially replacing Mina's mother, Savi. Aves doesn't seem to be able to conceive of a model in which a child might have more than one mother, and instead expects a complete break with the birth mother. Aves' model of replacement by a new 'mother figure' is also thrown into confusion here by there being two female adopters. For me, this kind of break/replacement model of adoption is implicitly heteronormative, since it does not allow for the possibility that Mina might retain contact with her mother, Savi, whilst living with Marisa and Judy. David Eng has argued that such 'psychic' possibilities must be acknowledged if we are to exceed 'traditional notions of marriage, family, and social alliances' (Eng, 2010: 137).

Aves also raises concerns about 'emotional and sexual development', which she clearly sees as threatened with 'confusion' by placement with a lesbian couple. Aves makes use of gender role model theory, referring to Mina's lack of 'good paternal figures', and interprets a lesbian adoptive couple as lacking in positive male role models – a point that I take up in detail in Chapter 5 on gender. Here, it is crucial to note that Aves suggests Mina might develop a confused 'sexual identity' because she has lesbian carers. These two arguments – that lesbian/gay parents cannot provide proper gender role models, and that they might cause emotional and sexual identity confusion in children – are frequently used to oppose gay parenting, and here they form part of what I would interpret as Aves' heteronormative expectations about family/adoptive life.

In 1999, Marisa and Judy wrote two responses to the Aves piece (Marisa and Judy, 1999a, 1999b), which they have allowed me to quote and analyze. These raise some very interesting responses to, and different perspectives on, the case of Mina. First, the couple argues that they had been shown a report from the psychotherapy clinic 'which described Mina as being totally identified with her birth mother, unable to detach from her, and therefore highly unlikely to be able to cope with adoption' (Marisa and Judy, 1999a: 2). This seems to chime with Aves' concerns about Mina's ability to make an emotional break with her birth mother. Marisa and Judy describe their experiences of the clinic as 'hostile to the adoption and dismissive of our abilities to help Mina deal with her past', in part because they did not expect Mina to make any such break with her birth mother. They say, 'it was our clear contention throughout this process that we did not expect Mina to make this kind of break immediately and that we were committed to working with her over a long period to reconcile her feelings for Savi with her move into a new family' (Marisa and Judy, 1999a: 5).

Second, Marisa and Judy objected to the idea that they ought to be seen as replacement 'mummies' for Savi. They say that, in their approach, 'there were no rigid expectations placed on her [Mina] that a traditional nuclear family might have had of her. We told her from the beginning that she didn't have to call us Mummy, which came as an enormous relief to her as she clearly felt calling us Mummy would be disloyal' (Marisa and Judy, 1999a: 3).

Third, the couple took issue with Aves' concerns about male role models and the potential for Mina to develop a confused emotional and sexual identity:

Corinne [Aves] raised concerns about a lack of male figures in our lives, forcing us to explain the positive relationships we have with the men in our lives and the positive relationships Mina was developing with our male relatives, especially Marisa's father, and with various of our male friends. Mina has no problems relating to men and we have explained that her sexuality will emerge in its own way and she may be bisexual, heterosexual or gay and that any of these is fine. Indeed she knows that to be true as we have friends who identify in all these ways. It seemed to us that there were much more central questions to be addressed, around our ability to understand Mina's frame of reference and meet her where she was in order to help her move forward, than the quality of the male role models we had to offer, and we wondered to what extent the … Clinic has done work with its own staff around homophobia and stereotyping of lesbians and gay men. (Marisa and Judy, 1999a: 4)

This point contests the supposed need for parental gender role models and the association of gay/lesbian parenting with a confused – read 'gay, lesbian or bisexual' – sexual identity in children, a point that Marisa and Judy later characterized as 'homophobic. It runs contrary to all the available research ... and it also carries the implication that it is preferable for children to develop heterosexual identities' (Marisa and Judy, 1999b: 2).

Finally, Marisa and Judy objected to what they saw as psychologization of themselves by the clinic/professionals in this case. They say there was 'an assumption that we had come for therapy or support ourselves. We were indeed open and shared in good faith some of our anxieties and concerns around parenting Mina. We found ourselves being reassured and analysed in a way that felt patronising and objectified us' (Marisa and Judy, 1999a: 4) – exemplified, for me, in Aves' description of some of Marisa's 'fears' as 'extraordinary fantasy' (Aves, 1998: 35). Of course, this point might be disputed, and that is exactly one of the problems with Aves' piece, as I see it. Although she names her article 'the child's perspective', I would argue that the piece is quite clearly Corinne Aves' perspective, just as Marisa and Judy's points are theirs, and this overview account is mine. That is, *none* of these is actually Mina's perspective at all. A letter from the journal editors to Marisa and Judy asks them to maintain a focus on the child's experience, but the couple says, 'the point of our article ... is to present the prospective adopter's perspective. We also take issue with Corinne Aves' claim to be presenting the child's perspective as she is manifestly presenting her own' (Marisa and Judy, 1999b: 1). As they say, the 'whole point is that therapy *is* contested' (Marisa and Judy, 1999b: 1).

This vignette nicely illustrates some themes key to my analysis in this book. My approach differs markedly from that of Aves', since I am troubled by her insistence on the psychologization of concepts. Debates about the possible meanings of Marisa and Judy's adoption of Mina are turned into interior states such as confusion, fantasy or unconscious processes, none of which may be proven but all of which are asserted by Aves as though merely descriptive. Marisa and Judy object to this, and the approach I take in this book objects to such narrative realism too, since it allows a therapist to present her own heteronormative concerns about gender and sexuality as reasonable whilst excluding the concerns of others as 'fantasy', for example. In addition, I would argue that Aves' piece rejects the possibility of extended relational forms beyond the conventional family through her notions of the impossibility of having more than one mother, or the concerns about the potential intensity and damage that a lesbian couple might personify.

There are also questions of what Jonathan Potter terms 'stake' here, since for Aves to claim to speak 'the child's perspective' is to inoculate herself against accusations that she is, in fact, speaking in her own interests (Potter, 1996: 125). Aves attempts to head off accusations of homophobia, or of speaking in her interests, by suggesting she speaks *for Mina's*. This book pays attention to claims and contested claims about gay parents because there are questions of power and hierarchy involved in who speaks and who speaks for others. To speak *for* an adopted child, to speak *for* lesbians, is a powerful act that also involves the exclusion of other voices (as 'fantasy', for example). This is clearly a problem with psychoanalytically-based accounts, in my view, since these involve claims or interpretations about the interior states of others – and the idea that such interior states exist – as though factual.

Lesbian/gay parenting and discourse

My research engages with narratives and practices concerning lesbian and gay parenting within everyday contexts, and this means that I pay attention to how concepts and categories are produced and put to use. Christian right-wing authors have accused me of merely presenting 'self-congratulatory testimonials' (Morgan, 2002: 49), another exclusionary practice of knowledge, whilst other researchers working in the field of lesbian family studies suggest that I am 'overly sensitive to status claims in everyday language' (Perlesz et al., 2006b: 233). But my 'sensitivity' is part of a commitment to consider how 'phenomena arise in, through, and from actual people's here-and-now, located, and coordinated practices' (de Montigny, 2007: 98). By this, I mean that concepts and categories – such as kinship, family, race, gender, sexuality, lesbian, gay, and so on – matter, or are made to matter, within what George Smith termed the 'concrete, sensuous world of people's actual practices' (Smith, 1990: 633). That is, they are social – rather than psychological or personal – categories, which require we not take them for granted. Using an evocative phrase taken from the work of C. Wright Mills, I would hope readers, when encountering such categories, feel 'as if suddenly awakened in a house with which they had only supposed themselves to be familiar' (Mills, 2000: 8). This book, then, questions *familiarity* on many levels.

Paul Baker has called for:

> a critical consciousness of the power of everyday language in all its forms to shape discourses of gender and sexuality, the ways that the dozens of different types of 'texts' that we encounter on a daily basis inform, persuade, normalise and taboo. (Baker, 2008: 263)

And so, in this spirit, this book treats narratives and images of lesbian/gay parenting not as mere descriptions of events or attitudes, but rather as performative. That is, they are engaged in the work of assertion, claim, counter-claim, and so on, a process that includes my text – this text – as much as any other (Stanley and Wise, 1993). As Paul Atkinson has argued in relation to personal narratives, these are 'as conventional and as artful as any other mode of representation' (Atkinson, 1997: 341; see also Stanley, 1992), and so it is important to analyze how and why narratives are made to work and what work it is that they are doing. Michel Foucault's account of discourses describes these as forms of talk or regulated statements and practices that produce 'the objects of which they speak' (Foucault, 2002: 54), which are involved in processes of exclusion, prohibition, claims to the ir/rational and truth/falsity (Foucault, 1981). This means that we are subject to discourse, or that we have to find a place within discourse, and this may become problematic for gay/lesbian parents for two reasons. First, at the level of words, it becomes hard to describe new relational forms adequately: what are we to call the adopted child's two lesbian parents? What words can be used to describe the non-biological (or non-birth) lesbian mother? What are friends-as-family or important, primary friend-relations to be termed? There are plenty of creative and interesting responses to these questions, yet most of these remain unrecognized within wider discourses. Second, subject positions must be taken up within discourses, and so to be recognized as a legitimate subject may be to make use of traditional or dominant conceptions of family, relationality or parenting, at times.

Knowledge is a social form in which questions of hierarchy are relevant, and so this book also considers the co-production of meaning within discourse. The dialogue between a gay adoptive applicant and a state social worker, or that between my research participants and me, are the contexts in which meaning is produced. And those contexts are also examples of the ways in which questions to do with race, gender, sexuality and so on, are made relevant. That is, the presentation of self/identity as a lesbian/gay potential foster carer or adopter, for example, is made sense of through state welfare organizational practices. Or, as Christine Cocker has put it, it's a case of the 'state being in your sitting room' (Cocker, 2011: 158). For that reason, my book considers discourses 'outside of' the immediate text/conversation (Wetherell, 1998), since I am interested in how the taking up of subject positions is influenced by wider discursive and institutional forms. As Judith Butler notes, 'one invariably struggles with conditions of one's own life that one could not have chosen. If there is an operation of agency or, indeed, freedom in this struggle, it takes place in the context of an enabling and limiting field of constraint' (Butler, 2005: 19).

However, it is important to examine language-use in context too, since the taking up or imputing of categories and subjectivities occurs within narrative complexity. Susan Speer reminds us that we should avoid treating concepts like 'homophobia' merely as pre-existing, fixed 'attitudes' held by particular individuals (a point that I develop in Chapter 5 on gender), since this is not 'something one can easily identify in specific prejudiced terms or utterances prior to an analysis' (Speer, 2005: 173). Neither would all concerned agree on something called a 'homophobic' incident or piece of talk. Further, my book also draws upon aspects of category membership analysis, since I am interested in the ways in which category work – the taking up or naming of others as gay, lesbian, black, Asian, masculine, feminine, and so on – is used to make and remake identities and ways of knowing about the social world. Dorothy Smith has reminded us of the importance of not taking such categories as 'already given' (Smith, 1990a: 159), and Peter Eglin and Stephen Hester suggest that 'categories are interactionally deployable in formulating locations, doing accusations, making excuses, allocating blame, finding a motive, telling a story, and so on' (Eglin and Hester, 2003: 9).

Queer theories

Foucault's *History of Sexuality, Volume 1* asks us:

> to account for the fact that [sex] is spoken about, to discover who does the speaking, the positions and viewpoints from which they speak, the institutions which prompt people to speak about it and which store and distribute the things that are said. What is at issue, briefly, is the over-all 'discursive fact,' the way in which sex is 'put into discourse'. (Foucault, 1990: 11)

This requires us to treat 'sexuality', not as 'a kind of natural given which power tries to hold in check, or as an obscure domain which knowledge tried gradually to uncover', but rather as 'the name that can be given to a historical construct' (Foucault, 1990: 105). Foucault's point was, in part, that relations of power have established sexuality as an object of knowledge, and that sexual 'types', similarly, designate ways of thinking and talking about persons, bodies and desires. These notions have been taken up within queer theories, in order to ask how hetero/homo-relations have been used to structure forms of knowledge (Sedgwick, 1994a; Turner, 2000) and to posit 'heterosexuality and homosexuality as categories marking the truth of selves' (Seidman, 1997: 93). Thinking back to Aves' suggestions about Mina's potential emotional/sexual identity confusion due to adoption by a lesbian couple (Aves, 1998), for example, we have a:

> heavily psychologised model of sexual subjectivity – which knits up desire, its objects, sexual behavior, gender identity, reproductive function, mental health, erotic sensibility, personal style, and degrees of normality or deviance into an individuating, normativizing feature of the personality called 'sexuality' or 'sexual orientation'. (Halperin, 1998: 97)

That is, a heteronormative account of proper sexual identity development in adolescents is at risk due to the imagined gender/sexual deviance inherent in Aves' account of the lesbian adoptive couple. Gayle Rubin has pointed out that 'sexuality is political. It is organized into systems of power, which reward and encourage some individuals and activities, while punishing and suppressing others' (Rubin, 1993: 34), and so queer theory must also ask how sexual 'types', such as the lesbian adopter, are produced and put to work in the knowledge-making activities of institutional practices such as state social and psychological welfare. But we also need to ask how heteronormativity is not solely related to questions of sexuality, but also to ideas about ways of life, relationships and parenting as a whole (Berlant and Warner, 1995; Jackson, 2006; Jackson and Scott, 2010).

Research by Jeffrey Weeks, Brian Heaphy and Catherine Donovan has argued that there are difficult topics/practices 'where society remains most anxious about non-heterosexual ways of life, where the boundaries are still most heavily policed. Parenting...remains on this disputed border' (Weeks et al., 2001: 186). As I will argue in this book, gay and lesbian parents are often positioned at the borders of what is seen to be conservative/radical, same/different, private/public, natural/social, immoral/moral, familial/queer, invisible/visible, personal/political, racially unmarked/marked, or intimate/disconnected. That is, the categories of 'lesbian parent/gay parent' are used to stand for, and to make claims about, questions to do with knowledge, morality, society and hierarchy. I have made use of aspects of queer theory that I take to be concerned with challenging the 'facticity' (Kessler and McKenna, 1985: 99) of claims about lesbian/gay parents, since I am keen to indulge a 'historicized reading of categories that begins with a refusal to accept the "naturalness" or inevitability of those categories...[one which] involves the effort to find the choices, accidents, and circumstances that brought particular categories into use as means for dividing up persons into types' (Turner, 2000: 32).

Queering children, queering parenting

For some theorists, the figure of the gay/lesbian parent (and often the adopter, in particular) serves as a personification of the anti-queer, since they argue that all gay parenting is assimilative, a conservative form of politics that wishes gay people to emulate heterosexuals and to disappear into mainstream ways of living. Bell and Binnie, for example, suggest that arguments about chosen families are a form of privacy politics, and that 'many of' these people 'would count themselves as hostile towards...queer forms of alternative citizenship' (Bell and Binnie, 2000: 136). They describe most arguments for gay parenting as 'buying into the ideology of the family as the organizing logic of intimate and social life' (Bell and Binnie, 2000: 138).

I also find similar dismissals of lesbian/gay parents as non-queer/anti-queer in work by Judith Halberstam. She says, 'when so many middle-class gays and lesbians are choosing to raise children in conventional family settings, it is important to study queer life modes that offer alternatives to family time and family life' (Halberstam, 2005: 153). Halberstam also argues for 'a "forgetting of family" ... in order to allow for the possibility of other modes of relating, belonging, caring, and so on' (Halberstam, 2007: 317). This notion that the lesbian/gay parent stands for a return to conservative kinship and family politics is also present in other queer theories, and so it is part of the purpose of this book to ask why gay/lesbian parenting cannot be a queer practice. That is, I ask why it is that *some* theorists/narratives fix gay/lesbian parents into anti-queer positions, and I suggest, instead, that the complexities of gay/lesbian parents' lives – and the many different subjectivities taken up by those within that category – allow for queer possibilities.

Of course, Bell, Binnie, Halberstam and others are asking important questions about a kind of conservative citizenship politics that is based on recognition of particular forms of gay relations only, the couple (preferably state registered, possibly with children). In addition, Halberstam is challenging the notion that all lives (all recognizable lives) must be lived according to standard notions of temporality, the idea that only those who form long-term relationships and who go on to have children are properly 'mature'. The infantilization of gay and lesbian lives ('the boys', 'the girls') is just one of many ways in which heteronormativity works. But to assume that all lesbian/gay parents take up, or wish to take up, a conservative/mainstream subject position is to ignore the complex dynamics of relationality that are enacted within the category of 'the gay parent': how mainstream is the single, lesbian foster carer, really? Or, the gay couple and the bisexual woman who live together and have three children? Or, the single gay man who has fostered over 40 children and adopted three? Or, the racially mixed lesbian couple with three adopted Asian girls?

There are advocates for gay parenting who promote a respectable/mainstream position, of course. Dan Savage has said that many gay parents 'have decided that we want to fill our time with something more meaningful than sit-ups, circuit parties and designer drugs. For me and my boyfriend, bringing up a child is a commitment to having a future' (Savage, 1998: 95, cited in Edelman, 2004: 75). Ben, a gay father by surrogacy in Ellen Lewin's book *Gay Fatherhood*, says:

> you see these older gay men participating in the party scene and you wonder. Some of this is sort of pathetic, and you wonder how long are we going to want to be in that part of the gay scene and not sort of finding reward and value and pleasure exploring different aspects of gay life ... You know, the priority of getting to the gym and looking good and going out. And then the restaurants, and then this and that. And it's just such an antithesis of what we're doing. We're just trying to make it through the day and make sure these kids are both okay. (Ben, in Lewin, 2009: 108 and 169)

Lewin comments, 'it is not unusual for fathers to declare their new lives as parents to be morally superior to being gay – less selfish, more adult, more constructive. These men often disparage gay life as frivolous and lacking in real significance' (Lewin, 2009: 184). David Strah, in *Gay Dads*, has argued:

> One of the men profiled ... says that gay men having children is a sign that they are growing up. I agree with him. If coming out was the first step and forming a movement the second, then perhaps asserting our fundamental right to be parents is the third step in our evolution as a community. It's a step out of the ghetto-like colonies many of us understandably walked into when we came out as gay men. (Strah with Margolis, 2003: 7)

For me, these statements promote hierarchy and moral superiority between gay people. These particular gay dads pick on and, as Lewin says, disparage certain aspects of *some* gay lives (the gym; the gay scene; sex; drugs; even, horror-of-horrors, restaurants) in order to seek recognition for their own status as gay fathers, a position that is described in terms of selflessness, maturity, futurity and meaning. And here, queer theorists, such as Lee Edelman, are right to point out that the association made between parenting/children and the future good of society is a commonly used trope designed to create 'the queer' as a figure of repulsion or abjection (Edelman, 2004). So, part of my argument in this book will be to ask difficult questions about morally superior stances taken up by some gay parents, when they occur.

But to position all gay parents as conservative/respectable types, as some queer theorists do, is just as problematic I think. Apart from ignorance of the complexity of positions or claims taken up by gay/lesbian parents, this does not take account of contexts in which claims to respectability or even normality might be understandable. Yvette Taylor's research on working class gay/lesbian parents demonstrates this point, since those on low incomes or state benefits struggle to achieve any kind of 'respectability' and may wish to pass, or be taken as, 'normal' at times (Taylor, 2009). That is, to be accepted by others – to be recognized as a legitimate subject – is something that we all participate in, even those who are interested in a transgressive version of queer theory/lives. In addition, why treat all lesbian/gay parents as a homogenous group (Bell and Binnie's 'many of' them; Halberstam's claim that they are all 'middle-class')? And why assume that all gay parents are hostile to the queer? Isn't the rejection of gay parents by other gay people just as hostile or exclusive? Aren't there just as many trans, bisexual, lesbian or gay non-parents who perform conservative or assimilative practices and claims? Do all gay parents really 'buy into the ideology of the family'? Certainly, the narratives of the lesbian/gay parents in this book are far more complicated – with many, for example, deliberately asking questions of and challenging standard notions of the family. And, in relation to those who have fostered or adopted children, those questions come not only in the form of questioning the heterosexuality of standard family notions, but also a questioning of relationalities based upon blood/genetics and 'marriage-like' ties.

The particular strand of queer theory that I am objecting to – and it is only a strand, since there is plenty of queer theory in this book – is one that has developed in response to Leo Bersani's 'anti-social' thesis in *Homos* (Bersani, 1995). Part of Bersani's argument was that attempting 'to "resignify" the family for communities that defy the usual assumptions about what constitutes a family ... while valuable, can have assimilative rather than subversive consequences' (Bersani, 1995: 5). He suggests that attempts by some gays to blend into straight society involve claims to be 'good parents' among others (Bersani, 1995: 42), and proposes, instead, that we question 'the value of community and, even more fundamentally, the notion of relationality itself' (Bersani, 1995: 52).

This argument has been taken up more forcefully, and specifically in relation to questions about children, by Edelman (2002, 2004, 2006, 2007). In *No Future*, he argues that to be in the (best) interests of children has become an unquestioned social value linked to the notion of 'reproductive futurism' (Edelman, 2004: 3). Edelman's argument is that the queer must oppose this kind of standpoint, since 'queerness *should* and *must* redefine such notions as "civil order" through a rupturing of our foundational faith in the reproduction of futurity' (Edelman, 2004: 17). In Edelman's argument, it is pertinent that the lesbian, gay, bisexual or trans parent becomes a symptom of anti-queer assimilation; he says the 'appeal of futurity [and] ... the temptation to reproduce' are hard to 'resist', since *all* queers, he says, are 'psychically invested in preserving the familiar familial narrativity of reproductive futurism' (Edelman, 2004: 17). Instead, Edelman argues for a queer disturbance of social organization, since he suggests that, while right-wing theorists wish to eliminate queers, the left 'seeks to normalize queerness ... as merely a type of "sexual expression"' (Edelman, 2002: 184). He argues, rather, for 'a project that's willing to forgo the privilege of social recognition and so is willing to break the compact binding the image of the human to a social order speciously conflated with kinship and collectivity, the compact adduced to foreclose dissent from reproductive futurism by assuming the ontologized identity of futurism and sociality itself' (Edelman, 2007: 473).

John Brenkman's response to Edelman's thesis makes the point that there is no gay or lesbian life outside of the social (Brenkman, 2002a), and he objects to Edelman's casting of 'all social and political reforms as in essence perpetuations of the anti-queer imperatives of the social-symbolic order', with queer somehow 'beyond politics' (Brenkman, 2002b: 176). He says, 'while queer sexualities are obviously in this historical moment anti-social, it does not follow that they are the very embodiment or enactment of asociality or the asymbolic. What has given, for example, anonymous sex its value in the gay community – what has made it worth fighting for – is its role in creating an alternative sociality' (Brenkman, 2002b: 180). This is an important point since, for my purposes, there can be no sociological account of, or interest in, lesbian/gay parenting or, indeed, in questions of queer theory/practice, outside of the social or outside of some form of inter-action and relationality. Of course, it's important not to simplify Edelman's arguments here; it is particular forms of social recognition – the representa-tion of the responsible parent as (invested in) the future – that he is queer-ing, yet his argument for a space outside of politics and for a practice of negativity seems to cast queers outside of any subjectivities that might take up questioning, playful, contradictory and connected positions.

Lynne Fanthome has argued that Edelman is, of course, right to note that associations of the queer and the child are used to 'produce powerful homo-phobic effects' (Fanthome, 2007: 2):

> I agree with both Lee Edelman and Judith Butler that to urge for social and political change by attempting to 'humanise' the queer may not only fail, where empathy and recognition are denied to those maintained beyond recognition, but also may more insidiously bind into normative schemes of recognition. (Fanthome, 2007: 3)

But Fanthome also argues against Edelman's 'urging to *ditch the child* because this act fixes "the child" in an injurious and antagonistic rela-tion to the queer' (Fanthome, 2007: 3). She makes the important point that actually 'the child', just like the queer, can represent uncertainty and instability in relation to supposed normative schemas of human develop-ment, and reminds us that 'the "childish", irresponsible queer' (Fanthome, 2007: 6) is a key trope that associates the two figures outside of proper human development, as evident in the examples from the gay dads, Savage, Strah and Ben, that I discussed earlier (pp. 17–18). Fanthome also questions Halberstam's embrace of 'the terms of immaturity' and argues that het-ero/homo differences – or even anti-queer/queer ones – are 'performative rather than ontological' (Fanthome, 2007: 6). That is, there are no simply or straightforwardly queer subjects or practices. Finally, Fanthome ques-tions Edelman's embrace of 'social death', since this seems to place 'the injured/murdered queer as the centre of queer subjectivity'. Instead, she argues 'against a position that appears to disdain the idea of an ethical *and* liveable life' (Fanthome, 2007: 6).

Other work has asserted the queerness of the category 'child/children' (Bruhm and Hurley, 2004; Lesnik-Oberstein and Thomson, 2002; Stockton, 2002, 2004, 2009). Kathryn Bond Stockton, for example, argues that 'the child from the standpoint of "normal" adults is always queer...the child can only be "not-yet-straight," since it, too, is not allowed to be sexual' (Stockton, 2009: 7), and she reminds us of the many ways in which the gender/sexuality of children is under constant monitoring and policing through concerns about proper femininity/masculinity and heterosexuality. Foucault also made this point when he noted the role of parents, families, educators, doctors and psychologists in taking charge of 'this precious and perilous, dangerous and endangered sexual potential' (Foucault, 1990: 104). This, of course, relates to one of the key arguments against gay parenting, or any association between the 'not-heterosexual' and the child, which suggests that children will be corrupted or tainted by such association (see, for example, Morgan, 2002). In addition, it relates to Eve Kosofsky Sedgwick's argument, in *Tendencies*, that 'everyone who does gay and lesbian studies is haunted by the suicides of adolescents' (Sedgwick, 1994b: 1):

> I think many adults (and I am among them) are trying, in our work, to keep faith with vividly remembered promises made to ourselves in childhood: promises to make invisible possibilities and desires visible; to make the tacit things explicit; to smuggle queer representation in where it must be smuggled and, with the relative freedom of adulthood, to challenge queer-eradicating impulses frontally where they are to be so challenged. (Sedgwick, 1994b: 3)

Sedgwick's point is, in part, to allow space for *queer* children, and it is the category of the standard 'family' that she questions in order to disengage 'the bonds of blood, of law, of habitation, of privacy, of companionship and succor – from the lockstep of their unanimity in the system called "family"' (Sedgwick, 1994b: 6). For her, queer refers to 'the open mesh of possibilities, gaps, overlaps, dissonances and resonances, lapses and excesses of meaning ... [including] performative acts of experimental self-perception and filiation' (Sedgwick, 1994b: 8–9).

This leaves me with a number of questions for queer theory, which this book tries to address through detailed investigation of lesbian/gay parents' everyday lives. It's not that theorists like Edelman, Halberstam, Bell and Binnie don't have an important point – they do, because there are limiting and conservative ways of thinking, talking and practising familial and relational politics that attempt to exclude some queer ways of life. Of course it is vital to question standard and conventional relational forms (Edelman's 'familiar familial'), but to expel all lesbian/gay parents and those who might refer to themselves as a 'family' from this possibility seems itself very exclusive to me. Further, the idea that the experiences of a single lesbian adopter, a mixed race lesbian couple with two children by donor insemination, or a gay man with over 40 fostered children can be captured by the phrase 'buying into the ideology of the family' is simplistic. Indeed, Edelman's, Halberstam's, Bell and Binnie's questions about 'the family' *are largely my participants' questions too.*

In addition, I find Edelman's reliance on a 'psychoanalytic context' (2004: 7) for argument – with its assertions about the psychic investment in the familiar familial – very limiting, since this tends to ignore or overlook the *social* form and context within which claims about belonging are made. Those claims are never individual, they are always dialogic, and they relate to wider and powerful discursive forms that allow or disallow the possibility of subjectivity. Try living outside of connectivity or sociality for a while (an impossibility, of course), and one soon becomes a non-subject. Sedgwick's argument is, contrary to Edelman's, about carving out a queerer future and one that allows for experiments with relational styles, so that queer-eradicating forms – the kinds that produce queer children who do not believe that they deserve a future and liveable life – are themselves eradicated.

This lack of attention to what might be termed the messy realities of everyday life in some queer theories raises both epistemological and methodological questions. This book brings queer theory in contact with social and political dynamics, since an emphasis on '[d]yke anger, anti-colonial despair, racial rage, counterhegemonic violence, punk pugilism' (Halberstam, 2006: 824) or 'pervy sex and bodily fluids' (Binnie, 2004: 74) as the proper objects of queer theory seems to specify only particular forms of life as adequately queer and assumes that those dynamics are not present in the everyday lives of gay parents. As José Esteban Muñoz has argued, a version of the radical that 'merely connotes extremity, righteousness, or affirmation of newness' (Muñoz, 2006: 825) may avoid engagement with the mundane and with hostile contexts in which passing as 'normal' may become necessary.

A queer theory that is sure that it is the most radical, or one that ascribes an anti-queer stance to certain categories of person, seems to be one that is, itself, about hierarchical positioning and one that avoids careful engagement with the mundane. As Back has argued:

> the political value of sociological work lies in being open to unsettling dialogues with humility. This is not a good way to produce a stirring manifesto, but it perhaps has the merit of greater honesty with regard to the truths that are touched, if not wholly grasped, through sociological endeavour. (Back, 2007: 162)

This point has also been made by Rubin, who has argued that it 'is an exercise in futility to anoint any particular critical stance or political movement with permanent transgressive or revolutionary status (Rubin, 2009: 370). She says, 'we should be giving due consideration to humility: humility about the inevitability of change [and] humility about the imperfection of our formulations' (Rubin, 2009: 371).

'Adoption Nazis'

In 2009, the British Association for Adoption and Fostering (BAAF) published Nicola Hill's book, *The Pink Guide to Adoption for Lesbians and Gay Men* (Hill, 2009). Part of the book consisted of interviews with gay and lesbian adopters and, in response to a question about what advice they would give to others considering adoption, Laurent and Goudarz (adoptive parents of two boys) said:

> And most importantly, don't worry about society. Children need good parents much more than retarded homophobes need an excuse to whinge, so don't let your worries about society's reaction hinder your desire and ability to give a child a loving, caring home – we've done it, and the reactions, even from strangers, and our kids' church-funded school, has been brilliant! (Laurent and Goudarz, in Hill, 2009 [original print run, now deleted])

This was immediately picked up by the *Daily Mail*, a UK newspaper, in an article, 'Slurred by the adoption Nazis: Critics of gay parenting are branded "retarded homophobes"' (Doughty, 2009). Steve Doughty's piece attributed Laurent and Goudarz's comments to the British Association for Adoption & Fostering (BAAF), 'the state-funded national adoption agency', and suggested that BAAF had described any person with 'concerns about the adoption of children by gay couples' as 'retarded homophobes' and as 'whinging' (Doughty, 2009). Under a generic, model-posed, library photograph of a gay couple shopping for designer cushions, one of whom can just be seen with his hand on a baby-buggy, the piece went on to castigate the adoption organization for using 'insulting' and discriminatory language, and to suggest that BAAF otherwise rejects potential adopters who are not of the 'same race' as a child or those who are 'overweight, or because they smoke...[or those who are] judged to be "too middle class"' (Doughty, 2009). Patricia Morgan, author of a book opposed to *all* gay parenting (Morgan, 2002), published by the Christian Institute (UK) – an organization that campaigns against gay adoption (Christian Institute, 2002) – is quoted as saying, 'they do not wish to discuss the pros and cons of gay adoption...They do not appear interested in evidence about the outcomes for children' (Doughty, 2009).

BAAF immediately released a press statement from their Chief Executive, which read:

> The quote attributed to the British Association for Adoption & Fostering (BAAF) in today's *Daily Mail* was in fact the words of one gay adopter, out of many who featured in our new *Pink Guide to Adoption*. These words

are not the views or policy of BAAF. We deeply regret the use of the word 'retarded' and apologise for any offence that it has caused. The use of this word is unacceptable in any circumstances. The fact that this was part of the quote that went to print was down to a human error for which we apologise. We are correcting the error. (British Association for Adoption & Fostering, 2009)

Following this, the original print run of Hill's book was deleted, and a new version published, with the phrase, 'much more than retarded homophobes need an excuse to whinge', removed (Hill, 2009: 188).

This example raises a number of methodological and ethical dilemmas: should we censor a respondent's words in this way? What is happening when a direct challenge to homophobia is defused? Why are the words of one person transformed into the view of an entire 'state-funded national adoption agency'? How is it that the white middle-class (as well as smokers and the 'overweight'), rather than lesbian/gay adopters, emerge as the truly discriminated against here? Why is an image of gay men as 'stylish consumers' used as representative? What is happening when the word 'retarded' is treated as offensive, yet the words 'adoption Nazis' are not? What kind of power reversals are at work when a gay adopter's voice is silenced, yet 'adoption Nazis' is used to suggest that powerful people in the professional adoption field favour black and gay people unfairly over the white, middle-class? Why is Morgan, author of a book opposed to all gay parenting, allowed to suggest that gay adoption is some kind of unquestioned orthodoxy which 'they' all support?

Genealogy, methodology

The kinds of questions provoked by the 'adoption Nazis' episode are addressed in this book through a concern with how conceptualizations of lesbian/gay parenting have come about, and with what work those categories are made to take up. The word 'genealogy' is relevant here, as my book not only investigates questions about possible lines of descent and connection, but also is indebted to Foucault's account of a genealogical method. He referred to genealogy as concerned not with origins, but rather with a 'history of the present' (Foucault, 1991a: 31), and he suggested that, instead of looking for the essence of things, we consider 'an unstable assemblage of faults, fissures, and heterogeneous layers' (Foucault, 2000b: 374). He also insisted that a genealogical approach ought to concern itself with 'various systems of subjection: not the anticipatory power of meaning, but the hazardous play of dominations' (Foucault, 2000b: 376). With regard to the notion of 'sexuality', Foucault argued:

Refusing the universal of…'sexuality' does not imply that what [this notion refers] to is nothing, or that [it is] only [a chimera] invented for the sake of a dubious cause. Something more is involved, however, than the simple observation that [its] content varies with time and circumstances: It means that one must investigate the conditions that enable people, according to the rules of true and false statements, to…arrange that a subject recognize the most essential part of himself in the modality of his sexual desire. ('Florence', 2000: 461–2)

The government of individuals (a point that is taken up and developed in Chapter 7 on state) objectifies the subject as a subject of 'sexuality', so that she or he begins to see the self as requiring some kind of sexual typology, character or culture. Further, institutions 'act upon the behavior of individuals taken separately or in a group, so as to shape, direct, modify their way of conducting themselves' ('Florence', 2000: 463). This does not mean that subjects are merely passive – Foucault was keen to investigate forms of ' "reverse" discourse…[in which] homosexuality began to speak in its own behalf' (Foucault, 1990: 101) – but it does imply that notions such as 'the good/approved gay/lesbian adoptive/foster carer', as used by state social work agencies, must be analyzed for their part in producing notions of gender, race, sexuality, or the good/adequate/'non-risky' subject.

My methodological approach in this book is inspired by aspects of feminist, interactionist, queer and discursive sociologies, all of which are concerned with the everyday circumstances within which knowledge and subjects are produced, with complexity and contradiction, and with people's daily practices, those 'many little *some*things worth noting in the direct composition of the ordinary' (Stewart, 2007: 48). For example, rather than imposing psychological/interior states and feelings onto subjects as though 'real', I examine how and why claims about subjectivity and feeling are taken up. This doesn't mean that I do not consider questions of affect or suggest interpretations of subjects' narratives. But, rather than treating people as symptomatic of norms, roles or values, I ask about 'actual people's doings under definite material conditions', how those 'are coordinated', a process 'always in motion', and in which the 'phenomena of language [are] integral to the investigation of the social' (Smith, 2005: 70). I try to be 'a stranger to the "life as usual" character of everyday scenes' (Garfinkel, 1984: 37). In relation to the field of state childcare, this is one of the reasons that I treat 'sexuality' and its categorization into various types as an epistemological and powerful process that has material and social consequences. I do not treat social work's approach to the assessment of lesbian or gay foster or adoptive carers as simply a case of working more fairly with sexually diverse populations, as some might describe it. Instead, I ask how and why social work institutional practices produce and make use of particular conceptions of sexual subjects.

Such an approach has several implications: for example, my text rejects what Alvin Gouldner called 'the myth of a value-free sociology'

(Gouldner, 1973: 3), and embraces my own commitment to challenging heteronormative ideas about families, parents and relationality. For example, I was the co-founder in 1994 of a support and campaigning group for lesbians and gay men interested or involved in the fostering or adoption of children (the Northern Support Group, based in the north of England, UK, 1994–2010); I have been involved in various campaigns and events to raise awareness and to challenge discrimination in this field; I have carried out research in this area since 1991; and I was – for a short time – a state registered foster carer for a disabled boy.

Although the book contains many autobiographical accounts by lesbian and gay parents, I do not treat these as authentic and unquestionable. My data are largely generated from dialogues, and that means that the research participants are influenced by what I say and what kinds of questions I ask, just as they influence me. This is *'sociology as a relational practice as well as a means of developing theories of relationality'* (Smart, 2009: 3). Although I have asked the gay and lesbian parents in this book to comment on my thoughts and, in some cases, have identified areas in which we disagree, the book remains a statement of my interpretations. I'm fascinated by what my participants have to say, but I am not interested in presenting 'the authentic voices' of lesbian/gay parents, since this would suggest some kind of homogenous group, fix what they have to say in time and place, and imply that my interpretation of their accounts is somehow absent. Rather, their stories become 'topics of investigation in their own right' (Plummer, 1995: 12).

There are no innocent, unmotivated, uncommitted voices here – including my own – and so my book asks why and how positions in discourse are taken up. As Gouldner argued:

> the notion of contaminated research presupposes the existence of uncontaminated research, and this is pure folly. All research is contaminated, for all research entails relationships that may influence both sociologist and subject. The aim of the reflexive sociologist is not to remove his influence on others, but to *know* it. (Gouldner, 1973: 77)

All of this means that my book is not some kind of dispassionate, objective account, but rather one that is motivated by a political desire to challenge heteronormativity and to ask some hopefully complicated questions about the ways in which we think about questions to do with kinship, family, everyday social relations, gender, race and state welfare practices as these relate to lesbian and gay parents.

2
Kinship

> I am sick to death of bonding through kinship and 'the family,' and I long for models of solidarity and human unity and difference rooted in friendship, work, partially shared purposes, intractable collective pain, inescapable mortality, and persistent hope.
>
> (Haraway, 1997: 265)

Donna Haraway's plea suggests, perhaps, that kinship has had its day. That it may no longer be either a helpful or interesting way to make sense of human relationships. But, at the same time, it is a wistful plea that suggests – as one lesbian adopter put it to me – 'a feeling of hopelessness before the enduring power and pervasiveness of kinship'. Given the range of contemporary practices that challenge kinship defined by blood or by marriage/law, these are pertinent and vital questions. But, if it is really defunct, then what happens, as Janet Carsten asks, 'after kinship'? (Carsten, 2004). And why, despite such claims, are reports of kinship's demise so greatly exaggerated?

What is kinship?

Kinship is generally taken to mean a system that organizes and approves particular forms of human relationships. Standard definitions from Europe and America emphasize that kinship recognizes ties based upon blood or marriage/law (Allan, 1979; Carsten, 2004; Schneider, 1980, 1984; Stone, 2006). Thus, immediate family (our parent(s) and siblings) and extended family (grandparents, aunts, uncles, cousins) are traditionally recognized as relatives. Further, we also recognize the forming of new families through marriage or other marriage-like means; 'marriage-like' because, in some contemporary societies, there is recognition of heterosexual, non-married couples, step-relations, and lesbian/gay couples through civil partnership or other partnership registration schemes.

David Schneider's work, *A Critique of the Study of Kinship*, argues that, given the array of possible human relations, kinship:

> constitutes a selection from them which are given sociocultural value; sociocultural relationships are added to the biological relationships which are recognized and valued (and which are, therefore, themselves sociocultural). Since these relations all start with those of reproduction, and assume incest prohibition, two kinds of relationships emerge as fundamental: relations of consanguinity and relations of affinity. These in turn provide a genealogical grid in terms of which different sociocultural systems can group and classify, make distinctions, and create a relational system of both kinds or categories of persons. (Schneider, 1984: 55)

Schneider's quotation raises a number of points that emerge as problematic: first, any system based on 'valued' biological reproduction will prioritize heterosexual relationships. Second, as Schneider argues, the genealogical grid is a system for classification and distinction and, therefore, exclusion. Third, the quotation identifies 'the pre-given analytic opposition between the biological and the social on which much anthropological study of kinship has rested' (Carsten, 2000a: 4). As we shall see later, this nature/culture split has been called into question.

One of Schneider's most important points was to insist that anthropologists and other researchers should not treat kinship as a given or privileged social form. He argued that we should 'take kinship as an empirical question, not as a universal fact' (Schneider, 1984: 200), a point that Elizabeth Freeman suggests contributes to the 'queering' of kinship studies (Freeman, 2007: 299). Schneider's argument has inspired the investigation of contemporary kinship *practices*, with much of the new wave of kinship studies responding to Schneider's work. This understanding of kinship as practice has led to the examination of what Sarah Franklin and Susan McKinnon term its 'classificatory technology,' the ways in which some relationships are signified as connected/included and others disconnected/excluded (Franklin and McKinnon, 2000: 277). That is, how is a version of kinship, based upon the adage 'blood is thicker than water' (Schneider, 1984: 176), used to warrant particular ways of life and to define 'proper' human connections?

Biogenetic linkage, based upon assumed reproductive relations, is used to signify belonging and to privilege those relationships (such as parent/child) over others. This means that kinship is not a descriptive system but is, rather, a socially achieved *and enacted* one. A range of social practices, including textual and visual representations, work to designate a hierarchy of human relationships. This results in the formal and informal recognition of some connections, even some lives, over others. This sense of practice, of 'kin work' (di Leonardo, 1987), is present in all human relationship systems and it involves the statement and repetition of ties.

The study of contemporary forms of lesbian or gay kinship has been used to illuminate these questions of privilege, since heterosexual relations are upheld as a norm within systems based upon the creation of 'natural' gender differences. Gayle Rubin, for example, argued just this, and added that a kinship system, based on an assumed complementarity of the sexes, creates homosexual taboo (Rubin, 1975). A case of this hierarchy of relations may be found in the work of Brenda Almond:

> it could be argued that heterosexual unions are in general intended as the foundation of families – in most human societies that has been their *raison d'être* – while gay unions appear, again in general, more commonly intended for adult companionship. (Almond, 2006: 110)

For lesbians and gay men, kinship practices are a problem because it is *heterosexually based ties*, based upon blood or marriage, which are privileged. Where lesbian or gay couple relationships are recognized by the state through civil partnership (or equivalent) legislation, these do not enjoy the status of marriage and such laws recognize only one relationship form. Other forms, including families of choice or non-couple-based relations (as well as most non-sexual ones) are not counted at all. Because lesbian and gay relationships are assumed to be non-procreative, then they are likely to be designated as mere 'companionship' and not 'the foundation of families' (Almond, 2006: 110). Heather Murray has also pointed to the ways in which the discovery of a gay son or daughter by heterosexual parents is frequently spoken of in terms of death metaphors, such as death of aspirations, of the child that they had known or of hopes for grandchildren (Murray, 2010: 132).

The assumed biological/procreative link within kinship also means that lesbian and gay parenting is subject to curtailment and containment. Gay adoption, for example, is allowed in some countries, but there are places where it is prohibited and where access to assisted reproductive technologies is denied to lesbians (Brodzinsky et al., 2002, 2003; Gates et al., 2007; Gross, 2006; Mallon, 2004, 2006, 2007; Reilly, 1996; Ryan and Cash, 2004; Tobias, 2005). Some countries forbid transnational adoption by known gay or lesbian couples (Dorow, 2006; Tan and Baggerly, 2009). In addition, gay and lesbian parenting has been misrecognized as a 'pretended family relationship' in the UK's Section 28, and has been described as dysfunctional and damaging to children (Morgan, 2002; Phillips, 1999). In such accounts, procreation is assumed to flow from marriage and/or gendered heterosexuality. Finally, lesbians and gay men experience an 'ambiguous relationship with family of origin' (Weeks et al., 2001: 49). Blood kinship ties may be severed when someone comes out as lesbian or gay or, at least, become strained.

John Borneman argues that a kinship system based upon blood and marriage/legal ties doesn't work for lesbian, gay and other non-heterosexual adult or adult–child relationships. He describes two cases from Berlin, Germany in the 1990s. In the first, a 55-year-old man, Harald, applied to adopt 35-year-old Dieter because, after developing a terminal cancer, Harald argued that 'he cared for Dieter like a son and friend and therefore wanted to leave his house and other property to him. Adoption was the only legal means by which he could do this' (Borneman, 2001: 33). Harald and Dieter had lived together for 12 years and had been in a sexual relationship. The court hearings centred on the nature of the relationship between the two men: since, essentially, according to the principles of kinship, those in an adult (sexual) relationship (affinity) cannot 'convert' that relationship into a (non-sexual) 'adult–child' adoptive one (legal descent). The couple therefore had to deny that they had ever had a sexual relationship in order for the adoption to be approved. Borneman argues that this is an interesting example in which 'the initial kinship logic had been effectively stretched out of recognizable shape' (Borneman, 2001: 34). But he also argues that 'the enforcement of the incest taboo for purposes of social reproduction' is not relevant as a structuring device for most gay male relationships (Borneman, 2001: 35): 'The relationship between Dieter and Harald resembled neither marriage nor parentage, while containing elements of both over time' (Borneman, 2001: 37).

In a second case, he describes a lesbian couple, Bärbel (aged 42) and Mirka (53). Mirka's son, Martin (34) is married to his mother's partner, Bärbel, 'out of loneliness, out of flight from homosexual desire, and due to the strong "recommendation" of the local Communist party boss that he normalize his domestic relations' (Borneman, 2001: 38). The three lived together, and so one of the 'relationships in this household inverted the anthropological/legal gender-sex paradigm: lesbian lovers, mother-in-law–daughter-in-law sex. The other extended the mother–son bond well beyond the culturally expected age of parental care' (Borneman, 2001: 39). Borneman argues that this relationship was neither about reproduction nor the possibility of descent, but rather 'extended the meanings of descent and affinity in new directions' towards relations of 'affinity based on care alone' (Borneman, 2001: 40). Borneman argues for anthropological attention to 'the actual situations in which people experience the need to care and be cared for' (Borneman, 2001: 43), since 'the connections of marriage and the family – the principles of descent and affinity – to the assertion of privilege, abjection, and exclusion are rarely seen and, therefore, rarely examined' (Borneman, 2001: 30). As we have seen, these questions of privilege, abjection and exclusion are particularly relevant to lesbians and gay men.

Two responses to the exclusion of lesbians/gay men

Writings by Cheshire Calhoun and by Butler provide two differing responses to this dilemma. Calhoun argues that it is not the case that heterosexuals make use of 'natural' (blood/marriage) kinship ties while lesbians/gay men use 'cultural' ones (chosen families). She says that both versions of kinship are present in heterosexual and lesbian, gay and other non-heterosexual relations. Chosen kinship is present in heterosexual arrangements too (through marriage, step-families, adoption and so on). Concomitantly, bio-genetic kinship is present in gay and lesbian family forms (through maintenance of family ties as kin, ideas about parent–child relations). She says that 'both straight families and gay and lesbian families employ both the principle of choice and procreatively secured biological ties to determine kinship' (Calhoun, 2000: 158).

However, for Calhoun, the question is about social and legal entitlement, and she believes that lesbians and gay men are displaced to the margins of civil society:

> The central political problem is not that the conventional understanding of family excludes the principle of choice, but that lesbians and gay men are denied social and legal entitlement to use *either* kinship principle. Social and legal arrangements are built on the assumption that kinship, *however determined*, is for heterosexuals only. (Calhoun, 2000: 158)

For Calhoun, this situation is remedied via lesbians and gay men seeking access to civil recognition through marriage (or the right to marry) and through the right to be defined as family, though she is careful to argue that neither of these necessarily has to mean traditional forms. However, she concludes that 'lesbians and gays will not be fully equal until the law recognizes same-sex marriages and equally protects lesbian and gay family life' (Calhoun, 2000: 160).

Butler's argument, in 'Is Kinship Always Already Heterosexual?', is very different. Like Calhoun, Butler recognizes that variations on 'kinship that depart from normative, dyadic heterosexually-based family forms secured through the marriage vow are figured not only as dangerous for the child but perilous to the putative natural and cultural laws said to sustain human intelligibility' (Butler, 2004b: 104). But, unlike Calhoun, Butler raises questions about seeking access to recognized kinship forms for lesbians and gay men. This is because, in seeking state recognized legitimacy, other types of relations will always remain illegitimate. Or, to put this another way, lesbian and gay marriages or civil partnerships offer recognition only to specific relationship forms, and also carry out definitional work in terms of what gets counted as a 'relationship' in the first place. For Butler, this raises a problem: we may wish to oppose homophobic arguments that deny the legitimacy of gay and lesbian relationships, but this does not mean that we should necessarily support solutions like marriage or civil partnership (Butler, 2004b: 109). This is further complicated in relation to the specific question of gay and lesbian parenting. Butler notes that in France or Germany, for example, legislation allowing registration of lesbian and gay partnerships specifically prevented adoption and access to reproductive technologies. So, in these examples, legal recognition of a particular form of gay or lesbian relationship does not include the right to state-assisted parenting.

Here, then, we have a problem with the solution to lack of recognition being seen as resting with access to existing kinship forms. First, registration of an adult gay or lesbian relationship does not necessarily confer the right to become a legitimate family – so much for the 'equality' proposed by many supporters of state recognized relations. Second, such recognition relies upon the illegitimacy of other human relations, those that lie outside of *normative dyadic homosexuality*. For these reasons, as Butler argues, 'it is crucial that, politically, we lay claim to intelligibility and recognizability; and it is crucial, politically, that we maintain a critical and transformative relation to the norms that govern what will and will not count as an intelligible and recognizable alliance and kinship' (Butler, 2004b: 117).

For Butler, the traditional kinship system rests upon a notion that heterosexuality guarantees the continued reproduction of cultural norms through children. She shows that arguments against lesbian and gay parenting often use this idea – that children will not be properly acculturated – and that this demonstrates the heteronormativity of many kinship claims. Butler's concern, which I will return to later, is that, in seeking normalcy through traditional forms of kinship recognition, lesbians and gay men will not question the 'defining framework' of kinship itself (Butler, 2004b: 129). She argues that:

> a more radical social transformation is precisely at stake when we refuse, for instance, to allow kinship to become reducible to 'family,' or when we refuse to allow the field of sexuality to become gauged against the marriage form. For as surely as rights to adoption and, indeed, to reproductive technology ought to be secured for individuals and alliances outside the marriage frame, it would constitute a drastic curtailment of progressive sexual politics to allow marriage and family, or even kinship, to mark the exclusive parameters within which sexual life is thought. (Butler, 2004b: 129–30)

Butler is therefore arguing that contemporary kinship takes many forms other than just 'family', and that it would also be dangerous to support only those relationships that take marriage or marriage-like forms as their basis. A progressive sexual politics for Butler does not rest upon access to, and approval under, state registered forms of adult and adult–child relations. Whereas Calhoun argues just this – equality achieved through access to marriage and family recognition – Butler argues that a reliance on kinship as a social technology limits sexual life.

Calhoun and Butler's arguments respond to the heteronormativity of kinship systems (a point that I will return to later), but one limitation of this work is its tendency to disregard the field of contemporary kinship studies, much of which argues that kinship nowadays is no longer like 'kinship'. That is, standard blood/marriage-type definitions do not account for the diversity of current forms or, rather, how people enact their relational lives.

'New' kinship theories

Marilyn Strathern's *After Nature* (1992) is a key text for contemporary kinship studies. She argues that the nature/culture split, used to distinguish what counts as proper natural kin, no longer holds. An element of choice is present in what were formally regarded as entirely natural relations, so that, for example, any individual person's notion of kin has boundaries. That is, a choice is made to stop relating, somewhere. As Strathern argues, 'relatedness – "blood ties" – can thus be cut by failure to accord social recognition (someone is forgotten), just as social relationships can be cut by appeal to biological principles (dividing "real" kin from others). So in practice one does not trace connexions for ever' (Strathern, 1996: 530). Further, nature is now given a helping hand in a whole range of ways, in order to assist reproduction, for example. Nature has been 'enterprised-up' (Strathern, 1992: 30). Contemporary practices of assisted/new reproductive technologies, step-parent and other recombined families, surrogacy, open adoption, gay/lesbian parenting and so on have all contributed to this breakdown of the nature/culture divide in kin theories.

Here, we might return to the concept of 'kin work' (di Leonardo, 1987), as contemporary kinship theories analyze the ways in which kinship relations are claimed and enacted. This may be observed in at least three fields: first, the demise of the nature/culture split, as described above, has resulted in the undermining of claims to a purely natural kinship. Haraway's work is relevant here, as she has argued that ideas about kinship, based upon reproduction, nature and sex difference, have been replaced by concerns about replication and genetics (Haraway, 2004). The phenomenon of lesbian/gay parenting is a case in point here, as opponents frequently raise concerns about this being unnatural and about lack of proper sex/gender role differences. As Haraway notes, ideologies of 'sexual reproduction can no longer reasonably call on the notions of sex and sex role as organic aspects in natural objects like organisms and families' (Haraway, 2004: 21). We live now with what Haraway terms 'natureculture', since '[c]yborg figures – such as the end-of-the-millennium seed, chip, gene, database, bomb, fetus, race, brain, and ecosystem – are the offspring of implosions of subjects and objects and of the natural and artificial' (Haraway, 1997: 12). In modern times, Haraway argues, the family tree has been overshadowed by genetic databases and the human genome project, blood kinship by the genome, and natural heterosexual reproduction by the new reproductive technologies, to the point where heterosexuality is no longer a stable basis for reproduction.

Haraway's analysis is important because it identifies a range of technologies that complicate modern kinship. The term 'natureculture' helpfully extends Strathern's analysis, but it is necessary to remember that Haraway does not suggest that ideas about natural kinship have disappeared. Other work, too, reminds us that dominant ideas about kinship relations remain strong, for example, when used either to oppose or even to support the phenomenon of lesbian/gay parenting. That is, there is a danger of overstating the idea that modern kinship has completely broken with all claims based upon blood, marriage and nature. As Daniel Miller has argued, 'there is ... a danger, as is so often the case with attractive new ideas, of swinging the pendulum too far in the opposite direction until the other end of the kinship spectrum, that concerned with formalisation, normativity and fixity, in turn disappears below our gaze and we actually lose the appropriate sense of balance' (Miller, 2007: 537).

Consider, for example, the biologically-based connection claims made by many lesbian parents using assisted and donor insemination techniques. These claims both challenge and reinforce the idea of blood kin and, as Lynn Jamieson has noted, 'dominant uses of reproductive technology do not take the possibilities of separating social, biological and genetic parents to their limits' (Jamieson, 1998: 172). This is a restricted practice or field from which lesbians (and even single women) may be barred, and it may also reinforce biogenetic claims to kinship. Laura Mamo, for example, notes:

> The women I interviewed selected socially and physically dominant donors, assuming that their sperm would help 'build' socially dominant offspring. At times, the women chose donors they felt could enhance familial shortcomings (e.g., by choosing a tall donor when the biomother was short). In addition, women looked for social health (such as education, hobbies, interests) in donors ... Whether the donor characteristics were personality traits, cultural ancestry, personal health status, family health history, or physical appearance, they were constructed as inheritable. (Mamo, 2007: 214/219)

A second aspect of kin work relates to the given/chosen split. As I have already noted, Strathern has argued that 'there always was a choice as to whether or not biology is made the foundation of relationships' (Strathern, 1993: 196). Carol Stack's study of black kin relations in 'The Flats', a poor section of a USA Midwestern city, shows that 'chosen' kin are crucial to daily life and the care of children. She argues that her subjects established 'socially recognized kin ties' (Stack, 1997: 29), a complex web of 'mutual aid domestic networks' (Stack, 1997: 61). The fostering of children, for example, was common, not unusual, and childcare was 'not necessarily a role required of a single individual' (Stack, 1997: 68). Stack does not romanticize this – she shows that there is conflict between friends, family and parents – but she also argues that distinctive kin relations, largely a response to poverty, contradict the 'negative features attributed to poor families, that they are fatherless, matrifocal, unstable, and disorganized' (Stack, 1997: 124).

The work of Janet Finch and Jennifer Mason (Finch, 1989; Finch and Mason, 1993, 2000; Mason, 2008) is important here, too, because they also argue that kin relations and responsibilities are not given but, rather, negotiated. Kin work involves the maintenance, avoidance, and even severance, of ties. Finch and Mason argue that English kinship does display patterns; for example, parent–child relations and those between 'spouses' (their term) are held as primary, over and above other relations. This is a crucial point – kinship is not a 'free for all', it is constrained for all of us by expectations, ways of thinking and practising. But Finch and Mason also conclude that kinship exists in negotiated, relational practices, which include the ways in which kin stories are narrated and remembered (Finch and Mason, 2000). Michael Young and Peter Willmott's classic 1957 study, *Family and Kinship in East London* (2007), also reminds us that social factors (geographical location, proximity, associations over time, income, class) affect the formation of enduring relations and 'kin'.

The third field of kin work is that which identifies the ways in which people's actual kin practices contradict the rules of kinship, or the idea that kin is founded upon structural rules. Carsten's work on adoptees seeking out biological relatives, for example, demonstrates the ways in which her respondents saw kinship as earned through love and care over time (Carsten, 2004: 149). Lesbians and gay men in Kath Weston's study make the same point – that true kin are those who have been there for you over an extended period (Weston, 1991). In Carsten's research, adoptees often valued the love and care that had been given to them by their adoptive parents over birth connections; indeed, re-established connections with birth parents were often disappointing, and the adoptees argued that biology itself was not sufficient a basis for connection (Carsten, 2000b: 691–2). This contrasts with the adoptees in Judith Modell's study, who cited 'satisfactions … (knowing the facts of one's past)', even when 'the relationship failed to meet expectations, when one or the other or both struggled with the "map" for further interactions' (Modell, 2002: 59). But, here, it is worth noting that Modell's research subjects were members of a national adoptee support group, a group that emphasized the need or 'right' to search for birth parents, and in which the reunion narrative was key. Even where a reunion relationship didn't go well, adoptees were told to 'work at it' (Modell, 2002: 59). Thus kinship is performed and also constructed through the auto/biographical accounts that people give of themselves and their connections. Kinship is practical work (Edwards, 2000: 27; Featherstone et al., 2006: x), and the notion that all adoptees ought to seek out birth (blood) relatives tells us that there is a social imperative to be properly connected. Taking up subjectivity or identity seems to require expected connections.

In addition to the acknowledgement that all kin ties must be made through work, contemporary kinship studies also focus on the creation of elective or chosen relations, such as friends as family, families of choice and chosen social networks (Beck-Gernsheim, 2002). This implies the creation of new kinship forms. One area in which this has been much analyzed is the development of 'families of choice' amongst gay and lesbian people. Research on lesbian and gay social networks and kinship has argued that relationships not traditionally recognized as kin – friends and other social contacts that have no blood or 'marriage-like' ties – play a crucial role. Indeed, many lesbians and gay men argue that their friends *are* their significant others or even their family (Giddens, 1992; Levine, 1998; Nardi, 1999; Perlesz et al., 2006a; Stacey, 1996, 2004; Weeks, 2007; Weeks et al., 2001; Weston, 1991). This highlights two important kin work processes: lesbians' and gay men's friends may perform roles usually associated with kin – emotional and practical support, social activities – and those people are redefined as significant, and even as family. Peter M. Nardi, for example, notes that the gay men in his study used familial terms – 'brother', 'sister', 'family', 'mother', 'auntie' – to describe their gay friends (Nardi, 1999: 52–3). These linguistic devices create family-like bonds, even if frequently suffused with irony or camp.

Weeks et al.'s study, *Same Sex Intimacies* (2001), identifies families of choice as a key dynamic and concern of their lesbian, gay and non-heterosexual respondents. For many lesbians and gay men, friends become their core network or kin, and – as with other research discussed earlier – the respondents saw these relations as based upon mutual care and commitment. Weeks et al. suggest that 'family' is used by lesbians and gay men to name 'kin-like networks of relationships, based on friendship, and commitments "beyond blood"' (Weeks et al., 2001: 9). However, it is crucial not to romanticize or even essentialize these ideas. First, some lesbians and gay men do not see friends as family or kin, they may not be in a position to make such choices, or they see this as something of a community myth (Carrington, 1999; Gabb, 2004, 2008). Second, couples and (assumed) sexual relationships are frequently prioritized over friendships by lesbians and gay men, as much as by anyone else. Third, many heterosexuals develop friend-focused networks too (Budgeon, 2006; Roseneil and Budgeon, 2004; Spencer and Pahl, 2006). And, finally, most networks, groups or communities involve some element of *exclusion*.

Liz Spencer and Ray Pahl have argued that seeing friend-based relationships as chosen, in comparison with kin-based ones as given, is too simplistic. Instead, there is a 'process of suffusion' which blurs these boundaries – some friends play family-type roles and may be chosen, but others feel given and may imply obligations; some family members become friend-like and we choose to spend more time with them (Pahl and Spencer, 2004: 216; Spencer and Pahl, 2006: 112). That is, kin relations are neither simply given nor freely chosen; friends and family are not 'polar opposites' since 'kin and non-kin can occupy similar positions' (Spencer and Pahl, 2006: 125). As we have seen, this was also identified in earlier kinship studies (Finch and Mason 1993, 2000; Hayden, 1995; Strathern, 1992), and is raised by sociologists who concur that 'choice' is not an appropriate term for relationships that are affected by material and social factors (Allan, 1989; Jamieson, 1998; Mason, 2008; Smart, 2007). A focus on the idea of elective kin may over-privatize analysis, seeing social relations as individual choices, whereas it is important to remember that lesbian and gay claims about kin and friends as family take place within a context of heteronormativity. This was Weston's (1991) crucial point – it is not that friends as family are freely chosen but, rather, act as an intervention by lesbians and gay men into a kinship field that tries to discount their forms of relating. They, too, are kin work.

What gay and lesbian chosen families respond to, then, is kinship as a technology of classification and exclusion that devalues their relations. That is not to say that lesbian and gay kin claims are not also based upon classification and exclusion, as they surely are. But lesbian and gay communities make use of a wider and more diverse set of relational terms, some of which struggle to name otherwise unacknowledged social forms: 'fuck-buddies', 'friends as family', 'exes who are still friends', 'the non-biological mother', 'the co-parent', and so on. As Carsten notes, 'relatedness (or kinship) is simply about the ways in which people create similarity or difference between themselves and others' (2004: 82) and so, just as heteronormative kinship practices exclude lesbians and gay men, whether that be denial of the value of those relations or literal exclusion from 'the family' when someone comes out, so gay men and lesbians, too, construct their difference from heterosexuals through new kinship forms such as the idea of families of choice. As Haraway has noted, kinship 'is a technology for producing the material and semiotic effect of natural relationship, of shared kind' (1997: 53). And it is these processes that need analysis:

> Left largely untheorized are questions about how kinship ideologies arise, how people bring them into play in everyday arenas of dispute, the effect of specific lines of argumentation on power relations between dominant and subordinate groups, what possibilities emergent ideologies open or foreclose, how contests of meaning are themselves socially structured, and how social struggles to legitimate particular forms of kinship end up reshaping the very ideologies they deploy. (Weston, 1998: 61)

New lesbian/gay kinship forms?

When I spoke to Jean, in 1998, she was living with her partner, Trixie, and they had been together for about five years. They had four children: Georgia and Max, Trixie's birth children, each with a different father; Claire, fostered by Jean for about nine years, but who had just moved into a residential care home; and Joshua, a child born to Jean's ex-partner via donor/self-insemination, but who lived with Jean and Trixie under the terms of a legal order. Jean talked to me about James, a disabled boy that she had fostered until he died suddenly, aged two, due to a degenerative, terminal condition:

Jean: What do I think about networks of support? That can cause worries for those of us whose families cannot, or will not, accept our sexuality. Trixie's family are utterly brilliant about us, but my own isn't. My mother won't have any mention of my 'queer so-called family nor my queer so-called friends,' although my father and my brother's family are as accepting and supportive as they can be. But my networks of support are my friends. My views about whether there was a supposed 'lesbian community,' and whether it would support me as a parent, used to be somewhat cynical, but most of my friends were lesbians, and we certainly supported each other as much as we were able. I was unsure whether this constituted a community though. My view of this changed when James, my foster son, died quite suddenly.

The most significant thing I can take away from that experience, as I see it now, is that there really is a lesbian and gay community and it really does work for us. People, who I knew vaguely, and their friends, and partners and children appeared and consulted with those I was close to. They really helped. They took the children out, they made practical arrangements that were tedious and unthinkable for me at the time, but were necessary. They sent cards, they sent 'rescue remedy', they all gave what they could and it really helped.

I have brought away from that experience a real sense of respect and belonging that I never had before. I know there is a community that will help me on my terms when appropriate, and not make demands on me afterwards. These people are not my 'family' but offer a network of support that is real and tangible. I have close friends who are indeed my first line of support, but the community is important and demands to be taken into account in any social work assessment. Don't underestimate the power of friendships!

Jean's story asks a number of complicated questions about kinship, which have also been raised in research on lesbian and gay relationship forms. First, Jean and Trixie have a complex family, including children from former relationships, fostered children and a child conceived via donor/self-insemination. These complications provoke questions about new forms of kinship, and they demonstrate that this does not have to be based upon biological/blood links. Karín Lesnik-Oberstein has argued that parents with children 'not their own' are 'often judged as exceptional, extraordinary, self-sacrificing, heroic' (Lesnik-Oberstein, 2008: 180), since there is a strong cultural imperative that children should be biologically related to their parents/carers. Jean and Trixie question this imperative through their parenting of children 'not their own', and through refiguring such bonds as legitimate. But, at the same time, it is possible to see a story about fostering a child with a terminal illness as taking up subjectivities to do with self-sacrifice or legitimacy. That is, some lesbian parents may be forced to take up such positions in narrative in order to achieve personhood in the face of family prejudice and cultural misrecognition. I am not suggesting that Jean's motivation, here, is to do with seeking a 'heroic' status, and, as will be seen in my discussions with a group of single lesbian adopters later in this chapter, some actually reject this 'extraordinary' label. But, at the same time, the stance of the self-sacrificing carer is one that gay and lesbian parents may take up. Simon's story in *Lesbian and Gay Fostering and Adoption*, for example, is entitled 'Heavy-duty Kids...?' as he talks about fostering young men from children's homes that 'couldn't cope', and later describes this as 'a very selfless task' (Hicks and McDermott, 1999b: 32 and 36).

Jean's story asks provocative questions about who counts as 'family': she shows that her own blood kin includes a mother who rejects Jean's 'queer so-called family' and her 'queer so-called friends,' and others who are more supportive. Here, then, is a demonstration of the 'ambiguous relationship with family of origin' (Weeks et al., 2001: 49), which Jean contrasts with a kin-like network of friends. She talks about close lesbian friends as her everyday support, and then about others from the 'lesbian community' who offered practical and emotional support at a time of crisis.

Jean describes a certain suspicion of the 'lesbian community,' possibly based upon the hostility that can be shown towards gay/lesbian parents by some lesbians and gay men, possibly upon a distrust of the idea that a group of women categorized as 'lesbian' would actually have much in common. But Jean's experiences lead her to state that 'there really is a lesbian and gay community and it really does work for us.' She claims 'a real sense of respect and belonging that I never had before.' These ideas suggest a family or community being claimed on the basis of kin work (care and support), with reference to a shared sexuality, and contrasted with problematic blood kin relations – ideas that also feature in Weeks et al. (2001). The question of 'belonging' that Jean identifies is a crucial one related to the claiming of kin-like connections, but it is also one that relates to questions of subjectivity. I shall return to the question of belonging later in this chapter and in Chapter 6 (Race) but, here, it is important to note that it figures as a way not only to locate a subject (amongst friends, within a lesbian community, amongst others like the self), but also to create a subject (since those who belong or who are connected are more easily recognized). This is a point that Elizabeth Povinelli has taken up in arguing that 'kinship [is] a persistent and relevant category of social life' (Povinelli, 2006: 66), one that is both creative and normative – as in Jean's case – since to count as a legitimate person is to be seen to belong.

Finally, Jean offers a challenge to state social work/welfare, reminding us that any assessment of a lesbian or gay potential foster carer ought to take community and friends (not just blood family) into account when considering support networks and kin. Jean is asking for a wider conception of kinship within social work and family placement practice. This is vital, because lesbians' and gay men's ideas about human relations are 'constrained by the state regulated field of family placement' (Hicks, 2006b: 773). This highlights complex questions about what happens when lesbian and gay challenges to heteronormativity seek recognition within state welfare institutions, a point that is central to debates about gay and lesbian foster care and adoption, and to which I return in Chapter 7, which deals with childcare/welfare practice.

Jean's story demonstrates both a rejection of some forms of standard/blood kinship and a redefining and claiming of kinship ties or belonging. Like many other gay and lesbian relationship and parenting narratives, Jean's neither completely rejects nor accepts kinship, since, while her story challenges heterosuperiority, it also places Jean within a family and community. We all want to belong. Like others, I have argued that gay and lesbian narratives usually demonstrate both conformity and rebellion claims (Hicks, 2005), since to move 'beyond oversimplified arguments that "alternative" families either totally mirror or completely counter "hegemonic" forms of kinship requires a less dichotomized understanding of the dynamics of ideological change' (Weston, 1998: 61). Mamo makes a similar point: that the kinship practices of lesbians using technologically assisted reproduction:

> both 'trouble the normal' and reinforce the normalization of traditional gender, sexuality, and family constructs...how, and in what ways, do these practices construct new and old ways of knowing about kinship, of becoming related, of being recognized as belonging to social life, and of being and doing gender, sexuality, and family[?]. (Mamo, 2007: 6)

New and old ways of knowing about kinship feature in theorizations of lesbian and gay relationships. Giddens, for example, in *The Transformation of Intimacy* (1992), argues that lesbians and gay men are pioneers of new relationship forms – 'the prime everyday experimenters' (Giddens, 1992: 135) – in which equality and '*plastic sexuality*, severed from its age-old integration with reproduction, kinship and the generations' is demonstrated (Giddens, 1992: 27). This version of lesbian and gay relationships as a challenge to old kinship forms is present in work which claims these as egalitarian, questioning of gender roles, not dependent upon biological links, based on families of choice and affinity ties (Sullivan, 2004; Weeks, 2007; Weeks et al., 2001).

But these ideas are also challenged: Weeks et al., for example, also note that Giddens' book pays little attention to 'socio-economic factors that may constrain people's ability to participate in the transformation of their intimate lives' (Weeks et al., 2001: 108), while Jamieson argues that seeing all lesbian and gay relationships as 'pure' is a 'strong generalization' (Jamieson, 1998: 154). Gay and lesbian relationships may demonstrate inequalities and the reinforcement of gender roles. They may be primarily focused on the couple and on links with blood kin. Essentially, there is a danger in assuming that any relationship form is inherently radical or egalitarian (Hicks, 2006a), and it is vital to remember that most gay and lesbian relationships are accounted for in ways that seek to create some form of kin-like bond. These accounts frequently draw upon a combination of challenge to heteronormativity mixed with some reference to socially expected kinship ties. As Miller says, 'evidence for complexity and diversity does not preclude an equal and abiding emphasis upon normativity and formal ideals' (Miller, 2007: 550). This is the construction of 'affinity ties' and 'relatedness' in action (Mamo, 2007: 231), with people using complex ideas that, at the same time, draw upon 'deeply rooted and familiar ways of forming and claiming kin,' whilst 'simultaneously extending the reference of the kinship terms that [are] being disambiguated through the strategies' (Thompson, 2005: 177).

Lesbian and gay adoption

Mary, Liz, Michelle and Sarah are four single lesbian adoptive parents who met at a national support group for gay and lesbian foster carers and adopters. All have adopted children, and in 2004 they wrote a short piece for the UK-based *Pink Parents Magazine* (2000–4). At that time, Mary had a birth child, Susan (aged six) and an adopted girl, Amreen (aged one); Liz had an adopted daughter, Kayleigh (six); Michelle had an adopted girl, Tina (four); and Sarah had adopted siblings, Julia (three) and Kyle (14 months):

Michelle: We meet up once a week to take turns cooking for each other and our kids, to drink, swap news, stay over, and have a laugh...

Liz: Our commitment to each other has evolved as we have got to know each other and the kids. It's not only a social event central to my life, but supporting each other through the different stages is also an exciting and rewarding experience...

Sarah: The others have supported me right through the adoption process. They have been a lifeline for me, providing practical and emotional support through the ups and downs of becoming a parent … We have created an extended family for our children. Two years on, we are four adults, four adopted children aged 20 months to three-and-a-half years, a birth child and, we hope, another adopted child on the way!

Mary: Our kids are all cousins to each other. They are very much a part of each other's lives. They are all adopted kids, or siblings of adopted kids, with lesbian mums, and if that makes them special, then having each other will make them ordinary too. I think we all need to be a little bit special and a little bit ordinary.

Michelle: Children need to know other children who are like them. They actively look for similarities. They need to belong. By keeping these close links between us, we are helping to make them secure in their own identities. Family structure and family history is a key issue for them. Our kids have birth mummies, foster mums and adoptive mums. This is a core part of their identity, and the fact that they will know other children with similar early experiences should be a source of strength to them as they grow up.

Sarah: It is important for our children that they understand that families are made up in all sorts of ways. My daughter knows other children who have one or more mums, and some children who have dads too! (Mary et al., 2004: 40).

Mary, Liz, Michelle and Sarah's discussion *is* kin work: they identify emotional and practical support given to each other over time, what Liz terms 'commitment', and they use words that claim likeness, similarity, being 'cousins' and an 'extended family'. Like Jean, Michelle says that people 'need to belong'. But here, that sense of kin and belonging relates not only to being a lesbian parent, but also to being an adopted or fostered child with a lesbian parent. This is why Mary talks about a sense of needing 'to be a little bit special and a little bit ordinary'. Kin work is what both Modell and Signe Howell call 'self-conscious' (Howell, 2006: 38; Modell, 1994: 226), not only for gay and lesbian relations, but also for adult-fostered/adopted-child ones (Jones and Hackett, 2010). Sarah, Michelle, Liz and Mary are acknowledging that being fostered, adopted and having a lesbian mum is special, but they are also making this ordinary through kin work that allows their children to mix with others in a similar family situation. It's no accident that Michelle uses the words 'like them', since likeness is a classic kinship trope.

Anthropological research into adoption and kinship parallels work on sexuality as it, too, deals with the process of what Howell has termed 'kinning' (Howell, 2006). Howell's Norwegian study of transnational adoption emphasizes the kinning process, by which biological ties are rendered insignificant and social ones made all-important. This she describes as 'highly self-conscious' kinship (Howell, 2006: 38). While there are some parallels here between social/self-conscious and chosen/elective kinship, Howell also notes that adoptive families do make use of biological tropes (for example, narratives about the early parts of the adoption process often draw upon a 'pregnancy-like' stages model) (Howell, 2006: 67/70). Savage's book, *The Kid*, is an example of this. Even though it's a story of gay adoption, the book is subtitled 'what happened after my boyfriend and I decided to get pregnant,' and has sections entitled 'fertilisation,' 'gestation,' 'birth,' and 'afterbirth' (Savage, 2000).

Howell emphasizes the work that adoptive families have to do in order to establish their kinship ties, but she notes that this kinning process is achieved through all parties: the adoptee, the adopters, the birth family and the state (Howell, 2006: 228–9). She draws on the work of James Faubion, who has argued that kinship is 'a system – or array of systems – of subjectivation, if perhaps many other things as well' (Faubion, 2001: 13). Faubion draws upon Foucault's work on subjectivation, defining it as 'all those processes through which individuals are labelled or made into subjects of one or another kind,' and 'all those processes through which individuals make themselves into subjects of one or another kind' (Faubion, 2001: 12). This is an important argument as it suggests that kinning is a process by which individuals are compelled to locate their auto/biographies of self within a socially approved form, kinship. Part of becoming a subject involves both being recognized, and accounting for oneself, as a kinned subject.

Modell's work on American adoption argues that biology-like models of kin links are used, but that blood ties make this problematic. So, like Howell, Modell argues that adoption is 'self-conscious' kinship (Modell, 1994: 4). One example of this is the matching process used by social workers and adoption agencies; here, a potential adopter is matched with a child, and Modell argues that this draws upon ideas about likeness, 'in order to re-create a semblance of real kinship in the contrived family' (Modell, 1994: 36). Kin work on the part of all involved is necessary to maintain the fiction of true kinship; or, what Modell terms 'a *paper* kinship' (Modell, 1994: 226).

Modell examines the move towards open adoption, in which all parties are made aware of the adoption from the start and in which some form of contact between the child, adopters and birth parent(s) is encouraged. Interestingly, Modell argues that this very openness about adoption 'is disturbing because it does not allow adoptive kinship to be just like biological kinship' (Modell, 1994: 231). That is, it draws attention to the active creation of kin bonds between adopted child and adopter(s), and also potentially those between adopter(s) and birth parent(s), since some form of relationship is created here too. It also maintains a biologically-based link between the adopted child and the birth parent(s). Modell argues that 'individual actors in adoption are currently redesigning the *fiction* of their kinship. Reunions, openness, and blended families form the basis of a new kind of kinship, in which genealogy is only one way of constructing parenthood' (Modell, 1994: 238).

In her later work, *A Sealed and Secret Kinship* (2002), Modell examines the practices of open adoption further. Some of her earlier terms, such as 'fictive' or 'paper' kinship, are replaced with 'culturally *non-ordinary* kinship' (Modell, 2002: 13) in order to challenge its 'presumed "not real," fictive, and liminal quality' (Modell, 2002: 179). She is critical of some aspects of open adoption because she notes that it may, in fact, reinforce biological ties as foundational, as it sees 'something essential about a birth relationship' (Modell, 2002: 70). But she notes that there are elements of both ordinary (biological) and non-ordinary (social) kinship to American adoption:

> while adoption works on an individual level because adults believe they can raise a 'stranger' child, it is also true that many of those adults request information on the child's 'natural endowment' in order to raise her well. And while adoption works on a societal level because of a cultural conviction that transplantation into a fresh environment will benefit a child, in practice the child's traits (however designated) determine where he or she is 'best' placed. (Modell, 2002: 186)

Yet, Modell holds out the hope for adoption to expand, rather than narrow, 'the meaning of a parent–child relationship' (Modell, 2002: 199), and it is telling that one of her examples of new adoptive parents is that of 'two men pushing a baby carriage' (Modell, 2002: 193). Her example of gay adopters is used to signify extraordinary kinship via the confounding of usual gender/ sexuality expectations (the notion of women as carers and the heterosexual couple as family); the gay couple seems to represent new adult/child connections; and it challenges not only expectations of adult/child blood links but also those of adult affinity.

Mary, Liz, Michelle and Sarah ... revisited

I carried out an interview with Sarah, Liz, Michelle and Mary in 2009, five years on from their original magazine piece. Mary had adopted another girl, Katie (aged 18 months at the time of the interview), and Michelle had a birth child, Tom, in 2006. I asked them about their original magazine piece, how they thought things had changed, and how they made sense of their connections. When I asked about the children, Mary said, 'I think that they do feel like each other, Amreen's got a very strong attachment to her "cousins" ...' and Sarah noted that the children sometimes refer to the group as their 'family'. The group talked about offering support to each other as adults and wanting to create a 'bond' between their children. However, they also talked about how this had changed within the group over the years; they said they did not meet up as much as they used to, they got together on Friday evenings but didn't do 'sleep-overs' any more, they still went away on holiday together every year. The group acknowledged these changes and made sense of them in terms of children's development/ages and how their own lives as parents had altered. Mary and Michelle both had another child, most of the group talked about developing contact arrangements with adopted children's birth families (a version of Modell's 'open adoption'), and they mentioned other demands on their children's time. Nevertheless, they still emphasized the everyday support they offer to each other:

Michelle: We do some Friday nights and Christmases and holidays, and there's quite a lot of birthdays...

Sarah: We still do Friday nights but we just do a meal.

Michelle: And we go to [lesbian families group] and we're all there...

Liz: And we see each other in between.

Sarah: And another thing that has changed and developed is because we have various different arrangements with maybe one other person to do things, so Mary takes Kyle to swimming because Julia is at choir, and I meet up with them and Michelle meets Kyle at school and I usually take Tina swimming.

As with the respondents in Weston's (1991) study, Sarah, Michelle, Liz and Mary emphasize being there for each other over time. However, I also asked them what they thought of the rosy picture of lesbian/gay family life presented in some accounts. Here, of course, it must be remembered that I introduced this topic via a deliberately ironicized reading of Giddens (1992). That is, I suggested that Giddens presents an overly positive view of lesbian and gay relationships as egalitarian. The group agreed with me. Michelle pointed out that this picture was misguided and said, 'it's real life, and being a parent is quite stressful, and you've got all those pulls on your time and you feel like you've not seen your adult friends that you love very much and so on...but it ebbs and flows really.' Liz also said, 'we've been very close and we've had our dodgy moments with each other.' The group talked about 'being huffy' [annoyed/irritated] with each other at times and feeling they could say anything to each other, which they saw as ordinary and, in a sense, part of being close. They pointed out that their children fall out with each other at times too, but Michelle said, 'that's what families are like, aren't they? There's ups and downs and they fall out for a bit with all the stresses and the strains, and they carry on doing it...', another example of the normalizing of their experiences.

When I asked them about kin work, this concept made sense to the group. Mary said, 'We talked about ourselves in those terms at first, didn't we, we were very conscious of the fact that we were getting together to support each other around adoption issues.' The group talked about a 'triple-whammy' effect; that is, having to create a sense of belonging as adopters (not based upon biogenetic adult/child links), as single people (not in recognized 'relationships'), and as lesbians (not based upon socially sanctioned adult relations). Sarah said:

Sarah: In a way I think that makes it easier. In some ways it might be easier for us as lesbians to adopt because I don't think we have those fixed notions of biological/genetic family, and even if you've had a birth child you have to think about who the dad is going to be and all that stuff and bring that in ... 'even if you've had a birth child', you know I don't mean it like that! But I think we're more open I suppose to other ways of thinking about things ...

Steve: Well you've also had to think about your place in the world as a lesbian. How do I fit in? Who do I relate to? How do I relate? How do I create my family or my friends or ... so you've already had to do that, so maybe you've thought about some of those things when you come to adopt anyway?

There were inevitable contradictions here too. Whilst the group was clear in its recognition of kin work and the creation of bonds, this contrasted with ideas about identity. Sarah talked about being a middle-class adopter with working-class children, and she and Mary joked about the children being 'mixed-class'. Sarah said that it seemed ridiculous to think of a child, adopted at 14 months, to 'have' a class, but Mary said, 'Oh but you do ... You've got a background, where you come from, it's your identity. You can't get rid of your identity and – you know – that imprint that's your birth. You can't get rid of it, it's there.' So, for some people, there is a sense in which an adopted child brings a fixed identity into a new family. In addition, it's rare that class gets talked about very much in relation to lesbian/gay parenting (Taylor, 2009), but it is highly relevant to questions about mobility – the notion of a child moving across or being trans-class, but also the idea of a self-conscious and reflexive adopter – and to notions about how kin is created, since class has played a crucial role in notions of kinship (Young and Willmott, 2007).

Modell's contradictions of kinship also come into play here; there is a sense of an 'ordinary/biological' link as well as a 'non-ordinary/social' one (Modell, 2002: 186). And this contradiction is strongly felt, even by those who are clear in their acknowledgement of the importance both of adopted children's links with others and of their own self-conscious kin work. Liz, for example, said:

Liz: Kayleigh does remember her birth family and I do get from time to time, well it's not exactly 'jealous', but I do think she's not … well, all of her isn't my child, there's a big chunk of her that belongs to another family and always will and she's not all mine, not in a possessive sense.

Sarah: And maybe it's an age thing because Julia was three-and-a-bit and she's still very attached to her foster mum and she still has a strong thing about that and she still sees me as like a second or third mum … whereas the others were adopted when they were little …

Liz: I've certainly had twinges of quite strong feelings of – you know – it's different from having a birth child and I'm sharing her, in a way, and I'll never be the 'mum' that I would've been if I'd had her, you know.

Michelle: You *are* her mum.

Steve: But those feelings are …

Liz: … well they're weird …

Steve: … they're weird but they're normal.

Liz is conscious of the multiple links her adopted daughter has, but, elsewhere in the interview, she was clear that Kayleigh referred to her as 'mum' and talked about Liz's father as 'granddad' too. The notion of sharing connections demonstrates an awareness of kin work, but Liz also uses tentative language to express her feelings. The sense that she might be jealous or possessive is tempered ('not exactly "jealous" … not in a possessive sense'), which indicates that Liz is open about feelings that are probably quite common to adopters, yet may be difficult to express for fear of opprobrium. Although I attempt to emphasize the 'normality' of these feelings – partly because I am very aware that, both as lesbian parents and as adopters, Liz, Sarah, Mary and Michelle may be subject to disapproval or denial of their connections – acknowledgement is hard. Liz is saying that, in certain contexts, she may not be seen as a proper mother, and that – at times – this hurts.

Finally, when I asked the group about whether they felt that they were pioneers of new ways of relating, they made a number of interesting points. First, they told me that their social workers had been very impressed by the support they offered to each other. All four women were adopters for the same agency, and they joked that social workers had wanted to refer other potential lesbian adopters to their group. Liz says, 'we were made to feel a bit like "pioneers" of new family forms by the reactions of others. Social workers would say, "Oh we've heard of you and we know what you're doing. What a good idea and can it spread?"' Second, there was some opposition to the idea of the nuclear family:

Sarah: I suppose I feel I'm not doing the 'nuclear family' thing and I've never felt particularly like I've wanted to go down that nuclear family route, and I think when I made the decision … well I know a lot of lesbians who've said, 'I'd really like to have children but I'm not going to do it until I find the right partner because I don't want to do it on my own,' and I think I've never felt like I've had to create that thing with a partner and having children with them as a prerequisite. I think a lot of lesbians and gay men who I meet in both things like [gay and lesbian foster and adoptive parents support group] and [lesbian families group] are actually creating nuclear families but that just have two people of the same gender as the parents, rather than two people of different genders and that to me doesn't kind of challenge the nuclear family thing, which I don't think is a particularly healthy family structure…

Mary: But why isn't it healthy? Why isn't a nuclear family healthy?

Sarah: I don't think it's necessarily a better or healthier thing than having … I think extended families are …

Mary: Which is healthier, a single parent family or a nuclear family?

Sarah: Well it depends on the people in the family!

Mary: Yeah. I'm talking about models, not about individuals.

Sarah: I think being a single parent without any support is a pretty difficult thing to do.

Mary: Well yeah. But nuclear families that are warring are equally difficult.

Sarah: And because we've chosen to do it as single parents and we've looked outside the immediate thing of what we're doing and made connections with other people to create … well, what I feel we've created is an extended family which is what I like about it because it enables the children to have relationships with different adults and each other and all that kind of thing. So to me it's that which I think is quite pioneering really.

Liz: But I don't think for me, I didn't go out there to 'challenge nuclear families', I found myself in this situation of being able to have a child which I'd always wanted to do, and here I was single and suddenly it was a possibility … and, I wanted to do it on my own but I didn't want to be isolated.

Sarah: Yeah, that's the same for me, I'm not saying I did it to make a point, I like the way we've done it, and I feel there are people I know who will regret not having children because they are waiting for the right circumstances to do it. I feel what I've done is created the circumstances around me rather than wait.

Sarah's comments about a challenge to the nuclear family model provoke a debate within the group. There is a sense of creating new ways of relating that does challenge accepted models, but also a sense in which any family form is not necessarily better than another, it depends on how that family life is lived. Liz doesn't see her adoption of a child as a challenge, since she frames her story here as about realizing a lifetime's wish to become a parent. In response, Sarah is forced to say that she did not become an adopter to 'make a point'. Here is a clash of ideas; the group's approach does seem to challenge ideas about expected kinship, yet they are wary of the danger that lesbian (or gay) parents may be condemned for 'making a political point' rather than really caring for children, an insidious and simplistic binary. Neither does the group really accept Giddens' pioneering label, summed up by two responses. Michelle said, 'I don't feel like a pioneer, but whenever I'm explaining my family situation to people outside of it for the first time, it feels a bit like "oh gosh!"…people are a bit surprised…but often admiring or envious of it.' And Liz said, 'Is Giddens a gay man…well, what does he f***ing know then?!' This humour is used to undercut the notion that lesbian or gay parents are essentially pioneering or 'brave' (an idea that the group rejected) or egalitarian. If anything, the group used the notion of parenting as labour ('hard work') to challenge what they saw as rather utopian ideas. They emphasized the 'triple-whammy' effect, having to create legitimate bonds as lesbians, as single people, and as adopters, but they also talked strongly about the ups-and-downs of ordinary life. This relates directly back to their original magazine piece, 'a little bit special and a little bit ordinary' (Mary et al., 2004: 40).

'Queering' kinship?

What will be the topoi of queer 'kinship'? Will they devolve from 'choice' (Weston, 1991)? Or 'care' (Borneman, 2001)? Will gay kinship require constitutive prohibitions? Will it be, as it evidently is for revelers at gay discos, a practice of freedom? A form of ethical subjectivation?

(Faubion, 2001)

Is it an ambivalent mimicry of heterosexual norms? Or is gay marriage and kinship the sign of a normative subjection, a kind of melancholia, in which persons remain compulsively attached to forms of love from which they have been violently excluded? Why indeed do gays and lesbians continue to subjectivize themselves and their relationships in familial terms, where 'gay mother' might refer to a lesbian with children or to a drag queen and her coterie of devotees? What does it mean? We will not be able to say without inspection.

(Strong, 2002: 415)

I have suggested that a traditional blood/marriage-type version of kinship excludes others, including lesbian and gay relational forms, and have discussed differing responses (Butler, 2004b; Calhoun, 2000). I have also noted that contemporary kinship is much more diverse and includes forms and practices that question standard ideas. However, kin work exhibits patterns based upon social expectations, ways of thinking, talking and acting. New kinship studies are interested in how it is practised, and these have made use of data from research on new reproductive technologies to show that kin work involves both challenge and conformity. Weston has suggested that:

Lesbian and gay families cannot be dismissed as a fiction predicated upon a heterosexual model for constituting kinship. Yet they have incorporated prevalent symbols and appeals to authenticity in ways that make it difficult to separate dominant from 'alternative' constructions of family. (Weston, 1998: 81–2)

This is an important point because we need to remember that any dismissal of such kinship claims as misguided, or as mere acquiescence to heteronormative standards does not recognize the mixture of challenge and acceptance found in these narratives and practices. Neither does it recognize the need to belong. However, what is interesting about kin work performed by lesbians, gay men and adoption participants is that these practices may be said to queer kinship in that they act as an ethnomethodology, or demonstration of the methods by which kinship is produced. That is, they demonstrate kin work in action and show that, first, *all* of us are engaged in kin work; and, second, that this work involves practices of exclusion. For example, birth parents in Modell's original study had no 'sympathy for adoption by gays, even gay couples. The desirable family was not just heterosexual, it was also an old-fashioned family, in which the father worked and the mother stayed home with the children' (Modell, 1994: 82). Of course, this may have changed somewhat, and there are now birth parents with positive views of gay adopters. But it is easy to fall back onto traditional images of 'family life' when imagining kin, especially for a child given up.

To rethink kinship for lesbians and gay men has provoked a range of responses. As we saw, Calhoun's argument is that lesbians and gay men will only acquire kinship entitlement through legal and social recognition of 'marriage' and 'family' (Calhoun, 2000: 160). However, Weston argues that, if 'gay people begin to pursue marriage, joint adoptions, and custody rights to the exclusion of seeking kinship status for some categories of friendship, it seems likely that gay families will develop in ways largely congruent with socio-economic and power relations in the larger society' (Weston, 1991: 209). Weston is critical of seeing kinship as based upon access to 'marriage' and 'family' (basically, the old legal/blood ties version), as this restricts who counts as kin. Her solution is to widen the forms of relations that get called kinship.

Butler's position is more critical still, because she promotes a ' "breakdown" of traditional kinship that not only displaces the central place of biological and sexual relations from its definition but gives sexuality a domain separate from that of kinship' (Butler, 2004b: 127). Like Butler, others have argued that 'kinship' restricts the kinds and forms of human relations that are seen to matter (Berlant and Warner, 1998; Heaphy, 2007; Warner, 1999). Povinelli suggests that, as 'kinship and affinal relations proliferate, ... this proliferation seems only to elaborate and more thoroughly disperse the genealogical grid' (Povinelli, 2002a: 227). That is, acquiring recognition as kin for wider relationship forms means that having genealogy or intimacy becomes the basis for legitimate persons. To be without these 'is to risk being dehumanized' (Povinelli, 2002a: 234), which is to say that kinship claims rest upon exclusivity and insularity.

Faubion's point about kinship as 'subjectivation' (Faubion, 2001: 13) is crucial here. A sense of belonging is relevant to everyday life, and so we engage in kin work, using stories, artefacts, practices, in order to create a sense of our place in a social and relational world. But this also subjects us to kinship; that is, we are lost without it. Further, kinship draws upon heteronormative and hierarchical forms of knowledge in which some lives seem not to count. The 'sad old lonely single person' (a trajectory that is often imagined for gay people) is just one of a series of 'types' that are created to police the boundaries of proper kin. Another would be the 'adult man who still lives with his mum', an acknowledged kin relation that is treated as an illegitimate way of living and as a code for 'gay man', since the 'sphere of legitimate intimate alliance is established through the producing and intensifying regions of illegitimacy' (Butler, 2004b: 105). Indeed, Eng has argued that adoption has now become a 'popular and viable option ... for homosexual couples and singles seeking to (re)consolidate and (re)occupy conventional structures of family and kinship' (Eng, 2003: 1). I will return to Eng's argument in more detail in Chapter 6, since his piece deals specifically with the racial politics of transnational adoption. But he, too, is essentially concerned with how we might promote a queer or 'poststructuralist kinship' (Eng, 2003: 32).

I shall end this chapter with discussion of an interesting piece by Julianne Pidduck, 'Queer Kinship and Ambivalence', which analyses video autoethnographies by two USA artists, Jean Carlomusto and Richard Fung. Pidduck's piece is one of the few that acknowledges that any queering of kinship must work with its everyday claims but also question its foundations. Kinship remains '*vital*, an ontological common denominator shared by queers and nonqueers. Nonetheless, the relationship between kinship and lesbian, gay, and queer experience, politics, thought, and cultural production is an anguished and contested one' (Pidduck, 2009: 441). Anguish and contest are present, or made use of, in narratives by gay or lesbian adopters and foster carers (Hicks and McDermott, 1999b; Hill, 2009) and in the accounts given in this chapter by Liz, Mary, Sarah, Michelle and Jean.

Pidduck's analysis of *To Catch a Glimpse* (1997) and *Shatzi Is Dying* (1999) by Carlomusto and *My Mother's Place* (1990) and *Sea in the Blood* (2000) by Fung reads 'against hegemonic kinship narratives of continuity across space and time, of heredity and progress' in order to highlight 'motifs of displacement, illness, death, and loss [which] produce fractured and affectively ambivalent kinship documents characterized by disruptions, silences, traumas, and gaps' (Pidduck, 2009: 444). These motifs are found in works that make use of video, photographic, spoken and written texts, and that investigate the complex situation of lesbian and gay people within their kinship networks. Pidduck's analysis reminds us that 'relatedness is forged not only on our own terms [but also] within conditions (and relations) not of our own making' (Pidduck, 2009: 446). Crucially, she notes the 'centrality of practices of mediation – storytelling, domestic photography, and home movies – in forging kinship relations' (Pidduck, 2009: 451). That is, kinship is claimed or practised, as we have seen with narratives by Jean, Mary, Liz, Michelle or Sarah. I develop analysis of storytelling and photography in the next chapter.

Pidduck's interest in Carlomusto's and Fung's works is motivated by a concern to highlight 'painful silences and gaps that haunt family memory' (Pidduck, 2009: 454), and she argues that autoethnography 'returns again and again to the moments where kinship falters or breaks down' (Pidduck, 2009: 457). Pidduck's point is that, in their investigation of such ruptures, Carlomusto and Fung challenge 'genealogies based on heredity, continuity, and property' (Pidduck, 2009: 461), the stuff of more usual kinship claims. Pidduck uses the term 'ambivalence' to capture this in two senses; it sums up questions of affect for lesbian, gay and queer people 'on the cusp of kinship', and it pinpoints the 'fragmented and discontinuous kinship ontologies' explored in the video works (Pidduck, 2009: 463). Pidduck argues that 'autoethnography helps us understand (queer) kinship as a set of performative practices' (Pidduck, 2009: 464). This returns us to my earlier argument that queer kinship practices are an ethnomethodology because they demonstrate kin work carried out by everyone, part of which includes the assertion of power relations.

Pidduck's piece is also helpful because it does not adopt an either/or approach to questions of kinship as they relate to lesbians, gays and queers. That is, she does not suggest that lesbians and gay men are either simply inside (assimilative) or outside (radical) of kinship. They are simultaneously both, as Mary, Liz, Michelle and Sarah argued, a point also made by Weeks:

> The language of 'family' used by many lesbian and gay people may be seen as both a challenge to conventional definitions and an attempt to broaden these; as a hankering for legitimacy and an attempt to build something new; as an identification with existing patterns and a more or less conscious effort to subvert them. (Weeks, 2007: 180)

The kinship claims of lesbian adopters, for example, must be made or performed within the constraints of a state-sponsored childcare system, one that makes use of standard ideas about relationality and one that sometimes condemns queerness, a point that I shall return to in Chapter 7. But, like Pidduck's silences and gaps, the challenges and contradictions of kinship were highlighted by Liz, Mary, Michelle, Sarah and Jean. Liz's confession about 'jealousy', or the debate the group had about challenging/not challenging the nuclear family, are examples of ambivalence. And this arises because to be subject to kinship means to find a way to narrate or create relations within the terms of recognition by a dominant discourse; a kinned subject is created through some reliance on restricted notions of relationality. Of course there is room for creativity and challenge, but these constitute difficult work, in the sense both of finding the resources for such creativity but also taking up positions that may not be recognized as belonging. As Mason argues, 'people do not have a completely free hand to create what they desire, but neither do they simply follow geneticist or biological versions of kinship, origin and consequence' (Mason, 2008: 37). A queerer kinship would work with these gaps and contradictions in order to avoid relational hierarchies and to allow for the production of what Foucault called 'new alliances' (Foucault, 2000a: 136). But Foucault also warned against defining a programme of new relational forms since this was bound to curtail creativity. For us, this provokes a dilemma: how do we acknowledge the development of new and interesting kinship forms whilst still guarding against their possible exclusivity?

3
Family

It has become an essential ritual of our societies to scrutinize the countenance of the family at regular intervals in order to decipher our destiny, glimpsing in the death of the family an impending return to barbarism, the letting go of our reasons for living; or indeed, in order to reassure ourselves at the sight of its inexhaustible capacity for survival.

(Donzelot, 1997: 4)

Lesbians and gay men have been at the centre of contemporary debates about the family. For some, they are pioneers of new relational forms; for others, they represent a threat to the family, a symptom of its decline, or assimilators who wish to disappear into a virtually heterosexual lifestyle. As Jacques Donzelot (1997) notes, thinking and talking about the family presents an opportunity to imagine a better, more family-centred, past or – equally – to glimpse in new ways of living family life the tenacity of an essential form. Lesbians and gay men might represent a threat to the family, or they might just be the family in a new incarnation. Perhaps neither of these is a very satisfactory account.

This raises the question of 'The Family' versus what we might refer to as the living of everyday family life. There have been various attempts to theorize this difference and, in those approaches that I favour, sociologists and others have begun to examine how family is achieved, done or enacted in the everyday. Asking whether lesbian and gay parenting and other relations count as 'The Family', then, may not be very useful since it probably tells us very little about those lives, and it does not ask how and why family claims are put to use in various contexts. Further, all claims about family status take place within a hierarchical context in which lesbians and gay men are held accountable in some way. To do everyday life as a lesbian or gay family is to risk being held accountable to gender/sexuality norms.

'The Family' *versus* families

John Gillis says that each of us has two families, 'one that we live *with* and another we live *by*' (Gillis, 1997: xv). The family that we live with is our everyday one, but the family we live by is an imagined version, how things ought to be. Gillis says that families we live with 'are much less reliable than the imagined families we live by. The latter are never allowed to let us down' (Gillis, 1997: xv). But, crucially, 'we are being encouraged to see the good family life as a "world we have lost"' (Gillis, 1997: xvii). This 'world we have lost' version may be found in some accounts of contemporary family change, where there is both nostalgia for, and an attempt to reassert, 'The Family', always a heterosexual and usually a nuclear (dad, mum and kids) model. This is partly a response to changes in family structures or ways of living, since contemporary life consists not so much of the nuclear but, rather, what Bob Simpson terms the 'unclear' family (Simpson, 1994). Yet, it is also important to remember that this 'golden age' of the nuclear family *versus* today's new forms is itself an unreliable contrast structure. Extended, diverse and non-biologically based relations, as well as hardship, poverty and higher infant and adult mortality may be found in both past and contemporary family lives (Gillis, 1997; Stack, 1997; Young and Wilmott, 2007). Of course, this is not to say that nothing has changed but, rather, those who lament the decline of the nuclear family wish to re-establish its primacy. For them, the two-parent, heterosexual, married couple is the proper place to bring up children.

This perspective, represented in the UK by writers such as Almond, Morgan or Melanie Phillips, is a contemporary version of functionalist sociology (e.g., Parsons, 1956a, 1956b) because it sees 'The Family' as serving the best interests of children, adults and society as a whole. Almond, for example, argues that a biological pair bond between a man and a woman is the proper basis for the raising of children. She also claims that relationships other than marriage are transient, and that marriage is there to model the 'pre-ferred relationship' for children (Almond, 2006: 168). According to Phillips, marriage socializes men (not just children), since they are encouraged to adopt more settled and responsible lives, and it provides the 'otherness' of the opposite gender, which all children need for identity development:

Sons learn from their fathers about male responsibility and achieve-ment and relating to girls. Without their fathers, the influence of the peer group takes on disproportionate importance. From their fathers, girls learn how to relate to men and to appreciate their own femininity (p. 108) ... Women and men need each other to play complementary roles. Children need both of them. Mothers cannot function without exten-sive support networks. Men can. If they cut loose, everyone will suffer. (Phillips, 1999: 359)

Like many who defend 'The Family' in contemporary times, Phillips displays a concern not only to uphold this way of life, but also to promote distinct gender roles, a point I analyze in detail in Chapter 5. In particular, it is men – or the role of men – that garners most attention. First, in modern times, men's role within the family has been thrown into question, but, for Phillips and other writers, this is a symptom of modern decline or crisis (Blankenhorn, 1995; Dennis and Erdos, 1992; Morgan, 2002; Popenhoe, 1996). Second, in Phillips' work, men are potential 'savages' who require the socializing influence of women and 'The Family'. Phillips' view of the family, then, is a functional one in which gender roles are necessary, complementary and distinct. She insists that children learn to relate to the opposite sex, and she defines key roles for boys and girls to learn from men. However, whilst boys learn active public roles ('responsibility' and 'achievement'), girls learn only to 'relate to men' and to be feminine.

These writers also oppose lesbian and gay relations, since, for them, such ways of life represent all that is wrong with the decline of 'The Family' and the proper gender order. Morgan says that children do much better in heterosexual homes, and even that mathematical ability 'in children of homosexual cohabitants [is] below the average scores for all students and well below that for the children of heterosexual cohabitants and married couples' (Morgan, 2000: 44). She also suggests that gay men and lesbians use children as 'trophies', to 'make political statements' (Morgan, 2002: 133), a charge that Liz and Sarah referred to in Chapter 2.

Writing by sociologists, such as Giddens in the UK or Stacey in the USA, has argued a very different point of view. For these theorists, lesbian and gay relations exemplify all that is positive about changing family forms. For Giddens, gay men and lesbians are relationship 'innovators, often in a hostile environment' (Giddens, 1999: 6). Stacey similarly argues that queer families display 'features of improvisation, ambiguity, diversity, contradiction, self-reflection and flux' (Stacey, 1996: 143). Lesbians and gay men seem to demonstrate egalitarian couple relationships and a commitment to the 'pure relationship,' which Giddens defines as 'a situation where a social relation is entered into for its own sake, for what can be derived by each person from a sustained association with another; and which is continued only in so far as it is thought by both parties to deliver enough satisfactions for each individual to stay within it' (Giddens, 1992: 58).

However, Giddens tends to overlook wider social inequalities, especially in terms of gender; and his emphasis on the pure relationship 'feeds into a therapeutic discourse that has sometimes been the antithesis of empowering for women and gays' (Jamieson, 1999: 490). See, for example, his ideas about women's 'co dependence' on 'womanising' men (p. 87) or his view of 'male sexual violence' as stemming from 'insecurity and inadequacy... a destructive reaction to the waning of female complicity' (Giddens, 1992: 122).

In addition, his account of lesbians and gay men imputes psychological insecurity or lack: gay men adopt 'roles' (p. 123) and 'cope with' a general 'resentment towards women [that] is part of male psychology' by 'detaching themselves from it altogether' (Giddens, 1992: 146), while lesbians 'have difficulty in gaining a sense of security' in long-term relationships (p. 135), even though lesbian sex is held up as 'more successful than heterosexual activity' (p. 142).

Stacey's ethnography of gay men's relational lives, centred on Los Angeles, suggests a 'cruising culture' that:

> yields social and familial consequences far more complex and contra-dictory than most critics (or even a few fans) seem to imagine. The gay cruising arena of unencumbered, recreational sex certainly does disrupt conventional family norms and practices. At the same time, however, it also generates bonds of kinship and domesticity. (Stacey, 2004: 183)

She describes a series of adult and parenting relationships that cross and mix classes, races and cultures, and that 'simultaneously reinforce and challenge conventional gender and family practices and values' (Stacey, 2004: 193). Stacey also argues that 'many gay men can more readily separate physical sex from romantic and domestic commitments', and so 'they enjoy greater latitude to negotiate diverse terms for meeting their sexual and emotional needs within and beyond dyadic couple arrangements' (Stacey, 2005: 1926). This is an important point, one that is not best served by a defensive 'but gay men have long-term, committed relationships too' response, and one that I take up in Chapter 8. Stacey's argument is that non-normative, non-dyadic relationships are present within these gay men's relational communities, but may have interesting implications for all practices of relationality.

However, Neil Gross reminds us that 'many of the intimate practices of such "arch inventors," (Weeks et al., 2001: 20) not to mention the practices of their more obviously conventional counterparts, continue to revolve as much around debts to tradition – as tradition has been reshaped by other forces such as capitalism – as around autonomous principles or prefer-ences that are individually or collectively negotiated' (Gross, 2005: 306). Christopher Carrington's ethnographic study of lesbian and gay family life, for example, raises some key problems with the over-generalized view that such relationships exemplify new, egalitarian forms of intimacy. He shows, first, that, in practice, many gay or lesbian families or couples are not as egalitarian as they would have us, or themselves, believe. One person often does most or all of the day-to-day planning and running of a household, and some couples divide jobs or roles in a typical worker/breadwinner-carer/homemaker fashion (Carrington, 1999: 34). Crucially, material factors are highly relevant. Carrington argues that wealthier, urban gay people have more resources (income, space, domestic help, and so on) with which to develop wider friends-as-family networks, while those with limited resources are more self-sufficient, since they have to be. They work longer hours, have smaller homes, do their own housework, and often don't, or feel unable to, entertain at home (Carrington, 1999: 211).

The sociology of gay and lesbian relations and questions of family ought to retain a concern with these material questions. As Stevi Jackson argues, we should keep in mind 'the material social contexts in which cultural products and practices emerge, in which discourses are deployed and sub-jectivities are constituted' (Jackson, 1999: 3). This means that social rela-tions – heteronormativity, for example – are relevant to claims or narrative about family status, or, put another way, accounts of family/sexuality have to make sense within a given context, and that context consists of hierar-chical power relations. It also means paying attention to hierarchies *enacted within* families. Feminist work on the family has argued that it is women who still bear the burden of unpaid or undervalued caring work (Brown, 2009; Delphy and Leonard, 1992; Hanscombe and Forster, 1982; Lewis, 2003; Segal, 1983; Somerville, 2000), and has reminded us that, far from being the 'the safest environment in which a child can grow up' (Almond, 2006: 141), 'The Family' is the site of most of the abuse and violence towards women and children.

In response to these questions about exploitation, many theorists have blamed 'The Family' and have advocated less restrictive relational forms including communal life, freely available child care, shared care, and the valuing of adult relationships not solely based upon the (sexual) couple – yet, in practice, many of these have been difficult to achieve and, amongst all sections of society, the couple is still prioritized (Gabb, 2008; Wise and Stanley, 2004). Part of this has to do with the point that it is much easier to live in a socially approved relationship. As Gross has noted:

> while those who deviate today from the practices of LISM [lifelong, inter-nally stratified marriage] are subject to fewer and less intensive social sanctions than in the past, the image of the form of couplehood inscribed in the regulative tradition of LISM continues to function as a hegem-onic ideal in many – perhaps most – [American] intimate relationships. [American] intimacy also remains beholden to the tradition of romantic love. (Gross, 2005: 288)

There are material, as well as discursive, reasons for this.

In the UK, for example, governments have emphasized the primacy of marriage within family policy (HM Government, 2007; Home Office, 1998), and in 2010 initiated tax breaks for married couples (Cabinet Office, 2010). Although UK law was amended to allow joint adoption by unmarried couples (including lesbians and gay men) and the Civil Partnership Act 2004 allowed registration of gay and lesbian couple relationships, policy has, nevertheless, clearly asserted that 'the stability associated with marriage usually provides the best environment in which to bring up children' (HM Government, 2007: 3). In 2005, for example, the UK Government allocated some £25 million to voluntary sector work supporting marriage, relationships and parenting (HM Government, 2007: 21). In the USA, too, similar work goes into the maintenance of the primacy of the heterosexual couple (Mink, 1998), with policies that give 'strong endorsement, even in an implicit sense, to the conservative construction of ideal identities and kinship formations' (Smith, 2007: 43).

Family discourse and family practices

A sociology that moves away from 'The Family', or even merely asking about different forms of the family, would need to question the ways in which a sense of family, of entitlement to being recognized or named as such, is enacted. A Foucaultian notion of family discourse is one in which the concern is not solely with texts, but also with material practices, with how family is enacted and delimited within a range of circumstances. Foucault, for example, argues that nineteenth-century disciplines of medicine, psychiatry and sexology concerned themselves with the policing of motherhood, involving parents in the monitoring of children's sexuality and the family in responsible procreation. The family, he says, was an 'active site of sexuality' (Foucault, 1990: 109) and a form of what he calls sovereign power (Foucault, 2006) in which order was produced. Types, such as 'the nervous woman, the frigid wife, the indifferent mother – or worse, the mother beset by murderous obsessions – the impotent, sadistic, perverse husband, the hysterical or neurasthenic girl, the precocious and already exhausted child, and the young homosexual who rejects marriage or neglects his wife' (Foucault, 1990: 110) were brought forth and responded to by doctors, educators, psychiatrists, priests and so on. The 'dreadful secret', that the family 'was the germ of all the misfortunes of sex', was discovered so that it should be endlessly examined (Foucault, 1990: 111). Family discourse involved practices of inclusion/exclusion and ab/normality:

> Through the various discourses, legal sanctions against minor perversions were multiplied; sexual irregularity was annexed to mental illness; from childhood to old age, a norm of sexual development was defined and all the possible deviations were carefully described; pedagogical controls and medical treatments were organized; around the least fantasies, moralists, but especially doctors, brandished the whole emphatic vocabulary of abomination. (Foucault, 1990: 36)

Foucault's work implies that we should pay attention to family discourse as it is implicated in, first, a sense of what is right/valid and usual/normal. People's family activities relate to what they see as a moral course of action, 'doing the right thing' (Charles et al., 2008; Finch and Mason, 1993), but also their activities are used to define what is usually expected. For example, in Charis Thompson's study of assisted reproductive technological clinics, 'the ability to provide a stable family environment was frequently discussed in terms that had to do with class, via references to patients' assumed wealth, stylish dress, sophisticated demeanour, or professional rank. There was broad agreement that anyone seeking treatment should be heterosexually partnered although not necessarily married' (Thompson, 2005: 86).

Second, family discourse is a set of practices with consequences. This observation is derived from David Morgan's important shifting of family sociology towards an analysis of practice (Morgan, 1975, 1985, 1996, 1999, 2011). This involves asking how family is done rather than what it is, moving away from family's 'thing-like' status towards its constructed, interactional nature. Morgan suggests that we take family as an adjective, 'to refer to sets of practices which deal in some way with ideas of parenthood, kinship and marriage and the expectations and obligations which are associated with these practices' (Morgan, 1996: 11). This notion may be broadened, or perhaps challenged, to include gay and lesbian relational practices – as Morgan later notes (Morgan, 2011) – but, still, interest will lie in what kinds of activities, claims, narratives, images and so on, are used to take up family status.

Third, family discourse gives meaning; that is, through making sense of situations, family status is either confirmed or denied. For example, James Holstein and Jaber Gubrium suggest that practices of care can be used to override a purely biological basis for family, something that is evident in gay and lesbian family claims (Holstein and Gubrium, 1994: 235). Finally, Foucault's argument that discourse works through practices of exclusion is also clearly relevant to family accounts, since stories are used to ostracize those who don't measure up, and a 'white nuclear version of familialism' is used to find other forms wanting (Chambers, 2001: 2), a point I return to in Chapter 6 on race.

This last point is central to the argument made by Dorothy E. Smith, in her piece, 'The Standard North American Family: SNAF as an ideological code' (Smith, 1999). Smith is interested in how discourses, 'skeins of social relations, mediated and organized textually, connecting and co-ordinating the activities of actual individuals', are taken up by people, and how they order 'practices and courses of action' (Smith, 1999: 158). What Smith terms the 'Standard North American Family' (SNAF) refers to a:

> conception of The Family as a legally married couple sharing a household. The adult male is in paid employment; his earnings provide the

economic basis of the family-household. The adult female may also earn an income, but her primary responsibility is to the care of husband, household, and children. The adult male and female may be parents (in whatever legal sense) of children also resident in the household. (Smith, 1999: 159)

SNAF is an ideological code because it refers not to a real and specific family but to a universal. Smith compares SNAF with, for example, Stack's ethnography of kin relations amongst black American families (Stack, 1997), and notes that such ways of life remain 'marginal to the ubiquity of SNAF' (Smith, 1999: 160). SNAF works to produce other family forms as 'deviant instances' (Smith, 1999: 160), and Smith gives the examples of single-parent families, families without fathers, and black families, all of which are so characterized. Black families, for example, are frequently referred to as 'matriarchal' or 'female-headed', in order to identify them as deviant but also to locate women as the source of family decline (Smith, 1999: 166). Smith says:

> SNAF-infected texts are all around us. They give discursive body and substance to a version of The Family that masks the actualities of people's lives and inserts an implicit evaluation into accounts of ways of living together in households or forming economically and emotionally supportive relationships that do not accord with SNAF. (Smith, 1999: 171)

Gubrium and Holstein have argued, too, for a social constructionist account of family. In *What is Family?*, they suggest that 'the everyday reality of the familial is produced through discourse. Thus family is as much a way of thinking and talking about relationships as it is a concrete set of social ties and sentiments' (Gubrium and Holstein, 1990: ix–x). Further, this discourse is a 'social process by which "family," as a social form, is brought into being as a matter of practice...[There are] myriad social processes through which persons in the course of everyday life produce and organize "family" as a meaningful designation for social relations' (Holstein and Gubrium, 1999: 4).

  Holstein and Gubrium's work is opposed to research that takes the family as given and then attempts to understand what happens within that unit. Instead, they argue for a view of family as 'an idea or configuration of meanings, thus problematizing its experiential reality'. They wish to understand '*how* family meanings are assembled and *used* in any site or social location, and *how* this situated process of interpretation gets transmuted into concrete domestic life' (Holstein and Gubrium, 1999: 5). People are creative about their use of 'family' and it is put to use in different ways depending on context. However, Holstein and Gubrium remind us that 'people do not construct their lives completely according to their own desires', since the process is 'mediated by the interpretive resources and circumstances at hand' (1999: 7).

An important example of this would be the shift in thinking identified by many lesbians and gay men who move from seeing parenting as an impossibility (or, perhaps, not even imagining it as a possibility at all) towards an understanding that their desire to care for children is achievable. Weeks et al. discuss this when they identify 'stories of impossibility' moving towards 'stories of choice' (Weeks et al., 2001: 161–8). Liz, the lesbian adopter introduced in Chapter 2, also talked in these terms:

> I felt totally out on a limb at first … um, except that I knew Michelle. She was my – um – my person that enabled me to see that [adoption] was a possibility for me, where I hadn't even realized before. I literally didn't know that it was feasible … I think the main thing for me was that I didn't think social services would give somebody like me a child.

Or Richard, who has adopted with his partner, Paul, says:

> I have a clear memory of when it hit me as a teenager that I would not be able to have children of my own. Embarrassing as it is to admit it, I remember crying about it on one occasion in bed at night. It seems amazing now, more than thirty years later, that I could have had such a clear perception at that young age. Like a lot of teenagers, I was struggling with issues of 'abnormal' sexual feelings and sexual identity 'problems' … Anyway … I decided that even if I couldn't have my own children I would be able to work in the child-care field … I'm not sure when it first dawned on me that I might one day be able to join the ranks of foster carers … (Hicks and McDermott, 1999b: 54–5)

Here, there is a time and place in which gay parenting was not claimable as a possibility. Impossibility is not just about thinking that it is not feasible to realize a desire to parent, but also – crucially – it is about anticipating discrimination. These narratives typically employ a contrast structure, in which a new context allows for possibility. Often, explicit reference is made to the influence of hearing about other gay parents, or meeting them, or taking part in lesbian and gay parenting support groups. That is, there is a shift of 'interpretive resources and parameters as *local culture*' (Holstein and Gubrium, 1999: 8), which allows for the possibility of a gay parenting, or even family, claim. However, the story *itself* – that is, the narrative that contrasts the past with the present – acts as a claim about relations: 'I now think of myself [or I *am*] a [lesbian/gay] parent and/or we are a family.' This is important, as the context in which the story itself is heard (maybe within a lesbian/gay parenting group, amongst friends, with other family members, or even within a research interview), is relevant to the claims made.

This idea of a local culture, however, does not refer to a set of rules. Holstein and Gubrium describe it as 'a situationally assembled array of resources and conditions for interpretation, not a monolithic set of injunctions or absolute directives' (1999: 8). Within the context of a lesbian/gay parenting group, for example, the idea that lesbians and gay men can be parents is not questioned but, rather, is taken as a morally approved stance. However, outside of such contexts, in everyday life, then the family retains 'an ethical and normative prescriptive stature' (Gubrium and Holstein, 1990: 133) which, as Smith noted, works to maintain some forms as 'deviant instances' (Smith, 1999: 160). Gubrium and Holstein note that some discourses work to establish limited forms (such as the nuclear structure) as 'The Family', but these also work hard to be 'taken to be merely descriptive so that ... partisan motivations are hidden' (Gubrium and Holstein, 1990: 133). Designating any relation as familial involves the assertion of power, or powerful assertions, and it is these processes that Holstein and Gubrium argue require analytic attention.

Love Makes a Family

Kaeser and Gillespie's book, *Love Makes a Family: Portraits of Lesbian, Gay, Bisexual, and Transgender Parents and Their Families* (1999), makes family claims on a number of interconnected levels – as auto/biography, as photobook, as commentary on the 'lesbian, gay, bisexual and transgender (LGBT) family' and as an exhibit. It is an example of what Finch terms family 'display' (Finch, 2007). The text contains narratives by LGBT parents and their children, Kaeser's photographic portraits, essays and information about the associated touring exhibition 'Love Makes a Family: Living in Lesbian and Gay Families' (Gillespie, 1999: xiv). In addition, the format uses professional photographs that, although having a 'coffee-table book' feel, remind the reader/viewer of a domestic family album, a crucial point to which I shall return. The book represents family on many levels, and it is important to consider its claims within the context of its production and exhibition, as well as thinking about the auto/biographical, visual/photographic and academic/political narratives it contains.

Love Makes a Family is variously described as a 'contribution to information about who we are in all of our diversity' (comment by Barney Frank, House of Representatives, United States Congress, on the book's back cover) and as an exhibit that:

> seeks to challenge and change damaging myths and stereotypes about LGBT people and their families. At the most basic level, *Love Makes a Family* combats homophobia by breaking silence and making the invisible visible. By encouraging people of all ages – beginning in early childhood – to affirm and appreciate diversity, this travelling rental exhibit

contributes to the process of dismantling the destructive power of prejudice and intolerance, thereby making the world a safer place for all families. Designed for audiences of all ages, *Love Makes a Family* challenges stereotypes about LGBT people and helps dismantle homophobia. (Family Diversity Projects, 2004–8)

The book has accompanying essays by Minnie Bruce Pratt (1999), whose poetry collection *Crime Against Nature* (1990) detailed her struggle as a lesbian mother who lost custody of her two sons; by Weston (1999); and by April Martin (1999), author of *The Lesbian and Gay Parenting Handbook* (Martin, 1993). These essays claim that *Love Makes a Family* represents ordinary people and that love is what counts (Gillespie, 1999; Martin, 1999). But, at the same time, they argue the collection does not represent *all* LGBT families, and that dealing with homophobia is a key difference (Gillespie, 1999; Pratt, 1999). Weston highlights the authenticity and diversity of the photographic portraits, yet she is also clear that these are posed. This is 'not a collection of "action shots" that propose to capture the look on the face of a parent who has just spent the last six hours doing the laundry' (Weston, 1999: 5). This is interesting, as it shows an awareness of the composed nature of the portraits. At the same time, Martin argues that the pictures 'are not sentimental "Hallmark" [a USA greetings card company] images of people looking their best for the camera' (Martin, 1999: 252), which seems to suggest 'realness'. This raises again the question of authenticity, the notion that the portraits are, or are not, real accounts. This has always been a problem with any 'positive images' approach; for any suggestion that an image is necessarily positive or accurate does not allow for acknowledgement that it is actually open to interpretation and that it is posed.

The exhibit is funded by a number of organizations listed on the website, and is supported by an extensive advisory board that includes young people (Family Diversity Projects, 2004–8). Finally, a number of published testimonials talk about questions of diversity, and the idea of love and caring expressed within LGBT families:

The success of the exhibit *Love Makes a Family* is its immediacy in establishing the love and humanity in all types of families. The exhibit cuts through all the political arguments and rhetoric right to the heart of the issue by showing the love, caring and connection that are so basic to all families. (Maldonado, 2000: 1)

For many who have been unable, because of bias and discrimination, to be visible as LGBT families, the photographs of *Love Makes a Family* confirm their existence, speak for them, humanize them and announce their 'normalcy', establish familiarity and demand attention. The multiracial selection of photographs speaks to the diversity within our community and influences everyone who sees them. (Wolpert, 2006: 1)

The simple and straightforward portrayal of LGBT families in *Love Makes a Family* celebrates the range of family structure that exists and sends the powerful messages simultaneously that *different is wonderful* and *we're not so different after all*. Whether looking at the photos and reading the interviews at an exhibit venue, perusing the new book version of *Love Makes a Family*, or exploring Family Diversity Project's online resources, students, educators, and community members are challenged to confront stereotypical understandings of LGBT people in the light of honest and moving depictions. (Jennings, 2000: 1)

A number of important claims are brought together through these accounts of the book/exhibit, most of which are concerned with establishing the idea of *family diversity*. This is a claim that challenges 'The Family' and, instead, proposes a representation of many family types. Second, they argue that *Love Makes a Family* challenges myths, stereotypes and homophobia, and presents an account of the love, humanity and 'normalcy' (Wolpert, 2006: 1) to be found within LGBT families. Here, alongside the idea that all families are the same and are about human essentials such as love, the notion of difference also arises. As Kevin Jennings notes, *'different is wonderful and we're not so different after all'* (Jennings, 2000: 1). A simultaneous acknowledgement and denial of difference, very much like 'a little bit special and a little bit ordinary' (Mary et al., 2004). The claims about humanity and love are reinforced by Lisa Maldonado's notion that 'political arguments and rhetoric' have been avoided (Maldonado, 2000: 1). She asserts a sense of ordinary, human life, rather than politics, perhaps also responding to the claim that LGBT parenting is solely a political tool. Finally, there is the question of visibility, raised a number of times. The book and exhibit make visible LGBT families, and this counters ignorance and invisibility within visual and narrative representation.

Before considering why and how such claims have come about, I would like to offer some critiques. The idea of family diversity itself acts as an assertion of difference and multiculture, but this raises a number of problems. First, LGBT families are subject to forms of homophobia. Of course, *Love Makes a Family* is overtly challenging this – that is partly its point, but a diversity model suggests that a level playing field will be achieved through acknowledgement of difference. But, whenever any new and different version of the family is allowed, then there will always be some others excluded; that is, *Love Makes a Family* may participate in establishing the 'good homosexual' family life whilst maintaining its other, the 'dangerous queer' (Smith, 1994: 18). This brings us to a related problem with diversity models. In relying on difference *within the family*, rather than questioning the *family form*, then types may be established, 'the LGBT family' for example, or 'the black family'.

This also relates to concerns about the visibility/authenticity trope used in claims about the publication. 'Here is the LGBT family', the arguments seem to say, as though this is a real depiction of LGBT parents and their children's lives. But the claims within the narrative and visual text of *Love Makes a Family* are artful; they are posed, careful, motivated, and they may conceal and much as they reveal. And the idea that they are necessarily positive depictions is highly suspect, for this does not allow any space for interpretation or reception, a point that I shall return to in relation to the photographs themselves. Finally, the notion of challenging 'myths' is also a problem, as what this does not admit is that the versions being challenged are not mythical at all but, rather, powerful claims about how family life ought to be. It is not simply that people carry around in their heads uninformed myths about LGBT families but, rather, that they can and do draw upon heteronormative discourses in making everyday claims about what are, in fact, objections to LGBT lives. As Homi Bhabha has argued, the stereotype is not simply a false representation; rather, it is an attempt to fix something or someone in place that requires constant repetition. Indeed, he suggests that we shift our focus away from argument about whether any image is necessarily positive or negative towards 'the *processes of subjectification* made possible (and plausible) through stereotypical discourse' (Bhabha, 2004: 95).

Bhabha's work also helps me to raise questions about the diversity discourse surrounding *Love Makes a Family*. He argues that one of the major problems with any cultural diversity argument is its very reliance upon the idea of separate cultures. Diversity relies upon 'the separation of totalized cultures that live unsullied by the intertextuality of their historical locations' (Bhabha, 2004: 50). Thus, the 'LGBT family type' is added in to existing or dominant notions of the family, but it seems to occupy a particular, cultural form. It relies on what Steven Epstein has termed the 'ethnic identity' model of sexuality (Epstein, 1987), one in which 'the LGBT family' is seen as a distinct type with particular characteristics.

In addition, this notion of diversity doesn't help us to ask how a claim for the LGBT family is achieved, since it has to draw upon and make use of certain ways of speaking or looking in order to work. Potentially, *anyone* can claim a family status, but this does not mean that all such claims will be heard or agreed. Particular ways of talking, behaving or appearing must be used. The very notion 'love makes a family', for example, draws upon sentimental or idealized imagery. It suggests sameness, but it inevitably excludes other ways of living (even though the book itself is careful to include a range of family forms), since normality is achieved through the creation of abnormal others.

These concerns about some of the claims made in and through *Love Makes a Family* are crucial, but I also need to ask whether they are wholly fair. Arguments for the LGBT family, for its inclusion or representation, for its ordinariness, are made, we must remember, in the face of homophobia. This is pointed out by some of the contributors. Bonnie says, 'the fact that people fear us does make our lives significantly different' (Kaeser and Gillespie, 1999: 38), and Perry says, 'I get very angry when people say that it is horrible for children to be brought up in a gay family and that gays are absolutely sick people. There's a lot of hatred against us and our families' (Kaeser and Gillespie, 1999: 226). In addition, it's worth remembering that the exhibit itself was the subject of court action to prevent its display in some schools. This sense of complexity is important, and it emerges as I analyze the essays, narratives and photographs in the book.

The auto/biography of LGBT family life

Turning now to the written stories in the book, Liz Stanley's work on auto/biography argues that life writing is always 'highly selective…artful construction' (Stanley, 1992: 128), and that any account of a life is a product of its author, context and reader(s). This latter point is crucial here; my reading of *Love Makes a Family* is just that – *my* reading, and many others will disagree. But, as the work is presented as an authentic account, then it is necessary to ask how the stories work as such. That is, it is important *not* to treat the accounts given as real, but to consider their claims. My analysis of the narratives in the book finds a number of recurring or common threads, though this is not an exhaustive list '(see Table 3.1).'

The first of these, love makes a family, draws upon the title of the book/exhibit to argue that all families are the same and that what defines them is love and caring, rather than sexuality. This recalls arguments in Chapter 2, whereby chosen kinship was often defined by longer-term caring and sharing of experiences, rather than blood (Weston, 1991). But it also argues that all families are ultimately defined in this way, through caring work. It is therefore a claim for family entitlement and legitimacy. Rob says, 'It's very important for people to understand that love makes a family. Without love, there's no family. Gay families do the same thing straight families do – which is to love each other. Gay parents have the same power of love as

Table 3.1 Common stories in *Love Makes a Family*

Love makes a family/'we're all the same'/the mundane labours of family life/ordinariness
Family diversity and difference (within *all* families and within the LGBT family)
A 'coming out and coming to terms' story: 'I always wanted kids/didn't think I could/realized I could…'
Extended and non-biological/chosen families (with some links made to ethnicity)
Queer community/groups versus prejudice of birth family
Gender roles/models and prejudice
Use of family rituals/celebrating family and identity

anyone else. All they do is love their children and try to do their best to raise a family' (Kaeser and Gillespie, 1999: 67). These claims draw upon a recognizable and even sentimental story about the family as concerned with love, care, respect and commitment. This appeals to an everyday notion of family life, which is, nevertheless, a rather mawkish one at times: 'Respect is love's equal partner', says Shirley (Kaeser and Gillespie, 1999: 199).

Many contributors list parenting's mundane labours in order to challenge the notion of LGBT parents as 'other'. Joann says, 'What makes me a mother is baking muffins at 11:00 p.m. for Sol's school party, comforting her when she's crying, creating a "math dog" to make math fun, and saying "no," even when it's disappointing to Sol' (Kaeser and Gillespie, 1999: 153). Regina uses similar examples to challenge the equation of lesbianism with sex: 'If the thing that defines us and makes us different is who we have sex with, then I can hardly find time to be a lesbian! Cooking, doing laundry, taking the kids back and forth, fussing at somebody who didn't do their homework, going to a teacher's meeting, taking the animals to the vet. That's our day' (Kaeser and Gillespie, 1999: 78). However, many of these lists exist alongside claims *for* difference. Beth says, 'Karen and I are normal, everyday people: we are parents; we run a business together; we are fortunate enough to have a mortgage to pay; we do laundry; we pay the bills; we've started a family support group in our area with a monthly newsletter that goes out to about six hundred gay, lesbian, bisexual, and transgender families and allies...I am not trying to say that we are "normal," as in, "just like straight people." I mean we are normal lesbian parents' (Kaeser and Gillespie, 1999: 29–30). Listing is used to emphasize sameness, but a contrast structure (sameness/ difference) is either implied (really we're just the same as others) or employed (we're the same...but different).

The second thread links to the overall diversity stance of the text. Here, the stories suggest that diversity within *all* families must be recognized through adding in the LGBT family, but also that there is diversity *within* the LGBT family category. Barbara argues, 'It is important to understand that families come in all shapes and sizes' (Kaeser and Gillespie, 1999: 14) and Allan, a teacher, talks about his work in the classroom: 'in addition to the traditional nuclear family we will also learn about all kinds of alternative families, including families with gay and lesbian parents' (Kaeser and Gillespie, 1999: 23). Diversity within the LGBT family is largely expressed via the many family forms and racial backgrounds of the contributors, primarily made evident through the photographs, to which we will return. Here, the claim is largely for the recognition of difference.

Third, a 'coming out and coming to terms' story is a regular feature. Typically, this story follows a structure: 'I always wanted kids/but I realized I was gay so thought it was impossible/then I had an epiphany or crisis that led to realizing that it was a possibility.' Robin, for example, says, 'When I was five I already knew that I wanted to be a mom...Imagine my surprise when it began to dawn on me that I wouldn't be June Cleaver or Donna Reed. For years, I went through scenario after scenario of just how I could realize my dream of having a family without being in a traditional heterosexual relationship. It took me quite a while to know that I could stay true to myself, love a woman, and have the family I wanted. I was so excited that I could hardly contain myself' (Kaeser and Gillespie, 1999: 14). There are other instances of this kind of story in the book, mirrored by the trans men's accounts of a gender journey (crudely summarized as: 'I always felt in the wrong body/I was always like a man/I realized I could become a man'). These formats echo Ken Plummer's analysis of the 'dominant narrative' in coming out stories, which are 'usually "modernist tales" in that they use some kind of causal language, sense a linear progression, talk with unproblematic language and feel they are "discovering a truth"' (Plummer, 1995: 83). Plummer notes a typical form too: 'an unhappy childhood with a sense of difference/a crucial moment and a discovery of being gay/resolution of problems and an emerging sense of identity'.

There are a number of reasons why recognition of this story type is important. First, reliance upon this kind of story structure allows for credibility; that is, the format affects the believability of an account. Second, the story of becoming a gay parent mirrors coming out narratives, and so has a sense of the familiar. Third, the 'I always wanted to be a parent' claim is very similar to a born-gay type explanation. Indeed, these also appear in the text: 'Being gay is not a choice,' says Allan (Kaeser and Gillespie, 1999: 24). This allows for confirmation of the 'natural' – wanting to be a parent seems natural, even biological. Finally, as Plummer has argued, the telling of the story itself is a part of *'inventing identities'* (Plummer, 1995: 128). It makes a claim for the teller's identity as a gay parent, but it also feeds into the creation of an LGBT parent/family group or community identity.

The fourth trope relates back to issues raised in Chapter 2 on kinship, as it deals with the extended and the non-biological family. Dorothy says, 'We've constructed a family – and it's a family of people who have become related by dint of having a child together. It's also a family of friends, which is pretty much something I discovered in the lesbian and gay community' (Kaeser and Gillespie, 1999: 17). John also argues, 'People often assume that I have a biological link to Sol, but I don't. A lot of us who are part of the extended families of love for gay and lesbian families with kids are creating new family roles based on love, not on biology' (Kaeser and Gillespie, 1999: 156). Here, the words 'construct'/'create' are used to suggest new forms, and the familial is produced out of friendship, love and community, rather than biology. Some of the parents make links with questions of ethnicity, here, drawing upon the idea of extended and constructed family within particular racial communities. Lillian says, 'There's an African saying, "It takes a village to raise a child." I think this attitude has been instilled in our Puerto

Rican culture as well. If you need something, you can rely on aunts, uncles, and cousins to help ... People deal with each other as one big family' (Kaeser and Gillespie, 1999: 118). Of course, the danger in such claims is that they elide conflict and prejudice towards gay and lesbian community members, and suggest a rather rosy picture of 'culture'.

Crystal, of Chinese heritage, and Nancy, of mixed race/Japanese heritage, highlight some of these questions. Crystal argues that sexuality is not spoken about amongst her Chinese community and says that most Chinese gay people 'are most often not out to their families because they're really afraid of shaming them' (Kaeser and Gillespie, 1999: 142). Nancy recounts that she had mixed reactions from Japanese people when she came out as a lesbian – 'I'm even out to my family in Japan, although they don't really understand my being a lesbian. These relatives think it's a phase, and they still ask my mom when I'm going to get married' (Kaeser and Gillespie, 1999: 143). Whilst these comments highlight mixed reactions and the problems that some gay and lesbian people face in coming out within a community, they also tend to present family reactions *as cultural* reactions, which may not be the case. That is, Japanese 'community' members are more likely to have a wide range of reactions to lesbian parents. These stories are used, then, to highlight exclusionary practices. Nancy's 'even' – 'I'm *even* out ...' – is an example of this; although she is open about her lesbianism, she claims a difficult position within her Japanese family.

The next story-type compares queer community/family with prejudice from family-of-origin/birth family. Karen says that she has not spoken with her mother or sister in a decade due to their homophobia, and Bonnie describes her parents as 'invested in a homophobic system of beliefs ... I was a sinner for whom there would be no redemption ... My mother tried to figure out what had "gone so wrong" in my life that caused this "perversion"' (Kaeser and Gillespie, 1999: 37). Doug recounts a family funeral: 'Michael's parents have never accepted the fact that we are a family. They met Justin just once, but they have never met Zach. Recently Michael's father died and we all attended his funeral. There were relatives at the funeral who didn't even know who we were. They asked us, "Who are you to the family?" Others walked past us purposely and wouldn't speak to us, and there were some relatives who were very nice. It went from one extreme to the other' (Kaeser and Gillespie, 1999: 86). Contributors like Karen or Dominique also raise the issues of those who are not out to family, and the violence and abuse that can exist within the nuclear family. These claims act as critiques of 'The Family', they highlight homophobia and the denial of some ways of living. Doug's funeral story is particularly strong in this respect. These points are also used within a contrast structure – the found queer community *versus* the prejudiced birth family – and, here, some of the parents also talk about their membership of LGBT family/parent and other groups. Sunshine mentions a lesbian parent network and a diversity in education group; Mary Ann describes a lesbian mothers' group; Dana mentions Gay Pride; Karen and Beth run a LGBT family group.

Concerns about gender role models are also discussed. But this does not mean that gay and lesbian parents are necessarily challenging of traditional ideas about gender. Jonathan and Rob's account, for example, talks about their daughter, Jessica, wanting to play soccer, but mainly being into ballet, makeup and dressing up. Their son, Daniel, is a 'rough-and-tumble type', into computers and tennis. Rob, who describes himself as a 'househusband', looks after the children and has taken Jon's last name, but he also says, 'Some people think there has to be a mother for the daughter to become a woman. But Jessie is doing just fine,' and, at a 'get-together with a lot of moms…I feel like there is no difference. We're all just parents' (Kaeser and Gillespie, 1999: 66–7). Here, then, the account draws upon gender, at times confirming traditional gender roles but at others undercutting them. 'We're all just parents' denies the importance of gender, but there is also an awareness of standing out amongst a 'lot of moms'.

Leonard, who had two children when formerly married, also raises the concern about adequate gender role models for children. He says, 'There isn't a lot of information out there that says two men can successfully raise children, so I was particularly concerned about raising a little girl without a female role model in the home. But I knew that Michelle still had her aunts, her grandmothers, and other female friends of ours in her life' (Kaeser and Gillespie, 1999: 242). Leonard uses the notion of gender role models in two ways here: he is concerned about it, but he also answers his own concerns and those of (perceived) others through providing an adequate response. The concern about role models is not challenged or questioned, instead it is duly addressed.

Finally, there is the use of and reference to family ritual. Gillis' work has identified that families are a 'world of their own making' (Gillis, 1997), in that they employ ritual (birthdays, weddings, get-togethers, gift-giving, naming and so on) in order to create and cement an idea of family connection. Kathy, one of the respondents in Carrington's study, says, 'Well, we eat with them…They are people who invite us over for dinner and people with whom we spend our fun times and because of that, I think of them as family' (Carrington, 1999: 64). The rituals identified by the narrators of *Love Makes a Family* include commitment, marriage and adoption ceremonies; a special 'counselling' role for 'Two-Spirit people' within Native American communities; name changing; baby blessing; equinox and solstice celebrations. Sunshine says, 'we recognized the power of creating a family life with rituals that reflected our values and affirmed our family identity in a culture that marginalizes us by rendering us invisible' (Kaeser and Gillespie, 1999: 151).

These various tropes are used in order to connote authenticity. The narrative forms used are familiar, and the parents speak from and refer to experience. They take up various positions or claim stakes, such as 'natural', 'loving', 'for children', 'non-prejudiced' and so on, and they adopt category membership ('a good parent', 'a concerned citizen', 'a properly gendered person') in order to achieve entitlement to family. Partly, this is arrived at through emphasizing ordinariness, but also the prejudice that has to be confronted; partly through listing everyday family activities; and partly through the working up of a new identity (the LGBT family). Achieving the category 'family' is not easy; it involves careful work with recognizable forms.

Visualizing LGBT family life

> The photograph appears to have a more easy access to the truth...The 'beingthereness' of the photograph gives it this quality, and yet...photographs can't deliver the whole truth. The truth moves on them and the truth moves on us. (Stuart Hall; in Hall and Back, 2009: 658)

Love Makes a Family's concern with making the LGBT family visible works, not only through statements about bringing such families to public attention and giving them a voice, but primarily through photographs, which appear in the exhibition and most of which appear in the book. These photographs aim to challenge invisibility, to represent the LGBT family and, crucially, to create space in which homosexuality (or, rather, LGBT people) can exist alongside the child. In part, I think that this can be read as a response to the notion that the non-heterosexual (or even just the sexual) does not really belong in everyday/public space, and, in particular, in spaces/places which are assumed to be those of children and/or the family.

Phil Hubbard, for example, has noted that, 'displays of heterosexual affection, friendship and desire are regarded as acceptable or "normal" in most spaces, ... [but] homosexuals are often forced to deny or disguise their sexual orientation except in specific (and often marginal) spaces' (Hubbard, 2000: 191–2). Homosexuality is frequently regarded as suspect if and when it is present in what are seen as everyday/public and family spaces, and concern about causing offence to 'The Family', women and children specifically, is often cited (Hubbard, 2002; Riggs, 2010). *Love Makes a Family*, however, challenges this on a number of levels since it represents LGBT people and children as family within the photographic shot, puts these images out into public circulation and – crucially – exhibits these images in community settings such as schools and colleges, spaces primarily associated with children and young people.

Gillespie reminds us that, when the *Love Makes a Family* exhibition was planned to be shown in four schools in Amherst, Massachusetts, five local families took the superintendent of schools and principals to court to prevent the show on the grounds that it 'would "sexually harass" their young children' (Gillespie, 1999: xv). A Federal Court judge dismissed the case and the exhibition was displayed for two weeks without incident, but it is certainly interesting to imagine the view of homosexuality and its representation that suggests *photographs* are capable of sexual harassment. Adult offence taken in relation to an image (or, perhaps, an imagined image) is claimed to damage children through sexual harassment, words that conjure up sexual advances or sexually inappropriate pictures. That is, some heterosexuals are offended by the very idea of the LGBT family, and attempt to police what they see as family spaces in order to protect and maintain the dominance of heterosexuality within everyday life.

The photographs of *Love Makes a Family* attempt to counter these concerns through the notion of positive images, the idea that the families represented are ordinary/everyday and that the scenes depicted are of good, moral, caring folk. Nevertheless, this is also a problematic aspect of the publication's message. It suggests that all negative ideas about the LGBT family can be countered – rationally and completely – by a positive response. Yet, homophobic discourse is far trickier than this, since simply countering a negative with a positive does not question the normative form of family representation, or the idea that a family life is a proper one. In addition, positive images often work by attempting to copy a norm. So, positive images of lesbians and gay men are usually those that are seen as respectable and responsible and akin to heterosexuality. This is a key claim of *Love Makes a Family*, the 'we're all the same under the skin' approach. Further, there is a tendency with positive representations to be strongly generalized, and rather rosy or even dull. And finally, and most importantly, the idea that an image – any image – is positive is a problem as it fixes, or attempts to fix, the meaning of that image and leaves little, if any, room for the role of interpretation and debate. Many of the images in *Love Makes a Family* may strike some readers/viewers as anodyne or conservative; and, if they do, then that response must be allowed, too.

In thinking about how the photographs work, the question of in/authenticity is immediately raised since they are staged and professional pictures, yet remind the viewer of a family photo album. That is, the photographs, although carefully managed, have the feel of domestic and everyday snapshots. This is achieved by shots that appear to capture ordinary life, those which are a posed version of it, or those that resemble family group portraiture. Even the shot of Dominique, Laurie, and Chris with their extended foster family of eight children/young people (p. 164) recalls the format of larger family portraits. Gillespie's response to my argument, interestingly, was to say that the photos are not 'posed…we did go to these homes and very casually really ask the families to assemble however they wanted to' (Gillespie, personal communication – feedback on my work, 2009). My suggestion that the pictures are staged does not imply that they are somehow false but, rather, that the assemblage taken up by members has to do with display of what counts as a family, so I think that use of domestic and exterior/garden space and positioning of people is part of the ways in which 'family' is achieved.

A number of features of these pictures make reference to the family album as genre. The chaos of everyday family life is made coherent, and the pictures are 'carefully coded', as with most family portraiture, to project family life as it ought to be (Williams, 1994: 13). As Marianne Hirsch argues, because the 'photograph gives the illusion of being a simple transcription of the real, a trace touched directly by the event it records, it has the effect of naturalizing cultural practices and of disguising their stereotyped and coded characteristics' (Hirsch, 1997: 7). This is a crucial point; what is in fact cultural (a practice called 'the LGBT family') appears natural (an ordinary family), and what is in fact highly artful (staged/posed) appears authentic (real). But it is necessary to remember this point about artfulness, since even though the photographs aim to challenge dominant versions of family, all such photographs 'construct a set of familial roles and hierarchies, [and] reinforce the power of the notion of "family".' These conventions draw 'borders around a circumscribed group... strengthening its power to include and thus also to exclude' (Hirsch, 1997: 47).

In analyzing these images I have turned to Erving Goffman's work, *Gender Advertisements*, since he provides an interesting analysis of how gender dynamics work across a series of photographic/pictorial representations. Goffman argues that gender is a form of 'display'; that is, it must be enacted: 'Gender expressions are by way of being a mere show; but a considerable amount of the substance of society is enrolled in the staging of it' (Goffman, 1979: 8). Goffman uses the analysis of advertisements in his book because he asks us to remember that we are *all* engaged in doing gender; we must consider 'what we ourselves might be engaged in doing' (Goffman, 1979: 27). The photographs in *Love Makes a Family* are involved in similar processes; that is, they stage or display gender, race, family, sexuality, care (and a lot more besides), but involve the viewer/reader in asking how far he or she might, or might not, resemble those pictured. Any representation of a family will provoke reflection on how far it is similar or different to our own. As Weston notes in her associated essay, the images 'participate in [a] bid for recognition' (Weston, 1999: 6). When we look at these pictures, do we see a recognizable self, a family, an LGBT person, an LGBT family, 'like us, like all of us' (as the text is trying to suggest), or do we see an 'other', someone different to us, not a 'real' family, an LGBT person/family that is different from us in an abject sense? Or perhaps a combination of both – 'people who are different to me, yet that I can recognize as family'?

Goffman's analysis of family as it appears in gender advertisements is that, usually, all members 'can be contained easily within the same close picture, and, properly positioned, a visual representation of the members can nicely serve as a symbolization of the family's social structure' (Goffman, 1979: 37). In this sense, the images in *Love Makes a Family* confirm standard family portraiture; all members are contained within the frame, and their positioning says something about a rejection of standard gendered forms and about structural dynamics that do exist within LGBT families. Goffman's analysis points out that, in advertising images, it is the nuclear family that is usually represented:

> the allocation of at least one girl and at least one boy ensures that a symbolization of the full set of intrafamily relations can be effected. For example, devices are employed to exhibit the presumed special bond between the girl and the mother and the boy and the father... [but] there is a tendency for women to be pictured as more akin to their daughters... than is the case with men... Often the father (or in his absence, a son) stands a little outside the physical circle of the other members of the family, as if to express a relationship whose protectiveness is linked with, perhaps even requires, distance. (Goffman, 1979: 37–9)

The images in *Love Makes a Family* reject many of these conventions. Take, for example, the photograph of Jaqué, Roberta, Nabowire and Edwian, used as the book's cover image (Figure 3.1). The standard gendered family image is questioned by the presence of two female parents, yet it is also possible to see Roberta taking up the role of protector, as her arm is around Jaqué and the twins lean into her. Goffman's boy/girl balance is also disrupted, as it is not really possible to tell the twins' genders from this image. In a later image of the family (p. 123), however, Edwian and Nabowire are more clearly gendered as boy and girl. There are images of gay men in the book that ask questions about gender through picturing them in caring (traditionally female) tasks; for example, Perry changing Julian's nappy on p. 226, or Michael dressing Adam on p. 109. Indeed, there is very little in these photographs that confirms traditionally gendered ideas. Marcelle, one of the trans men, is shown in a protective role (towards son, Kai and partner, Loree) in one picture (p. 58), but later is shown holding his son (p. 60). Whilst both Marcelle and Kitt, another trans man, use appearance to signify masculinity (facial hair, dress), both are shown in stances that disconfirm traditional male tasks. And whilst it is possible to read some of the adults in the photographs as confirming fairly regular gendered patterns of appearance, stance, occupation (e.g., Ken appears on the back cover in his police uniform, holding his daughter, Annie), others appear to question expectations. This is not to say that gender is not relevant, of course. A 'non-traditional' image of gender nevertheless makes use of conventions, even though it inverts them, and all of the images signify gender in some way or another.

Figure 3.1   The front cover of the *Love Makes a Family* book
© Gigi Kaeser and the University of Massachusetts Press, reproduced with permission.

In terms of context, the images make use of natural or domestic settings. Nature is signified through placing families alongside trees, in gardens (Figure 3.2) or with animals (a goat, dogs, cats). Hirsch argues that this technique of 'nature over culture' has been used to diminish 'pronounced differences due to culture and history, and also thus naturalizing and sentimentalizing the institution of the family' (Hirsch, 1997: 56). That is, images of nature are used to confirm these are just ordinary families and to minimize any sense of difference. This ties in with arguments in the autobiographies about sexuality and the desire to parent also being 'natural'. Domestic settings (home interiors) are frequently used, and these express a sense of authenticity or ordinariness. Interestingly, such images also expose a private space to public scrutiny (we rarely see inside the homes of most people that we meet), inviting the viewer to look inside as though to confirm the status of 'home'.

Goffman's work on 'relative size' argues that this is used in pictures to echo 'social weight – power, authority, rank, office, renown' (Goffman, 1979: 28). In *Love Makes a Family*, however, parents are frequently shown to occupy the same level/space. It is common in the photographs to show parents standing over or acting protectively towards their children (through positioning, holding, touching), signifying a sense of authority and care, but there is little sense of rank between adults. Children, however, are sometimes pictured as active, which can be seen as a 'function ranking' (Goffman, 1979: 32); that is, their activities confirm their status as (playful, active) child. In relation to function, Goffman also noted that, in advertisements, men are rarely pictured in 'the domains of the traditional authority and competence of females – the kitchen, the nursery, and the living room when it is being cleaned'. When he is pictured in these places, then the man will be seen as 'engaged in no contributing role at all, ... avoiding either subordination or contamination with a "female" task', or he will be presented as 'ludicrous or childlike' (Goffman, 1979: 36). In *Love Makes a Family*, however, men are seen holding their children, changing nappies/diapers, and teaching sign language. That is, gay fathers are pictured as competent in 'female' domains.

Subjects sometimes gaze directly at the camera/viewer, but this is more frequent with children rather than adults. In some pictures, a child is the only person to gaze directly at the viewer. In many pictures, however, the gaze is turned inwards, towards a partner, towards the group as a whole, reinforcing a sense of family inclusivity, but also, therefore, exclusivity. Adults or children may mirror each other's gaze, and there are also photographs in which adult and child mirror not only gaze but also pose, so that they seem to reflect a likeness of each other. All of these poses suggest typical family shots, and are used to signify affinity, care, likeness and a group bond.

Smiling, which Goffman noted was present far more in women than men, is frequently used in *Love Makes a Family*. Family members smile at each other, far more so than with most domestic family photographs, in which subjects usually smile outwards at the camera. The book often uses intra-familial smiles to express a sense of sharing, bonding and even exclusivity.

Figure 3.2 Madison, Jon, Michael and Adam, from the *Love Makes a Family* exhibition
© Gigi Kaeser, reproduced with permission.

The 'shared joke' image of Jay, Al, Kerry and Mark, for example, signifies familiarity and creates a group scene. The viewer is allowed to look but cannot participate. Smiling, however, is not associated more with women than with men. Head or eye aversion, suggestive of conflict or 'concealed' feelings (Goffman, 1979: 63) hardly appears at all. The only photograph that potentially expresses conflict is that of Mary Ann, Keely, Bryna and Melinda (Figure 3.3). Melinda wears a wry smile, and both she and Bryna, Mary Ann's biological child, look into the camera. Keely, Melinda's biological child, is absorbed in drawing, while Mary Ann stares rather blankly into space.

The picture seems to suggest some disharmony (very unusual for this publication), and we learn from the text that Mary Ann and Melinda were former partners but have now separated. This picturing of family conflict is vital, but features rarely in a publication that works hard to present a positive image of LGBT family life. Gillespie, however, takes up this point:

> I did try to include some difficult family stories as we didn't want it to be all positive, perfectly happy families... the original photo of the Cofrin/Shaw family [Mary Ann, Keely, Bryna and Melinda] was before the split up – they didn't look too happy, but they sounded happy, so I was surprised that they split up... If I had the ability to revise the book, I would mention this... that like all families, there are divorces, terrible split ups, etc. (Gillespie, personal communication – feedback on my work, 2009)

Figure 3.3   Mary Ann, Keely, Bryna and Melinda, from *Love Makes a Family*
© Gigi Kaeser, reproduced with permission.

This is an important point, as it indicates that my reading of the Cofrin/ Shaw photo may see disharmony only because I have read in the accompanying text that the couple later split, although it still strikes me as a very uneasy picture. Gillespie makes the point that the book is not all about 'positive, perfectly happy families', and she is clear that conflict ought to be part of any discussion of lesbian, gay, bisexual and transgender family life, as this is an aspect of being ordinary, 'like all families'. As Mary, Sarah, Michelle and Liz argued in Chapter 2, conflict is claimed as part of ordinary family life.

Ethnic diversity is signified in the book in many ways, through inclusion of people from a range of ethnic backgrounds, inclusion of racially mixed families, and people with mixed racial origins. However, racial signifiers other than skin colour are used as well. Consuelo and Falcon's photographs, for example, signify their Native American (and mixed racial) heritage through artefacts – blankets, clothes and jewellery. The book also includes children adopted from other countries and with racial backgrounds different to that of their parents. Here, skin colour signifies difference within families, but poses are used to suggest unity. Once again, racial dynamics are rarely commented upon in the text, although this is occasionally picked up – usually in reference to ideas about cultural attitudes towards homosexuality, as in Crystal and Nancy's account.

To sum up my analysis of *Love Makes a Family*, I have argued that the text works primarily to suggest likeness, not only between family members, but crucially between all family types. The LGBT family is akin to other families; it is, in this sense, ordinary. This sense of likeness is achieved, not only through narratives that describe recognizably everyday activities, but also through imagery that recalls the domestic family album, through literal family 'display' (Finch, 2007). The central narrative, that 'love makes a family', recalls a (supposedly) common experience, chimes with dominant discourses about how families work, and counters concerns about LGBT people as parents. The mundane labours of parenting are regularly listed in the narratives, and represented in the photographs, in order to confirm likeness – parenting is parenting.

However, the publication does raise the potential differences of LGBT families, challenging some ideas about gender and power dynamics, and raising homophobic discrimination. But this notion of difference sits alongside sameness – 'we're all the same deep down'. Take gender, for example. Whilst it is possible to read some of the photographs as questioning of the kinds of traditional pictures that Goffman found, standard ideas about gender feature in the text. Concerns about gender role models are raised and addressed. A further example of potential difference occurs in relation to sex. Whilst LGBT sexualities are clearly represented through stories and pictures, the question of adult sexual activity is rarely discussed and is even downplayed.

Diversity, another key message of the publication, is represented through stories and photographs that figure a range of family structures, racial mixing or multiculture, and through a central claim for inclusion; that is, 'The Family' should include LGBT people and their children. This inclusivity trope is backed up via authenticity devices, to situate the book's subjects as ordinary families. Authenticity is signified through auto/biographical narratives that make use of standard genres, and through images that represent groups in familiar ways. This is perhaps one of the most interesting aspects of *Love Makes a Family*; photographic images of LGBT parents and their children are, still, relatively rare, not least because of fears about potential discrimination or harassment.

The text also works hard to present a respectable account of LGBT family life. In addition to the ordinariness figured in the stories and pictures, the book and exhibition draw upon academic essays, a university press, an organizing board, and testimonials. These work alongside positive stories that rarely mention questions of conflict (although there are some examples). But we need to remember, here, that *Love Makes a Family*'s purpose is to challenge homophobic ideas and the kinds of discriminatory practices mentioned by some of the parents and children. Gillespie reminded me of this point:

> We were trying to counter homophobia... [The] rather happy feel... is a step towards 'normalizing' these families in the eyes of people who are unfamiliar and prejudiced about LGBT people having children and families... if you are expressing pride about being gay, it's fine to show all the forms of gay life taken from promiscuous sexuality to more heteronormative married life. But in the name of getting equal rights in this country [USA], it is probably 'better' to just portray the more traditional gay/lesbian families and not focus on for example a family that is involved in a group marriage or multiple partners, etc. (Gillespie, personal communication – feedback on my work, 2009)

This countering of homophobia happens, primarily, through positive images. However, I have argued for the need to disrupt attempts to freeze the meaning of any image/narrative. And here, of course, it might be objected that my readings of the text could be wrong too. My claims about the text/photographs are not statements of fact, and other readers/viewers will have a different take on the publication. But my argument, in part, is that a positive images approach to accounts of LGBT family life will constrain the form and content of narratives and pictures to the familiar, as Gillespie's comments also suggest. It may even constrain possible 'family' forms. As Holstein and Gubrium state, '[n]ot just anything or anyone is called "family." Family is not constructed out of "thin air." Descriptions must make sense' (Holstein and Gubrium, 1994: 236).

Family complexity?

Valerie Lehr asks whether:

> it is time for those of us outside of communities with a history of alternative family life to stop using the language of family politically, thus challenging these ideas: (1) there is an essential connection between people because of sexual identity; (2) families are essentially places of emotional closeness, rather than socially defined institutions in which power operates; and (3) that familial connections are preferable to other kinds of close, nurturing commitments. (Lehr, 1999: 75–6)

We have seen how LGBT parents and their children respond to these problematic ideas. In the face of heteronormative practices, they have good reason to stake a claim as family, since this has largely to do with a sense of legitimacy, rather than normality, or what Weeks terms 'validation, not absorption' (Weeks, 2008: 792). The creativity that is present in some forms of queer relationality – worked up via neologisms, different structures, peculiar rituals, challenging imagery, and the deliberate occupation of public/family space – can result in shifts in thinking about how a family, or even ways of relating, might be achieved.

But Lehr is right when she suggests that 'family' may not always be the better claim. That is, we need to allow for the creation of new relational forms within a context that might, one day, become less hierarchical than at present. For, however creative LGBT parenting arrangements are, nevertheless, the doing or claiming of a family status is to be held accountable. This accountability involves being measured against heteronormative standards, and against norms of gender/sexuality. This has implications for the ways in which a LGBT family life may be claimed. To make sense of this as 'families of choice' may be to over-generalize, both in the sense that there are many other forms of contemporary family diversity and in the sense of being overly positive about the challenging role of the LGBT family. In addition, the use of 'choice' itself may be in danger of ignoring, or suppressing, material and contextual questions. The claims made in *Love Makes a Family* are frequently about legitimacy, but they are also constrained to repeat many standard ideas about relational forms. They use claims to sameness, normality, diversity, being ordinary, being based on love, being authentic and positive, alongside an emphasis on care over sexuality/sex and potential denial of conflict and problems. They repeat concerns about gender role models and rely upon familiar story/narrative/pictorial forms. And this is because, in order to achieve ' "family" as a meaningful designation for social relations' (Holstein and Gubrium, 1999: 4), then expected forms must be used.

At the same time, it is churlish to write off LGBT parents' and their children's claims to be 'family' as merely conservative or assimilative. In some contexts, LGBT parents display remarkably queer, creative ideas/practices, but in others they are responding to homophobic denials that they will ever live a recognizably familiar life. Morgan reminds us:

> While accepting all the criticisms of family life and, in particular, of constructions which appear to present a normative version of 'the family' it is also the case that family life continues to be important for many people for much of the time. Further, even at the level of discourse and representation, matters are not so straightforward. While there continue to be many political or popular representations of a particular version of family life based upon heterosexual marriage there are, equally, popular accounts which present a more complex and finely nuanced perspective in which multiple partnerships, bi-nuclear households and gay relationships coexist with more 'conventional relationships' (a lot of soap operas and sitcoms for example). In discursive or ideological terms, competing versions of what family and intimate relationships are or should be about are to be found. (Morgan, 2011: 173)

4
Everyday

> The EDL [everyday life] is the pedestrian and mundane life that is so commonly recurrent that its participants scarcely notice it. EDL is the seen-but-unnoticed life…sociology's distinct function is to liberate EDL from the neglect that is the fate of the commonplace. Which is to say, its task is to focalize the seen-but-unnoticed.
>
> (Gouldner, 1975: 423–5)

If we are to represent lesbian/gay/queer parents' lives in all their complexity, then it seems vital that we pay attention to the quotidian, the doing of everyday life and the settings in which it occurs, since statements about those parents are made within a disputed, situated and interactional context. As Damien Riggs argues, 'we are always in the process of "becoming" and "doing" family' (Riggs, 2007a: 28). In addition, if we are to understand what doing/being a lesbian or gay parent involves, then we will need to ask how that very category is brought into being (or made relevant) for various everyday settings (Zimmerman and Pollner, 1973). This chapter does this by using sociological theories of the everyday in order to understand the mundane aspects of LGBT parents' lives. It tries to 'produce a deep wonder about what is often regarded as obvious, given or natural' (Pollner, 1987: ix).

Ethnomethodology, institutional ethnography and the everyday

Harold Garfinkel has described ethnomethodology as the analysis of 'everyday activities as members' methods for making those same activities visibly-rational-and-reportable-for-all-practical-purposes, i.e., "accountable," as organizations of commonplace everyday activities' (Garfinkel, 1984: vii). This means that any everyday scene comprises its members' methods or activities and their accounts of those. To put this another way, being a lesbian or gay parent is actually about the *doing* of various activities, and accounting for them, within various settings, the home, the street, at school, at work, and so on. In fact, the question of lesbian or gay parenting must be made relevant or produced within a setting, otherwise it will not have relevance for the people ('members') present. Lesbian and gay parents are acutely aware of this, as they talk about situations in which sexuality/parenting are not overtly relevant (situations in which they 'pass'), scenes in which they are always and openly referenced, and others in which they are suddenly made relevant.

Ethnomethodology asks us to consider a scene and then take three steps:

1 Notice something that is observably-the-case about some talk, activity or setting.
2 Pose the question, 'How is it that this observable feature has been produced such that it is recognizable for what it is?'
3 Consider, analyse and describe the methods used in the production and recognition of the observable feature. (Francis and Hester, 2004: 25–6)

This means sticking with 'the concreteness of things' (Rawls, 2002: 2), asking what people do and say, and how they do these things in order to achieve an everyday setting that makes sense to its participants, a supermarket, a school, a university, a home, and so on. It also means asking what methods people use to achieve this; that is, how they become adequate doers of that scene.

Actions include talk, and David Francis and Stephen Hester remind us that people 'do not talk to one another as anonymous "actors", but as occupants of situationally relevant identities or membership categories' (Francis and Hester, 2004: 14), of which 'parent', 'mother', 'father', 'child', 'gay', 'lesbian', and so on, are prime examples. In Harvey Sacks' classic study, the opening of a child's story, 'The baby cried. The mommy picked it up', is used to illustrate how we hear the second category, 'mommy', as relevant to the first, 'baby'. We hear it as the mommy of the baby, even though this may not be the case (Sacks, 1995, vol. 1: 236). This is because 'mommy' and 'baby' are 'two categories from one collection, the collection you could roughly call "family" ... [and they are] categories-that-go-together' (Sacks, 1995, vol. 1: 238). We:

take the set of categories of the collection, treat the set of categories as a unit, and put people into cases of that unit, where what you don't get is seven daddies, six babies, three mommies, etc., but you get sets of people who are organized into more or less complete units. (Sacks, 1995, vol. 1: 240)

Sacks also argues that there are 'category-bound activities' (Sacks, 1995, vol. 1: 241), such that crying sounds like an activity of babies, and picking crying babies up sounds like something that a 'mommy' would do. These also act as norms in which pairs of actions may be related. We assume the mother picks the baby up because it is crying and because this is something that mothers 'ought' to do. Thus, categories are 'culturally available resources which allow us to describe, identify or make reference to other people or to ourselves... [but] there are strong expectations and conventions associated with them' (Hutchby and Wooffitt, 2008: 35–6). This will be very relevant for my analysis since 'lesbian' or 'gay' do not ordinarily seem to belong to a collection 'family' that includes 'child', 'baby', 'mother' and so on; neither does the collection 'family' ordinarily allow for more than one 'mother' or 'father', as Sacks notes. Further, the gendered nature of expectations means that 'gay *men*', for example, is not assumed to go together with caring for children. This is because 'the assignment of a person to a category ensures that conventional knowledge about the behaviour of people so categorized can be invoked or cited to interpret or explain the actions of that person' (Hutchby and Wooffitt, 2008: 36). One question this chapter seeks to address, then, is how the category 'lesbian' is made relevant in relation to 'children'/'family'.

Garfinkel and Robert J. Stoller's 'Passing and the managed achievement of sex status in an intersexed person, part 1' (Garfinkel, 1984: 116–85) is an ethnomethodological analysis of the doing of gender and sexuality, concerned with Agnes, a male-to-female transsexual. For my purposes, the importance of Garfinkel's work is that, from the 'standpoint of persons who regard themselves as normally sexed, their environment has a perceivedly normal sex composition. This composition is rigorously dichotomized into the "natural," *i.e.*, moral, entities of male and female' (Garfinkel, 1984: 116). Garfinkel says that people are held to be essentially, and so always, either male or female, figured through 'insignia' such as '[a]ppropriate feelings, activities, membership obligations, and the like' (Garfinkel, 1984: 122–3). There are assumed sex characteristics (appearance, dress, ways of speaking, moving, and so on) and 'persons are held to compliance with them regardless of their desires, *i.e.*, "whether they like it or not"' (Garfinkel, 1984: 125). However, this production of a 'normally sexed' scene requires work, done by all persons ('members'). This work has a 'routinized character' (Garfinkel, 1984: 118), in that it is quotidian, and so Garfinkel's argument is that, in studying Agnes, this mundane labour is made clear. That is, the ways in which *all of us* do gender are revealed.

Agnes had to create a believable auto/biography in which she was always essentially a female, and she also had to learn to act and feel 'like a woman'. She used 'shrewdness, deliberateness, skill, learning, rehearsal, reflectiveness, test, review, feedback, and the like' (Garfinkel, 1984: 165), distancing herself from any association with homosexuals or cross-dressers. Garfinkel describes Agnes as '120 per cent female' (Garfinkel, 1984: 129) and calls her a 'practical methodologist' of sex status (Garfinkel, 1984: 180), although it is also important to remember Garfinkel's own research/textual involvement in the creation of Agnes' story and femininity (Denzin, 1990, 1991; Germon, 2009; and see Garfinkel's 'Appendix', 1984: 285–8). Agnes was 'doing being a woman (presenting an unambiguous, consistent display of feminine attitudes and comportment) and evading answers to questions that would jeopardize her claims to female sexual status' (Zimmerman, 1992: 195). That is, 'sex status' (or 'gender' or 'sexuality') must be achieved and maintained through everyday work:

> normally sexed persons are cultural events in societies whose character as visible orders of practical activities consist of members' recognition and production practices ... members' practices alone produce the observabletellable normal sexuality of persons. (Garfinkel, 1984: 181)

In relation to questions about sexuality, gender and parenting, three key aspects of ethnomethodological theory are highly relevant for my research; first, that people's interactions assume the relevance of identity types or membership categories. Sacks argued that ways of categorizing people (by sex, occupation, status, class, and so on) are 'inference rich', in that they imply knowledge about a person ('you can feel that you know a great deal about the person') (Sacks, 1995, vol. 1: 40–1). Any category member, such as a 'lesbian/parent' for example, also comes to represent those categories for the purposes of knowledge or inferences that they imply. In one example, Sacks shows how a man invokes a 'subset of occupational categories, "hair stylist ... fashions ... and things like that," which constitutes an adequate basis for inferring homosexuality' (Sacks, 1995, vol. 1: 47). That is, the category 'homosexual' is inference rich and implies stereotypical knowledge, or an activity such as hair styling or fashion may invoke the category 'homosexual' when performed by men. Thus, categories are moral devices.

Second, mundane work also has a moral purpose; that is, distinctions on the basis of race, gender or sexuality hold people accountable to those expected categories, even though many do not live up to those expectations and may even choose to ignore or flout them. Doing gender involves the production of hierarchical and moral ideas. Finally, for a person's gender, sexuality, parental status, race, and so on to be present to a scene, ethnomethodology argues that such points have to be made situationally relevant. They must be produced and used in some way.

This raises a complicated problem within ethnomethodological theories, since the point at which 'gender', for example, is relevant to a scene is disputed (as, indeed, it is by members in everyday life). For some, gender is only relevant when it is commented upon, when it is part of the 'orientations of the participants in the data itself' (Francis and Hester, 2004: 65); but this may be a limitation of some ethnomethodology. Some and not others may read gender into a scene, and it may be present in places other than in a verbal or written narrative. This is a point to which I will return, since many gay or lesbian parents talk about what might be termed a *background category presence*, the feeling or experience of sexuality always being relevant, even when it is not referenced overtly.

Smith's institutional ethnography is partly inspired by ethnomethodology, and she refers to Garfinkel's writings to argue for analysis of 'the coordering or concerting of actual activities by actual individuals [that] is continually being worked out in the course of working together, competing with one another, conversing, and all the other ways in which people coact' (Smith, 1987: 123–4). Smith differs from some of the ethnomethodologists in arguing for a method of inquiry that considers social relations 'not fully present in the...observation' (or data) (Smith, 1990b: 150); that is, relations beyond the text. She talks of everyday life 'as arising in an ongoing organization of practices that continually and routinely reaffirm a world in common at the most basic grounding of our life in the concrete daily realities as well as in more complex social forms' (Smith, 1987: 125).

Smith's work develops a problematic of the everyday, and by this she means, first, avoiding a sociology that takes up 'a viewpoint of society and social relations that [is] extralocal, something like a bird's-eye view, a viewpoint not situated in the local and particular places and not located in actual, particularistic social relations' (Smith, 1987: 77). Instead, she argues for sociology concerned with actual, material, social relations. Gender and sexuality, for example, should not be treated as 'already given' (Smith, 1990a: 159), since to do so would be to treat them as concepts rather than engage with how they are *done*. This treatment of social/material practices *as things* is the 'blob-ontology' exhibited by much sociological and other thinking (Smith, 2005: 56). Second, the everyday is made problematic through consideration of standpoints of the excluded (here, Smith talks about women, working-class people, 'women and men of color, of native peoples, and of homosexual women and men', 1987: 107), directing our attention 'to a possible set of questions that have yet to be posed or of puzzles that are not yet formulated as such but are "latent" in the actualities of our experienced worlds' (Smith, 1987: 110). That is, the sociologist must consider how the everyday world is related to what Smith terms the 'relations of ruling' (1990a).

This phrase refers to 'the complex of extralocal relations that provide in contemporary societies a specialization of organization, control, and initiative. They are those forms that we know as bureaucracy, administration, management, professional organization, and the media' (Smith 1990a: 6). Ruling relations are, therefore, present in, and organize, people's 'everyday/ everynight activities', the 'intersection of everyday local settings and the abstracted, extralocal ruling relations' (Smith, 1999: 73). For my purposes, homophobia might be thought of as an obvious or prime form of ruling relations, but it is here that institutional ethnography presents us with an interesting challenge.

Smith's colleague, George Smith, who worked alongside her in the early years of the development of institutional ethnography (see Smith, 2006), argued that the concept 'homophobia' is very limited as a form of analysis. He analyzed a police raid on gay saunas ('steambaths') in Toronto in 1981, in which over 300 men were arrested, with a focus on not just the local, but also extralocal, 'regulation of sex' (Smith, 1988: 165). Speculation about the reasons for the police's actions often resulted in the idea of 'homophobia', but Smith suggests that the explanation lies 'beyond personal bigotry' (Smith, 1988: 166). Smith calls for what he terms 'an ontological shift' (Smith, 1988: 166; 1990: 633), a focus on '*how* it is that this sort of thing happens to us [gay men]' (Smith, 1988: 167). This ontological shift involves institutional ethnography's 'change from a generalized world of conceptual and theoretical explanations to the concrete, sensuous world of people's actual practices and activities' (Smith, 1990: 633). This is because:

> the social processes which impinge on our lives do not appear miraculously, but are constituted in the activities of people, and...our experience of police oppression arises in how these activities are put together. (Smith, 1988: 167)

Smith used Dorothy Smith's work on textual analysis (expanded upon in Chapter 5) in order to ask how police documents express and are a part of the social forms of their activities (policing sex, carrying out raids, and so on). What he means is that police activities (any person's activities) 'are neither random nor chaotic, but rather constitute particular social relations' (Smith, 1988: 169). Smith shows that the activities of the police officers are very differently socially organized to those of the gay men in the saunas. The police officers' work relates, extralocally, to the requirements of enforcing criminal law, and it 'transforms a scene of sexual pleasure into the site of a crime'. As Smith puts it, 'jacking off comes to be described as an "indecent act"' (Smith, 1988: 171 and 174).

Police reports appear 'as an "objective" form of knowing where the analysis and description arising out of them is not articulated directly to the actual social organization of the bath, but is constructed in terms of what is important about this setting for the purpose of ruling it (i.e., regulating sex)' (Smith, 1988: 173). An objective, third-person reportage is used ('it was noted') so that reports seem factual and devoid of actual police officers doing their work. These are a part of sexual regulatory relations or a 'ruling apparatus', the purpose of which 'is to enforce heterosexuality and to ensure that people's sexual activities take place in private familial settings' (Smith, 1988: 178).

Smith's argument, here, is that an explanation of 'the mental state (i.e., homophobia) of individual officers' (Smith, 1988: 179) is inadequate, since there is a lot more going on than a simple face-to-face interaction between gay man/police officer. The police actions relate to reinforcement of heter-onormative law, and explanations of events in terms of 'homophobia' end up attributing agency to that concept rather than looking at events that are 'actively produced by people in concrete situations' (Smith, 1990: 634). This kind of thinking is a problem for institutional ethnography:

> Because it does not have a concrete grip on how things function, this kind of theorizing is not much help in effectively challenging or chang-ing the workings of a *regime.* (Smith, 1990: 634)

That is, simply labelling some people, or attitudes or actions as homophobic does not ask about the concrete, mundane activities of people that result in the establishment of particular sexual/social relations. Dorothy Smith, too, has noted:

> the concept of homophobia forestalled investigation of how the regime worked to enable such actions [as the bathhouse raids] ... [George Smith] did not deny, of course, that there was homophobia, but held rather that it was a dead end politically, to use the term as an explanation for all the oppressions that gays experienced. (Smith, 2006: 21–3)

Thus, for institutional ethnography, 'the social *is* people coordinating activ-ity; language is part of that' (Smith, 2005: 80), and it is these everyday prac-tical actions of people and how they intersect with ruling relations that I am interested to consider from the standpoint of gay and lesbian parents. That is, *how* do gay and lesbian parents' experiences, actions or views link to wider sexual regulation? And how might some of their actions lead to changes in institutional and regulatory frameworks?

Everyday life as lesbian adopters: Nita and Clare

I first met Nita and Clare in 1994 when I was the co-founder of a support and action group, based in the north of England, for lesbians and gay men interested in foster care or adoption. I carried out research with them and with their social worker in 1994/5 (Hicks, 1998), and I re-interviewed them in 2009/10 for this book. When I first met Nita and Clare in 1994, they had been approved as adopters but were still waiting for a child. Subsequently, they went through a very difficult process of consideration and rejection by a social services agency as potential foster carers for a group of seven Asian sisters (described and analyzed in Chapter 6 on race). They then went on to adopt Lubna, Neelam and Saima, three mixed-race Asian girls, at separate times and from different agencies.

I asked them to think about how and why sexuality and parenting were made relevant in various contexts, since I wanted to know how this impacted upon the day-to-day. 'What does it mean to be lesbian adopters or lesbian parents in terms of home life?' was my first question. It's worth pausing here to think about how other parents might answer a similar question, 'What does it mean to be heterosexual adopters/parents in terms of home life?' My hunch is that many heterosexual parents would not know how to answer such a question, in the sense that heterosexuality is likely to be so mundane as to be virtually invisible, something that is never, or very rarely, commented upon. Nita and Clare had no trouble talking about relevance, although they did have to give it considerable thought, and they used practical examples of how 'lesbian' matters:

Nita: It figures a lot actually...

Clare: Yeah, yeah...

Nita: It's always...it comes into our conversations with the children a lot. And they'll bring it in, like, Neelam says really funny things, I don't know, like...

Clare: When I brought you that toast in bed...

Nita: Yeah...'Isn't she a lovely wife?'! *[all laughing]*...she'll tell us how to behave with each other, you know, like, 'Give your wife a hug,' or something! you know, 'Give Clare a hug' or 'Give Nita a hug' or...They're aware of our relationship as part of the family life I suppose, and they're aware that it's a lesbian relationship and that it's different from others. It's hard to pin down the ways that they talk about it and acknowledge it but they do very much acknowledge it and we do talk about it and we talk to them as well...

Clare: And I think the intensity of parenting, I think that because, you know, a lot of their friends have either got split up parents or they've got heterosexual parents where their dad just isn't around, so they get...I mean I can remember Lubna used to come and complain that she'd got too much parenting! you know, that she used to go, 'Oh god why can't you...I've just explained this once! why can't you just be like other parents?!' *[all laughing]* 'Coz it's like, rather than in a lot of families where you've got one parent who's responsible for most things, they've got two parents so they feel that brings good and bad 'coz it can be like...

Nita: As if you're hounded...

Clare: Neelam will say, 'Don't get involved!' you know, if you're *[Nita]* in some dispute with her and then I say, she'll be 'Don't get involved. It's not yours!' And also she's at that age now, she's 13, where there's this kind of 'cool-ness' about having two mums, you know, 'Ooh, my friend Sally thinks it's really cool I've got two mums,' they get a bit of kudos!

Steve: Again, that's interesting because it's changed hasn't it from when she was younger? She's repeating the story but in a different way, she's making sense of it again and again and again at different ages. I wonder if you can remember when they were younger how they used to make sense of it?

Clare: Well, Saima the other day said, 'You're not gay are you, you're lesbians?' and we had to say, 'Yeah, but we…that is "gay"…"gay" can mean lesbians,' and she went, 'Oh?!' *[all laughing]* But like you say, they're making sense of it…

Nita: Yes, she'd worked it out so she'd tested out that theory but 'Oh?! No…okay, right, I got that wrong, let me think again …' sort of thing…

Steve: So, it's changing in their minds as they get older?

Nita: And maybe because she's heard 'gay' used pejoratively at school…

Steve: At school…

Clare: Yeah…

Nita: So, something's happened where either she's said or somebody has said, 'Oh, but that's not your parents because they're lesbians'…

This extract shows that Nita and Clare's lesbianism is made relevant by them, and by the children, in different ways; it may be referred to in a normalizing way (Neelam's notion of 'Isn't she a lovely wife?'), drawing upon standard talk about coupled relationships to locate this one, or its difference from heterosexual relationships may be highlighted (the 'coolness' of having lesbian mums). Being a lesbian adopter/parent is not mundane in a wider, societal context and so this makes the status of Nita and Clare's relationship, or, rather, their sexuality, relevant. This relevance is emphasized through words about frequency – 'a lot' (repeated), 'always' and 'very much'. But this relevance is also indexed via relationality (Nita and Clare's relationship, the children having two mums). That is, an understanding of being lesbian adopters is derived from references to the family and its relationships, rather than a more abstract notion of sexuality in society.

The couple's talk is rather tentative in places ('I suppose…It's hard to pin down…') because, first, I am asking them to think about an everyday family practice and, second, because, within the family itself, questions about lesbianism and adoption – although clearly talked about openly – have been normalized. It is striking that it is in relation to the 'outside' world, to the reactions of others, that these questions have to be justified. Lesbianism may be thought of as 'cool', for example.

This raises the question of indexicality; that is, the ways in which words like 'gay' or 'lesbian' are used to mean, or make meaning, in given contexts. In a particular context, amongst schoolgirls of a certain age, then, having lesbian mums may be described as 'cool', but, at the same time, the word 'gay' may be used pejoratively in the school context to mean bad, naff, 'uncool', and so on. Children (and adults too) may describe things as 'gay' to ascribe negative value. And this may account for Nita and Clare's story about Saima asking if they were 'lesbians', rather than 'gay'. She may have heard 'gay' used in a negative way, to describe things rather than people, and so was struggling to make sense of her two mums as 'gay'. Perhaps, in Saima's mind, she made the distinction between gay and lesbian to distance a picture of her mothers from the negative use of 'gay'. This, of course, is a story that many lesbian/gay parents will recognize and one that I have heard many times; having to deal with moments at which their children hear 'gay' or 'lesbian' (or other associated words) used pejoratively, either to suggest something bad or to suggest that being gay/lesbian is bad. Nita and Clare's story indexes this problem – anti-gay prejudice is experienced outside of, and yet is brought into, the home and has to be made sense of.

This led on to a discussion about how sexuality/parenting was relevant in the children's school(s) context:

Clare: Every time they move class, you have to make sure you go and see the teacher and say, 'Hi, I'm Clare. I'm one of Neelam's mums,' you know…

Steve: Do you always do that?

Both: Yeah, yeah.

Nita: At the beginning of the year, we both go…and because I'm away next week I won't get to go until the week after, but she's got two teachers and so at least one of them might be under the misapprehension that she's only got one mum and so when I get back from Scotland I'm gonna have to go in and make sure that they understand that I'm the other mum, you know?

Clare: And like you went to that thing at the hospital with Neelam for the hearing impaired, and I tend to take her for her hearing impaired appointments just because it's easier if one person does it, otherwise it gets really complicated and I've tended to have more time during the day…and you met the Consultant that I've seen a million times before and you said that you were Neelam's mum and she went, 'What?!'

Nita: And so I said, 'She's got two mums,' and of course everybody else there knew but the Consultant had missed that bit so she was a little bit flustered! But she was OK, I think she was embarrassed she hadn't known, that she'd displayed that reaction because she thought she should have taken it in her stride …

Clare: But most people, you just say it to people quite openly.

Steve: So, would you say that you do deliberately bring it up?

Both: Yeah …

Nita: Yeah, we do bring it up and we try to establish it very early on in any new relationship or anything that's going to be significant to them.

Steve: Rather than wait for it to come up?

Clare: Yeah, definitely.

Nita: Because otherwise they end up dealing with it or it ends up with some misunderstanding that's not helpful to them so we always make sure everybody knows.

Steve: So, in the school context it's really crucial?

Both: Yeah.

Steve: In the sense that you bring it up with their teachers, but how else does it come up in relation to school? Do they come back with stuff? Do they say, 'so-and-so said this,' or 'so-and-so said that'?

Nita: We've hardly …

Clare: No …

Nita: We've had so little of that it's quite incredible really.

Clare: When they … I can remember was it Neelam when she started in reception *[first year of primary/elementary school]* and I can remember some of her friends coming up … I think it was Neelam or was it Saima? … her friends coming out and saying, 'Oh Neelam says she's got two mums, is it true?' and we said, 'Yes,' and they went, 'Oh right,' and then ran off …

Nita: I don't know if it's to do with the sorts of schools they've been at where … or to do with the fact that we've just been present, both of us, all the time, right from the beginning and from nursery really …

Steve: Have you been involved in their schools yourselves much, have you been involved in the PTAs *[parent teacher associations]*?

Nita: No, not that kind of involvement, but because we always pick them up and take them then we're always in the playground and that's another reason, well there are many reasons for not having used after-school clubs and so on, but one of them is that we wanna be seen in the playground or with the other parents.

Here, Nita and Clare talk about making their lesbianism relevant in the school context. They are clear that they want the children's teachers to know that they are lesbian parents and also adopters. Clare even talks about this in 'you have to...' terms, which suggests that she thinks of this action as almost unquestionable, it is simply something that must be done. This phrase is repeated and associated with 'every time', 'make sure' and their emphatic, joint 'yeah, yeah' when I ask whether they always talk to teachers about their sexuality. In addition, 'you have to' is echoed by Clare's 'you just say it', a form of talk that Sacks refers to as an 'object... [that] cuts off the basis for the search for an account' (Sacks, 1995, vol. 1: 23). That is, I am asking Clare to account for her actions, but her use of 'you have to/you just' expresses an assumed commitment to the event. She brings us all into her speech, creating a situation in which making lesbianism clear is just something that is done. However, I think that 'you have to' has another usage here, too, which is that lesbianism has to be made clear, otherwise people may assume that the children have one mother and/or heterosexual parents.

Nita and Clare use the story of the Consultant's epiphany to illustrate this very point. The Consultant is familiar with Clare as Neelam's mother. When Nita turns up instead, and says that she is also Neelam's mother, the Consultant is confused. Nita duly explains the situation but there is talk of the Consultant being 'flustered'. This is an example of a scene in which a person must make a sudden adjustment to see two lesbian parents, rather than whatever had been assumed (a single mother, a heterosexual woman, and so on). Nita and Clare excuse the Consultant, they understand her reaction, because she is thrown and because it is a situation in which they had not managed to make their position as two lesbian parents clear. They then go on to emphasize that they usually try to do this early on in any new relationship with adults in their children's lives. This is a very interesting point – for Nita and Clare, part of the reason to make sure that adults know they are lesbian adopters is to avoid their children having to deal with this or having to deal with 'misunderstanding'. Nita says, 'we wanna be seen in the playground or with the other parents,' which involves two actions; being seen as lesbian parents and making lesbian parenting/adoption relevant to an everyday scene. This is expressed in Nita's 'we've just been present', the idea of making lesbian parents ordinarily part of a daily situation.

When I ask about teasing, Clare and Nita say they have had very little of this. Nita describes this as 'quite incredible', which may express a reaction to the assumption that the children of gay or lesbian parents suffer merciless teasing, an argument used by some to oppose gay parenting (see Morgan, 2002). In an earlier interview, Clare and Nita told me that their children have had to cope with far more racism than homophobia. Nita's 'incredible' anticipates the problems that their children might have experienced due to others' reactions to their having lesbian mums, but Clare's follow-up story about Neelam's friends is also used to suggest that most children do not make an issue of it. This talk references the potential for prejudice that is always present for lesbian parents and their children – it's always possible that someone might make negative comments. Nita and Clare anticipate this, and so deal with it by taking on the responsibility of making their lesbian parent/adopter status clear.

I went on to ask how this translated to situations outside of school, to being out and about:

Steve: What about in the street? How does being a lesbian adopter matter outside?

Nita: Well, again, I'm always aware of asserting something as we move around, you know, if we go into a restaurant or um it's not a deliberate thing but it's just…I don't know, I suppose I'm just aware that we're out as a family and we're saying something to the world about, 'Here we are, this is our family', not deliberately attracting attention 'Hey, look at us!' but um…

Steve: So, are there ways in which people are more likely to see 'it'? Get it?

Nita: They're more likely with Neelam and Saima, partly because they call us 'Mummy'…

Clare: And they might say 'Mummy Clare' or 'Mummy Nita'…

Nita: And because they're quite vocal! They have lots to say and you can't go many minutes before the word 'mummy' will come out and you don't have to spend more than half and hour with us for it to be said at least once to both of us.

Clare: And also you can just see by the dynamics of how things are going on, you know, where you might be saying to Neelam, 'Don't do that,' and I might be saying to Neelam, 'Don't do that', so, if you were watching, you would know that both were parents because one wasn't a guest, you would see by the dynamics.

Steve: Are you aware of people looking sometimes? Are you aware of being read as a lesbian family, or is it just that you are conscious…?

Clare: I think I probably would be if I looked for it but I'm probably too busy looking at what we're doing, but I think if I was that way inclined, I probably would notice if I sat there and looked around.

Steve: There's a sense that there's a possibility that you might be…?

Both: Yeah, yeah.

Nita's 'I'm always aware of asserting something as we move around' is a key phrase and it returns me to my notion of a background category presence. That is, to be a lesbian parent/adopter is to be aware of potential difference, and to carry this around as a relevant category, even when it may not be explicitly referred to in talk or actions of an everyday scene. On this point, I differ with some ethnomethodologists, such as Francis and Hester (2004), who argue that an issue such as sexuality is only relevant to members when it is spoken about or referred to in the scene or data. But Nita is 'always aware', the question of lesbianism never goes away, and she is 'asserting something' because, as she says, 'I'm just aware that we're out as a family and we're saying something to the world about, "Here we are, this is our family"' This sense of a background category presence is also highlighted by April Martin, who talks about being pregnant:

> Even worse, for me, was the experience of having everyone regard me as heterosexual. I was tempted to get a maternity blouse inscribed with the words 'How dare you presume I'm heterosexual!' It felt uncomfortable to walk past a lesbian couple and fail to get the ordinary flicker of recognition and kinship I was used to getting. A pregnant woman evokes a constellation of traditional associations for most people, and my nontraditional identity was not being affirmed. (Martin, 1993: 68)

Martin retains her own background category lesbian in situations in which she thinks she is seen as heterosexual. As a pregnant woman, she evokes traditional ideas about parenthood and so people, including other lesbians, may assume she is heterosexual. They no longer acknowledge her lesbianism through a 'flicker of recognition and kinship'. Yet, for Martin this creates discomfort as she wishes to assert her lesbianism, and it is always relevant and present for her, even if not for others.

This also came up in my discussions with Michelle, Sarah, Mary and Liz, the lesbian adopters I introduced in Chapter 2:

Liz: Yeah, well I get mistaken for her grandmother, only last week somebody said, 'Oh your nana's come to get you' *[laughs etc.]*...whereas you're fairly inconspicuous really as a single lesbian mum because people don't...well, and that's an issue in itself...

Sarah: You have to kind of come out that's the issue about being single, because if you're in a lesbian couple that's the other thing that's different isn't it, it's about talking about being a lesbian with the children or with other parents or at school, you know people say, 'Aren't you out at school?' and I'm kind of like, 'In what circumstance should I be out?' you know, I don't go around and say, 'Oh by the way I'm a lesbian' you know.

Michelle: But it does come out, you know, when your child's in reception and they talk about families, you know, or my child's family looks like this. I wrote a letter to the school outlining his situation and background and...

Sarah: But did you say you were a lesbian?

Michelle: Yeah, because I thought it was important that the teacher should know, so that when they did group work in the class that the teacher could, you know, incorporate that family model into the discussion that they had... or even about adoption too...

Liz and Sarah argue that lesbianism may not be recognized, as they are single adoptive parents. Liz refers to this as being 'inconspicuous' and Sarah says you 'have to kind of come out'; that is, make lesbianism relevant. Interestingly, she then goes on to say, 'I don't go around and say, "Oh by the way I'm a lesbian" you know,' which indicates that she does not always make her lesbianism relevant to others in all situations. She is judging situation-by-situation. Nevertheless, lesbianism is still very relevant for her. This contrasts with Nita and Clare's situation as a lesbian couple – they are able to talk about being 'two mums' and to be seen in the school playground as such, whereas, for Liz and Sarah, being a single adoptive parent may obscure lesbianism to others. Michelle picks up on this and, like Nita and Clare, talks about making her lesbianism relevant to her children's teachers.

This relevance is referred to in two other ways. First, Nita and Clare make the point that, although they do not refer to their lesbianism in many public contexts, it is possibly seen or read by others. The couple also notes that their children call them both 'Mummy', and that others will hear this. In addition, they use a parallel claim, about the 'difference' of their children, to make the point that they feel others may notice them – their children draw attention through being 'quite vocal', 'loud', 'funny', 'unlike other people's children', and so on. This point interested me a lot because I have also noticed it used by other foster carers and adopters. Here is an exchange from my discussion with Liz, Michelle, Mary and Sarah:

Sarah: I probably have more in common with people who have got kids, who have that kind of maybe adopted or some other kind of issues that mean that they are less secure, than I would about some kind of you know nice lesbian couple in *[inner-city suburb]* who've got very precious perfect kids and I actually find that slightly intolerable actually; whereas the people who've got slightly...

Liz:	Wonky kids...
Sarah:	Yeah, wonky kids...
Michelle:	You want to hang out with people who've got similarly wonky children, don't you...
Steve:	Otherwise you feel judged all the time?
All:	Yeah.
Steve:	'Coz there's that hierarchy of parenting isn't there?... You know, about is your kid going to the right school, is he playing the violin?...
Mary:	And even just how they're playing with each other, you know, because if you've got these perfect kids and this perfect couple then you know in *[inner-city suburb]* children are very nicely sharing together and doing lovely things! ...you know, and yours is apoplectic in the corner bashing everyone over the head!
Liz:	They're not always like that!
Mary:	Well, I'm sorry but sometimes Amreen is!
Sarah:	Yeah, and most of the time Kyle is.

Here, the claim has to do with children who have been adopted or fostered being 'different'. Sarah talks about feeling judged in what she describes as a 'middle-class' parenting context, as she feels that the behaviour or actions of her adopted children may mark them out. Liz refers to this as having 'wonky kids', a phrase echoed or taken up by both Sarah and Michelle, since they immediately recognize this sense of being slightly bent or on the edge. There are suggestions of class difference here. Sarah's 'nice lesbian couple in [inner-city suburb]' references an area frequently referred to as middle-class, 'trendy', and so on, but also an area acknowledged to have many lesbian (parent) residents, and this is used to highlight moral distinctions that she feels are made *amongst* lesbian parents. She feels an outsider within a certain middle-class parenting context even though she is middle-class, since her children's behaviour sometimes marks her family out.

But these claims are also to do with having fostered or adopted children. These parents feel their children are somehow different, or another way to say this is that the parents are conscious of the potential for stigma. But, in making such claims, they are also marking out their children as special in some way. Their own sense of difference – of being made to feel different due to lesbianism and due to being an adopter – makes them conscious of how their children might be feeling or made to feel, a process that Goffman referred to as the 'management of spoiled identity' (Goffman, 1990a). Being marked requires the management of that potential stigma within the everyday, since a sense of 'deviance' is situational.

I asked Clare and Nita to talk to me about ways in which they had made the categories 'lesbian' or 'adopter' relevant to everyday life:

> **Steve:** I'm trying to get to the point of how far you think it's relevant in context really … So, let me say in a different way: describe a scene to me in which you have made being lesbian adopters relevant to that situation …
>
> **Clare:** When Neelam was really little, do you remember that time we had to go to hospital with her? And we were together and we went, I think it was her eyes, and there was that young woman who was the Consultant or whatever she was, and we thought that we had made it clear that we were both her parents and she said out of the blue, 'Well, which one of you gave birth to her?' … or something like 'Well which one of you's the real parent?' and we said, 'Well, she's adopted and we've both adopted her,' and she really couldn't cope with that at all, she really wanted to know *which* …
>
> **Nita:** 'Who am I to refer to as the mum?'
>
> **Clare:** 'We can only have one mother here' … !
>
> **Nita:** 'You can't have more than one mother, it's not allowed' … yes.
>
> **Clare:** It was extraordinary.
>
> **Nita:** It was it was very strange.
>
> **Clare:** It was very rude, the way she said it as well.

It is interesting that their response to the question of relevance makes use of a story in which one person – a Consultant at a hospital – cannot see both Nita and Clare as Neelam's mothers. Relevance is ignored or, rather, questioned. Clare says, 'we thought that we had made it clear that we were both her parents', which refers both to being lesbian mothers and to being adopters. Noticeably, their story makes use of a number of possible utterances by the Consultant ('Which one of you gave birth?', 'Which one's the real parent?', 'Who am I to refer to as the mum?') and implied statements ('We can only have one mother', 'You can't have more than one mother, it's not allowed'), some of which do not refer to actual statements made, but rather to characterizations of the Consultant's stance. This is an example of how something made relevant can then be denied by another because it does not fit with an expected category. That is, although Clare and Nita had made their status as two mothers relevant, the Consultant's version of the membership category of 'mother' does not include or infer 'lesbian' and the collection 'family' does not allow for 'two mothers' (Sacks, 1995, vol. 1: 240).

But the story also references heteronormative prejudice experienced in an everyday scene. The Consultant does not accept the possibility of a lesbian family/adoptive arrangement. She cannot allow its possibility; hence, 'You can't have more than one mother'.

In talking about the making relevant of the category lesbian to their daily lives, Clare used the term 'up-front':

> **Clare:** I think our experience has been that, the more up-front you are, the less it can be a problem later because you're up-front from the beginning and so you then get a clear idea about whether it's a problem with somebody. Most people go, 'Oh,' you know and it's surprise rather than revulsion and, if people have got a problem with it, you'll soon know because they won't ever talk to you again and that's fine because you've then identified them as problematic...

This notion of 'front' was used by Goffman, in *The Presentation of Self in Everyday Life* (1990b), when he talked about impression management. He said a person 'must mobilize his activity so that it will express *during the interaction* what he wishes to convey' (Goffman, 1990b: 40). 'Front' is about the way a self is presented to others, and refers not only to the notion of impression management, but also to acknowledgement that a presented self is a performed self; that is, one staged for others. Clare's use of being 'up-front' also acknowledges this – she talks about being 'up-front' about their lesbian parent status 'from the beginning', meaning as early as possible in any new encounters with significant others. This clarifies the position, anticipates misunderstandings, but also crucially gives the couple a sense of people for whom lesbianism may be a problem.

I then asked the couple whether they could think of situations in which their lesbian parenthood status was never relevant. They were clear that, for them, it was always relevant:

> **Steve:** What about the other way around, are there situations in which it isn't relevant ever?
>
> **Clare:** No.
>
> **Nita:** No, I think it's always relevant...
>
> **Clare:** I think it's always relevant...
>
> **Nita:** I mean we...
>
> **Steve:** Well, what would be a situation where it doesn't come up but it is relevant, if you know what I mean...
>
> **Nita:** Well, if I think about the swimming club, I think for a while, because of the nature of swimming training sessions and so on,

you don't get into social chit-chat, the business is swimming, so we went into it and the business is swimming and we got Neelam into the kind of…well, I think it probably took us a while to establish…

Clare: Don't you think it was at first, from just talking to people?

Nita: I don't know, I can't remember 'coz maybe you talked to Sharon at the beginning or something?

Clare: I think I made it clear.

Nita: Oh, yeah, so that wouldn't be…It's very hard to think of a situation where we haven't made it clear really early on really. I can think of lots of other people's situations where people might not think it's relevant, but we always think it's relevant and so we always bring it in.

Clare: I think going to the dentist, they probably don't know!

Nita: That's true yeah…because I take them to the dentist, don't I, and they just probably think I'm a single parent and they've been going to the same dentist for years and years and years, right from when we had Lubna on her own first and then as each one came along we've added them to the list, and so I've always seen that dentist with the children and there's never been any need or kind of situation in which we've needed to refer to the fact that there's another parent or anything, yeah it's true.

Steve: But is it still relevant?

Nita: It is relevant really because there might be an occasion where one of them needs to go to the dentist and I can't take them and then it will be relevant that you're…well, you know, that you have as much right to authorize treatment as I have.

Clare: Well, they have got my surname.

Steve: Of course, yeah.

Clare: And that's part of why they have got my surname, because the connection physically is more there with Nita than it is with me, so I have the connection with the surname and also mine's an easier surname than yours.

The couple's emphatic repetitions ('No/No I think it's always relevant/I think it's always relevant') at the opening of this section make it clear that they think their sexuality is always part of social scenes. Nita begins to talk about the swimming club as a possible scenario in which she has not been out as lesbian, but Clare's intervention changes the progress of this account. It becomes another story in which they believe they have made their sexuality clear. Nita's 'we always think it's relevant and so we always bring it in' shows that, even when they feel others may think sexuality is irrelevant, this does not mean it is irrelevant for them.

Even irrelevance raises the very question of sexuality in social contexts; that is, it is perhaps only certain people who may have the luxury of being able to say it is irrelevant. On Nita and Clare's account, this is not possible. Even going to the dentist with the children is a situation in which having two mums becomes a concern. This is crucial – both of their examples of situations in which sexuality might not be relevant transmute into accounts of relevance. As Sedgwick has written, 'an out gay person deals daily with interlocutors about whom she doesn't know whether they know or not; it is equally difficult to guess for any given interlocutor whether, if they did know, the knowledge would seem very important' (Sedgwick, 1994a: 68).

Finally, Clare raises examples of situations in which anticipated homophobia is contradicted. This is important because, here, lesbianism has been made relevant to all. In these examples, Lubna's former foster carer, Neelam's birth father and Saima's birth mother had been made aware that Nita and Clare are a lesbian couple, but homophobia has been anticipated on behalf of those people by others; in the first two cases, by social workers and, in the final case, by Clare herself:

Clare: But I was just thinking that in Lubna and Neelam's, in both cases, there have been things about homophobia that haven't been true because Lubna's foster family, do you remember, we were told that it would be a problem that we were lesbians? And it never was. Someone had decided that 'some' elderly, African Caribbean woman would think that they were bad and actually she was fine and said, 'Oh, I trained with them when I did midwifery'!

Nita: Yeah, the profession was full of lesbians!

Clare: And then, when we said we wanted to meet Neelam's birth father, there was a whole thing that we couldn't go and meet him because he was absolutely homophobic, he didn't want her to go to lesbians, and he was in prison anyway and we would have a really bad time and, when we went and met him, he was as nice as pie!

Nita: And he did say something like, 'I have difficulty with your lifestyle, I'm not totally OK with it,' and we said 'OK, that's fine'

Clare: But he never said he wasn't OK with us having her but he was perfectly civil.

Nita: He was quite emotional.

Clare: And Saima's birth mother chose us. Saima was 'accommodated' because her birth mother gave her up for adoption rather than have her taken, she was given four families to choose between, and I remember the conversation I had with the social worker where I said, 'This is a complete farce, why are you telling me about this child? This woman is not gonna choose us,' and she was, 'Oh I don't know ... ' dah dah dah, 'she wants someone that's got children already, she doesn't want her to be an only child, and she wants her to be in a family that reflects her ethnicity, and she doesn't want them to be Muslim but she wants her to know about Islam', and I was like, 'This is a joke', you know, I was really angry at her, and yet she *[Saima's mother]* chose us and she thought that we were the best bet. So, it's other people, often, that think it's a problem, isn't it?

Steve: Yeah, fears of what people might think or say or how they might behave.

Nita: So, I suppose in that sense Saima's birth mother thought that the fact that we were lesbians was not the relevant fact to her. The relevant issues were about there being siblings, a professional family, a house with books, stuff like that ... and she wanted a family that would be positive about her Asian heritage without bringing her up in a particular religion.

Clare: And she was very warm when we met her

Nita: Yeah.

Here, expected homophobic reactions do not play out, and it is noteworthy that Clare constructs categories ('"some" elderly, African Caribbean woman', a 'birth father ... in prison') that she suggests others have used to infer likely homophobia. This has connotations based upon race (the black foster carer, an Asian dad), age ('elderly') and even class, since Clare's point is that it is actually discriminatory to assume likely homophobia based on these categories. The story of the black foster carer is used to undercut such assumptions, whilst the story of the birth father recounts some friction ('I have difficulty with your lifestyle ...'), but within a context of his being 'nice as pie', 'perfectly civil' and 'quite emotional'. Ironically, Clare's 'So, it's other people, often, that think it's a problem, isn't it?' applies to the social workers in the first two cases, but cannot account for her own thoughts of likely homophobia from Saima's birth mother. Clare refers to this – 'I was really angry at her [social worker], and yet she [Saima's birth mother] chose us' – and Nita suggests that lesbianism may have been 'not the relevant fact' in choosing them as adopters. Indeed, she lists other relevant factors. Thus, these stories reference situations in which membership categories infer homophobia which does not materialize, and one in which it does not arise, as lesbianism is thought to be irrelevant to a birth mother, or because she accepts it. Lesbianism is always relevant to such situations – acknowledged through Nita and Clare's desire to meet with birth relatives and former carers – but reactions to this do not play out in expected ways. Nevertheless, Clare reminded me of possible reasons to anticipate homophobic reactions:

> In the case of Neelam's foster mother, she was so opposed to the adoption by lesbians that she wouldn't allow introductions in her home. They were done in a so-called neutral location, a home used for the disclosure of sexual abuse. The oldest foster brother threatened to come and kidnap Neelam once she was placed with lesbians. It is ironic that the person having to deal with the foster family's homophobia was Judith – the social worker for that family – who was herself a lesbian.

To sum up this section, my interviews with Clare and Nita were about asking how everyday life was affected by the relevance of being lesbian/adoptive parents. The couple was clear that their lesbianism was always relevant to the everyday. I have termed this situation a background category presence, since their lesbianism may be overtly referred to, or others may raise it, or it may suddenly be raised anew (by someone in a scene who is unaware, or by others who are anti-lesbian). Nita and Clare say it is always relevant because they feel that it is, and because they must anticipate its relevance to any new situation. They approach this through being as open as they can about their lesbianism, what Clare called being 'up-front' and what Nita referred to as 'asserting', and they are also acutely aware of 'standing out' as a family, as lesbian parents, as adopters in particular contexts. This is a process of identity management.

Anti-lesbian reactions may just happen in everyday life (the Consultant who couldn't countenance two mothers), or they may not happen when anticipated (the stories of the foster carer, the birth father and mother), but Nita and Clare talk of anticipating these situations. They use being open/up-front as a way to manage this, and refer to this as a way of helping their children (that is, preventing their children from having to deal with too many 'misunderstandings') and as a way to identify those who have a problem with their being lesbian adopters, a point echoed in various disclosure strategies identified by Amaryll Perlesz et al. (2006c). In this sense, the relevance of sexuality and kinship to lesbian adopters is a quotidian one and, for this reason, Nita and Clare make it a members' analysis through visibility, verbal accounts and language use.

Mundane 'homophobia'?

I have been focusing on the mundane, and so I would like, finally, to turn to situations in which anti-gay/lesbian prejudice suddenly, and ordinarily, enters into a scene. One of the potential problems with the concept of 'homophobia' is that it tends to suggest extreme and obvious practices, but this overlooks what Elizabeth Peel terms 'mundane heterosexism', 'incidents of the everyday' (Peel, 2001: 541). Peel argues that we should 'pay more attention to "mundane" unnoticed and (normatively) unnoticeable incidents of *hetero*sexism' (Peel, 2001: 541), since this is often subtly encoded into quotidian practices. For example, Peel suggests that lesbian and gay lives are devalued through forms of talk that may purport to be about equality. She discusses cases in which people argue that lesbians and gay men should be treated just the same as anyone else, saying, 'if your son was in a motorbike accident and lost his leg would you still love him the same', or 'there's always going to be something wrong in everyone's family but you … teach yourself that it's not wrong it's just different' (Peel, 2001: 546–8). These forms of talk are about acceptance, but acceptance of 'deficiency'. Peel notes that 'immediate and direct challenges to subtle forms of heterosexism are not easily made, because of the local interactional situation' (Peel, 2001: 551), since there are many ways that such challenges can be diffused, even ignored, in ordinary talk. Challenge itself can also be problematized in ordinary conversation too, with the result that the challenger is made to appear out of sync with others. This may be overt – 'You haven't got a sense of humour', 'You've a chip on your shoulder' – or more subtle.

Mundane heterosexism is also part of the need to assert heterosexuality in scenes, since it requires the work of reiteration. That is, heteronormativity requires practices of subtle dominance. I noticed in interviews with lesbian and gay parents that these moments were often referred to. Here, I'd like to turn to a story from Sarah about her adopted children's school:

Sarah: What happened was that it was at an informal thing, after a school event, and she *[the Headteacher]* said something to my next-door-neighbour, who's straight and has a child at the school, she was talking to her and she said something really homophobic, and my neighbour told me, she said, 'God, you won't believe what she said', she said something about, well, they were just talking about what was on telly and soaps *['soap operas'/television drama series]* and she said, 'Oh they see all sorts of things and homosexuality, for example, we wouldn't ever allow that to be taught …' She just came out with it.

Liz: Apropos of nothing at all the Head just said, 'Well, I won't be having people teaching homosexuality in my school.' And she then claimed – I mean I wasn't there so I don't know but this is what I heard – and then said 'I think it's against my …'

Sarah: She's a Christian … she said 'immoral'.

Liz: 'I think it's immoral.' Sort of thing, words to that effect.

Sarah: And it was reported to me – I felt really really, really upset – by my neighbour in a fairly flippant way, you she said, 'You won't believe what she's said now', and

Steve: Does she know you're a lesbian?

Sarah: My neighbour? Yes, and she was saying it to me in a support-ive way but, you know, like, 'God, she's so ...' whatever, because we had a new Head that had come in since the children started there, very evangelical, and so we all knew she had these fairly strong views and in a way it wasn't a massive surprise but ...

Liz: Well, that she actually had the lack of judgement to say it in an inner-city school ...

Sarah: So, I felt very upset, I got extremely upset about it and I um didn't know what to do, and I knew a parent who I thought would be sympathetic who was one of the parent governors, so I managed to catch her ... well, she was there during the conversation with my neighbour, this parent governor and the Head, so I phoned her up and she said, 'Oh, I think I know what you'll be phoning me about' 'coz she was obviously shocked as well, and I tried to take it to a governors' meeting, but they said the only thing I could do was make a complaint, well, go and see the Head first about it, and I said, 'I don't want to see the Head first about it'

Steve: That's terrible asking you to do that.

Sarah: And, 'I don't want to see the Head first' and so on, 'I want it raised' ...

Liz: You tried to do it anonymously.

Sarah: I tried to do it anonymously, the Chair of the governors, who's the local vicar, 'coz it's a church school, got involved at which point somehow they made a connection back to who it was, and he sent a letter to my house, me having tried to do it ... so I was completely outed to all the governors and to the Head

Steve: That's also that it's now become 'your' thing.

Sarah: Exactly, and I wrote a letter saying why I didn't want to deal with it, you know, it's not my, it's not an issue that belongs to me, it's an issue about everyone.

Steve: The whole school.

Sarah: The whole school, and I'd said on the phone, 'If it had been a racist thing, would you have made someone go in and say it on their own and say it had been one of the black parents? No, you wouldn't', you know, and, 'It's not an issue about me', and so it all went round in circles and nothing, in the end, I sort of lost the will to pursue it any further and apparently she was quite contrite, as the expression is, and she kept saying things like, 'Oh, I've got lots of gay friends', and you know all that! *[laughs]* And since then, she's treated me with some caution and gets completely flustered whenever she has to call my name, she goes, 'Mrs. XX, Miss, Ms, Mrs...'!

Michelle: Freak woman strange lesbian! *[laughing]*.

Sarah: Who shares my name, she's got the same surname as me.

Liz: I think she realized she'd made a serious gaff.

This story emerged during a discussion about how schools were trying to reflect or acknowledge a range of family types, including lesbian and gay parents, in their curriculum. A feeling of progress is suddenly undercut by a reported 'homophobic' event. Although Sarah introduces her account, it is noticeable that Liz joins in on several occasions, completing sentences for Sarah at key points and adding further comment. This may be a feature of turn taking in a group interview situation – that is, it may be unwise for one speaker to hold the floor for too long – but it also helps to emphasize the story. It is as though a discussion of anti-lesbian prejudice needs corroboration. A second speaker adds evidence to the account and increases believability, what Smith refers to as the addition of an independent 'witness' (Smith, 1990a: 29). Liz takes up this role to back up Sarah's account, even though she actually says, 'I mean I wasn't there so I don't know but this is what I heard.'

Sarah's 'what happened was' introduces the character of the homophobe/ Headteacher. Sacks noted that story characters often appear 'on cue' (Sacks, 1995, vol. 1: 182), since, 'when a character who has some proper grounds for occurring and some proper thing to do, has its cue, then there's no need to account for how they happened to have come on the scene' (Sacks, 1995, vol. 1: 183). The Headteacher just appears as the story takes place at school, but also the 'homophobe' just appears too. I would suggest that, in these stories of mundane heterosexism, there is no need to account for why 'the homophobe' appears. Rather, lesbian and gay parents expect this story to occur at some point – it has familiarity. Of course, there is some questioning of this character in Sarah and Liz's account – the category 'Headteacher' is not supposed to infer 'homophobe', and so this is made sense of as a 'serious gaff'. But, at the same time, there is something simultaneously shocking and expected about the Head's views – 'She just came out with it' and 'we all knew she had these fairly strong views and in a way it wasn't a massive surprise'.

I think that the account itself is designed to undercut the Headteacher's views. Melvin Pollner has pointed out that, when there are competing versions of events or 'reality', then what he terms 'mundane reason' must account for this disparity by making one account appear 'inadequate' in some way (Pollner, 1987: 29). The classic way to do this is to 'ironicize' one account by giving another:

> one experience, tacitly claiming to have comprehended the world objectively, is examined from the point of view of another experience which is honored as the definitive version of the world intended by the first. The irony resides in the subsequent appreciation that the initial experience was not the objective representation that it was originally purported or felt to be. (Pollner, 1987: 71)

Thus, Sarah's work in this account (including contributions by Liz and, to an extent, by me, too) is to ironicize the Headteacher's views. She must cast the Headteacher in the role of a mistaken or inadequate actor. This is done in a number of ways. First, the Head is categorized as 'Christian/evangelical'. This categorization infers 'anti-gay'. Second, the Head's views are categorized as unbelievable ('you won't believe what she said'), and Liz characterizes the Head's actions as a 'lack of judgement' and 'a serious gaff', implying they are unprofessional. Third, the incident and its effects are undercut by humour (Michelle's ironic 'Freak woman strange lesbian!') and laughter towards the end of the extract. That is, an upsetting and disturbing incident is reworked into one that can be laughed off in this particular context, a group interview with three other lesbians and a gay man. It's 'just' anti-gay prejudice, something that we are all used to.

Sacks' lecture 'Doing "being ordinary"' (1995, vol. 2: 215–21) makes the point that, 'in ordinary conversation, in reporting some event, people report what we might see to be not what happened, but the *ordinariness* of what happened' (Sacks, 1995, vol. 2: 216). The ordinariness of life, or being seen to be ordinary, requires work and so it is 'the usual aspects of any possibly usual scene' that are reported (Sacks, 1995, vol. 2: 218). My view of Sarah and Liz's story is that it makes use of many devices in order that the account appears ordinary or believable. It has a sense of (justifiable) outrage, but it also emphasizes aspects of ordinary conversation (overhearing things, a chat with a neighbour). It is the work of mundane reason to achieve believability, but it is also the work of gay and lesbian parents to account for everyday life as a scene of mundane heterosexism.

If this is simply called 'homophobia', then, in Smith's terms, this seems to be about individual prejudice (Smith, 1988). Indeed, in Sarah's story, the reactions of the parent governors and the vicar (asking her to go and see the Head and to make a complaint) are about making the incident into Sarah's problem and, at the same time, publicly identifying her as a lesbian. A question about heterosexism within a school context is turned into an individual lesbian parent's concern or 'problem'. Sarah – rather than heterosexism – becomes the problem. This also means that any challenge to the Head's remarks is easily diffused. Dealing with the wider implications of events is prevented through turning the problem into Sarah's, and the Head herself is able to retract her remarks through contrition and the 'I've got lots of gay friends' statements. But the Head's remarks do not indicate a merely mistaken and individual prejudice:

> social frames of consciousness regarding homosexuality as a 'social danger' or as 'sickness' are not simply backward ideas in some people's heads. Rather, these are actively organized within the worlds of official discourse and ruling relations. (Kinsman, 1995: 80)

Institutional ethnography reminds us that Sarah's story indicates something more than just face-to-face interaction. The ruling relations of a school context may be said to displace lesbian and gay people/parents; that is, the school is a scene in which the categories of gay/lesbian are not assumed to be present or to necessarily have a place, hence the attempt to prevent exhibition of *Love Makes a Family* in schools, referred to in Chapter 3. This is a complex situation, of course – there is work by some educators to include lesbian and gay people, and there are lesbian and gay people who make their presence felt, either as parents or as teachers, governors and so on. But still, the scene reminds us of the background category presence felt by lesbian and gay parents; relevance must be made, something must always be asserted. For this reason, lesbian and gay parents use the word 'homophobia' in the everyday, as it is a way to seek recognition of prejudice and it is a word that is more easily used than 'heteronormativity' or 'heterosexism' because it has more currency. The word itself is more widely recognized. But this does not mean, in analytic terms, that we should fall into the trap of seeing Sarah's story – or, indeed, accounts given by Nita and Clare – as merely examples of individual prejudice.

The production of lesbian and gay families as *not* an 'acceptable and normal alternative', as Liz puts it, shows that, within this particular school setting, the best that gay parents can hope for is to be seen as just another type of family, alternative to an assumed norm. At worst, they are not 'acceptable' or, rather, a Headteacher feels that it is acceptable to say that homosexuality has no place in her school. Smith has analyzed a similar set of processes in relation to single parents in the school setting. She says that single parents 'were viewed at school as defective families; defective families produce defective children; any problem our children might have at school indexed the defective family as its underlying interpreter; we were always guilty' (Smith, 1999: 163). The single parent family is produced as a deviant case. This applies to Sarah's story too; she may be produced as deviant because she is a single parent and because she is an adopter, but, in this instance, it is primarily as a lesbian that she is marked by the Head, governors, the vicar and others. That homosexuality should be thought of as a thing that must not be 'taught' in schools refers back to the UK's Section 28. But it also forms part of an educational discourse that fears homosexuality; it constructs the idea that homosexuality is a thing that may be passed on to children, that children should be diverted from any association with homosexuality and that the school is a place free from such associations.

Through giving attention to the everyday life of lesbian and gay parents, I have highlighted how they must deal with mundane heteronormative practices. Examples of particular scenes or moments have been used to show how those parents manage their identities and potential reactions to that, and I have also argued that what they term 'homophobia' is likely to arise in a quotidian way. It would be tempting to see these processes as merely encounters with individually homophobic people and situations, but this does not really account for the complex management of emotions, discussions and prejudice that lesbian and gay parents engage with. They are held accountable for their actions in terms of discourses to do with sexuality, gender, race, class, and so on. An everyday set of scenes is encountered, in which the routinized and moral work that goes into producing notions of a sexed/gendered being is always present. Their stories reference not just the particular instance, but also a wider set of ruling relations. Local events are situated within extended ruling relations concerning sexual regulation. But, as Kathryn Almack notes, 'being visible as lesbian parents in interactions with others... can challenge implicit social judgements and stigma. In this sense everyday actions are turned into political actions' (Almack, 2007, para. 8.8).

5
Gender

> Damaged children need both male and female role models, a mother and a father. Homosexual adoption would deliberately place some of the most damaged children in a home without either a father or a mother. Is that in the interests of the child?...How would they feel if their friends knew that they had either two dads or two mums? It is likely that they would be mocked and made to feel even more different.
>
> (Baroness O'Cathain, UK House of Lords debate on Adoption & Children Bill, 16th October 2002: column 884)

Ideas about lesbian and gay parents typically make use of ideas about gender, about versions of femininity and masculinity and – as in the example above – about the notion of gender role models. My earlier work in this field (Hicks, 2000, 2006c) didn't really consider what might be termed the micro-doing of gender in talk and practices, and so here I want to get closer to complexities and contradictions, as well as asking how lesbian and gay parents position themselves as gendered subjects. Whilst I pay some attention to those who, like O'Cathain, are opposed to all gay parents and who make use of gender socialization theory in order to bolster their arguments, I am more interested in everyday theorizations of gender that occur when social workers talk about potential lesbian/gay carers or when gay parents talk about themselves.

To theorize 'gender'

My work is opposed to the notion that 'gender' is a thing or characteristic that is either acquired through socialization or inheres in women ('femininity') and men ('masculinity'). One of the reasons that I take this view is because, if we are to shift expectations about who can be, or ought to be, a parent or carer, then we must shift the notion that this is a role that belongs to (heterosexual) women. But this also means shifting gendered ideas about parenting roles or – more specifically – activities, since the notion that children need 'mothering', and that men cannot 'mother', is an unhelpful, but obstinate, view. And it is not necessarily a view solely held by conservative thinkers. Some feminist work on mothering, for example, holds fast to the view that it is only women, even the woman who is biologically connected to the child, that can mother (Baraitser, 2009; Hollway, 2006; Park, 2006).

A further reason to challenge fixed views of gender is that lesbians and gay men are still regarded as gender deviants; that is, failed examples of femininity and masculinity. Gay men caring for children, for example, are often seen as gender inverts, associated with the feminine, and therefore as failed men who are likely to pass on such ways of being to their children – so much so, that some gay fathers report 'gender role strain', stress caused by the felt need to conform to expected notions of masculinity (Benson et al., 2005: 3; Schacher et al., 2005). As Halperin argues, whilst modern ideas about gay people have moved away from a gender inversion model, 'this conceptual transformation has not been either total or absolute. Many people nowadays, both gay and non-gay, continue to draw a direct connection between gender deviance and homosexuality' (Halperin, 2002: 132).

Yet, at the same time, gay and lesbian parents may pose some interesting challenges to traditional conceptualizations of gender. This is not to say that all gay parents are automatically gender rebels. Whilst there is some work that does argue lesbian and gay parents always question gender conformity in a positive or radical sense (Nelson, 1996; Sourbut, 1996; Sullivan, 2004), my view is that such families express both conformity and rebellion in their doing of gender, a view suggested by others, too (Dalton and Bielby, 2000; Mamo, 2007; Ryan-Flood, 2009). Indeed, the more pressing and difficult question is not whether gay/lesbian parents are gender conformists or radicals but, rather, what 'gender' refers to within a given context. What version of gender do we use when we imagine lesbian and gay parents? And what versions do we produce through those imaginings? Or, as Butler puts it, 'Am I a gender after all? And do I "have" a sexuality?' (Butler, 2004b: 16).

Butler's work is crucial for my purposes because she argues:

> The heterosexualization of desire requires and institutes the production of discrete and asymmetrical oppositions between 'feminine' and 'masculine,' where these are understood as expressive attributes of 'male' and 'female.' The cultural matrix through which gender identity has become intelligible requires that certain kinds of 'identities' cannot 'exist' – that is, those in which gender does not follow from sex and those in which the practices of desire do not 'follow' from either sex or gender. (Butler, 1990: 17)

Butler's argument is that heterosexuality *requires* the production of gendered difference, rather than the other way around; that is, the more usual assumption that natural differences between the sexes result in heterosexuality. This point rests on her claim that gender is enacted, a 'repeated stylization of the body, a set of repeated acts within a highly rigid regulatory frame' (Butler, 1990: 33). But her argument extends further than this, in that she is also saying that gender is not simply a learned or cultural product either. It is not the result of gender socialization, since this implies an ultimately fixed characteristic, too. We may produce the 'illusion of an abiding gendered self' (Butler, 1990: 140), but much everyday work goes into its production, a point that is the bedrock of earlier, ethnomethodological theory. Butler describes gender as the 'forced recitation of norms' (Butler, 1993: 94), and, as Moya Lloyd says:

> The norms that are repeated are thus both deeply imbricated in relations of domination, reprimand and control (think of the risks that attach when gender is done wrongly) *and* they are inescapable…It is also the fact that they must be repeated, however, that creates the space for them to be repeated differently and thus is also the condition for the possibility for action. (Lloyd, 2007: 63 and 65)

Butler argues that it is through a process of subjection and regulation that the gendered person appears, since gender is 'the apparatus by which the production and normalization of masculine and feminine take place' (Butler, 2004b: 42). Here, then, is another reversal of the usual assumption. Rather than gender being built upon, and the result of, sex differences, those differences are the result of gender's work. Gay men and lesbians pose a problem for heteronormative ideas, then, because they represent identities that are not supposed to 'exist' since they do not conform to heterosexual desire. Since gay men and lesbians do not desire the 'opposite sex' in heteronormative terms, then their gender, or their masculinity/femininity, is rendered suspect. Whilst it may be the case that few people today would argue that a lesbian is a man trapped in a woman's body and a gay man *vice versa*, nevertheless, ideas about gender problems prevail. Gay men may be seen as insufficiently masculine, lesbians as insufficiently feminine, and both may be regarded as inappropriate or inadequate parents who may pass on some kind of queered gender to their children.

This idea of proper gender 'passed on' is highly problematic, not least because many heterosexual women and men don't conform to expected gender roles either. I will return to the question of gender role models in some detail later but, first, I would like to suggest that such reification of gender may be challenged by models/theories which see gender as enacted within particular social scenes, as discursive *and* relational (Germon, 2009). Treating gender as a discourse – that is, ways of talking, thinking, behaving

and acting which are not simply freely available but actually highly pro-
scribed – is a way to ask about the politics of gender as these are put to use
in debates/narratives about gay parenting. Subjects are multiply positioned
within gendered discourses, discourses that both constrain and enable,
which means that, although subjected by dominant accounts of gender,
there is also the possibility of resistance. Gay and lesbian parents, for example, are usually highly aware of gendered expectations and often very critical of them. But they also use humour, irony and other means to take up
positions that offer pleasure, resistance to the dominant, and sometimes a
sense of normality.

A crucial point developed in the work of Candace West and Don
Zimmerman was that of 'accountability':

> a person engaged in virtually any activity may be held accountable for
> performance of that activity as a *woman* or a *man*... to 'do' gender is not
> always to live up to normative conceptions of femininity or masculin-
> ity; it is to engage in behavior *at the risk of gender assessment*. (West and
> Zimmerman, 2002: 13)

West and Sarah Fenstermaker have also pointed out that accountability does
not mean a person simply being blamed for an activity because of their
gender, race or class, as in, 'Well, she would do that, she's a woman'. Rather,
it is 'the ever-present *possibility* of having one's actions, circumstances, and
even, one's descriptions characterized in relation to one's presumed membership in a particular category' (West and Fenstermaker, 2002: 541). They
make this point to show that being held accountable is an interactional and
institutional, not just individual, process.

Jackson has argued for a material analysis of gender, one that considers a
structural account of hierarchical relations:

> I find it depressing that much of what passes as radical these days does
> not envisage the end of gender hierarchy or the collapse of institutional-
> ized heterosexuality, but simply a multiplying of genders and sexualities
> or movement between them. (Jackson, 1999: 181)

Nevertheless, we need to avoid the assumption that hierarchies of gender or
sexuality are simply already there or given, and ask, instead, how these work
in everyday contexts. And, whilst I would agree with Jackson that simply
adding in new versions of gender/sexuality categories does little to challenge
hierarchy, it may be possible to detect some interesting and questioning
ideas/practices in the reworking of gender narrated by gay and lesbian parents. Gay fathers calling themselves 'Mummy/Daddy parents' (Benson et al.,
2005: 19) may rely upon old gender categories, but this also ironicizes those
categories and suggests their inadequacy for talking about new practices.

Ethnomethodology and gender

Suzanne Kessler and Wendy McKenna's notion of 'gender attribution' suggests that 'we decide whether someone is male or female, every time we see a new person', a process that *forms the foundation for understanding other components of gender*, such as gender role (behaving like a female or male) and gender identity (feeling like a female or male)' (Kessler and McKenna, 1985: 2). It is important to note that their explanation of gender role specifically talks about 'behaving *like* a female or male'; that is, behaving in ways that are recognizably gendered and recognizably female/male, rather than some supposedly natural or fixed way of being. Kessler and McKenna's language is about acting ('behaving') and achieving ('like').

Kessler and McKenna also ask, 'How is a social reality where there are two, and only two, genders constructed?' (1985: 3), since – as ethnomethodologists – their job is to suspend or bracket this belief. They go on to outline three key terms relating to gender: 'assignment', which occurs at birth, so that a child is instantly labelled a girl or a boy; 'identity', which refers to 'an individual's own feeling of whether she or he is a woman or a man' (1985: 8); and 'role', which 'is a set of expectations about what behaviors are appropriate for people of one gender' (1985: 11). Under a two-gender social system, if any of these do not fit together, then there is a problematization of the individual. That is, if a child labelled a boy does not feel or act 'male', then that child – rather than a two-gender system – will be labelled a problem.

For Kessler and McKenna, a socially achieved, two-gender system results in the establishment of supposed biological or psychological 'facts' about differences between women and men, rather than the other way around. They call this the 'objective facticity of gender' (1985: 99) – the notion that separate genders simply exist and can be scientifically proven. In order to challenge or question this model of gender as 'fact', Kessler and McKenna – like Garfinkel (1984) – consider transsexuals in order to show how gender identity/role is achieved and 'an ongoing process of "doing" ... in everyday interactions that we all engage in' (Kessler and McKenna, 1985: 126).

In the final chapter of their book, Kessler and McKenna report on a study in which they showed various sketches of figures with mixed and, sometimes, ambiguous gender cues to 960 adults, who were asked to label each figure 'male' or 'female'. They found that more figures with covered genitals were described as 'male', and the presence of a penis was a powerful indicator of 'male' (96%). The presence of a vagina, however, did not produce a powerful 'female' attribution. About one third of their respondents were able to ignore the vagina as a 'female' cue. Kessler and McKenna argue that, in this case, gender attribution 'is, for the most part, genital attribution; and genital attribution is essentially penis attribution' (1985: 153). They point out that, in everyday life, genitals are not visible for use in gender attribution, and so other cues (dress, hairstyle, speech, and so on) are used alongside an assumed genital configuration. Kessler and McKenna develop a schema, which is, '*See someone as female only when you cannot see them as male*' (1985: 158). By this, they mean that the gender system sees male characteristics as more obvious than female ones, and:

> The condition of failure for being seen as a woman is to be seen as having a concrete 'male' characteristic. The condition of failure for being seen as a man is to be seen as not having any concrete 'male' characteristics. In the social construction of gender 'male' is the primary construction. (Kessler and McKenna, 1985: 159)

Relating this point to theorizations of gender in regard to lesbian and gay parents, I would suggest that childcare is seen as a 'female/feminine' characteristic. It is viewed as an insufficiently 'masculine' activity. Even within the range of activities associated with the care of children, gender distinctions are made. For example, Jake, a respondent in Andrea Doucet's *Do Men Mother?* says:

> I do some things that are typical of fathering. I throw a ball and play catch, mini golf, take him on the roller coaster, watch movies, play sports. But I also do non-typical things. I let him cry; I am physically demonstrative. I want to break that generational cycle. I let him play with dolls, watch women superheroes. (Doucet, 2006: 123)

Doucet notes that most 'men, even sole-custody fathers,... cling to the view that in spite of their most ardent efforts, they can never be mothers or replace the *mothering* done by women... It is notable that most... gay fathers... recognize the need to consider both masculine and feminine in mothering and fathering and to emphasize the importance of traditionally feminine qualities in fathering, particularly in the raising of sons' (Doucet, 2006: 123). Male parents feel very self-conscious about their role and about its gendered implications. Even to 'watch movies' supposedly is typical of 'fathering', or – rather – it is claimed to be, since to be a male primary carer of children is a 'condition of failure for being seen as a man' (Kessler and McKenna, 1985: 159).

Gender role models

One of the ways in which these arguments surface with regard to lesbian and gay parents is that of gender role model theory. Gender role (or sex-role socialization) theory argues, in essence, that children learn to be a woman or a man (to be a properly gendered being) from interactions with, and modelling of, two parents of either sex, a mother and a father. According to Raewyn Connell:

> the first generation of sex role theorists assumed that the roles were well defined, that socialization went ahead harmoniously, and that sex role learning was a thoroughly good thing. Internalized sex roles contributed to social stability, mental health and the performance of necessary social functions. To put it formally, functionalist theory assumed a concordance among social institutions, sex role norms and actual personalities. (Connell, 1995: 23)

Within gender role theory, the sexes are assumed to perform essentially discrete and complementary roles. Talcot Parsons, for example, argued that 'the man takes the more instrumental role, the woman the more expressive' (Parsons, 1956b: 23), and also that, even though the assumed content of masculinity and femininity might change over time, nevertheless, the roles were clearly differentiated. Socialization theory sees gender as a learned phenomenon and children are assumed to acquire the correct role through interaction with parents. Parsons argued that gender is a part of the personality that 'must be "made" through the socialization process' (Parsons, 1956b: 16). As Liz Stanley says, within socialization theory, 'it is assumed, "gender" is somehow "laid down" through the pattern of interaction between the child and its social and physical environment' (Stanley, 2002: 37).

Socialization theory sees gender roles as learned primarily within 'the family'. Parsons argued 'the differentiation of the sex roles within the family constitutes ... a major axis of its structure' (Parsons, 1956b: 22). This theory further argues that children require both a male and female parent in order to achieve correct socialization. Any deviance from traditional or standard versions of masculinity and femininity (even though these may change over time) is a problem, an example of 'incorrect' socialization. Thus, Parsons argued that homosexuality is prohibited within the family in order specifically to reinforce sex role differentiation, and also to emphasize that any future relationships should be analogous to marriage (Parsons, 1956a). As Stanley and Sue Wise argue, exceptions to the usual sex roles can only be explained as 'deviance'. Socialization theory 'sees *feminism*, along with lesbians, "effeminate" men, career women, and a myriad of other people, as "mistakes" whose existence can't be explained except by reference to "mal-socialization"' (Stanley and Wise, 1993: 102–3). And, as Connell suggests:

> The socialization model seems to miss the *pleasure* which is obvious in much gender learning, the enthusiasm with which young people take up gender symbolism (e.g., sexy clothes) and construct gendered relations (e.g., teenage dating). Nor does it give much insight into the *resist-*

ance which many young people put up to the hegemonic definitions of gender: the boys who hate sport, the girls who want to be astronauts, the teenagers who recognize themselves as gay. It also seems to miss the *difficulty* which is involved in constructing identities and working out patterns of conduct in a gender order marked by power, violence and alienated sexualities. (Connell, 2002: 78)

Commentators who wish to oppose lesbian or gay parenting, however, frequently use the notion that children 'need' a male and female gender role model within the home. For example, Lynn Wardle argues:

Among the most important reasons why heterosexual parenting is best for children is because there are gender-linked differences in child-rearing skills; men and women contribute different (gender-connected) strengths and attributes to their children's development. (Wardle, 1997: 857)

Phillips argues that heterosexual marriage supports the division of 'complementary' gender roles that serve both men and women's interests. In relation to children, she claims that gender roles provide the 'otherness' that children need for the development of a gendered identity (Phillips, 1999: 107). Morgan also suggests that, amongst the children of lesbians and gay men, gender 'confusion seems to be rife, with daughters of lesbian mothers more likely to value and exhibit male sex-typed traits, and sons more female-valued traits' (Morgan, 2002: 78). She adds that the sons of lesbian mothers experience 'threats to masculinity' (p. 84).

There are a number of points that can be made about these arguments. First, it is important to remember that writers like Wardle, Phillips and Morgan favour heterosexual marriage, and are opposed to gay and lesbian parenting. They argue for a society that promotes and upholds one specific family structure, the 'nuclear' heterosexual family with a married couple at its head. Second, they write about 'gender role' as though this refers to an obvious and naturally occurring phenomenon – the idea that men are naturally one way and women another, or that they naturally are better at, and favour, particular tasks, roles and functions. Any questioning of this is described as 'confusion', an attack on the family, and a result of attempts to 'feminize the state' (Phillips, 1999: 85).

Third, Morgan's assertion that research demonstrates gender 'confusion' in the children of lesbians and gay men is not a fact but is, rather, an interpretation or claim. She is actually discussing a study by Beverly Hoeffer (1981), which used social learning theory to suggest that children acquire a 'sex-role'. Hoeffer studied children's toy preferences, toys that were predetermined as gender-typed by her, and, based on this, suggested a sex-role type for each child. Putting aside my very serious qualms about such 'sexrole' determination and its methods for a moment, Hoeffer actually reported that there were no significant differences in toy preferences between the children of heterosexual and lesbian mothers, and that most of them chose traditionally gender-typed toys (Hoeffer, 1981: 542). However, she argued that some lesbian mothers were less likely to insist their children play with traditionally gender-typed toys, which, in Morgan's account, becomes 'evidence' that children with gay or lesbian parents suffer terrible gender confusion.

The gender role model notion is by no means confined to right-wing theorists and those opposed to gay parenting. Richard Redding's article supports gay parenting, yet also says, 'most of us probably have the intuition that children benefit by having two parents of the opposite gender' (Redding, 2008: 166), and that 'differences in how mothers and fathers parent appear to matter' (p. 167). He adds that 'it is likely that children learn about appropriate gender role behavior by observing and internalizing the behavior of their parents', and that 'father involvement predicts children's short- and long-term psychosocial adjustment, even in adulthood' (p. 169).

On this last point, it is worth noting that Redding's main source for such claims is David Popenoe (1996), a writer who opposes 'fatherless families'. Redding also adds that 'it may be particularly important that lesbian parents provide male influences and role models for their boys' (Redding, 2008: 174). This point is interesting as it indicates that Redding, like many of those who write about the need for gender role models, focuses nearly all of his attention onto concerns about boys who lack a male parent (see also Rosky, 2009). He gives just one brief paragraph to the relevance of fathers to girls. Although Redding adds the caveat that 'it is difficult to draw strong conclusions' about gender role, he then states, 'research suggests that mothers and fathers each make a unique contribution to children's (particularly boys') social, emotional, and intellectual development' (Redding, 2008: 175). Language use is telling here; the idea of gender role is based on 'intuition' and Redding says it 'is likely' that gender is learned in this way. These are subtle terms that suggest or encourage agreement between reader/author on the notion of gender role. Later, Redding uses much more concrete terms to indicate clear 'evidence' for the importance of gender role in research studies. Thus, he says that father involvement 'predicts' better outcomes, or that 'research suggests' that the two genders make a different but important contribution to child development. Gender role theory seems to occupy a commonsense position, and that is why it is so easily drawn upon.

Gender role models in social work assessment

In the field of gay and lesbian foster care and adoption, questions about gender role models are ubiquitous (Cocker, 2011; Folgerø, 2008; Hicks, 2000, 2008a, 2009b; Hicks and McDermott, 1999b; Riggs and Augoustinos, 2009; Ross et al., 2009; Taylor, 2009). Pete and Peter, a gay couple who had adopted a three-year-old boy, talked to me about their home study assessment:

Peter: She *[the social worker]* did ask us quite a lot about role models, and female role models and 'Who would you have as a kind of a source of…?' and then we'd just say that we had loads of different friends and…

Steve: What sort of other things did she ask you about that, do you remember? Did she just say, 'What kinds of role models would there be?' or did she ask you specifically who…?

Pete: Who our family was made up of and how much contact do you have with people and how much contact with friends, 'coz we see Ruth and Liz *[a lesbian adoptive couple]* regularly and other contact with female friends…

Peter: The thing is that Rachel *[the social worker]* was lovely and it must be difficult when you're in that kind of job and they've got set questions they have to ask and there's that form…

Steve: Yes, it's quite prescriptive…

Peter: Yeah, and it's a bit 'Who does this, who does that?'

Steve: I'm interested, and I don't know whether you know this, but was she worried about the gender role thing or do you think it was the Panel that she had to satisfy?

Peter: It was a mixture of the two, I think it was a mixture of the two. I think she struggled with it slightly… But the Panel one was the name thing… They struggled with our names because we're both called Peter. 'What would a child call you?'

Pete: Especially one member of the Panel, she just kept going on about it, and the Chair eventually had to say, 'Let's move on'.

Peter: I said to her, what was it I said, well, I said to her something about, 'Look, we're both called Peter but we've never struggled with that with my nieces and nephews or with Ruth and Liz's children, when they want us they'll prod or they'll say Pete or Peter and we'll know which one they mean, and in some way you just know which one they want'.

Pete: Or they say, 'Big Peter' and 'Little Peter'.

Peter: Yeah, they do that, and when I said that to her, she said something along the lines of, 'But you've got to remember when a child is small and they're that age, they need to know who you are and what to call you, you need to have a definite…' and she wouldn't let it go, she was like a dog with a bone really… and we got a little bit frustrated with that, and I don't know what that was around.

Pete and Peter identify concerns about gender role as a key component of their adoption assessment. This is evident in language that invokes quantity; they are asked 'quite a lot' about gender role and one panel member goes 'on about it', is 'like a dog with a bone'. Similarly, contact with female role models is described in terms of quantity – they describe being asked about 'source', 'how much contact' (twice), 'who', and their response is to talk about 'loads of different friends', 'other contact' and so on. That is, the concern about gender role becomes a measuring effect, as though a certain amount of contact with women will pass the gender role model bar. The couple is frustrated by these assumptions but, nevertheless, duly provides answers to the concerns. Indeed, at one point Peter makes allowances for the social worker's questions, as do I – Rachel is 'lovely', it 'must be difficult', she has 'set questions' and the form is 'quite prescriptive'. That is, our dialogue recognizes gender role theory as a typical concern. We make allowances for Rachel, as we do not see her questions in individualistic terms but, rather, we know that there are layers of organizational expectation here that draw upon, and expect, answers about female role models. Frustration about gender role is an effect of narrative construction that aims to highlight and challenge this idea, and our allowances do similar work in that they indicate attention to context and to institutional expectations. Crucially, the research interview itself provides a specific occasion for talk, one in which an analysis of gendered expectations is possible.

The couple refers to one panel member's concern that they are both called 'Peter'. This is an interesting example as Pete says the woman 'kept going on about it' and that the Chair had to intervene to move discussion on. The couple portrays her concern as to do with an adopted child not knowing what to call them, and again they duly provide answers to this concern through examples. But they are clearly impatient with the question. For this reason, I ask them further questions about this episode since, in my view, the concern about the two Peters actually stands for a concern about two gay men; that is, the concern is doing work other than just expressing a focus on the what children 'need'. I offer this as a possible explanation, but with a get-out clause attached ('if you were being a little bit paranoid') in case the couple does not agree:

Steve: I think that's really interesting because you could, if you were being a little bit paranoid maybe!, you could see it as a concern about two men.

Peter: Yeah, two men.

Steve: It's really about that but she's using the 'Peter' thing as a concern about the 'Mum and Dad' thing... 'coz a lot of gay couples get asked, you know, 'Well, what are they going to call you?' Or 'You can't both be "Mummy"'.

Peter: Yeah, but why can't we both be 'Mummy'? In fact, I think that when he *[their adopted son]* came to us, I would have preferred it maybe if he'd used our names really, but we got used to 'Daddy' and 'Pops'. That's what he calls us.

Pete: But that came from them, the 'Pops' came from them.

Peter: Because they said he can't...

Steve: Really?

Peter: Yeah, we were always given that and in some ways I quite like it now, I've grown used to it, but I always wanted... well, he does call us Pete and Peter now.

Pete: Sometimes, but in the main...

Peter: ...in the main, it's 'Daddy' and 'Pops'...

Steve: So, they suggested 'Daddy and Pops'?

Pete: Yeah, the social workers suggested it, but they had another gay couple where they used 'Daddy and Pops', so we're all losing our identities!

This section of dialogue raises the ways in which 'difference' is created and imputed to gay parents. My suggestion that the concern about forenames is really about two men is immediately echoed by Peter, and takes us into discussion about the notion of a lack of gender 'difference' in gay couples. The idea of a lack of a mummy and daddy (Butler's 'symbolic order' – 2004b: 118), which also echoes Nita and Clare's example of the Consultant's 'You can't have more than one mother, it's not allowed', raises concerns about difference – a lack of gender difference and an imputation of difference for the child.

I find Peter's response here fascinating – 'but why can't we both be "Mummy"?' He takes up a position that many men would not. For example, in both Doucet's study of male parents and Lewin's study of gay dads, most did not see or refer to themselves as 'mothers' (Doucet, 2006; Lewin, 2009). Yet, Peter's response challenges gender fixity (he opts both himself and his partner into a category usually retained for women), and it challenges the need for obvious difference. Peter sees the role as something either or both of them can take up, and there is no need for another complementary member category. I also find Peter's 'when he came to us, I would have preferred it maybe if he'd used our names' telling, since this questions the requirement that adopted or fostered children should have to call their new carers

'Mummy' or 'Daddy'. This is, in part, an attempt to de-gender roles. Other gay and lesbian carers have suggested that this is also a pressure on children who may already have adults that they think of, or refer to, as 'Mummy' or 'Daddy' or may be wary of using these terms at all. Others, however, use these terms and find that their children wish to use them. But my point, here, is that, in Pete and Peter's case, there appears to be a need to insert some kind of 'gendered' difference through naming practices. Thus, the social workers suggest using the Americanized 'Daddy and Pops', which is a way of reintroducing difference, one that is also used by some gay fathers (see, for example, Symons, 2002).

Pete's assertion that another gay adoptive couple were referred to as 'Daddy and Pops' by social workers leads to his comment, 'so we're all losing our identities!' Pete recognizes that an answer to the concerns about difference is now being applied to gay adoptive couples as a group. Just as most heterosexual parent couples will be known as 'Mum and Dad', so gay parent couples may be called 'Daddy and Pops'. But Pete's point is that this is imposed, it's not a phrase that he would choose, and it is ironically creating a lack of difference between gay parent couples. Will they all become known as 'Daddy and Pops'? Of course, such phrases – Daddy/Dad, Daddy/Pops, Daddy/Papa – may simply be ways of distinguishing between two male parents, and are used by gay dads and their children, but I have made more of it here because the 'what will a child call you?' question is often raised with gay or lesbian couples and, for me, it has to do with disruption of usual or assumed gendered difference.

I asked Pete and Peter more about what their social worker raised:

Steve: What kind of stuff did she ask you about, I mean did she try to pin you down on who does the cooking?

Pete: Oh, yeah.

Peter: Oh, yeah, and we almost at the end of it came to a decision where we wouldn't argue with it. I mean we'd argued that and I think, well, all couples do have arguments about who does the cleaning!

Steve: Yeah...

Peter: We don't define who does what, we kind of muck in, and we do argue about it, but we almost felt as though we couldn't when she was there because we thought she would say, 'Well, you've not really got this managed quite well. If you can't manage a rota of who does what, then how will you find it when a child is introduced to that? You need a lot clearer ideas of who does what, who does the ironing'... It was a bit strange really, it was almost as though she wanted us to be these stereotypical roles.

Steve: So, when you said you weren't or that you do bits of everything, and you work it out between you, how did she respond? ... I've not put that very well! Did you just end up having to go along with it and say yes?

Pete: We tried to argue it for a while but then we just had to give up.

Peter: Yeah, I was a bit kind of like it was a defeat! and we just went along with it.

Steve: It's so common, I've spoken to lots of people who say exactly the same thing, they've ended up 'going along' ... or in their mind they've made a compromise just to shut the person up almost!

Peter: You get the end result. We didn't lie to her in any way, but I don't think we told her we're disorganized and we hate cleaning and we hate certain things. It was a bit, 'Pete does the cleaning and I do the cooking,' and it's not really like that ... Those gender roles used to get on my nerves really.

Pete and Peter talk about a decision not to 'argue with' gender roles, and about giving up. Peter says, 'it was a defeat! and we just went along with it'. They express this in terms of (a) having to hide or avoid certain discussions (e.g., having rows about housework); (b) recognizing that the social worker 'wanted us to be these stereotypical roles'; and (c) going along with this to achieve an 'end result'; that is, their desire to adopt a child. As I state in this extract, this is a common story amongst gay and lesbian adopters and foster carers, having to 'go along with' or giving up opposition to ideas like gender roles. There is much resistance here but, ultimately, the applicants cave in or 'give up', as they want to be taken seriously by a panel. If certain roles are an institutional expectation, then applicants 'go along with' this, even though it clearly creates discord in their narrative accounts of that process. Pete and Peter are not happy to 'give up', but they do. And when Peter says, 'It was a bit, "Pete does the cleaning and I do the cooking," and it's not really like that,' a standard discourse of gender dominates ('Those gender roles used to get on my nerves really'), yet it is also resisted. A view of the gendered gay couple is created through a dialogue between social worker and applicants, yet this is co-ordinated with institutional expectations or ways of working. To borrow from Smith, the account of Peter and Pete in terms of gender 'articulates a moral order' (Smith, 1990a: 171).

I also asked Mark about questions of gender role. Mark has been a foster carer for over 15 years, has fostered more than 40 children, and adopted one of the lads. Mark's account is interesting, as he says that gender role wasn't a particular concern for the authority that originally assessed him:

Mark: I was thinking about this because you had asked me to think about issues like this, and my recollection with the *[local authority]* was that they have treated me like anybody else. A single carer, the fact that I was gay wasn't an issue, so there hasn't really been a question mark about preconceived ideas or whatever. I really genuinely felt that I was assessed on my own merits as a person who was able to look after some of the young people ... I think I've been comfortable being gay for so long and I don't really come across, you know, as a gay man, I'm a man who happens to be gay ... so really there was no ... I think in the assessment we did talk about, 'would it be safer for me to be approved for girls', in terms of safe care. It's less of an issue for a gay man looking after girls than for a gay man looking after teenage boys. Well, you could also argue that a single man would find it a lot more difficult looking after teenage girls, because there's a lot higher risk of allegations and things.

Mark's talk is centrally concerned with gender and sexuality, but in a way that emphasizes his identification as a (single) male carer, but not as a gay man. He identifies himself as having been treated 'like anybody else ... assessed on [his] own merits', and he says that being gay wasn't really an issue for the authority that assessed him. He describes himself as single and then as 'a man who happens to be gay ... I don't really come across, you know, as a gay man'. There is a lot of work about gender going on here – for Mark, the primary issue is about being a male carer (with potential suspicion from others that this implies), rather than about being a gay carer, and yet his talk is saturated with reference to the category 'gay'. Partly, this is, of course, because I asked him to talk about this, but it is interesting to note that he says he doesn't 'come across' gay. This raises notions of stereotypical versions of gay men, which Mark wishes to challenge through his identification as an ordinary man. Being gay is not a particular focus of his life, he says, and he is also comfortable that the social workers that originally assessed his application to care for children did not focus on his being gay either. However, this does not mean that gendered work was not a focus of Mark's assessment or of his talk with me:

Steve: So, they did consider you for girls?

Mark: My recollection is that we talked it through and that [local authority] were very open.

Steve: And did you have a preference?

Mark: Well, I said that I understand boys, you know, I don't understand girls at all! My affinity, and all the work I've done in youth work and all the rest of it over the years, was all male-led ... But I think the idea about not having girls is rather about conventional thinking. If you think about a teenage girl that has suffered at some level from a man in the past, being alone in a house with another man might feel quite threatening, but it depends if you're openly gay or not. You know, I've got a girl now and I have looked after girls in the past. My preference was to take boys because I like doing boy-stuff really. And it's certainly easier with the younger ones if you're taking them swimming or to the toilet, whatever, it's generally easier with a boy than with a girl. It's easier now, I guess, because changing rooms are more family friendly, but back then ... I think, though, that it may have been slight convention in seeing a single man as a higher risk than female carers in terms of allegations.

A number of gender claims are used here. First, Mark talks about wanting to care for boys and having 'affinity' for looking after them. He uses words to describe ease with boys – it's 'easier', he 'understands boys', he likes doing 'boy-stuff', and so on. At the same time, he challenges what he calls 'conventional thinking' and suggests that a man may care for girls as well. He has looked after girls and was looking after a sister and brother when I visited him. Third, he raises the question of 'allegations', a phrase that is regularly used within fostering and adoption circles to describe a situation where a child or young person claims that they have been abused by the carer that they are living with. This is seen as a particular concern for all male carers, since men are more likely to be suspected of and commit sexual abuse, and so allegations against a man may be treated more seriously (and, therefore, have more serious consequences). Mark raises the idea that 'convention' may have seen male carers as more appropriate for male children, yet this doesn't seem to follow for gay carers. I asked Mark about gender role models:

Steve: What about gender role models, did they ask you about that because gay men nearly always get asked that? Did they ask you what women there were in your life or what female role models were these children going to have, anything like that?

Mark: At the time, I think we did because ... well, I've had a female lodger here since but not at the time of the assessment, and I'm very good friends with, well I actually bought the house with one of the nurses at the hospital where I helped out, she knew I was gay and we bought it to actually try and see if we could work as a couple. So there were often women around in the house and in my life, but not as partners, and my mother was – is – but then even more so ... well, she only lives around the corner, and she has been quite involved, so I had quite a reasonable network I suppose of females which would have given sufficient, you know, well, sufficient…well, the female role figure around in the area or the home, sort of thing.

Steve: But it doesn't sound like *[local authority]* were particularly bothered by that?

Mark: I think *[local authority]*, in all fairness, have been very good with equal opportunities and the whole…you know, they have always been very supportive and very to the point, you know, 'Well, what's the issue here?' you know, 'You're someone who has the skills to meet these kids' needs.'…There's been a lot of discussion with Sarah, she's thirteen now, and there's been a lot of talk about how I can meet her needs and about what females are around. I used to have a female lodger here and she lived here for about three years and she is an incredibly experienced social worker…and she was great for Sarah. Sarah has female mentors and all that stuff, but in terms of her own personal development or whatever, I fulfil the 'parent' role, I probably talk to her more about growing up, but you know you can approach it, I've talked to her about puberty and about periods and I've bought them both books, you know, age-appropriate stuff. I think I have a fairly good relationship with her really so we talk, and we've gone off and bought all the things she needs like some bras and we went together to the store and got one of the younger female staff to have a chat and she went off and helped, so you know it's all doable!

Steve: That's very interesting because when people say they have concerns about her 'needs', when they say 'needs' in relation to her being a girl, what do they mean?

Mark: I think some of it's emotional needs but I think a lot of it has been perceived to be around her needs in terms of physical change, periods and things like that, you know and I don't know all about that and I've not grown up with sisters and I have a very male-focused life, but you know I talk to others at the support group and to other carers. Sarah has been having sessions with one of the clinical nurses so that she can just talk through some of the stuff. I think any parent who's reasonably tuned in to life picks up that girls have different mood swings to boys and all the rest of it. It's assumed that dads talk to their sons about puberty and mums talk to their daughters but there's no reason why…In terms of wanting answers to questions, she's more than likely to come to me than Mum.

This text is, similarly, full of gendered work. Like others, Mark duly answers concerns about female role models, talking about a lodger, his mother, friends, a woman he bought his house with, and so on. He says, 'there were often women around,' and elsewhere calls this 'a reasonable network of females'. Again, there is a sense of quantification here, as though a certain number of female contacts will pass the test. Mark's language here – 'given sufficient, you know, well, sufficient ... well, the female role ... sort of thing' – is hesitant and unsure. This could be read in a number of ways but, for me, it connotes the almost defensive position that gay carers are put in, having to create a notion of adequate 'opposite-sex' role models. Mark is answering a question that he doesn't really have concerns about.

Interestingly, Mark goes on to question this idea by actually suggesting he is able to take up the role of caring for an adolescent woman. He talks about Sarah's 'needs', but then lists tasks that he is able to perform as her foster carer, including dealing with issues that are classically thought of in highly gendered terms – talking about 'growing up', 'puberty', 'periods', buying 'bras' and so on. Mark's 'it's all doable!' indicates some degree of frustration with conventionally gendered thinking here. Although such tasks are often thought of as belonging to, and mainly performed by, women, Mark asserts his ability to do them, too. I ask him what people mean by Sarah's 'needs', since this is an area in which gendered discourses are dominant. As Steph Lawler argues, 'the very formulation "needs" invokes a moral/ethical compulsion' (Lawler, 2000: 127). Mark talks about 'emotional needs' and also 'physical change, periods and things like that', which indicates once more that ideas about the body, about puberty and about developing sexuality are all thought about in gendered terms. Mark is aware of possible limitations here ('I have a very male-focused life'), but he also claims to make 'effort', to 'talk to others', and says that Sarah is 'more than likely to come to me than Mum'. Mark has to work to show an ability to carry out caring tasks (to meet 'needs') usually reserved for, or allocated to, women.

Institutional ethnography and 'gender role'

Smith's essay, 'Femininity as Discourse' (Smith, 1990a: 159–208), analyzes the concept of gender in order to problematize its 'already givenness' (Smith, 1990a: 159). For example, she opposes the notion that women and men are simply socialized into proper gender roles, since gender must be accomplished in the everyday:

> Women are not just the passive products of socialization; they are active; they create themselves. At the same time, their self-creation, their work, the uses of their skills, are co-ordinated with the market for clothes, makeup, shoes, accessories, etc., through print, film, etc. (Smith, 1990a: 161)

That is, social relations relate to a discourse of femininity mediated by texts, such as advertisements, magazines, television and so on. Femininity, on this account, is not a normative order of the type proposed in functionalist accounts of gender role, but is 'a complex of actual relations vested in texts' (Smith, 1990a: 163). It must be produced, talked about, and noted in relation to something else called 'masculinity'. This suggests a hierarchical set of social relations in which the 'discourse of femininity articulates a moral order' (Smith, 1990a: 171). This holds women, and men, accountable, since versions of femininity are expected, and yet devalued, in women and so unexpected and, therefore, abhorred in men. Smith gives the example of 'looking good', an expectation for women reinforced through magazines, makeup, makeup tips and so on:

> Being desirable, being attractive, is a condition of participation in circles organized heterosexually; such circles intersect with the social relations of the discourse of femininity. (Smith, 1990a: 194)

Women (and men) must work at the production of the gendered subject, 'appropriately entered into local heterosexuality' (Smith, 1990a: 202). Yet, this does not mean that all women are passive dupes of heterosexual femininity; 'there is play and interplay' (Smith, 1990a: 203), in which women resist such subjection. At the same time, however, Smith argues that the constant comparison between:

> discursive images of femininity and the imperfect body generates that perpetual renewal of desire into which the texts tying desire to commodity are inserted. Women are returned again and again as consumers to the retail outlets that will remedy their ever-renewed textually reflected imperfections. (Smith, 1990a: 208)

Smith's account of femininity as discourse rejects the notion of gender used in functionalist accounts of role socialization, since they treat gender as some kind of thing to be acquired and passed on. A concept ('gender') is substituted for actual practices of gender, so that 'for every...concept, there is taken to be a something out there corresponding to it. The disappearance of people and activities is striking...Agency is assigned to conceptually constructed entities' (Smith, 2005: 56), the very same point that George Smith made when considering notions of homophobia (Smith, 1988, 1990).

Applying Smith's thinking to the notion of gender role models, I would argue that social work as an institution operates ruling relations that require the upholding of a properly gendered self. Where the two gender roles do not exist at home (a notion that is always applied to lesbians and gay men), they are looked for in the idea of gender roles and providing gender role models. This treats gender as already given, as a thing to be learned. Part of its being achieved is brought about through institutional forms of fostering and adoption assessment, questioning, and so on, which require – or look for – the reassurance of standard gender role ideas. That is, lesbian and gay parents, especially those who apply to adopt or foster, regularly encounter questions about gender role.

Gay male parents and gender claims

So far, I have been discussing the ways in which gender emerges as a relevant category in institutional assessment practices. I would now like to focus on gendered work *by gay male parents*, since it is also important to consider versions of the gendered self that occur in their narrative accounts, including my research interviews. Gender is not just a problematic category imposed upon gay or lesbian parents 'from the outside', it is also a prevalent feature of their own presentations of self, identity, and parenting.

Johnny Symons' documentary film, *Daddy & Papa: A Story about Gay Fathers in America* (2002), features gay dads talking about gender as a socially limiting category. For example, Doug talks about taking his son, Oscar, to see a *Rugrats* cartoon ('Mother's Day'), in which the character Chuckie wishes he had a mother. The cartoon features an extremely sentimental song, 'I want a mom to read me stories/and sing a lullaby/and if I have a bad dream/ to hold me when I cry/oh I want a mom that'll last forever' (Klasky-Csupo/ Nickelodeon, 1997), and Doug says:

> Once in a while, I think that Oscar does really miss having a mom. It was just a movie – it was the *Rugrats* or something like that, where Chuckie gets a mom, and I took him to see that not knowing that this mom theme was gonna be a major part of the movie. He was okay, but afterwards he said, 'Well, Chuckie got to have a mom, I don't get to have a mom, huh?' and I said, 'Well, no Oscar, but there's a lot of people that don't have moms and there's people that have a mom but don't have a dad'...I mean, I think every kid would ideally like to have, you know, a mom and a dad and two sets of grandparents and two brothers and sisters and a dog and a house in the country, I don't know, that's still the norm that our society imposes upon us at every turn. (Symons, 2002)

In the *Rugrats* episode, feeling good is associated with gendered convention. It is 'moms' that comfort, hold and soothe, an idea that encourages feelings of lack in children like Oscar, and feelings of frustration, and even guilt, in gay dads.

In another scene from *Daddy & Papa*, we see Johnny and William's adopted son, Zac, playing in high heels:

Johnny: People went out of their way to point out to us that Zac was one hundred per cent boy, but once in a while he threw us a

> curveball ... When he developed an attachment to the neighbour's girl's high heels, it was a whole new ballgame ...

William: If he did more traditionally feminine things, people would tie that to the fact that he has two dads. It's probably just internalized homophobia, but when stuff like that happens in public, I feel a little bit of – shame (Symons, 2002).

William's confession of shame, here, is linked directly to the notion of a failed gender presentation, even though much narrative work has already been done to situate Zac as a proper boy (the couple even jokes about bringing up a 'jock', and their language employs sports metaphors). But William's reaction to Zac's playing in high heels shows that he is painfully aware of those who would argue that gay parents produce gender-confused kids. He is ashamed, since there is an 'assumption that individual or social deviance is rooted in parent-child interaction' (Lawler, 2000: 68). This sense of gay shame is addressed by David Halperin, who argues that any notion of a positive or 'proud' gay identity must not:

> forget its origins in shame, that is still powered by the transformative energies that spring from experiences of shame. Without that intimate and never-forgotten relation to shame, gay pride turns into mere social conformity, into a movement ... with no more radical goal than that of 'trying to persuade straight society that [gay people] can be good parents, good soldiers, good priests' (Bersani, 1995: 113) (Halperin, 2009: 44)

I think that Halperin's use of the Bersani quotation is quite deliberate here – he is saying that some versions of the 'good parent' are not challenging enough of the reasons for gay shame, and that conformity to a conservative version of the gay parent will result in a wider political or social conformity. But, in William's case, there is a sense in which he cannot win. Zac's non-traditionally gendered play is seen as feminine and this creates, for both William and Johnny, a sense of uncertainty. They feel that they will be blamed as gay dads for their son playing with high heels. Pete and Peter also told me a story in which their son had kissed a boy goodbye at school, which led to a comment from a grandparent, 'Oh god, if my grandson did that, I would be really worried.' So, William's concern is understandable, but he recognizes that it is problematic when he terms it 'internalized homophobia'. That is, William understands that the gender system that requires boys *not* to play with high heels is wrong, but he uses 'internalized homophobia' because, rather than question the gender order, he turns the concern in on himself – it is his own psychological problem that dominates and results in feelings of shame. That is, he makes it into a psychological problem.

William lives with his shame about having a son who plays with high heels, and he wants to protect his son from prejudice. He does not want to confirm the arguments of those opposed to gay parenting that gender nonconformity is a costly outcome. A deed – playing with the wrong toys – transforms into an identity. As Sedgwick says, 'shame and identity remain in very dynamic relation to one another, at once deconstituting and foundational, because shame is both peculiarly contagious and peculiarly individuating' (Sedgwick, 2003: 36). William's shame is catching – it may spread to his whole family, to all gay dads – since it expresses a concern about being identified as aberrant. It also identifies subjection to the gender order. He takes up a position, an affect, within gendered discourse, one in which femininity – especially in a boy – equals failure.

Mark's account of gender is another fascinating example of such identity management, or what Goffman (1990a) calls the management of stigma and spoiled identity:

Mark: I usually talk to the kids fairly early on about how they'd like me to be known to their friends, and that's usually more often to do with whether I'm a 'Dad' rather than being gay, although it does get blurred. With Shaun *[his adopted son]*, I think he was finding it difficult potentially about me being gay, well, not about *me* being gay but what the friends at school would say. He struggled quite a lot – he still does! – with life and when kids are nine or ten they can be pretty nasty, especially if a kid's been in care and moved around a lot, so we played it down I think really. Some of the parents of his friends knew, but then it was generally when it was appropriate. You know, someone would say, 'Well, are you married?' and I would say, 'No, I haven't had a partner for quite a few years,' and it was part of the conversation. And Shaun's close friends, because they knew me, it wasn't an issue, I was Mark, not just a gay guy. I've had very little experience of being gay as being an issue and it doesn't actually crop up that much. Because often it's not really relevant. You know, I've been coaching some of the kids at school and someone will say, 'Oh is that your daughter?' and that's about whether I'm the dad rather than a gay dad.

Steve: Is there a situation where you would absolutely make it relevant?

Mark: About being gay?

Steve: Yeah.

Mark: Um, *[sigh]*.

Steve: Or made clear?

Mark: Well, some of the foster carers know, by and large, maybe some of the newer ones may not be aware, but I don't know whether I'm known as 'the gay carer'.

Mark's talk is about managing identity for himself but also for his fostered children. This raises the question of how he will 'be known' to the children's friends. Here, Mark suggests that he is known as a dad rather than as a gay dad, and in relation to his adopted son, Shaun, Mark says they 'played … down' his being gay. This is because lesbian and gay parents and their children engage in complex processes of identity management and claims. Deciding who to tell that a parent is gay is a key example. But this also links to Mark's self-presentation as a man who happens to be gay ('often it's not really relevant'). One reading of this talk would be that Mark's identity as a man or as a father might be compromised if he is known to be gay. As Pam Nilan notes, 'perceptions of sexual preference/activity are routinely used as criteria in judgements about the gender identity of an individual' (Nilan, 1994: 139). Mark must work to maintain his gendered position, otherwise this may be compromised, a process by which moral judgements will be made. Mark draws on what can be seen as an activity associated with masculinity ('coaching' kids) – like Johnny and William's use of sports imagery – in order to emphasize his position as a 'dad rather than a gay dad'.

In Chapter 4, Nita and Clare expressed the view that their being lesbians was always relevant even when unspoken, whereas Mark goes to some lengths to claim that his being gay is not always relevant. For me, this does not discount the question of background category presence since Mark's talk indicates that he is always aware of whether others know that he is gay. He is constantly involved in the work of identity management concerning his sexuality. He works hard to display characteristics of the category man/dad, much of which revolves around notions of the ordinary, and he is aware that this may be spoiled if his sexuality becomes known. This discussion hinges on epistemological questions, which Mark continues to develop:

Mark: But there are still some people that I know pretty well that don't know I'm gay. It hasn't crossed their minds, it hasn't come up, it's just not in their mindset.

Steve: It's not as though you come out to every single person you meet.

Mark: No, and I was talking to a counsellor that I know the other day, and we were saying, 'When do you say it? At what point in a conversation do you say you're gay?' Or do you just let it ride … and how do you do it? You know, if you go to a party or something, I think most straight people, well, the social handshake is, 'This is my wife,' or whatever, but unless you say it then, or you might say, 'I'm single,' because, well, I used to have a male partner... so we were just debating that about how comfortable or safe you feel to do that with people you don't know, and does it start a whole debate when sometimes you just don't want a debate! Whereas you can say, 'Oh I've got a couple of kids,' and that can just kind of get the conversation going.

Steve: You have to gauge situations as well.

Mark: I think you do. It doesn't worry me, but it's not so much a part of me. It used to be, I used to run a gay and lesbian social group in *[city]* and I would have about thirty guys come around here. So then I guess it was slightly more high profile for me, but it's not – apart from friends who know – it's not a big part of my life really. With the kids, I feel comfortable enough that they can say whatever they like to whoever they like and I'll deal with it, whatever comes back.

Steve: It's not a secret.

Mark: No, and I think that's really important with the kids is to dispel any feelings of power they might have over you about that. It's like, 'So what?... If you've got a problem with it, that's fine and we'll talk about it' but... I've been out with friends for thirty or so years and so I guess it's got past that point of when do you bring it into the conversation.

Mark knows people who don't know that he is gay. And my intervention ('It's not as though you come out to every single person you meet') raises the questions of knowledge/relevance. Mark takes this forward, using the story about chatting with a counsellor, to talk about how and when being gay is made relevant in a social scene or conversation and to highlight the work that this involves. He refers explicitly to what he calls, 'the social handshake... "This is my wife," ...' for heterosexual men and, whilst Mark may use this turn of phrase because he is thinking from his own position as a man in social situations, I think that his choice of words here indicates the heteronormativity of those social scenes. There is a sense in which it is men who introduce their wives to each other, a sense in which both heterosexuality and male dominance are unremarkable. To come out as a gay man in such situations would be to become absolutely marked.

This management of identity and of knowledge is described by Mark as having to do with questions of safety and comfort. Lesbians and gay men must judge the relative safety of a scene, and they gauge their own comfort in terms of whether to come out. But Mark also notes that to come out is to introduce new and perhaps unanticipated knowledge, something that may provoke 'debate'. To come out as a gay father or carer is to provoke questions about whether others find this acceptable, to put the self into a position in which that self is being judged. This Mark contrasts with talking about having 'a couple of kids', a remark that promotes normative conversational genres. Mark returns to questions about epistemology towards the end of this extract, since he links the notion of the importance of his children knowing he is gay with ideas about secrecy and power. He does not want his sexuality – or, rather, knowledge about his sexuality – to become a form of power to be used against him. Yet, at the same time, he refers to his long-term friends with whom the nature of his sexuality is not a question, it is not something that figures in conversation. In this sense, knowing that Mark is gay is not always a good thing – or, rather, not knowing may be more usual.

These questions are central to Sedgwick's account in *Epistemology of the Closet*, where knowledge, or 'the relations of the known and the unknown, the explicit and the inexplicit around homo/heterosexual definition' (Sedgwick, 1994a: 3), is key. Sedgwick argues that this homo/heterosexual definitional trope marks other categories, such as 'secrecy/disclosure, knowledge/ignorance, private/public, masculine/feminine, majority/minority' (Sedgwick, 1994a: 11) amongst others, all of which may be found in Mark's speech. His identification as a man who 'happens to be gay', with long-term friends who do not know about his sexuality, pivots on questions of knowledge/ignorance. Mark may be identifying as an ordinary man or father in public, as masculine or as part of a majority group of parents, yet he is also very conscious of the potential for disclosure. His sexuality may become known, it may even be secretly known or suspected by his friends, and he certainly wishes to avoid secrecy in relation to his children. In part, I think that this is because Mark knows that disclosure of his sexuality will spoil his identity as a father in the eyes of some. Ignorance of Mark's sexuality works not only to protect his identification as a father, but also to uphold notions of heterosexual superiority.

Here, then, it might be possible to argue that the gay father is a marked or spoiled category in a way that the (heterosexual) father is not. But, in relation to men who act as primary parents/carers and those who apply to foster or adopt, this is more complicated, since the category 'male' is problematized:

> **Mark:** I was at a conference in London the summer before last about foster carers, about men who foster, and I was saying I think we bring the problems on ourselves or some people do, because they're not quite clear themselves what they're doing or why they're doing it, sort of thing, and – you know – there's a lot of male nurses who are gay and they work with children. There's lots of other caring professions in which men are involved and

it doesn't seem to be a problem, and yet being a foster carer suddenly becomes a problem. Whether it's because it's at home or because it's just different in some people's heads? I think it's around self-doubts and self-confidence, perhaps, and in worrying about what other people think. I don't worry about what other people think because I know that what I'm doing is fine. If they want to challenge it..., you know, and if we come out and speak confidently and behave in a confident way and don't try and feel guilty... You know, when people come out and the press always say, 'they *admit* to being gay,' and it's like it's a crime or something... I suppose we have that same media mentality with 'gay', whereas most paedophiles are, you know, living in ordinary families or whatever. I think it's about us men – not gay men, just men generally – being confident in themselves that they are doing what they're doing for the right reasons and in a safe way, and you can stand up and say, 'I don't have a problem. What is the problem? Why are you concerned?' Maybe it's to do with their own parenting? I mean, my dad was stereotypically alpha male, you know, I remember him telling me at sixteen that I couldn't be gay – not that it worked! – he made it quite clear that that didn't happen! He was very rebellious when I had my male partner, he didn't speak to me for over six months and this was only, what, twenty years ago. But because I think that everyone else who knew me felt comfortable, he actually found that he was the one out on a limb and he was the one that had a problem. Both of my parents had gay friends and it was okay knowing somebody gay, but he was seen by his friends that he could actually produce the gay son. He said some stuff to my brother in the past that, 'real men only have sons' or whatever, you know... what?! But I guess there's still a lot of that around, it hangs around and that needs challenging on a regular basis.

Mark argues that all men caring for children are under suspicion, a point also made in Symons' film (2002), in research (Hicks, 2006c; Mallon, 2004) and other accounts by gay fathers (Green, 1999; Savage, 2000; Strah with Margolis, 2003). Mark mentions caring professions in which men work in order to suggest that this 'doesn't seem to be a problem' and he asks why gender is seen as a problem in the field of foster care or adoption. Yet, I think that in fields such as nursing, social care, social work, teaching and so on, gender is regularly featured as a concern (Christie, 2001; Pringle, 1995). Mark creates a story of 'confidence' here, the idea that male carers should feel confident in what they are doing, yet he also raises questions around 'safe' care. That is, he acknowledges a concern about potential abuse of children and, linked to this, he challenges notions of gay men as 'paedophiles'. I shall return to this suspicion about gay men as potential abusers in Chapter 7.

It is interesting to note that Mark follows this point with a story about his own father. He suggests that a lack of confidence about being a parent may stem from some men's upbringing. This might refer to a notion of gender socialization, but I take it to mean that men grow up surrounded by practices, images and talk about what proper masculinity ought to be. Mark's story about his father being 'stereotypically alpha male' suggests traditional notions of what men should and should not do or be, thus being gay is not allowed. This is interesting because Mark explains that his parents had gay friends, but suggests that his father's problem was with the idea of having a gay son, as though to 'produce' a gay son was a form of shame. This also links with his father's 'real men only have sons' comment. Here, there is a notion of proper masculinity begetting proper masculinity, and homosexuality acts not only as improper masculinity but also to taint the father's sexuality in his terms. This story is also used by Mark to account for some men's misgivings about the parenting role. Mark refers to the media, family background, perceptions, self-image, and peers as affecting ideas about men as parents/carers. As is also suggested in narratives by other gay fathers, imagined gender roles have to be rewritten (Benson et al., 2005; Green, 1999; Lewin, 2009; Mallon, 2004; Savage, 2000; Stacey, 2006; Strah with Margolis, 2003).

To sum up, I have argued that gay dads do gender in a number of ways: they may claim female contacts in order to address role model concerns, or they may reject the idea of gendered roles when applied to themselves (Pete and Peter). They may describe their parenting as gendered 'male', retaining a view of self as a male figure or 'father' who cares for children (Doucet, 2006; Lewin, 2009; Mark's account), or as gendered 'female', challenging the need to be 'masculine' and embracing the role of 'mother', if ironically (Brinamen, 2000; Peter's account). Or, they may combine the two, sometimes drawing on notions of androgyny and even de-gendering (Benson et al., 2005; Bigner and Bozett, 1990; Bozett, 1989; Doucet, 2006). For example, a study by Stephanie Schacher, Carl Auerbach and Louise Silverstein includes statements, such as 'I wouldn't call it a "mommy" or "daddy" role ... just primary caregiver' or 'It's not about gender', which the researchers describe as *'degendered parenting'* (Schacher et al., 2005: 39 and 44). Of course, this can be contrasted with other research that argues gay fathers do not adopt a 'mother'-type role, since 'viewing themselves in that light would demand shedding their gender identity as men' (Lewin, 2009: 134).

Gay fathers assert their ability to perform caring and parenting tasks, yet they may also make use of being an 'ordinary man' (Mark's account). They may refer to themselves as unusual (even 'revolutionary', as Johnny says in his documentary) because being a male parent is still regarded as abnormal, and they frequently express impatience with gendered expectations. At the same time, gay dads worry about confirming gender stereotypes (William's shame), yet they play roles of which they are acutely aware and implicitly critical. That is, they accept or embrace gender expectations sometimes. Mark's account also shows that some dads may worry that overt identification as 'gay' spoils an otherwise respectable subjectivity as a father/man, and most identify times when they avoid discussion or acknowledgement of their sexuality in order to protect their children and themselves from stigma.

Does gender matter?

I wish to finish this chapter with discussion of Biblarz and Stacey's article, 'How Does the Gender of Parents Matter?' (2010), a follow-up to their earlier piece (Stacey and Biblarz, 2001) discussed in Chapter 1. Stacey and Biblarz's work supports gay and lesbian parenting, and argues that research has 'not identified any gender-exclusive parenting abilities' (Biblarz and Stacey, 2010: 16). Yet, in both articles, sexuality and gender are treated as isolatable variables, as 'thing-like', in order to test their relative effects on child development. This means that not only is gender treated as empirically locatable, but also that the later article is full of gendered claims. That is, gender is assumed in order to look for its effects.

Biblarz and Stacey advocate for the examination of gender 'as distinct from the number, marital status, sexual orientation, or biogenetic relationship of parents', and suggest that it is possible to 'isolate the variable of parental gender' (Biblarz and Stacey, 2010: 5). But this is a reification of gender. In addition, I think that Biblarz and Stacey make very many gendered assumptions themselves, treating lesbian families as examples of 'fatherlessness', treating gay and lesbian families as automatically gendered male/masculine and female/feminine, treating some parenting behaviours as 'feminine' or 'masculine', and talking about 'feminine socialization' of women or the 'masculine development' of boys (Biblarz and Stacey, 2010: 6, 9, 11 and 12). Treating gender as an isolated variable not only reifies a social practice, but it also removes many other contextual aspects from the picture.

These problems are highlighted in the section of Biblarz and Stacey's article that deals with gay fathers. Whereas they treat lesbian mothers as always 'feminine' – or, rather, as displaying feminine parenting qualities – Biblarz and Stacey argue that gay male parents 'appear to adopt parenting practices more "feminine" than do typical heterosexual fathers' (Biblarz and Stacey, 2010: 12). Whilst their point that gay fathers' parenting 'more closely resembles that by mothers' (p. 12) echoes many of the comments made by gay men in this chapter, my argument has been that gay fathers are described or identify themselves in such terms because they talk and act using ideas, practices or props usually associated with women/mothers, not because of any essential feminine aspects to a caring/parenting role. Biblarz and Stacey say:

> gay male parents challenge dominant practices of masculinity, father-hood, and motherhood more than lesbian co-mothers depart from nor-mative femininity or maternal practice. (Biblarz and Stacey, 2010: 13)

But, if the act of parenthood is associated primarily with women, then this is a limited argument. There are lesbian mothers who challenge norma-tive femininity, but gay men obviously appear to be more gender deviant within a category that is usually regarded as 'feminine'. And, whilst some gay fathers may try to challenge dominant gender practices, not all do, or, rather, this does not always happen.

Responses to Biblarz and Stacey's piece have also picked up on the prob-lems with any attempt to isolate gender. Abbie Goldberg, for example, questions 'whether gender can ever be truly studied and understood inde-pendent of both the immediate (familial) environment and the broader (e.g., societal and legal) context', and also asks 'whether the gender that we observe in one environment or context is truly equivalent to the gender that we observe in another' (Goldberg, 2010b: 29). Drawing on research by Emily Kane (2006), Goldberg reminds us of the crucial point that 'gender con-formity' may be taken up by gay/lesbian parents and their children in some contexts 'because of concerns about accountability to others' (Goldberg, 2010b: 30). She also picks up on the limitations of seeing lesbian families as essentially (all) female or gay families as (all) male environments. The gendered worlds of children are likely to be much more complicated than this. Tasker, similarly, argues that much of what Biblarz and Stacey refer to has to do with attitudes towards and norms about, rather than core aspects of, gender (Tasker, 2010).

I would argue strongly against a version of gender that sees it as an isolat-able variable or as a factor affecting child development. Gender, masculinity or femininity are not properties of men and women, or of gay men and les-bians, that are passed on to children. In that sense, much of the Biblarz and Stacey article echoes socialization theory. Instead, any parent has gender at their disposal, since it is a social resource that we are all impelled to use. All social interaction involves the deployment of gender, and gender is used to make sense of identities, people, actions, talk and so on. For example, whilst I would not want to present gay and lesbian subjects as without agency or resistance to the dominant, the possibilities open to those who wish to locate themselves as a (potentially) 'good parent/foster carer/adopter' within social welfare practices are very limited, in terms of the likelihood of challenging standard gendered ideas. As Butler also states, 'one does not "do" one's gen-der alone. One is always "doing" with or for another' (Butler, 2004b: 1).

Gender is a discourse that positions all of us morally and hierarchically. Thus, it is fascinating to notice how often gay dads are seen as 'feminine'. As Sedgwick has stated, 'the *de*pathologization of an atypical sexual object-choice can be yoked to the *new* pathologization of an atypical gender identification' (Sedgwick, 1994b: 158). The feminine, whoever does it, is itself devalued, a point that Kessler and McKenna (1985) made, as is the work of parenting/child care. What, then, are the possibilities for lesbian and gay parents who wish to do away with gendered roles? Could we degender/ungender ourselves?

> After all, is there a gender that preexists its regulation, or is it the case that, in being subject to regulation, the gendered subject emerges, produced in and through that particular form of subjection? Is subjection not the process by which regulations produce gender? (Butler, 2004b: 41)

What would happen if we allowed any person to take on the identity of parent without saturating this role with gendered expectations? Is this a possibility that is emerging through gay and lesbian parenting, or is gender still too important a resource for the taking up of subjectivity? Challenging the 'assumptions that suggest good parents should raise children that are gendered in particular ways' (Riggs, 2006a: 61) becomes difficult work, and becomes a difficult life to live, when that challenge may place a person outside of the usual realm of recognizability. Indeed, the very notion of gender mobility or challenge may itself be a resource or possibility open to some people more than others. Yet, it still remains vital to ask why we need gender, really.

6
Race

Because of poverty, I am resigned to sever my parental links, for what mother could bear giving up her child without breaking to pieces inside? Because his ill-fated life started out without the man who made him and because as a single mother I cannot afford to raise him, I have to give him up. Now, since you will adopt him, he will escape a life of want and wandering.

(letter from Trung Phi Kim Hoa to Kevin McGarry; in McGarry, 2003: 29–30)

McGarry's book, *Fatherhood for Gay Men*, describes his experiences of adopting two boys, Andrew Phuong and Vincent Luc, from Vietnam. The letter from Andy's mother, Kim Hoa, expresses some of the emotional and political dynamics of transnational adoption, concerned as it is with questions of poverty, lack of opportunity, despair and fantasy about a better life in the United States. Her 'breaking to pieces inside' is a sobering and upsetting statement, since it reminds us that decisions about transnational adoption are made within a context of global inequality and local poverty. As Eng argues, 'This is a politics focused not on issues of social justice, material redistribution, and substantive equality, but on economic entitlement and the privileges of family for an emergent class of multicultural elites' (Eng, 2003: 13).

In this particular case, that multicultural elite includes lesbians and gay men who adopt children from poorer countries. That is, people who have the choice and money to do so. So, whilst there is overt homophobia within the field, such as national policies that prevent transnational adoption by gay men or lesbians (Dorow, 2006; Tan and Baggerly, 2009), at the same time, there are questions about power, money and privilege involved (Oparah et al., 2006; Trenka, 2009). McGarry, for example, is quite dismissive of relative power and opportunity (or, lack of it), using phrases like, 'if she [Kim Hoa] had chosen to keep him', and stating that the letter 'makes it clear that she is happy that Andy will have a dad' (McGarry, 2003: 29). For me, these are telling phrases, since I am not sure that choice and happiness are the kinds of words to use of someone who talks of poverty, severance, giving up and breaking to pieces.

In addition, McGarry claims that adopting a 'child who is of a different race can be a sensitive issue, but, so far, this has been a nonissue in our family. No one has ever said anything negative about our being different' (McGarry, 2003: 72). This indicates a number of points about the ways in which race is, or is not, spoken about within contemporary 'diversity/democracy' politics: to speak about it is to highlight a 'sensitive issue' – that is, according to some. To put this another way, those who do raise questions about potential racial discrimination within the politics of diversity and transnational adoption are made to feel that they have introduced an awkward dynamic. McGarry's tone, for example, anticipates questions of racial difference only as 'negative' ones. And, whilst McGarry does deal with difference as a gay male adopter, his 'our being different' here relates to the ways in which his boys will be treated rather than him – he cannot know, for example, all of the ways in which his boys will be positioned racially by others. To say that race is not an issue is an example of racial privilege, since race cannot – currently – be a 'nonissue', or rather, to say that it is expresses what Richard Dyer calls the 'powerful position ... of being "just" human' (Dyer, 1997: 2), the ability to believe that 'race' does not apply.

Transnational adoption by lesbians and gay men, especially when it is 'transracial', forces us to think about how questions of race are, in fact, always relevant to the ways in which gay parenting is conceptualized. Eng's discussion of Deann Borshay Liem's documentary, *First Person Plural* (Borshay, 2000), for example, reminds us that transnational adoption brings 'racial alterity and otherness squarely into the privatized space of the white American nuclear family' (Eng, 2003: 32), and his analysis of a USA insurance advertisement that portrays a white lesbian couple with an adopted Chinese baby – 'Insurance for the unexpected/Investments for the opportunities' – demonstrates how gay parents, who, in other situations, experience discrimination by commercial institutions, here represent 'an emerging consumer niche group – white lesbians with capital' (Eng, 2003: 11). Jasbir Puar has also suggested that, whilst some gay families/couples may now be welcomed into the arms of the multicultural and diverse liberal state, this 'benevolence toward sexual others is contingent upon ever-narrowing parameters of white racial privilege, consumption capabilities, gender and kinship normativity, and bodily integrity' (Puar, 2007: xii). Indeed, she cites 'the return to kinship and family norms implicit in the new lesbian "global family," complete with transnational adoptee babies' (Puar, 2007: xiv) as a key example of the ways in which racial dynamics and prejudices are now subsumed under the portrayal of a post-racist, multicultural nation in which white lesbian couples with transnationally adopted (Asian/Chinese) children figure or stand for (capitalist) choice and diversity.

In this chapter, I am interested in how questions of race and racism are talked about in relation to lesbian and gay parenting. My focus is on how notions of racial, cultural or ethnic groups are produced and put to work. But, crucially, I am also interested in the ways in which concepts that I have been dealing with in this book (kinship, family, gender, and so on) are racialized. Kinship, for example, draws upon notions of racial descent and 'purity', whilst desire may be figured as 'dark, uncontrollable, and irrational', cast across not only 'non-white' but also 'non-reproductive' bodies (Winnubst, 2006: 130–1). Genealogy, too, is built upon notions of racial specificity and, in some cases, hierarchy, and familial or national belonging works through exclusion of 'the other'.

My approach to these questions – as with Chapter 5 on gender – rejects race as an 'ontological status' (Ware and Back, 2003: 13), but in the sense that I do not treat race as 'really real', as the basis of people's behaviours, talk, attributes, and so on. This does not mean, however, that race is not *used as a way to account for behaviours, talk, attributes, and so on, in everyday life*. As will be clear from this chapter, race is regularly made use of as a category to explain social situations; it has to be reiterated. As Riggs argues, 'although it must be recognized that racial categories are the result of particular power relations and histories of oppression, they are nonetheless *constructed as mattering* – they are accorded a materiality that renders them foundational to subjectivities' (Riggs, 2008: 1). We need to ask difficult questions about the ways in which racial types are produced, otherwise there is a danger of taking these at face value. As Sara Suleri argues, 'there are limits beyond which an articulation of otherness could cause the discourse merely to ventriloquize the fact of cultural difference' (Suleri, 1992: 11). Further, we also need to think about ways in which race is *not* talked about (Barnard, 2003; Lorde, 1996; Riggs, 2006b; Sgambati, 2009) and about ways in which other concepts – culture, religion, belief, diversity, and so on – are made to stand for it.

I am also interested in the ruling relations of race, since my argument is that, within institutional practices of social welfare, black lesbians and gay men are often treated as 'different' to white norms and so 'to be explained', just as the issue of potential gender (role) difference had to be explained in Chapter 5. Black (and white) social workers, for example, may find themselves in the invidious position of having to explain or account for notions of cultural difference amongst black lesbian and gay potential parents, as though people fall into racial types. I also argue that black foster care or adoption applicants are made to feel as though discussions of their everyday lives are assertions of difference from white norms. That is, questions of racial difference become 'stuck onto' black people, so that they are described in ways that force them to take up 'authentic cultural difference' positions. Racial ruling relations convert the everyday actualities of black applicants' lives into racial types and cultures, 'discriminable (distinct) cultural difference … in a prepackaged form' (Povinelli, 2002b: 180).

How does race matter?

Toni and Justina are a lesbian couple with four children, two of whom are Justina's birth children and two of whom have been adopted by the couple. Toni is a black, mixed-race woman who was adopted by a white couple, and Justina is a black woman of African descent. When I asked the couple about questions of racial identity in their adoption assessment, they raised some interesting points:

Justina: It felt as if she *[their social worker]* was almost scared of us ...

Toni: Challenging or querying or ... yeah.

Steve: Because of being black, because of being a same-sex couple, because of being professionals?

Toni: All of the above!

Justina: Yeah, all of those [laughing], because we ticked every box that could make them feel nervous and I think that she was quite nervous of that really.

Steve: Do you mean in the sense that she was treading on eggshells a bit? She didn't know what she could and couldn't say?

Toni: Yeah, yeah.

Steve: Which is really difficult isn't it coz of the room for misinterpretation and assumptions.

Justina: Yes, it is and I guess that the big time assumptions were that we were professional women and we're a same-sex couple, we're black, you know, this poor woman didn't know which particular 'egg to tread on', you know, that if she did tread on she would offend. And so she ...

Toni: She skirted around things.

Justina: She skirted around things and didn't really delve into it. The second social worker *[for the subsequent placement of a child]* did delve into it and did ask some really challenging questions and really made you think ... I think we were *[the first social worker's]* nightmare! And we were her nightmare because we were articulate and because we understood and could question, because Toni worked in social services and child protection and all that and we were both professional, we were black, we were lesbians ... Oh my god, you know, what bit did she think she was going to trip up?

Toni: She actually said something about that at the beginning, didn't she, about feeling a bit intimidated. 'Having to get it right', or it was something like that, or, you know, 'Well, you know more about it than me.'

Steve: That's interesting because there's a way that you could say that which might be helpful and get you talking about that, but maybe she didn't say it in that kind of way?

Justina: She didn't. I don't feel she was sufficiently confident for us to have this kind of discussion. I think she was worried about saying the wrong thing in case one of us – probably me! – blew up at her. I think she was terrified of being called racist and all of that, for me, meant that I don't think she was as rigorous as she could have been. Because of the fear really…and I think you just need to kind of get over it.

Here, Toni and Justina identify the question of their blackness as a concern within the adoption assessment. That is, they suggest that their social worker avoids challenging and difficult questions about race for fear of 'being called racist'. This is interesting, as their point is not that their social worker made overt assumptions about race but that her assessment was compromised – not as 'rigorous' or useful as it might have been – as race was generally *not talked about*. They say that she 'skirted around things' in order to avoid causing offence, and they recognize the social worker's position. Justina, for example, calls her 'this poor woman' in order to acknowledge that for a white social worker to assess two professional, black lesbians raises several concerns about how to talk about sexuality and race in an assessment. Justina attributes feelings through the use of words that conjure up the social worker's 'fear' or 'nightmare'; she is 'terrified', 'worried', 'scared' and 'nervous'. I think that this is a way of acknowledging and excusing the avoidance of overt discussion about race/sexuality. That is, whilst Toni and Justina think that the social worker should have done a lot more to ask them more challenging questions regarding race and sexuality, at the same time, they allow for this. So, just as lesbians and gay men talk about having to raise issues about their sexuality with social workers or about the avoidance of such discussions, Justina and Toni suggest that both race and sexuality may be topics 'skirted around', something that they are very familiar with.

Justina contrasts this experience with that of a second social worker, who 'did delve into it and did ask some really challenging questions and really made you think'. This highlights the couple's appreciation of an assessment situation in which race and sexuality are overtly talked about and discussed. The couple are making a case for the need to talk about being black lesbians openly, yet, at the same time, they joke about being intimidating. Toni refers to the first social worker feeling 'intimidated' and also to a phrase about having to 'get it right'. This phrase was also used a number of times by social workers in my earlier PhD studies. One social worker, for example, said, 'maybe that was my anxiety about getting it right and feeling there was a spotlight on me', when talking about assessing a lesbian couple for adoption (Hicks, 1998: 224). This notion of 'getting it right' highlights a dilemma for the social workers; wanting to carry out an adequate assessment, yet also wanting to act in a way that does not overtly discriminate against people on the basis of race or sexuality. Or, to put this another way, it highlights the dilemma of how to talk about race and sexuality. The notions of intimidation and of a 'spotlight' suggest that some social workers feel uncomfortable about talking to black lesbians or gay men about questions of sexuality and race, but also that their talk, and their possible support of gay/lesbian applicants, will be scrutinized.

When I asked Toni and Justina about how race was talked about in their adoption assessment, they said:

Justina: They didn't really talk to us about racial identity at all.

Toni: I think the only time they talked about it was in relation to my growing up in a white family.

Steve: So, they did talk to you about that?

Toni: Yeah. Maybe they did that when they talked to me on my own.

Steve: Do you remember what kind of angle they took?

Toni: Um, I don't think we got as far as how would I perceive or parent somebody as a consequence, it wasn't like that, it was more how did it impact on me growing up. But, you know, they talked about understanding and same-race placements, but I suppose the 'same-race' bit was a bit fluid!

Steve: Yeah, what did they mean by that?

Toni: I think it was sort of fairly general, sort of black Caribbean maybe, you know, quite wide 'coz you could be coming from a different racial background but you're both black.

Here, Toni says that one of the few times racial identity was discussed was in relation to her background as a mixed race black child adopted by a white family. This centres upon the notion of 'consequence/impact', the suggestion that she might have a damaged racial identity, and also the contemporary notion of a 'same-race' placement, the idea that black children ought to be placed with black families (Rhodes, 1992). This is typical of discussions about race in social work assessment, in my view, since the notion of a racial identity becomes psychologized. That is not to say that growing up in a white adoptive family is not significant for Toni, but the suggestion here is that she might be carrying a damaged racial identity that she might pass on to adopted children. Even though Toni says, 'I don't think we got as far as how would I perceive or parent somebody as a consequence', this phrase indicates that she anticipates her racial and family background being seen as a potential source of 'impact' by some. Toni is expected to perform some reassurance work around her own blackness. As Derek Kirton has argued in relation to transracial adoptees, a 'spectre of deep pathology, of pervasive and widespread psychological damage' is often invoked (Kirton, 2000: 36), as though racial identity is easily fixed as positive or negative and as an interior matter.

Justina used a story about their adoption assessment in order to highlight problematic assumptions that can be made about 'cultures':

Justina: I think she *[their social worker]* misinterpreted stuff because we had to fill in part of the form and I remember saying to her that my parents weren't sort of toys-focused. As African parents, that was not their priority and so I didn't get lots of toys. But what came back was almost this deprived childhood where I felt really deprived because my parents didn't buy me toys, and I thought that is not what I meant … I think she misunderstood the cultural bit … Hence, when I said that my parents didn't buy me toys, well, that didn't mean they didn't love me. Their *[their own children's]* grandparents do not buy them toys now but they shovel them down with sweets and give them lots of money, you know it's different but that doesn't mean that they're …

Toni: … neglected!

Justina: … neglected, and the fact that they have shed loads of toys that they don't even look at! …

Toni: Like having to explain the whole issue about you being left in [African country] with your grandparents for about five years and then coming over here.

Justina: Yes I was five when I came, and Mum and Dad had been here for about two or so years when I came, and we had this bizarre conversation about did I resent my mother for having left me? and I thought, 'no'.

Toni: Well, probably about six out of ten of your cousins are the same and would have similar experiences.

Justina: Yes, my grandparents were not just grandparents, they parented us. Not because parents weren't there but because we lived in a big compound and we lived with others as well, like my aunties and uncles, and so when my mum was teacher training, she often went to her teacher training and she left me with her parents, it's not a big deal. When she had opportunities here, then she took the opportunity and she settled before bringing me, not a big deal. I didn't feel that I had suffered in any way...

Steve: But did you feel that you had to explain it like it was a deficit model?

Justina: Yeah. Precisely. Because the questions were around what was my relationship like with my mum when I came here – well, when I came here the relationship was normal, and did I feel resentful of her? Well, I didn't even think about it. It wasn't, 'Oh my god, my mum has left me and I'm really bereft,' and I just think she didn't understand different cultures and what parenting was like in different cultures. Or I think it's what Toni said really, you spent time explaining family norms and the model of family is very Eurocentric and English and nuclear, and I don't come from a Eurocentric, nuclear family, I come from an African, extended family, where there was nothing thought of an aunty raising a niece or nephew or a grandparent raising a grandchild. It wasn't a big deal, it didn't mean your parents didn't love you, it might be because actually your parents can't afford it or that another family member is thought to be able to give you a better life. It's a bit like adoption, isn't it? I think the framework used to train people here is an English framework and then you have children who are born into families that aren't 'English' but you're trying to place them on a Eurocentric model... I didn't want a misrepresentation of my family because we have a different cultural context.

Here, Justina uses cultural difference to explain that giving toys to children is not a priority for her African parents. She argues that African parents have other ways of showing affection towards children, and so she is making a case for cultural difference. However, she goes on to state that her social worker misinterprets this as deprivation. Justina's argument is that 'the cultural bit' can be misunderstood, but another way to put this is that suggested cultural difference might be interpreted in different ways, or used to make positive or negative connotations about cultural groups. Toni introduces another example, taken up by Justina, which is the practice of childcare by extended family and/or grandparents within some black/African communities mixed with histories of migration, a point that was also noted in Stack's (1997) study.

Justina says that her family practices are interpreted in relation to a white 'Eurocentric and English and nuclear' norm, and so her African extended family model is potentially viewed negatively, or she is imagined by the social worker to have suffered psychological damage (figured through words concerned with deprivation, neglect, resentment and suffering). Her racial identity is institutionally produced in similar ways to Toni's – as a potential source of trauma. That is, both Justina and Toni are questioned about the possibility of carrying racial 'damage' due to imagined difference on the basis of African extended family care and adoption by a white couple, respectively. This constructs Justina's family background, for example, as due to essential cultural difference, rather than having anything to do with questions about relative poverty, opportunity in different countries, migration, and so on. Justina objects to such 'cultural…misrepresentation' and also makes the point that extended family care of children is 'a bit like adoption'. Her suggestion is that it is ironic to treat extended family care of children as deviant in an adoption context. Why should an adoption system reinforce standard ideas about family bonds and care? This is a point that I take up in Chapter 7. It is also vital, here, to note that Justina's and Toni's arguments about how black families may be viewed highlight the ways in which unspoken assumptions about white families may be treated as a norm. 'Culture', then, seems to stick to black people in a negative way. They may be treated as carriers of a fixed and, by implication, lacking culture in ways that white people are not (although there are many versions of cultural deficit ascribed to the white, working class).

Louise has a (black) Jamaican, Chinese and (white) English heritage and describes herself as a 'woman of colour', as she wishes to question standard phrases, such as 'dual heritage', that do not encompass her own background. With her partner, Karen, she has two children, a two- and a four-year-old, conceived through donor insemination. Louise talked about how race matters in different situations:

Louise: I work with some people who I would say are very actively involved with their Afro-Caribbean communities and they would perceive me I think in a different way really. You know, I live in *[suburb]*, people around me are white, middle-class, and actually the stuff that I get exposed to is people who are not comfortable with the fact. So, the barriers I think that my kids will have to face are about someone who is lesbian, who looks non-white and…um…is overweight and big, dropping them off at school. And I think that my kids will have to…I don't want to sound like I've got a chip on my shoulder…

Steve: No, no…Like most people in that situation, you are very self-conscious or monitoring yourself in relation to your children. It's a kind of protection thing but also an awareness thing, isn't it, you have to be constantly…

Louise: …Well, yes, and you see on some faces, you know, well the lesbian thing is obviously something that some people don't see, and I have long hair so of course it's a bit of a shock! but I think that combined with being a lesbian, that I kind of stand out anyway being a woman of colour and then a lesbian and then overweight, not that ... well it's all the perceptions around that ... Because I've known people in the past, when I was younger, be referred to as 'coconut' ...

Steve: Oh, yeah.

Louise: Because they've been perceived as behaving 'white' even though they're from a black community.

Steve: That's when it's not read solely as skin colour but it's about behaviour.

Louise: Yes, because you're behaving 'like a white person'. So, I don't know what that means.

Here, Louise's story makes the point that context matters for race. In her predominantly white, middle-class and heterosexual local community, Louise feels different, or she is made to feel uncomfortable at times. Or, she notices that others 'are not comfortable' with her being black, lesbian and 'overweight'. For Louise, this also has to do with concern about her children, since she does not want them to experience such discomfort, a point that Nita and Clare also raised in Chapter 4, when they used the technique of being 'up-front' to anticipate and avoid stigma. At the same time, Louise's acute consciousness about questions of sexuality, race and body image is self-excused. She offers a repair (Schegloff et al., 1977) in her talk: 'I don't want to sound like I've got a chip on my shoulder.' This is because, to draw attention to the possibility of heterosexism, racism or questions about body image is to risk accusations of humourlessness, defensiveness, and so on from those mainly heterosexual, white people that surround her. Indeed, it may also be that Louise makes this comment because it is to me – a white researcher – that she is talking. She must anticipate and avoid these accusations. Or, as West and Fenstermaker state, '*speakers see themselves as accountable* for their remarks in relation to their race category or race and sex category membership' (West and Fenstermaker, 2002: 547–8).

Louise argues that she is able to pass, or she may be read, as heterosexual (especially as she does not conform to the stereotyped view of what a lesbian looks like), but her race and – for her – body size are always visible ('you see on some faces'). She is clear that the issue about being 'overweight' is about 'perceptions', but she asserts that being black is always remarkable. She may experience racism within predominantly white areas, and she may not be 'black enough' for some other black people. This is especially interesting as the notion of a black person 'behaving "white"' picks up on the notion that racial categories are practised. That is, to be accused of being 'white/like a white person/coconut' is to have behaviour and practices brought into question. Yet, at the same time, such ideas also raise the policing of the category 'black' that is used to define or delimit what a black person ought to be and do. As Back notes, 'absolutist notions of affirmative, syncretic black culture can act as a constraint' (1996: 153).

To belong?

Riggs has outlined the ways in which a sense of belonging may require recognition as 'family' within the terms of a national imaginary (Riggs, 2006b, 2006c, 2007b). That is, some gay parents may acquire greater recognition for their relational forms due to an unmarked whiteness. As Catherine Nash argues, the 'idea that people "belong to each other" because they share what belongs to them individually in the form of blood or genes is central to ideas of genealogical relatedness' (Nash, 2008: 19). These notions of belonging are related to ideas of race, nation and, more specifically, skin colour. For example:

Clare: We've got friends who are foster carers and one's Asian and one's African Caribbean and they haven't had one placement yet that hasn't been white. And every single child that they've had placed, on their care plan it says, 'needs white adopters,' and every meeting they go to they have to say, 'you know this care plan, you know where it says "needs white adopters"...'!! And it is relevant because when they go out, you know, people constantly say to them, they say things like, 'are they yours?' You know, these two little boys who are like two and four, 'are they yours?' and the little boy came back from nursery saying, 'I don't belong with you, do I? Somebody said I don't belong with you 'coz I don't look like you,' you know, and you're thinking there's a whole issue there that somebody hasn't thought about. One, it's a complete waste of a resource and, two, they do need white carers because they're feeling that as little kids, that...

Nita: ...that they're in the wrong house.

Clare: Yeah, because people are projecting onto them...and how difficult can it be to find a white placement?

Nita: ...and how difficult can it be to find Asian or African Caribbean children who need a home with those carers?

Here, questions of foster care, adoption and race are related to those of belonging and also resemblance. White children are made to feel that they do not belong with their black carers because they don't 'look like' them. But, at the same time, both Clare and Nita argue that, within a context of limited numbers of black foster carers, it seems a 'waste of a resource' that their friends are not being asked to care for black children. However, whilst

Clare argues that the boys 'do need white carers', it seems wrong to suggest that black foster carers ought not to be able to care for white children. That is, to what point is racial matching of children and parents/carers taken? If a couple consisting of an African Caribbean and an Asian parent are not appropriate for white children, then what perceived racial background is appropriate? Nita's point is not for an exact racial 'match' but, rather, than there must be 'Asian or African Caribbean children' needing foster homes. Yet, this also raises the question of how notions of racial matching actually reinforce traditional (biological) ideas about belonging.

Questions of belonging/likeness are crucial to this story. Difference in skin colour produces anxiety about belonging and being (literally) out of place ('in the wrong house'). Interestingly, this is linked to notions of ownership, as the parents are asked, 'are they yours?' Skin colour produces questions about parenting and about association, but, in addition, belonging has to do with notions of ownership and blood ties. As Nash has argued, '[t]hemes of possession and belonging traverse genealogy's public and intimate domains' (Nash, 2008: 19). In addition, although it is the white boys who are assumed to be out of place, it seems as if it is the black parents who are the most racially marked. The impossibility of producing white children is invoked to suggest inappropriate racial mixing.

Justina also talked about belonging in relation to racial heritage and skin colour:

Justina: A couple we know, who had been assessed after us, they had been placed with a dual heritage little girl. And we know there's a whole host of factors that are taken into consideration before a placement. And so I rang her and said we'd heard this (as we still didn't have a child placed) and I was surprised as we had been assessed and approved way before and yet... you know. And bless her cotton socks, she brought round details of a child that was being considered. Now, bear in mind we are a dual heritage family but we're not black and white or dual heritage and white, and she brought a baby who one of their birth parents was dual heritage, the other was white, and the baby had blonde hair and blue eyes and we were like, 'erm!' And it was that kind of, well, I think she was a bit, 'Oh my god, I'd better find them something,' whereas actually what you're bringing isn't... not that we couldn't care for that child but what we'd said is we need children that blend into our family, that could be either of our child, and doesn't, you know, stand out and you're showing us a child with blonde hair and blue eyes. You know, how are we going to explain?... well, not how are we going to explain, but it's obvious from day one...

Toni: They need to look like they belong…

Justina: …and wouldn't look like they belonged…So, let's just have the conversation about 'we have considered you for a number of children but you weren't suitable for x, y and z reasons', don't just bring around a child that we are not the suitable family for. I wouldn't say that the child is not suitable for us, but we are not the suitable family for the child, and I just thought those kind of things were daft!

Justina's point is that they could have cared for this child, but this seems a poor match, even though the child in question is of mixed racial heritage. Justina talks about a child that would 'blend into our family', which immediately invokes ideas about (skin) colour, and a child that would not 'stand out'; that is, look out of place. The couple's use of phrases such as 'could be either of our child', 'how are we going to explain?' and 'they need to look like they belong' also raises questions about belonging, looking like and fitting in. They want a child that might have been a birth child – or, rather, a child that does not provoke the need for explanations – but also see themselves as a positive (and perhaps rare) resource for black children needing adoption. Justina's 'I wouldn't say that the child is not suitable for us, but we are not the suitable family for the child,' is a way of justifying this preference, as it is couched in terms of the child's, rather than their, interests. My point, here, is not to criticize Justina and Toni's choice, but rather to note that it has to be justified in this kind of way by them in order to head off imputations of rigidity or racial inflexibility. In both cases I have just outlined, black carers have been, or would be, made to feel the inappropriate parents of white children.

To look like?

Barbara Yngvesson makes the point that adoption demonstrates a slippage 'between real and fictive belongings' (Yngvesson, 2010: 13), which may be highlighted when it takes place 'across' race. This brings me to further questions of looking, reflecting and looking like. Questions of likeness came up when I talked to Louise about how she and Karen sought a sperm donor:

Steve: In relation to your children, and please don't answer this if you don't want to, did you use a donor or…?

Louise: No, we went through a fertility service.

Steve: And did you think about race in relation to that?

Louise: Yes we did, yeah. We did discuss it, yeah, and I don't know if you know the process but they ask you what you might want, and we did 'um and ah' a bit and should we go for someone who's mixed race? But it just seemed really complicated and just thinking about working out what 'mixed race' you should have! And in the end, we just said, 'No just bring us a donor,' and they bring you a choice of three and then we went from there really.

Steve: You didn't have a kind of really specific racial requirement?

Louise: No, but we talked about it 'coz we were thinking should we get a mixed race donor but then we were thinking, if we both have children, they're gonna be different again 'coz we come with difference. So, we thought let's just see what they offer us and we'll go from there.

Steve: 'Coz what kind of 'mixed race' would you go for?

Louise: Yeah, would you go Jamaican or what? you know, and people can't work out what I am so I don't know that there would have been an easy answer, so no we didn't in the end, so we just waited to see what they offered us and went with that really.

Steve: And did you use different donors for the two children?

Louise: No, the same donor.

Steve: That's interesting 'coz you do get people who've got a very specific almost like a racial shopping list really when they go. 'We want someone who reflects this and that.' And that's really interesting to think about what those ideas are about and where they come from ...

Louise: Yeah, we probably just touched on it because I'm mixed race and we probably wouldn't have otherwise, but when we got there we just said, 'Show us', and we picked the best out of the options they gave us, the best that we thought. And absolutely amazing what you make up around these few key facts. We'd made a whole story about one of the donors! You know, 'Why does he want to do it?!' and it was just really funny!

Steve: My favourite ones are the people who choose somebody with a really high IQ or who's got a PhD 'coz they think that's gonna be passed on!

Louise: Yeah! But I must admit ours was an art student!

Steve: *[Laughing]* So, was there something around that?

Louise: Yeah, yeah!

Steve: Was that just liking that idea or did you think some of that might rub off?

Louise: Well, we didn't want the middle-aged man because we couldn't work out why he would have donated. We could see with the student he'd want a bit of extra cash or whatever, it made sense. And there were two students, one was science and one was art. Now, if it was IQ, you might have gone with the science student but he was bigger and taller and that was fine if we had a boy, but what if we had a girl and she was big and tall and fat?! You know, that would be awful for her, so let's go for middle, so the art student was middle height, middle weight, he had green eyes and brown hair. And, interestingly enough, our girls have got really light brown hair bordering on blonde-ish and they look very like us but different as well.

Steve: So, you do create a little story around it, everyone does, don't they?

Louise: For us, well it was an unknown donor and it was in a time before the law changed, so we did create a little story and now, if one of the children picks up an art pencil, we're like, 'Hey look!'...*[laughing]*...but I think some of that is a sense of security really, that your kids are gonna be alright you know.

Louise's story demonstrates that the choices lesbian prospective parents make concerning the race of a donor and a child are always complicated. Thus, even though she and her partner did not choose a black or mixed race donor, Louise says their girls 'look very like us but different as well'. As Mamo notes, 'looking like and being like someone accomplishes social legitimacy and erases the stigma that often accompanies apparent differences' (Mamo, 2007: 207). Respondents in Mamo's study talk about complex notions of racial matching when selecting sperm donors, yet these also betray fantasies about how likeness is made and, at the same time, about biological inheritance. For example, Shari (white) and Robyn (Latina) chose a donor 'three-quarters Spanish and a quarter Mexican, with green eyes, and that fits her [Robyn] most...We were choosing someone who was some Latino mix...nice, trim, athletic guy. He's educated' (Mamo, 2007: 209). Here, a Latina heritage – in itself, a complicated category – slides into notions about likeness, then body type and even intelligence or character. As Mamo argues, 'arbitrary lines between what is and what is not genetic' may be drawn (Mamo, 2007: 214).

But what is also interesting here is the figuration of race as a consumer choice, since fertility clinics market donors by racial 'type'. Race becomes a reproductive commodity and is marketed according to liberal notions of choice, as though the racial background of a donor is simply one of many decisions to be made. Yet, there may be specific reasons why black donors are chosen that have to do with wanting to reproduce or replicate racial features. And, to imagine that different racial backgrounds are choices on an equal footing does not take account of the 'preferences for tall, Caucasian, muscular, college-educated, and heterosexual sperm donors...reinforced by semen banking practices' (Agigian, 2004: 99), or that black lesbians are less likely to seek insemination/assisted reproductive services due to lack of 'choice' (Gartrell et al., 1996).

Louise's donor story is interesting in this sense because she describes the possibility of choosing a mixed-race donor as too complicated. She has questions about what exactly would be an appropriate choice in her situation, where a lesbian couple – one white and one black (mixed race) – are thinking about having children who would also have different birth mothers ('if we both have children, they're gonna be different again 'coz we come with difference'). For Louise, it is easier to leave the 'choice' of donors to the clinic. At the same time, Louise explains that they created characters out of scant donor details. When I joke about people assuming that intelligence may be genetically passed on – it is, for example, possible to pay extra for 'doctorate sperm' (Agigian, 2004: 94) – Louise tells the story about choosing an art student. Here, she creates a donor that appears to be motivated for the right reasons, of correct body shape and artistic. Thus she jokes, 'now, if one of the children picks up an art pencil, we're like, "Hey look!"' Heritability is present even in practices and jokes about them. Louise's final comment – 'I think some of that is a sense of security really, that your kids are gonna be alright you know' – ties in with Mamo's about social legitimacy. 'Looking like' or fitting in acts as a form of protection as much as recognition, and this also acts as a way of asserting that the right moral donor choice has been made.

Nita and Clare used the language of reflection and replication when we talked about questions of race:

Nita: We always said we would care for Asian or Asian mixed race children, that came from us, and because we were so proactive about looking at various children, the choices often came from us anyway.

Clare: And to be honest, a lot of the children were dual heritage anyway, but for us that was never about having a child that would reflect us, or the idea of a child if we had had a biological child.

Nita: But there are other people in the Group *[support group for lesbian and gay adopters and foster carers]* where they have almost assumed that because one of them is white and one of them is Asian or black that they will have dual heritage children and they've not looked at black children with two black birth parents. There was one lesbian couple – one white and one black – who felt they would be an inappropriate placement for a black child who had two black birth parents and we were just saying, 'Why?'! What if it's a black child where the race of the father isn't known?

Clare: For all you know it could be somebody white.

Steve: Or it might be a light-skinned child with two black parents or…

Clare: The racial history of the Afro-Caribbean community is so complicated anyway because of slavery and everything, you can't…you know, and they turned down some really suitable children.

Steve: Did they want a mixed race black child, then, a child that would reflect?

Clare: They were adamant…

Nita: Presumably they did want a child that would reflect…

Clare: They wanted someone that was lighter-skinned than [x]…

Nita: …and darker-skinned than [z], so that's what they went for. But that wouldn't have been our priority.

Steve: There's lots of that goes on isn't there, and some social workers do it as well, the notion of a 'correct' racial mix. It's really powerful.

Nita: And it's particularly strange in the lesbian or gay setting! Because you can't say 'If we had had a birth child', because that's not, it's not what you're replicating anyway, so why are you trying to…?

The couple discounts a need for children that 'reflect' them, since they do not wish to replicate a pseudo-biological link through likeness. They talk about lesbian or gay couples that attempt to reflect racial backgrounds by adopting mixed race children, but Nita and Clare reject this on two levels; because they do not want to replicate biological links with children, but also because they see 'race' as more complicated than the idea of a simple 'mix'. Nita's final comments are particularly pertinent here. She asks why lesbians or gay men would want to 'replicate' the situation of having a birth child if they are adopting or fostering, and she objects to the notion of replication in both the lesbian/gay and adoption/fostering scenarios. She is arguing for the embracing of fictive kin relations or belongings that Yngvesson (2010) identifies. This is a key dilemma, however, since wanting likeness and 'fitting in' for children (and the self) may conflict with openness about adoption and the embracing of relations of affinity.

A case study of race/culture/religion/ethnicity

I turn now to the story of Nita and Clare's original application to care for a sibling group of seven Asian sisters. I have chosen to focus on this case because it raises several important questions about how race, ethnicity, religion, and culture are produced as categorization devices. And, in relation to the possibilities for a less restrictive/oppressive institutional practice in the fields of foster care and adoption, asking critical questions about how racial typologies are produced through social work interactions is vital.

Nita and Clare were considered as the potential foster carers for the sisters, but were eventually rejected by a 'matching' panel (used to assess the suitability of approved carers for particular children). The reasons given were that birth parents were likely to object to such a placement 'on religious grounds' (Social Services Department, 1994: 1) and that there was 'a fundamental problem in seeking to do this in the context of a relationship which the Panel understood is not recognized in the Hindu faith' (Social Services Department, 1994: 2). My analysis is based upon interviews with Nita, Clare and their original social worker, Barbara – a black woman of African Caribbean descent – as well as analysis of their adoption assessment report, various letters between them and the authority responsible for the care of the sisters, and the report of an officer appointed to investigate the couple's formal complaint about the case.

Notions of race in an adoption assessment

Nita and Clare define themselves as an Asian woman of Indian descent and a white woman of Irish/English background. Under 'ethnic descent', Nita is described as Indian and Clare as white European on their assessment report. Questions of race are discussed a number of times on the assessment report in relation to Nita's background: there is reference to her family's Indian origins, to her experiences of racism at secondary school, to her work with black communities as a teacher, travels in India, Nepal and Pakistan, and to her work in an Asian women's refuge. During interviews, Nita talked about some confusion about her ethnicity:

Nita: My family actually comes from a community that is often called 'Anglo-Indian'. That means we are Asian but we have a mixed racial heritage. But when we saw the written-up Form F, I think Barbara had got it a bit wrong about my heritage. She hadn't understood what 'Anglo-Indian' meant, she thought I was dual heritage *[or what some people call mixed race]* and she didn't understand that 'Anglo-Indian' was a term that referred to a whole kind of multiple heritage community which goes back generations and that both my parents are part of.

Clare: She thought one of your parents was white and the other Indian.

Nita: Yeah, so we had to take her back over that, and that was actually very late in the process.

Clare: It was, and she didn't like it because the Form had already been done. She was like, 'Oh are you sure? Is it necessary?'!

> **Nita:** It does matter because people scrutinize details about race so much and so carefully in placements and matching. So you can't let it go through with the wrong information.

Here, we return to the complexities of racial definitions. Nita's use of the term 'Anglo-Indian' refers to a community of people with a mixed Indian (Asian) and British (white) heritage, a phrase that arose during the colonial era. An Anglo-Indian person usually has at least one ancestor who was white British, but this does not mean that all Anglo-Indian people are 'dual heritage/mixed race' in the sense of having one Asian and one white parent. This raises the problem of racial categorization phrases: of course Nita has a mixed racial heritage, but she is not 'dual heritage/mixed race' – as these are most commonly used – in the sense of having one black and one white parent. In trying to describe, or make sense of, Nita's racial background, Barbara made a mistake that, later, she was not keen to change. Nita's point, however, that 'people scrutinize details about race so much and so carefully in placements and matching' is crucial, as ideas about race are literally read only from carer assessment reports, a 'virtual' reality in which knowledge is textually mediated (Smith, 1990b: 62).

When I asked the couple about how race was talked and written about during their assessment, they made two points: first, that race was hardly mentioned and, second, that, when it was, the focus was on Nita being Asian. They said:

> **Nita:** I don't remember being talked to about race at all actually on my own.
>
> **Clare:** I think we were talked to together.
>
> **Nita:** We did have some discussions together.
>
> **Steve:** I remember you said that, before the adoption assessment happened, you went on that preparation course. Wasn't that for black people?
>
> **Nita:** Yes, it was for black single adopters. I went on it ostensibly as a black single adopter, because we hadn't yet told them *[about being lesbians]*.
>
> **Clare:** So, didn't you talk about race then?
>
> **Nita:** Well, no. They kind of assumed we didn't need to because we were all black. So I don't remember a lot of content about race on that course either. The way it was delivered was with an assumption that we were all coming from the same place.
>
> **Clare:** ...without saying what the assumption is!
>
> **Nita:** ...and also, well, I could have done with a lot more opportunity to discuss how we'd arrived at our black identities and what those identities were. And that wasn't really...

Steve: Well, 'coz that's always complicated isn't it?

Nita: Oh, yeah.

Steve: ...and the more you talk to people about that, the more complicated it is, and the more you realize – well, in my case anyway – the more assumptions you realize that you can make!

Clare: And with me, there was never a conversation, which I think there should have been, about 'How are you going to feel parenting Asian children?' I was never asked that.

Nita: No, you weren't.

Clare: The assumption was that because Nita was Asian, that was fine, but there was no thought down the line that, even if that was right, what if something happened to Nita? There was no mention of the possibility of there I was, being a white carer with Asian children. They talked to us together about it but they never talked to me on my own...There was an assumption that I was okay about race because of Nita. It was not pushed.

Steve: Was there ever any talk about whiteness?

Clare: No. No.

Steve: ...or you being Irish or...?

Clare: No, never.

Steve: If they did talk about race, was it all focused on Asian-ness?

Clare: Yes.

Nita: Yes.

This extract shows, again, that race is often *not talked about*. Nita makes the point that, on a preparation course for black applicants, race is not discussed very much. Instead, there is an 'assumption that we were all coming from the same place'. Nita's use of the phrase 'I could have done with a lot more opportunity to discuss how we'd arrived at our black identities and what those identities were' is crucial for me, as it demonstrates that a black identity is 'arrived at' and that those identities are not shared for all black people. This is important, as Nita is saying that thinking about a black self is a process and practice, rather than a fixed, obvious identity. A black self is practised and lived, and it is arrived at through interaction, the point that Justina also made. Nita means that there are different versions of a black self held by different people. That is why I make the point that it is very easy to make assumptions about a person's racial background and identification. Nita and Clare also say that, when race was discussed, it was largely focused on Nita being Asian and not on Clare's whiteness. Clare's example – what were the implications for her caring for Asian children? – is used to show that the couple felt Nita's being Asian is used as a default position. Clare also adds that she thinks social workers assumed she had 'acceptable' views about race simply because she has an Asian partner.

Clare and Nita's application to care for seven Asian sisters

After having been approved as adopters for two or three children, aged nought to seven years, Clare and Nita saw an advertisement, in a national newsletter, about a group of seven Asian sisters who needed long-term foster care. The girls were described as Asian, nominally Hindu (although they had, in fact, lived in Hindu, Christian, Christian Jehovah's Witness and Sikh households at various times), and from a Punjabi-speaking home, although the girls spoke English. The authority responsible for the girls' care had been directed to find a single home for them, as they were, at the time, split up in a number of white foster homes. The authority wanted a permanent home with at least one Asian parent, where the girls would be brought up with some understanding of the Hindu faith. Clare said the girls were described as 'confused and negative about their racial identity', some were involved in self-harm and one had tried to commit suicide in the past. The man living with the girls' birth mother, who was birth father of some of the younger children, had been convicted and imprisoned for sexually abusing them.

Nita and Clare offered to be considered as a placement for the girls and were prepared to help them with their various identified problems or 'needs' to do with racial identity, religion and culture. For example, the social workers told Nita and Clare that the girls 'hated being Indian. You're going to have a really hard time with them because they hate the idea of "Indian", they've had terrible experiences of being Indian, they hate themselves.' During the matching process, Nita and Clare were asked how they would explain their sexuality to the girls, and how they would provide for their religious, cultural and linguistic needs. Nita said:

Nita: They didn't really explain what these 'needs' were! But we spent ages talking about and writing down exactly how we would work to ensure the girls felt better about being Asian and how we would help them to develop an understanding of the Hindu religion. But when the social workers came to visit us, we ended up actually having to force these bits of paper with our answers on them, you know, 'Would you like to take these away with you? We've answered all your questions which we understood you wanted to know about, and maybe you'd like to take them to help at the matching panel?' We had explained how we would bring them up as Hindus, how we'd give Hinduism a high priority in our daily lives, how we'd develop the children's understanding and practice of their religion. We were also committed to developing their positive feelings about being Indian and about being Asian through our own family, friends, community, and my family contacts and roots in India.

Clare: But everything we said we'd do for their identity, the social workers came back to us and said, 'Well that's a waste of time because they all hate being Indian'! Everything we suggested they were like, 'No won't work, no won't work!' We were more concerned about it than they were.

Nita: Well, they'd kind of given up on them in terms of their racial identity. They just thought they felt bad about themselves as Indian children and that was a lost cause. I don't know but I wondered if they were also a bit worried that we were so articulate about it. And they were not comfortable about placing them with us anyway and so they were so negative about everything we suggested. They didn't want us to be 'good'.

A notion of 'meeting racial/cultural/religious needs' is created by social work processes and is duly addressed by the couple. It's notable that, for Asian children, religion is given a high priority in a way that it probably would not be for others. But it's also interesting to think about what versions of racial identity are in operation here, too: Nita talks directly about making the girls feel better 'about being Asian' and about 'developing their positive feelings about Indian and about being Asian', which is a response to social workers' claims that the girls were 'confused and negative about their racial identity'. This begs the question of what 'racial identity/being Asian' means in this context.

One response to this might be to ask whether the social workers were expecting Nita and Clare to resolve perceived problems based upon both past abuse in an 'Asian family' and current placements in white foster homes where issues about racial identity and religion were not being addressed in any way. Clare's comments are relevant in this context, as she states the social workers responded negatively to any proposals the couple made. This sequence – create a notion of racial/religious identity problems; expect answers from Nita and Clare; reject those answers as doomed – is one in which racial identity itself is operated by social workers and by social work processes in the abstract. That is, there is little sense of specificity. As Nita says, the social workers 'didn't really explain what these "needs" were!' In addition, it seems as though a sense of responsibility for a 'correct' racial/religious identity is projected onto prospective carers, as though this were an expected and easily resolved issue, one that seems to have no connection to how it has been defined and used by social work in the first place.

Here, the issue of lesbianism is also relevant, since notions of an easily passed-on cultural/racial identity are usually imagined in a heterosexual context. Heterosexual families are assumed to provide natural inheritance of, or socialization into, racial, ethnic and cultural forms/identities. Lesbians are imagined to be excluded from most 'cultures', and the category is not usually seen to include black women, and so lesbians are thought to lack – or to be outside of – cultural norms as those are constructed. Clare and Nita's application to care for the girls received a mixed response from the authority responsible for their care. Barbara, the social worker, told me that her initial contact with the authority was negative. She spoke to a social worker who said that she did 'not approve of adoption by lesbians', but who then went on to say that her own views were not 'departmental policy' and referred Barbara on to a manager. The manager was positive about the couple and said they would be considered as potential carers.

However, shortly after this, two social workers from the placing authority, an Asian and an African Caribbean woman, came to visit Clare and Nita. The couple described this visit as 'awful, they just didn't want to be here and they were really uncomfortable'. Finally, Barbara and a colleague, Usha, an Asian Hindu social worker, attended a matching panel at the authority responsible for the girls, where a legal representative told them that Nita and Clare could not be put forward as potential carers for the sisters since their lesbian relationship would not be recognized within the Hindu faith. Barbara described this meeting as 'a shambles ... over in about five or ten minutes', and Usha tried to engage the authority representatives in debate about what she saw as discriminatory statements about Hinduism.

The reasons given for their rejection

A letter from the authority responsible for the girls set out the reasons for Nita and Clare's rejection, and it is worth quoting the detail of this:

> The specific problems that faced the Panel related to two legal difficulties which arise from the case ... [T]hey provide the basis for the Panel's decision not to proceed with the match.
>
> 1   Under Section 22 of the Children Act 1989 the Authority is required, before making any decision with respect to a child whom they are looking after, to ascertain the wishes and feelings of the child's parents. In this case, given the parents' professed strong Hindu beliefs, it is our understanding that they would object to the placement on religious grounds. Although the Local Authority is not absolutely bound by the parents' wishes and feelings regarding placement, these do have to be given due consideration.
>
> 2   Under Section 22(5)(c) of the Children Act 1989 the Authority must give due consideration to the child's religious persuasion, racial origin and cultural and linguistic background in respect of children either accommodated or subject to a Care Order. For children subject

to a Care Order, the duties are made even stronger by Section 33 of the Children Act which states that a Local Authority shall not cause a child to be brought up in any religious persuasion other than that in which he/she would have been brought up if the Care Order had not been made. The Panel were clear that you would make various efforts to accommodate the girls' Hindu religious and cultural needs. However, there is a fundamental problem in seeking to do this in the context of a relationship which the Panel understood is not recognised in the Hindu faith. (Social Services Department, 1994: 1–2)

The reasons for rejection of Nita and Clare are concerned with lesbianism but attributed to 'legal difficulties' and to the parents' religious beliefs. That is, the arguments used by the local authority may be interpreted as attempts to place the responsibility for rejection of a lesbian couple *elsewhere*. The legal arguments used here are interesting, since they can be seen as devices used to prevent any imputation of discriminatory or homophobic thinking. For example, the authority must 'ascertain the wishes and feelings of the child's parents', yet it is not clear that the parents' views were sought at all in this case and an agency is not 'absolutely bound' by parents' views. Section 22 of the Children Act 1989 also directs an authority to seek children's wishes, yet this is not even mentioned. In addition, the authority suggests parents are strongly Hindu, but it is possible to argue that the parents' religious 'beliefs' were in some doubt.

Reference to Sections 22(5)(c) and 33 [(6)(a)] of the Children Act 1989 is also used to make the case for the girls being brought up as Hindus, yet the phrase used – 'The Panel were clear that you would make various efforts to accommodate the girls' Hindu religious and cultural needs' – is perhaps ambiguous. It acknowledges that Nita and Clare were able to meet the stated religious/cultural 'needs', yet it also perhaps suggests an insufficiently 'Hindu' couple. The words 'efforts' and 'accommodate', I think, do this. The letter goes on to use the 'paramountcy principle' (Reece, 1996), in order to justify rejection of Nita and Clare, stating that the decision 'was made in the best interests of the girls' (Social Services Department, 1994: 2). But it is on the question of lesbianism/Hinduism that the rejection ultimately hangs: 'a relationship which the Panel understood is not recognised in the Hindu faith'.

Clare and Nita wrote a detailed response to the authority's letter, which set out their own views on the decision made by the authority. They challenged the view that the decision had been in the girls' best interests, and raised concerns about the way that both questions of sexuality and also race/culture/religion had been handled. They said, 'it appears from the letter that our efforts to accommodate the children's needs might have been viewed favourably, but *the refusal of our application was based solely and entirely on our sexual orientation'* (Nita and Clare letter, 1994: 2, their emphasis). Regarding questions about race and culture, they stated:

> The children's social workers identified serious difficulties in the children's present placements; they had difficulty linking with Asian people, resisted anything Indian and were described by social workers as 'westernized'. We demonstrated in great detail how we would address these issues and we are concerned that more work is not already being done with them on these issues.
>
> ...[The children were described] as 'nominally Hindu although they have had various experiences of other faiths'. We were told they had experienced many different faiths, including the Sikh religion, being Jehovah's Witnesses and involvement in other Christian sects. They have been largely out of touch with Hinduism for the last two years and had a variable experience of it prior to that. The authority were explicit in not advertising for a Hindu family. We therefore question their rejection of us on the grounds of so-called incompatibility with the children's religion.
>
> ...Hinduism does not explicitly prohibit any sexuality; of all the major world religions it is the most liberal on questions of sexual practice. There are many lesbian Hindus in this country and India, and many are bringing up children. Our fostering worker, who attended the [authority] panel, is a Hindu and disagrees with the interpretation you have given...One of our referees is a practising Muslim, and Islam is much more prescriptive on this point than Hinduism, yet she finds approval of our relationship and our parenting abilities totally compatible with her faith, as do our many Hindu, Muslim and Sikh friends. There are as many interpretations of a religion as practitioners and the only way to establish the implications in an individual case is to talk to the parents and children involved, rather than making stereotypical assumptions. (Nita and Clare letter, 1994: 2–4)

Nita and Clare's arguments suggest not only that they were able to meet the stated religious/cultural 'needs' of the girls, but that they would also do more. They raise the question of racial identity, for example, arguing that they would help the girls to develop a more positive sense of themselves as Asian. They make strong arguments about racist and stereotypical assumptions on the part of the authority regarding the Hindu faith. They suggest the authority has a limited understanding of Hinduism and has allowed a homophobic version or interpretation to prevail. Nita and Clare make the argument that Hinduism is 'the most liberal on questions of sexual practice' in relation to other religions, and they suggest that there are Hindus who reject homophobia. They state there are 'lesbian Hindus in this country and India, and many are bringing up children', an argument that counters the categorization of 'Hindu' as not inclusive of 'lesbian'. Thus, the couple is asking what *version* of Hinduism is being suggested by the local authority since, for them, there are different versions/practices of Hinduism, some of which do not reject homosexuality. This question – whether there is a single 'Hindu belief' regarding lesbianism – became the subject of the complaint investigation.

Investigation of their complaint

The authority appointed a senior child protection worker, from within the organization, to investigate Clare and Nita's complaint. The investigator's report claims that, due to the parents' stated requirements for the Hindu faith, which included 'being taken to the temple', (not, in fact, a require-ment of Hinduism itself), the local authority became concerned about a possible 'legal challenge' to the potential placement of the children with a lesbian couple. The report also states that an additional reason for turning down Clare and Nita, indicated by a senior manager of children's social services, was 'the continuing national debate and media attention related to placement of children with lesbian and gay couples', since this 'would cause children in such placements to feel insecure' (Complaint Investigation Report, 1995: 6). The investigator then comments on five issues in this case: equal opportunities, legal issues, Hinduism/lesbianism, the panel decision, and guidance under the Children Act 1989.

Under equal opportunities, the report states that, '[o]n the face of it, the Authority has given the complainants less favourable treatment, but says this is justified as being in the Childrens [sic] interests, and that they are required to put those interests first' (Complaint Investigation Report, 1995: 7). The investigator's 'on the face of it' does a lot of work, in my view, suggesting that 'less favourable treatment' has been incorrectly implied. Once again, a 'best interests of the child' argument is used to anticipate any imputed discrimination. But, as Helen Cosis Brown has argued, the interests of children and those of gay/lesbian carers are con-structed as dichotomous (Brown, 1991). This presents the notion of acting in children's interests as incompatible with placement with approved gay carers.

Under 'legal issues', the investigator refers to an article in *Family Law* about lesbians in residence and parental responsibility cases (Beresford, 1994), using this to suggest that a court will always view lesbianism nega-tively in relation to parenting. Yet, this is not Sarah Beresford's point. She actually argues that, in some cases, lesbian parents are granted residence or parental responsibility for children, but that their sexuality is 'considered a legally relevant factor in a way in which [a] father's [hetero]sexual orien-tation [is] not'. Beresford calls this 'deeply entrenched cultural prejudice' (Beresford, 1994: 644). The investigator, however, uses one quotation from a court judgement in order to suggest that a court will always view potential lesbian parents negatively. This is a case of double discrimination, then, using a negative court judgement to justify the authority's rejection of Clare and Nita.

The report then tries to 'establish what is Hindu belief in this matter' (i.e., lesbianism) (Complaint Investigation Report, 1995: 8). I will quote this section in full, as it is central to my arguments about notions of religion, culture and sexuality:

> My conclusion is that a distinction between religion and culture does not exist in this matter, and that Hinduism may be described as a system of practice rather than belief. The test I have therefore put to a range of people describing themselves as Hindu has been what would be the attitude in a temple to attendance by a couple known to be lesbian. This ranged from 'They would not be allowed in' to 'In some temples they might be accepted'.
>
> The key question however may be – would a Court accept the parents [*sic*] view if they were to say this was contrary to their religion? Clearly, the view of [x] Social Services Department, based on experience with K [the youngest child, a boy, living with the parents after a care order was refused], is that the Court would accept the parents [*sic*] view. (Complaint Investigation Report, 1995: 8)

Here, the investigator suggests that there is no distinction between culture and religion, a point that is contradicted by Arvind Sharma, who says that we should 'distinguish between Hindu religious attitudes and Hindu cultural attitudes. As a religion, Hinduism is perhaps more tolerant of homosexuality than it is as a culture', since – as with many other communities – homosexuality is described as culturally 'other' by some Hindus (Sharma, 1993: 68). The investigator of the complaint, however, seems to treat culture as religion, which does not allow for different versions of religious belief. Chetan Bhatt makes the point that anti-gay values are common to fundamentalist or 'neofoundationalist' versions of Hinduism (Bhatt, 1997: 230), but he also reminds us that there are distinct parallels in all cultural versions of sexual purity. Giti Thadani also argues that dominant, contemporary versions of Hinduism work to abject femininity and homosexuality, with lesbianism described as 'Western', for example (Thadani, 1996: 87).

The investigator's discussion of religion as 'a system of practice' seems to acknowledge that Hinduism may be practised in different ways. For a moment, then, it seems as if the possibility of pro-gay Hinduism is allowed. Indeed, the evidence gathered by the investigator is inconclusive, even though asking whether lesbians would be allowed into a Hindu temple is a very strange way to find out about either practice or belief. It confuses being in a temple with being a Hindu, 'attitude' with culture/religion, and what a person says, in response to an unknown investigator's 'test', with belief. A person saying that lesbians should or should not be allowed into a temple does not speak for Hinduism. The second remark – 'In some temples they might be accepted' – actually makes this point. Yet, the word 'allowed' ('They would not be allowed in') is telling here, since this expresses a dominant view or account – lesbians are assumed to be outside of, or other to, the category Hindu and they may or may not 'be allowed' by a heterosexual majority.

In addition, the investigator's attempts to establish 'Hindu belief' are objectionable because he is permitting a dominant view to prevail and he is suggesting that there is a single version of Hinduism. This version of Hinduism was opposed by Nita, Clare, Barbara and Usha, in part using an argument that, 'of all the major world religions it is the most liberal on questions of sexual practice' (Nita and Clare letter, 1994: 4). Thadani's scholarship, too, argues for the place of lesbianism *within* Indian and Hindu tradition (Thadani, 1996). Yet, Ashwini Sukthankar, in a collection of writings by Indian lesbians, argues:

> One longs for the luxury to be impatient with the question of whether or not lesbianism is part of Indian tradition. Those of us who live out the twin truths of being Indian and lesbian know what we are and where we came from, and are too busy with the day-to-day struggles of our lives to yearn for lost utopias when women's love for women was celebrated on temple wall paintings and in ancient scriptures. (Sukthankar, 1999: xi)

This is a crucial point since what religion does explicitly support lesbians and gay men, really? The *dominant* accounts of most religions do not, and Sukthankar's point is that a lesbian life should not have to depend upon approval or justification by reference to a notion of ancient tradition/culture. It is possible to argue that all religions and all cultures are intolerant towards homosexuality, and so the authority's decision regarding Nita and Clare does nothing to challenge homophobia. But, in addition, it constructs Hinduism as a more reactionary or homophobic religion and culture than others. Hinduism is suggested as an intolerant religion/culture (these being treated as coterminous by the investigator) with the parents formulated as an extreme case in order to support the authority's decision.

Under the question of the matching panel's decision to reject Clare and Nita, the investigating officer concludes that this was 'based on the relevant information and … flowed from that information'. He states that the 'SSD [Social Services Department] had no other choice available to it in the light of the advice and information available' (Complaint Investigation Report, 1995: 8). His use of language is interesting here; the first phrase almost says nothing, yet also works to make the decision sound as though it was based upon facts, justifying the decision without actually expressing anything about the 'information' itself. The second phrase reinforces the decision by suggesting there were no other choices available, which again heads of any imputation of discriminatory ideas or practices. Yet, it also works to deny that other choices were possible.

Finally, with reference to the then relevant guidance on the Children Act 1989 (Department of Health, 1991), the investigator quotes paragraph 3.14, part of which states:

> It would be wrong arbitrarily to exclude any particular groups of people from consideration. But the chosen way of life of some adults may mean that they would not be able to provide a suitable environment for the care and nurture of a child. (Department of Health, 1991: 25)

He uses this statement to support his view that [x] 'SSD has operated both the spirit and the letter of this paragraph and has not arbitrarily excluded any particular group' (Complaint Investigation Report, 1995: 8). The quotation of paragraph 3.14 is used as a justificatory device here. The 'chosen way of life' phrase allows for the need to assess and reject some applicants, yet this is also used to claim that lesbians have not been 'arbitrarily' excluded in this case. Rather, their exclusion is defended by means of stating an opinion as though it is fact. References to 'relevant information' and to 'the spirit and the letter' work to suggest facticity/objectivity. Paragraph 3.14 nevertheless echoes or refers back to the original version that appeared in the 1990 consultation paper on foster placements, which stated:

> authorities and those interested in becoming foster parents must understand that an authority's duty is, unequivocally and unambiguously, to find and approve the most suitable foster parents for children who need family placement. It would be wrong arbitrarily to exclude any particular groups of people from consideration. But the chosen way of life of some adults may mean that they would not be able to provide a suitable environment for the care and nurture of a child. No one has a 'right' to be a foster parent. 'Equal rights' and 'gay rights' policies have no place in fostering services. (Department of Health, 1990, paragraph 16)

That is, originally the 'chosen way of life' phrase was explicitly collocated with references to equal/gay rights. This was part of the then UK Conservative government's attempts to prohibit gay and lesbian parenting. Even though the 'gay rights' phrase was removed from the published Children Act 1989 guidance, 'conservative boroughs could still use them to deny fostering to lesbians and gay men' (Cooper and Herman, 1991: 76). The investigator's discussion of 'the continuing national debate and media attention related to placement of children with lesbian and gay couples' (Complaint Investigation Report, 1995: 6) references this political climate, in which local authorities were wary of being criticized for placing children with gay or lesbian carers, as a justificatory device.

The role of 'culture'

Yoosun Park's work on 'culture' as a concept in social work discourse points out that the term has 'largely replaced the categories of race and ethnicity as the preferred trope of difference' (Park, 2005: 29). In my case study of Nita and Clare, culture and religion were conflated and used to talk about Asian and Indian race/ethnicity. Park also argues that culture is actually 'a relational demarcator whose usage is an inscription of differential positions and hierarchical identities' (Park, 2005: 12); that is, it is used to categorize people and to produce notions of cultural difference. This, of course, means that the usage of culture within discourse is an assertion of power. Choosing not to talk about race, or describing race as an irrelevance, for example, is itself a form of privilege (Riggs and Due, 2010a, 2010b). Park argues that culture is usually applied only to black and other ethnic minority people, and this process is linked to the assertion of cultural 'types':

> 'Culture' and cultural attribute are presented as reified characteristics – fixed difference rather than positional divergence – which can be attributed to groups of people, who in turn can be identified by those essential attributes. (Park, 2005: 23)

Thus, we have seen that 'the Hindu' may be presented as essentially heterosexual and anti-gay/lesbian, strictly religiously observant and reactionary. My argument is also that 'culture' is imagined to be something naturally given or socialized into children by heterosexual families. One of the reasons that lesbian carers may be rejected, therefore, is that they are not seen as adequate passers-on of culture; that is, they are not imagined to be part of cultural/religious categories and they are assumed to be outside of imagined cultural norms. Lesbians are frequently assumed to be white, and groups designated as 'cultural' (black communities, religious communities, and so on) are rarely imagined to contain lesbians or gay men. So, in my case study 'the lesbian' is positioned by the investigator and by representatives of the social work agency as outside of religious norms, Hindu 'belief', national feeling ('national debate' on the suitability of gay carers) and a normal 'way of life', since a 'chosen' one is deemed unacceptable in this case. Asking a few Hindu people whether lesbians would be allowed into a temple summarily assesses a culture/religion.

Povinelli has argued that notions of multicultural diversity in contemporary societies work by asking or requiring 'subaltern and minority subjects to identify with the impossible object of an authentic self-identity' (Povinelli, 2002b: 6). That is, in order to achieve some aspects of recognition, subjects deemed 'cultural' must adhere to usually narrow and fixed notions of authenticity. But 'the very discourses that constitute indigenous [or ethnic minority] subjects *as such* constitute them as failures *of such* – of the very identity that identifies them (differentiates their social locality from other social localities) and to which they expected to have an identification (affectively attach)' (Povinelli, 2002b: 48). Having to adhere to the notion that one's life is dictated by a set of cultural rules is 'a practice of dehumanization' (Povinelli, 2005: 178).

Thus, I would argue that Nita and Clare were asked to identify with notions of 'the Hindu' but were deemed failures, as 'the lesbian' cannot be an authentic carrier of this religious category. In addition, 'the Hindu' is also imagined to adhere to a set of distinct ways of life and a 'belief' system that excludes homosexuality; 'the Hindu' is used to exemplify the anti-lesbian so that those making the decision are protected from such positioning. This traps or dehumanizes both lesbians and Hindus (and lesbian Hindus) as culture is imagined to rule or dictate people's everyday lives. Of course, these practices are resisted: examples have included Hindus who have spoken out in support of lesbians; lesbian Hindus living in India or the UK; black and white lesbians who contest the narrow representation of their lives; and social workers who are keen to avoid these narrow usages of 'culture'. But dominant discourses regarding notions of culture or religion are more conservative in their approach to questions of sexuality.

The question of race

In this chapter, black and white lesbians have suggested that race is often *not talked about* in relation to their status as parents. I have suggested that notions such as 'culture', and also 'religion' (often referred to as religious or cultural 'needs' of children), are used in place of direct reference to race. That is not to say that race is never talked about. Black lesbian and gay parents report that race may be raised as an issue for them in ways that it is not for their white counterparts, and race is often a focus of discussions within foster care and adoption when thinking about the placement of black children. Yet, race is also an area rarely discussed in most research and writing on gay or lesbian parenting (Eng, 2010; Moore, 2008; Riggs, 2006b, 2006c, 2007b, 2009; Sgambati, 2009). Race matters, yet how do we ensure that we talk about 'race' without adopting narrow and rigid views of racial 'types' and without treating or constructing the 'racial other' as merely and only a representative of an imagined racial 'group'? And how do we ensure that black lesbians and gay men are not required to identify sexuality over race, race over gender, gender over race, and so on? As Audre Lorde said, 'I find I am constantly being encouraged to pluck out some one aspect of myself and present this as the meaningful whole, eclipsing or denying the other parts of self. But this is a destructive and fragmenting way to live' (Lorde, 1996: 168).

The lesbians in this chapter have identified ways in which notions about culture are used to create racial differences, whether those be ideas about cultural deficit, 'damaged' racial identities, white exclusions of the racial 'other' in local contexts or fixed cultural/religious types. For these reasons and for others, likeness and other claims about fitting in are significant features of their stories since the creation of belonging is a way of challenging racist exclusions. For example, ideas about the nation as family ('the family of man', a national culture, and so on) often rely on exclusivity in which black people may be sidelined or abjected. Or, on a more local level, it is possible that lesbian and gay parenting groups or communities may also fail to notice questions of race or exclude black members. As Riggs has argued, claims to familial status through 'love makes a family' type tropes may 'overwrite the ways in which only certain family forms are recognised as morally worthy or deserving of protection' (Riggs, 2010: 51).

This chapter has sought to ask how racial categories are articulated alongside those of gender and sexuality. One key trope has been objection to, or complication of ideas about, replication. Nita, for example, suggests that the desire for racial replication doesn't make sense in a context of lesbian and gay parenting, where biological bonds are often irrelevant. Louise's story about donor choice similarly provokes questions about the idea of racial inheritance. Yet, at the same time, the stories in this chapter make use of likeness/fit, and they are acutely aware of the racism that may arise when these notions are not readily available. 'Are those children *really* yours?' was a pertinent reminder.

For the families in this chapter, race is always a background category presence, since it is always relevant even when not commented upon. For example, Justina and Toni were conscious of the ways in which race was not talked about by the social worker that assessed them as potential adopters. Since blackness (or 'non-whiteness') is racially marked, then black lesbian/gay parents are made aware of its presence in all social situations, regardless of whether it is a topic of comment. As Louise said, 'you see on some faces'. Kessler and McKenna argue that 'most of the work is done for the displayer by the perceiver' (1985: 136); that is, others read off questions about race/sexuality from signs/talk. Or, as Justina argued, 'it's about how you interact with people, it's about how people interact with you'. Racial categorization is never the result of the author alone, it is formed by dialogue, and neither can most racial complexity been seen, which means that the perceiver's conclusions are often limited or influenced by dominant notions about racial types. Nevertheless, in wanting to *make* race relevant, black gay/lesbian parents may face the danger that they are only allowed to inhabit one social category – they might be seen as black (but not gay), as gay (but not male/female), as male/female (but not black), and so on. If the lesbian/gay self is highlighted, then there is a danger that others will not see questions of race, and if the black or 'culturally other' self is highlighted, then lesbian/gay/bisexual/trans people may not be allowed as a possibility. This is one reason why black lesbian/gay parents have to assert the complexity of their social identities/categorizations so often (Hill, 1987; Jones, 1986; Lorde 1996; Silvera, 1995).

Yet, as we have seen, these assertions create double binds for black and other ethnic minority parents. The desire to question racial and cultural norms creates traps in which races and cultures are imagined as authentic and singular entities (Povinelli, 2002b). One of my participants – Louise – also made this point in relation to my research, saying that one of the potential problems with the self as reported in a qualitative interview transcript is that this can fix the person in a particular place. Louise describes herself as a 'fluid person whose ideas change and who is open to influences'. And this point is an important one to bear in mind when thinking about participants' words. At the same time, I also need to be wary of presenting black gay/lesbian parents as always stuck in oppressive and damaging social relations. An image used by Justina – not walking around with 'the sack of potatoes of racism on your shoulders' – is a salient reminder that black gay parents' everyday lives are structured, but not dominated, by racist ideas and practices. This is one of the reasons that the neglect of questions of race, and of black voices, within research on lesbian/gay parenting is unhelpful, and also why my discussion can only make a very small contribution to broadening that constituency. Questions of race and racial diversity within gay and lesbian parenting need far more attention.

Queer theory's concern with epistemological questions has highlighted, in part, that the knowing of sexual selves creates hierarchies and typologies. And so, similarly, knowledge claims about racial/cultural/sexual selves involve assertions about, and the creation of, types and relative value. To accept, for example, the versions of Hinduism and lesbianism perpetrated by the social work agency in the Nita and Clare case is to accept forms of knowledge in which both are denigrated, and in which the Asian/Hindu is held up as the exemplary reactionary/anti-lesbian in comparison with a white, liberal norm. But it is also to accept a version of the lesbian that is outside of 'cultures' that are not white and unable to inhabit imagined religious or cultural spaces. But, as Roderick Ferguson points out, to 'assume that categories conform to reality is to think with, instead of against, hegemony' (Ferguson, 2004: 5).

7
State

> social work and social welfare ... are far from being socially neutral
> or limited to technical interventions; they are deeply implicated in
> the construction of power relations in sexuality.
>
> (O'Brien, 1999: 151)

Whilst it is true that all lesbian and gay parenting is, in some way or another, circumscribed by state practices and relations, this is particularly apparent in the fields of foster care and adoption, since these usually require some formal assessment of parenting ability/potential by social welfare practitioners. For example, in the UK any person wishing to be considered as a foster or adoptive parent must undergo an assessment by a social work agency, and this process of assessment usually involves: initial application/discussion; attendance at a foster care or adoption preparation group; a formal 'home study' by a social worker; taking up of references and criminal/medical checks; and a decision on whether to approve potential carers made by a foster care or adoption panel consisting of various community, political, and social welfare representatives. Foster care or adoption by lesbians and gay men therefore throws into sharp relief questions about how state welfare agencies deal with sexuality, and how social work practices produce and make use of sexual knowledge. Lisa Duggan's call to analyze 'the embeddedness of heteronormativity in a wide range of state policies, institutions and practices' (Duggan, 1995: 189) may, in part, be answered by close scrutiny of how gay and lesbian applicants are assessed.

Research into lesbian/gay foster care and adoption

The body of work in this field is still small, but it is possible to summarize a number of key themes that arise from existing studies. First, it is important to think about questions of social welfare policy and law, since although some states/countries now operate foster care and adoption systems that should not discriminate on the basis of a person's sexuality, this has not always been the case; and there are still places that prohibit gay men or lesbians from fostering or adopting children (Brodzinsky, 2011; Brodzinsky et al., 2002, 2003; Gates et al., 2007; Gross, 2006; Mallon, 2004, 2006, 2007; Pertman and Howard, 2011; Reilly, 1996; Russett, 2011; Ryan and Cash, 2004; Tobias, 2005). In the UK, for example, foster care policy did not explicitly mention questions of sexuality until guidance following the Children Act 1989 (Department of Health, 1991), and law in England/Wales did not allow joint adoption by lesbian or gay couples (and all unmarried people) until the Adoption and Children Act 2002. Prior to this, lesbian and gay people had not been legally excluded from adopting, but for couples this meant that only one of them could be the named adopter – a 'single person' in the eyes of the law (see examples in Hicks and McDermott, 1999b). In addition, a liberal foster care or adoption policy does not necessarily prevent discriminatory practices, including rejection, by social welfare agencies, on the basis of sexuality (Brown et al., 2009; Cocker, 2011; Downing et al., 2009; Downs and James, 2006; Hicks and McDermott, 1999b; Hill, 2009; Mallon and Betts, 2005; Patrick, 2006). Further, as David Brodzinsky et al. have pointed out, some social welfare agency representatives in the USA have actually assumed that gay adoption is illegal in their state, when it is not (Brodzinsky et al., 2002, 2003).

Existing research points to plenty of examples of anti-gay practices within foster care and adoption systems. Individual gay or lesbian applicants report that they have encountered negative reactions, refusal or discouragement (Brown et al., 2009; Downing et al., 2009; Downs and James, 2006; Hicks and McDermott, 1999a, 1999b; Mallon and Betts, 2005; Parmar, 1989; Patrick, 2006; Ryan and Whitlock, 2007; Saffron, 2004; Shelley-Sireci and Ciano-Boyce, 2002), and Richard Sullivan and Margaret Harrington's study found 'a persistent belief among social workers interviewed that gay and lesbian single and couples applicants are discriminated against based on their marital status and sexual orientation' (Sullivan and Harrington, 2009: 243). In the Brodzinsky survey of American adoption agencies, a third of agencies didn't give detailed responses as they refused to work with homosexual clients and, of those that did respond fully, 20% had rejected gay or lesbian applicants because of their sexuality (Brodzinsky, 2011; Brodzinsky et al., 2003: 19 and 24). The survey showed that public adoption agencies – those dealing with 'special needs' children, international adoption, and secular or Jewish agencies – were more likely to consider gay or lesbian applicants than those dealing with infants and Catholic/Christian agencies (Brodzinsky et al., 2003: 24 and 31). The authors conclude that:

> Concern about offending community standards, violating religious doctrine and/or alienating possible funding sources evidently leads many of these agencies to have, at most, a low-key approach to recruiting homosexuals as prospective adoptive parents. (Brodzinsky et al., 2003: 39)

Authors such as Scott Ryan argue that individual social workers show a range of responses to gay and lesbian adoption/foster care. He found that male and Christian social workers were generally more homophobic than female or non-religious ones (Ryan, 2000: 524), and Lisa Saffron's interview with a lesbian adoptive couple also shows that individual adoption panel members have sometimes opposed gay/lesbian carers on principal (Saffron, 2004: 21). Of course, there are also examples of social workers being supportive of gay/lesbian carers (Cocker, 2011; Hall, 2010; Hicks and McDermott, 1999b), and John Matthews and Elizabeth Cramer's piece argues that the way in which social workers interpret and act upon policy and law is crucial (Matthews and Cramer, 2006). Riggs argues that gay and lesbian applicants are in a difficult position within foster care and adoption systems as their 'difference' from heterosexuals may be exaggerated or assumed, so they will have to manage 'normative views about parenting, sexuality, and identities' (Riggs, 2007c: 141). This does not mean that gay and lesbian applicants do not find ways of resisting heteronorms. They are 'keenly aware of marginalizing practices, but...they often [feel] unable to talk about this for fear of being labelled "paranoid"'' (Riggs, 2011), just as the black parents in Chapter 6 noted when they raised questions about race or challenged white norms.

Research argues that foster care and adoption agencies have often overlooked or ignored gay and lesbian people; for this reason, the notion of lesbians and gay men as an under-used or neglected 'resource' for the care of children is often raised (Hicks and McDermott, 1999a; Mallon, 2006, 2007; Ricketts, 1992). There are also frequent complaints by gay or lesbian applicants that social workers lack insight into their lives and the prejudices they may face (Brooks and Goldberg, 2001; Dalton, 2001; Mallon, 2004; Ricketts and Achtenberg, 1987, 1990; Skeates and Jabri, 1988). This may be especially true for bisexual and trans applicants (Ross et al., 2009). Christina Spivey's survey suggests a correlation between traditional views about sex roles and opposition to gay adoption amongst student social workers and adoption practitioners, although overall this population was generally positive about gay adoption, women more so than men (Spivey, 2006: 48).

One response to this has been to talk about social worker attitudes and to suggest a 'myths *versus* facts' approach (Mallon, 2004, 2006, 2008; Mallon and Betts, 2005: 23; Ricketts, 1992: 49; Skeates and Jabri, 1988: 18–24). Gerald Mallon, for example, says that social workers need 'to be clear about the facts' (Mallon, 2006: 53) when thinking about gay and lesbian foster care and adoption. For me, however, this is inadequate since it appears to suggest that there is simply 'bad' knowledge ('myths') that can be corrected by 'good' ('facts'), and that the problem lies with ill-informed or errantly homophobic individuals – a kind of 'bad apple' type explanation. It also suggests that homophobic practice is easily spotted and agreed upon, and that exposure to corrective research 'facts' will shift bad attitudes.

What this does not ask is how homophobic practices or ideas emerge and are put to use within social welfare institutions and ways of working. Neither does it ask how aspects of what appear to be ordinary and everyday social work practices may actually reinforce sexual hierarchies. Rather than seeing the problem as merely homophobic individuals, what is needed is investigation of the complex, frequently disputed, practices in which all of us – to some extent – participate, and which are part of the organizational order of social work. A 'myths *versus* facts' approach also does not acknowledge that claims about gay or lesbian parents are forms of sexual knowledge, in which hierarchies and other forms of discrimination are produced. Replacing a bad idea with a corrective fact will not prevent homophobic practices because:

> The discourses of homophobia...cannot be refuted by means of rational argument (although many of the individual propositions that constitute them are easily falsifiable); they can only be resisted. That is because homophobic discourses are not reducible to a set of statements with a specifiable truth-content that can be rationally tested. Rather, homophobic discourses function as part of more general and systematic strategies of delegitimation. (Halperin, 1995: 32)

Research argues that, especially in the 1960–80s, lesbian/gay applicants or agency representatives often did not mention sexuality during fostering or adoption assessments (Mallon, 2000; Parmar, 1989; Ricketts and Achtenberg, 1987, 1990; Shelley-Sireci and Ciano-Boyce, 2002; Skeates and Jabri, 1988). Indeed, Jane Skeates and Dorian Jabri argued that those who were not 'out' or open about their sexuality were actually treated more favourably than those who were (Skeates and Jabri, 1988: 50). This 'don't ask, don't tell' approach is still reported (Downing et al., 2009; Matthews and Cramer, 2006; Patrick, 2006), with 20% of women and 18% of men in Chris Downs' and Steven James' interviews saying that they 'had avoided challenges with the child welfare system by hiding their sexual orientation' (Downs and James, 2006: 295). Several authors argue that this is not helpful, as it can lead to problems of secrecy about sexuality, it denies the importance of discussing sexuality during assessment, and it can give children a message that a gay/lesbian sexuality must be hidden (Brodzinsky, 2011; Brodzinsky et al., 2003; Hicks and McDermott, 1999a; Riggs, 2004a; Ryan et al., 2004).

Where sexuality is acknowledged during assessment, there is a problem with either an over- or under-focus on its importance (Cocker, 2011; Mallon, 2006, 2007, 2011; Mallon and Betts, 2005; Skeates and Jabri, 1988). Brown also suggests that social workers need to avoid either 'positive or negative' stereotypes about gay or lesbian applicants (Brown, 1991: 15); that is, an assumption that *all* lesbians or gay men automatically will make good or bad carers. Earlier research argued that, because of concerns about questions to do with sexuality, gay and lesbian applicants were 'scrutinized more care-fully and are held to a higher standard than ... their heterosexual counter-parts' (Ricketts and Achtenberg, 1990: 104), and this is still possible (Brooks and Goldberg, 2001; Saffron, 2004).

Some liberal/diversity-type approaches have argued that lesbians and gay men should be treated the same as anyone else during their applications (Romaine, 2003; Sullivan, 1995). This perspective stems from a desire not to discriminate on the basis of sexuality, but actually avoids thinking about key areas pertinent to lesbian and gay lives. Riggs also reminds us that sameness approaches actually discriminate against lesbians and gay men because they work with an implicit heteronorm, and they do not acknowl-edge 'the power dynamics that underpin heterosexual privilege' (Riggs, 2004b: 2). Brown's early writings in this field were crucial in arguing that additional areas related to living as an openly gay or lesbian person ought to be covered during assessment. Because lesbians and gay men experi-ence difference due to societal responses to their sexuality, this will impact upon their lives as potential carers/parents (Brown, 1991: 16; 1998: 103–4). This point is reiterated in work with Christine Cocker (Brown and Cocker, 2008), and, in a later article, is developed into the 'SPRIINT model', which covers sexual orientation; previous sexual relationship histories; current relationships; intimacy; integration into the community; 'not so nice bits' (digging below the surface to explore the long-term nature of relationships, coping with difficulties, stress, and disagreements); and thinking about the patterns and gaps within applicants' stories. Their model 'enhances the focus on sex, sexuality and relationships within assessments for all appli-cants', but also retains 'a specific focus on the distinctive experiences of lesbians and gay men' (Cocker and Brown, 2010: 26; see also Brown and Cocker, 2011).

This emphasis on open discussion of questions related to sexuality has been echoed by others (Mallon, 2000: 15; 2011), and is recommended in some practice guidance (Mallon and Betts, 2005: 37–8; Manchester City Council – Children's Services, 2007). Some argue for 'more stringent risk assessment of the safety issues for gay male applicants' (Alderson and Crane, 2004: 33), not because they believe that gay men pose a greater sexual risk to children, but because gay men are at greater risk of suspicion, and even allegation of abuse.

Gay men and lesbians who do become foster carers or adopters report that social workers, especially in adoption, are not good at recognizing that this route to parenting may be a first choice (Hicks and McDermott, 1999a: 149); that is, they have not come to adoption or foster care simply because they are 'infertile', or have been unable to conceive their own birth children. The tendency to expect lesbians and gay men to take 'hard-to-place', disabled or HIV+ children is a key theme in research (Brown et al., 2009; Downing et al., 2009; Hicks, 1996; Hicks and McDermott, 1999a; Lewin, 1993; Matthews and Cramer, 2006; Ricketts and Achtenberg, 1987, 1990; Skeates and Jabri, 1988), something that Judith Weeks, in Pratibha Parmar's short film, calls the 'second-class children for second-class carers' approach (Parmar, 1989). Lesbians and, particularly, gay men report that they are sometimes discouraged from adoption or taking babies and young children by social workers (Cocker, 2011; Downing et al., 2009; Hicks and McDermott, 1999a).

All adopters/foster carers have spoken about a decline in their adult sexual relationships after the arrival of children. Interestingly, Rachel Farr, Stephen Forssell and Patterson's survey of adoptive parents found that lesbians reported having sex the least, then heterosexuals and then gay men (Farr et al., 2010a: 208), but Mark Gianino reports a 'marked decline' in sexual relations amongst gay male adopters (Gianino, 2008: 219).

Finally, the comparative research literature shows no differences in family functioning, attachment, a child or young person's well-being, behaviour, adjustment or gender identity development amongst gay/lesbian and heterosexual adopters (Averett et al., 2009; Erich et al., 2005, 2009a, 2009b; Farr et al., 2010a, 2010b; Howard, 2006; Ryan, 2007; Tan and Baggerly, 2009). However, some authors have questioned the need for such comparisons, since they may reinforce a heteronorm and neglect areas of difference that may be present in gay and lesbian parenting/families (Riggs, 2004a, 2004b; Stacey and Biblarz, 2001).

Sexuality, social work and the neo-liberal state

Vicky White has argued that any analysis of social work will be limited if it is 'isolated from an analysis of the features of the organisational regime... that are associated with its location in the state' (White, 2006: 31). This means that discussion of lesbian/gay fostering and adoption must take account of social work's place within, and contribution to, state child welfare systems and, relatedly, what has been described as a neo-liberal or mainstream approach to sexuality (Duggan, 2003; Lehr, 1999; Richardson, 2005; A.M. Smith, 2009; Vaid, 1995). It is possible to argue, for example, that the neo-liberal emphasis on performance management, audit, accountability and standard measurement within social welfare has resulted in a conception of social work that should no longer concern itself with questioning and challenging oppressive social relations. Instead, the emphasis is on personal values and the maintenance of respect for diversity (Harris, 2003; White, 2006). That is, individual social workers may be entreated to develop respectful relations with clients and others within a system structured by hierarchy, competition, poor resourcing and power struggles. If we take sexuality as an example, this neo-liberal approach neglects any attention to institutional ruling relations and how these produce forms of sexual knowledge. It also neglects discussion of how individual social workers and other practitioners interpret, make sense of, and even subvert, institutional expectations.

With regard to social work theory/practice and sexuality, where questions about sexuality are addressed at all, then neo-liberal versions are dominant (Hicks, 2008b, 2009a), although in some contemporary work this is now being questioned (Brown and Cocker, 2011; Cocker and Hafford-Letchfield, 2010; Featherstone and Green, 2009; Jeyasingham, 2008; Mulé, 2008; Myers and Milner, 2007). Neo-liberal ideas about diversity/equality, for example, result in notions of sameness in assessments of lesbian and gay foster or adoptive applicants, the idea that lesbians and gay men ought to be treated no differently – or, rather, in the same way as heterosexuals would be. As I will go on to outline, however, this is not a helpful approach to thinking about sexuality, and about gay/lesbian issues, in adoption and foster care, and it may result in dangerous practice whereby social workers feel unable to ask lesbians and gay men searching or difficult questions due to anticipated accusations of oppression (Brown, 1991, 2008, 2011; Cocker and Brown, 2010; Cocker and Hafford-Letchfield, 2010; Parrott et al., 2007).

A neo-liberal approach to questions of sexuality in social work may be exemplified by Neil Thompson's stance in *Anti-Discriminatory Practice* (1997 [but now in a fourth edition, 2006]). Essentially, Thompson's text describes lesbians and gay men as a sexual minority identity with particular characteristics and, consequently, social welfare 'needs'. Homosexuality requires 'understanding' and is not 'deficient', just 'different' (Thompson, 1997: 138–9). As I have argued elsewhere, this *version* of sexuality theory, however, results in a view of sexual categories as fixed identities having discrete welfare needs, with the solution to anti-gay practices being seen as equal access to existing legal, policy and cultural systems (Hicks, 2008b). Heteronormative values and ways of working remain invisible in this conception, and homosexuality is imagined as somehow external to social work, something or someone 'other' to be known about or understood. What this also does, of course, is to divert attention away from questions about how sexual knowledge, categories and hierarchies are produced within and through social work itself. It is certainly possible to argue, for example, that a social work position of liberal tolerance towards lesbian, trans, bisexual or gay people requires assimilation into, rather than challenge of, heteronormative practices.

One example of the troubles produced through neo-liberal ideas is that of the UK Government's Equality Act (Sexual Orientation) Regulations 2007 (superseded by the Equality Act 2010). These regulations were produced as an addendum to the Equality Act 2006, and prohibited 'discrimination on the grounds of sexual orientation in providing goods, facilities and services' (Brown and Kershaw, 2008; Cocker and Hafford-Letchfield, 2010: 1999). This Act prohibited discrimination against any person on the basis of sexual orientation in all public services including social welfare. This meant that all adoption agencies were expected to treat lesbian, gay, bisexual and heterosexual applicants/clients fairly and equally but – as the state had also prohibited discrimination on the basis of religious belief – this caused problems when several Christian-based adoption agencies made explicit their refusal to work with gay or lesbian adopters (see, for example, Armstrong et al., 2007; Brown and Cocker, 2008; Hurst, 2007). The response to this acknowledgement of what had otherwise been everyday anti-gay adoption practice was interesting, as the then UK government allowed religious agencies exemption from the Equality Act until the end of 2008, so that they could consider their stance on the question of gay adoption (Department for Communities and Local Government, 2007: 16). However, at the end of 2008 all adoption agencies in the UK were expected to conform to equality legislation. This left the liberal state in the position of sanctioning homophobic practice for about 20 months, but this was described as a period of adjustment or transition.

In a debate on the regulations in the UK House of Lords, Baroness Andrews argued that they were not designed to impinge upon religious rights of individuals or of religious groups. Thus, it was described as lawful for a church, mosque or temple to refuse gay, lesbian or bisexual people to enter if that was not 'in accordance with its religious doctrine'. It was public services that the regulations were designed to cover. Andrews made a distinction in her speech between religious belief of individuals and the provision of publicly funded services such as education:

> For instance, a teacher will be able to say, 'As a Christian, I believe that homosexual practice is wrong' or 'The Koran teaches...' What is unacceptable, however, and caught by these regulations is for a teacher to turn a blind eye to homophobic bullying, to single out a lesbian, gay or bisexual pupil for criticism on the grounds of their sexual orientation (Baroness Andrews, House of Lords debate on Equality Act. (Sexual Orientation) Regulations 2007, 21st March 2007, column 1293)

For me, this highlights a key problem with a liberal/diversity perspective; that is, in defining some beliefs as protected (whilst most beliefs are, quite rightly, not), homophobia is allowed to be expressed and form the basis of discrimination in some situations. Here, the example of a church, mosque or temple turning away gay people reminds us of arguments made by the investigating officer in Nita and Clare's case in Chapter 6. A congregation is assumed to be homophobic, or rather a particular interpretation of religious belief is taken to stand for all its members. Anti-gay prejudice or ideas on the part of some people are allowed to stand for a whole. Further, Andrews' example does not see overt expression of homophobia by an individual schoolteacher as wrong or as part of what is labelled 'homophobic bullying' or 'criticism'. But surely an anti-gay statement expressed within a school setting would be experienced by any gay person (pupils, teachers, parents, and so on), and some others, as part of an anti-gay set of values?

Liberal tolerance, then, has its flipside, since the state has instituted situations in which anti-gay prejudice is lawful and tolerated. Even though the 2007 regulations were superseded by the Equality Act 2010, this Act allows for situations in which a religious group might 'justify restricting ... membership to heterosexual people to comply with the doctrine of the organisation, or to avoid conflicting with the strongly held religious convictions of a significant number of the religion's followers' (Equality and Human Rights Commission, 2010).

There have been some explicit challenges to neo-liberal/anti-discriminatory-type models within the social work literature. Nick Mulé, although supporting a view of lesbian, gay, bisexual and trans people as occupying 'a differently centred cultural group' (Mulé, 2008: 1/8), argues against mere rights claims-based and fixed sexual identities theorizing, since he comments on an 'insidious neo-liberal influence, an assimilationist agenda' within (Canadian) social welfare (Mulé, 2008: 3/8). He opposes these as they allow 'traditional heteronormative intimate relationships ... [to set] the standard by which' others are measured (Mulé, 2008: 4/8). For Mulé, 'neo-liberalism offers a neutralized recognition of multicultural existence, without contestation of dominant structures' (Mulé, 2008: 5/8). Dharman Jeyasingham has also opposed ideas like greater visibility as solutions to the ignorance of lesbian and gay people within social work, since simply talking about or having images of gay/lesbian people can become one more 'way in which we are turned into objects examined by those who do not themselves need to be defined in terms of difference' (Jeyasingham, 2008: 141). He discusses ways in which *not knowing* about sexuality may be used as a technique within liberal equality to deny the need for change or challenge. That is, claiming not to know that a person is, say, trans or bisexual may be used as evidence to suggest that the practitioner would not have behaved any differently had they known (Jeyasingham, 2008: 147). Jeyasingham argues that questions of homophobic 'aesthetics and heteronormativity work to police social relations and experiences of intimacy for most of us, not just members of sexual minorities' (Jeyasingham, 2008: 149).

Governmentality, narrative, sexuality

Foucault's term 'governmentality' is used to refer to an 'ensemble formed by the institutions, procedures, analyses and reflections, the calculations and tactics that allow the exercise of [a] very specific albeit complex form of power, ... resulting, on the one hand, in the formation of a whole series of specific governmental apparatuses, and, on the other, in the development of a whole complex of *savoirs* [knowledges]' (Foucault, 1991b: 102–3). This perspective requires us to examine social work/welfare as an institutional form with specific or familiar ways of working (procedures, analyses, reflections, calculations, and so on) that are, in part, about the rule or exercise of power in relation to particular populations, such as that of potential foster carers/adopters. Foucault's point is that such social institutions, linked, as they are, with wider forms of government, result in ways of working (assessing, approving or disapproving of potential carers) and ways of knowing ('*savoirs*'). One implication of this is that we cannot regard the social work assessment of lesbian/gay potential carers as an objective or merely descriptive activity but, rather, must ask how and in what ways notions of the acceptable/good gay/lesbian carer, and of sexuality categories themselves, are produced. As Nikolas Rose argues:

> The state cannot avoid intervening in the shaping of familial relations through decisions as to which types of relation to sanction and codify and which types of dispute to regulate or not to regulate. (Rose, 1999: 127)

Leslie Margolin adds that, because 'awareness of manipulation, self-interest, or hierarchical domination represents for social workers an "ontologically fatal insight" into their activities, social work survives only insofar as it hides from itself any awareness of what it is actually doing' (Margolin, 1997: 60). However, it is possible that the case is being overstated here, since social workers and their practices are more diverse and potentially resistant to domination than this. That is, whilst it is crucial that we do examine social work's surveillance functions, we also need to ask how and where resistance to heteronormative domination occurs.

Mitchell Dean reminds us that forms of subjectivity are elicited, promoted, facilitated, fostered and attributed, but not determined, by forms of governmentality. He adds that they 'are successful to the extent that these agents [clients of social welfare] come to experience themselves through such...qualities (e.g., as having a sexuality)' (Dean, 2010: 44). This is an argument that Peter Miller and Rose also make: that power 'is not so much a matter of imposing constraints upon citizens as of "making up" citizens capable of bearing a kind of regulated freedom' (Miller and Rose, 2008: 53). That is, governmentality is about asking subjects to produce and monitor themselves (in interviews, in written form, and so on) as a way of getting them simultaneously to compare themselves with norms, and to produce themselves as an expected subject of analysis. This means that gay or lesbian foster care/adoption applicants will usually be asked to talk about their sexuality ('having a sexuality') in particular ways, as I shall argue. One of these techniques, for example, is about producing the good, rather than bad, homosexual (Hicks, 2000, 2006c) so that the 'dangerous queer' is abjected (Smith, 1994: 18).

Mark Philp's 'Notes on the Form of Knowledge in Social Work' (1979) is important, here, as he argues that 'beneath the apparent theoretical freedom in social work there is a form, an underlying constitution to everything that is said. This form creates both the possibility of a certain form of knowledge for social work and also limits social workers to it' (Philp, 1979: 84). Philp's claim is that forms of social work knowledge are social products 'not immune from social conflicts and dominant interests' (Philp, 1979: 88), and he makes the case that such knowledge is structured and regular. That is, we might say that social work assessments of gay/lesbian carer applicants feature regular tropes (the gender role model example in Chapter 5) that regulate knowledge about sexual types in ways that are linked to hierarchical notions about family, gender, sexuality, and so on. A sexual 'subject' is produced through social work, and Philp's argument is that social workers must transform the generalized type into a 'social subject' (Philp, 1979: 92). This is a crucial point, as social work has clearly been part of the creation of lesbian and gay foster care and adoption as possibilities in the first place. Social workers have had to create the image of particular lesbians or gay men as good carers, yet, at the same time, these subjectivities are constrained by institutional and dominant versions of sexual knowledge.

In order to investigate these forms of knowledge, then, it is necessary to think about social work discourse in terms of talk, text, practice and interaction. For example, Anne Rawls et al. argue that 'persons engaged in constructing complex social interactions seldom realize the degree of detail involved in producing the recognisability of the situations in which they take part' (Rawls et al., 1997: 114). That is, the interactional detail of a social work interview, the writing of an assessment report or an approval panel meeting is crucial, since these all use recognizable forms and methods. Rawls et al. argue that social workers, however, frequently rely on the reportage of supposed 'feelings and emotional content [and] ... *invisible ... mental states* of interactants' (Rawls et al., 1997: 116), rather than thinking about how those ideas are produced in interaction between themselves and others. Gerald de Montigny also makes a similar case for attention to what people in social work say and do, since client's stories 'arise in and through ... the interactional, in situ, and face-to-face work' (de Montigny, 2007: 106). His argument is that interactions are converted into textual forms:

> Through textual work achieved as production of files, reports, running records, notes, and so forth social workers reproduce documentary exchanges, which as circulated, read, interpreted, and acted on set into place a world of 'facts' that can be studied, recovered, recombined to tell professional and organizational 'stories'. (de Montigny, 2007: 112)

Social workers 'inscribe everyday or mundane occasions as proper instances into organizational categories' (de Montigny, 1995: 28), a phrase that echoes Smith's arguments about ruling relations and her point that, 'in organizations concerned with processing people, characteristic forms of co-ordinating work processes focused on individuals are textual ... Individuals are known as "cases" under the interpretive aegis of their records. When decisions are to be made their "current status" is located in the textual traces of their past contained therein' (Smith, 1990a: 220).

The construction or performance of identity within social work narrative is also crucial here, since professionals are involved in making knowledge through their practice. Linguistic accountability, or indexicality, is present in how a gay or lesbian applicant talks about himself or herself, how this is made sense of and written up by a social worker, and how this is interpreted and negotiated at a fostering or adoption panel:

> These instances are interactional in nature, but they are also linked to institutional constructions of people and events which function as accumulative building blocks in the production of knowledge within social work and related institutional settings. Situated social work knowledge has relations to occasions and sites which preceded this one and has consequences for those that follow it. (Hall et al., 2006: 21)

Accounts of the foster care/adoption assessment process

Wayne [adoption social worker]:
I talked about the socialization [of the child], *you know, 'How do you believe you will explain that* [having gay carers] *to a child?' 'What if he comes through the door and sees the two of you kissing?' He'll probably see a man and a woman kissing on the TV or on the street and surely ... well, 'surely', ... perhaps I can't be too sure about that! But I think he would have a different perception of that than if he had walked in and seen the two of them* [gay carers] *kissing each other on the mouth, you know. 'Would you be embarrassed about that?' 'How would you explain it?' I would have to explore that because it could very well happen ... I mean he is living, or she or whoever – for the sake of this discussion, 'he' – 'he is living with the two of you as his parents, right – "mother"? ... wrong. As his parents, you can't be mothers, but he knows he has got a mother because he has a right to know that he has been adopted and he must have a mother. There are other children with mothers, so how come he has got two fathers?' ... 'That the two of you* [gay carers] *go to bed in the same room? He has got his bed next door, but what sort of messages do you believe he gets from that?' Hence I used the example, earlier on, of a man saying he did this* [having sex with other men] *for money. So is the child likely to take on the same orientation as that?*

When I spoke to social workers and managers for my PhD studies on gay/lesbian adoption/foster care (Hicks, 1998), I heard a range of views about gender role. Wayne's account treats this as crucial, as he explicitly talks about socialization as though this is an accepted and natural concept. This is an example of 'facticity', building up a claim as though it is a fact, and is present in Wayne's concerns about 'messages' and influence (the idea that the 'same orientation' might be taken on by a child), and in his talk about men and women as naturally having discrete roles. Wayne links these concerns with the sexual – he talks about a gay couple going 'to bed' and suggests that this scene, created as sexual by him, leaks into a child's bedroom – 'He has got his bed next door, but what sort of messages do you believe he gets from that?' In addition, this imagery is collocated with a story of male prostitution. For Wayne, being gay is analogous with having sex for money or, rather, his story about a man having sex with other men for profit suggests that anyone might be tempted into such behaviour.

Wayne's narrative also builds up the idea of normal/abnormal sexuality, an example of prohibitive 'procedures of exclusion' in discourse (Foucault, 1981: 52). Wayne presents heterosexual kissing as ordinary (it might be seen 'on the TV or on the street') while gay kissing is a potentially damaging scene. The story about the gay kiss is very different – it is shocking because discovered or stumbled upon (the child 'comes through the door' and walks in on the gay kiss) and explicit (the kiss is specified as 'on the mouth'). In addition, it is embarrassing and requires explanation, whereas the straight kiss is quite matter-of-fact. Further, Wayne sees gender roles as flowing naturally from sex, so men here cannot mother children: '... "mother"? ... wrong.' Mothers are clearly women for Wayne, and they are located elsewhere; that is, the adopted child is imagined to have a mother elsewhere, which Wayne links with a notion of children's rights (the 'right to know' the 'real' mother). Having two dads is constructed as abnormal in Wayne's account, as it needs explanation and is different from most other families.

However, other social workers objected to standard gender roles in families, but still felt constrained to address these. This was exactly Barbara's point to me about her assessment of Nita and Clare. As a feminist, Barbara did not want to repeat expectations about gender roles, yet she was highly conscious that the Adoption Panel would expect her to address this question, especially as Nita and Clare were the first 'out' lesbian couple ever to be taken to that panel. Other social workers made the same point:

> **Annie:** It's the whole thing about role models which people are obsessed with; that, if you are a lesbian couple, there's no male role model, or with gay men that there's no female or indeed male role model, and I don't agree and I don't really understand it because it doesn't take much brain to see through it.

and:

> **June:** If I was assessing a lesbian couple, would I be worried that they were going to turn their girls into a man-hating little person, is that the kind of thing you're asking?
>
> **Steve:** Yes, that's certainly something lesbians get asked ...

June: Oh yes, 'Do you like men? Can you prove it? Will this child grow up to be a man-hating girl?' ... No, I wouldn't take that approach I don't think.

Annie and June are both careful analysts of gender, yet they told me that they had to address gender roles in their reports, and were questioned about this at fostering or adoption panels. Any gay or lesbian applicants that were perceived as too challenging of standard ideas about gender roles might be rejected. And it's not even that this rejection necessarily did happen; rather, the social workers anticipated it as a possibility where gender role was a concern. This reminds me of something that Steven Lukes says in his work on power: 'power is at its most effective when least observable' (Lukes, 2005: 1).

In Nita and Clare's case, an expressed preference to care for girls was treated as an anticipated problem. Usually applicants are asked whether they have a preference in terms of the gender of a child, and such preferences are 'normally' accepted. But, because Nita and Clare are lesbians, their report expressed concern about gender role:

> The couple have made a first preference of a girl child as they feel they have something to offer, to enable a girl to grow up as a strong individual with self esteem and a good, clear sense of identity. They also feel that they know more as women what it is like to be a girl, having had some shared experience, whereas they wouldn't feel quite the same with a boy. They emphasized that they have not got a problem with boys and they know several boys and would consider one as a second placement if a sibling to the first child placed.

Here, the preference has to be justified, and there is a rather defensive (because repeated) emphasis on 'not having a problem with boys'. On the question of gender roles, the report continues:

> The couple have contact with several males and have commented that they are all positive, healthy figures who would make good role models for a child to look up to and they certainly would not include aggressive, macho figures to be amongst their friends. Nita and Clare are not anti-men, and their being lesbian is something that they feel inside is a natural state for them.

The report addresses a concern about male role models through reassurance ('several males') and also positions men as to be looked up to. Men are neatly divided into discrete good man/bad man types ('positive, healthy' versus 'aggressive, macho'), which indicates an unacknowledged problem with role model theory: in these terms, what 'type' of man exactly provides a positive role model? The figure of the man-hating lesbian is invoked and addressed (the couple is 'not anti-men'), and, finally, the notion of lesbianism drawn upon here is a natural/biological one ('they feel inside is a natural state'). This diffuses the idea that lesbianism might be seen as a political or social choice and challenge to heteronormativity (a 'chosen way of life'). There cannot be too much questioning of traditional gender. Or rather, Barbara, the social worker, knows that traditional gender can, and should, be questioned. But she is also aware that the Adoption Panel will ask her about balanced gender role models. In interview, Barbara told me that she had to represent the couple as 'not too feminist.'

In my interviews with Nita and Clare, we talked about the assessment of 'gender':

Steve: OK, how did [Barbara] 'do' gender?

Clare: She asked us whether…well, there's something on the form where it asks about, 'Are jobs allocated or do you have roles that are…?' So we said how we didn't have male and female roles and how we thought it really important for children not to, and all that sort of stuff…and the other thing that came up with gender was that we wanted girls.

Nita: Yes, we talked quite a lot about that really, because she wanted us not to say that…

Steve: What did you have to say in the end?

Nita: Well, we said that we'd want to have a girl placed with us initially, but if that girl's birth mother then had a boy and we were asked if we would take the next sibling, that we would consider him…and that's all we said really!

Steve: But in a sense it was something that you had to say on the form as well as for Panel's benefit…

Nita: Yes…

Clare: And at the beginning of the assessment, Barbara said there was no problem, she said, 'Oh yes, it's really common for people to say they only want boys or they only want girls…No problem' sort of thing, but it wasn't until…Well, I got the impression that it was when she went back and she had team meetings and people played devil's advocate with the Panel…and she then became sort of more and more anxious about it and pushed it, and certainly the second social worker pushed it as well, so that was when we…

Nita: …caved in!

It is important, here, to note that a question – initially added to standard assessment forms (British Agencies for Adoption & Fostering, 1991 [now the British Association for Adoption & Fostering, 2005]) in order to *avoid* the reinforcement of rigid gender roles amongst children – is transformed into a concern about gender dysfunction amongst lesbians and gay men. Clare recognizes this as a game, having to meet required expectations, when she says, 'all that sort of stuff'. Barbara knows that, although a preference for a girl would normally be fine, here it becomes a problem *because Nita and Clare are lesbians*. My suggestion that the answer given in the report is for 'the form as well as for Panel's benefit' also shows that all four of us – Nita, Clare, Barbara and me – recognize this as part of an institutional order. That is, whatever we think about gender role models, this question must be addressed and concerns reassured. Barbara becomes more anxious about the need to address this as her colleagues remind her of this, and Nita's comment about caving in – which echoes Pete and Peter's 'give up/went along with it' – also acknowledges that the gender order is part of institutional processes.

Respondents identified other key areas of assessment that I would similarly describe as forms of governmentality; that is, they are regulatory practices that take the form of repeated and familiar concerns and ways of working, which produce ideas about sexuality and gender *as these ought to be, or are imagined to be, lived*. The first example of this is questions about infertility (and, specifically, 'coming to terms with' infertility) directed at lesbian potential adopters. This is a feature regularly identified by lesbian applicants, and it often stands out for them, as it seems irrelevant (see also Woodford et al., 2010). Whilst many potential adopters do come forward after failing to conceive a birth child, for lesbians and gay men, this is sometimes irrelevant. They have not sought to have a birth child, they are not concerned with questions of fertility, and they may have come to adoption as a first choice (Brodzinsky, 2011; Brodzinsky et al., 2003; Mallon, 2006, 2008, 2011; Mallon and Betts, 2005; Ryburn, 1991). Nita and Clare talked to me about this point:

Clare: Infertility did come up in the assessment, but they kept trying to push it as a negative, you know, and we kept saying, 'But we must be even better than people that normally come for adoption because we're not coming to it as a second-best, we're coming to it as our first choice.' In the assessment, there were all these questions about, 'Are you fertile? When did you find out you weren't?' and we were going, 'Well, we don't know!'

Nita: ...and we're not interested in whether we are or not...

Clare: And they kept coming back to it. When the second social worker came, she kept coming back to it, didn't she, saying, 'Well, why aren't you?' And so then we started talking about it properly and we said, 'If you want to talk about it, let's talk about why we don't want to "have" children.'

Barbara addressed this in her assessment report on the couple:

> As lesbians, they could have chosen artificial insemination, but they see adoption as a more sensible and valuable way of providing a home for a child who has already been born and needs a happy, secure home. They feel that AID [alternative insemination by donor] has so many problems. For instance, if the donor is known, then the father's involvement can be unclear or change over time causing problems, and if the donor is unknown, there are problems of what to tell the child. They would feel uncomfortable with the involvement of a person in them having a child who is not part of their loving relationship [*sic*]. Neither feels the need to experience pregnancy in order to become a parent, which they know that some women do. [Nita and Clare] have not specifically investigated the possibilities for themselves as it is not what they want to do.

And, on the health information section of the report, the question 'Reason for infertility' is answered for both Clare and Nita as, 'Miss [x] is unmarried.' Here – as with gender role – the question of infertility is duly addressed by Barbara, as it is both a formal and usual expectation of adoption assessments. Barbara's language is quite defensive, and she has to outline potential problems with donor insemination, even though this is not an option considered by Nita or Clare. That is, Barbara has to justify adoption as a first choice for parenting, and she has to explain away the issue of infertility. The heteronormativity of these expectations is also highlighted by the doctor's use of 'Miss [x] is unmarried' to answer a question about infertility. Infertility is an expectation applied to most (heterosexual) people/couples applying to adopt, and so being 'unmarried' is taken as an answer to this question. This, of course, avoids discussion of lesbianism and, at the same time, reinforces notions that those who have otherwise 'failed' in their attempts to have children would only consider adoption as a last resort. This seems a bizarre idea to reiterate within adoption practice, yet it stems from assessment of heterosexual couples and the requirement by most adoption agencies that adopters ought not to be seeking to have birth children, a requirement that has shifted in some agencies that now accept 'fertile' adopters (Brodzinsky et al., 2003).

Another question asked of applicants is about their support networks, friends, family and community. I was interested in this question because I wondered whether social work would reinforce notions of family contacts rather than friends, and whether social workers would ask lesbian/gay applicants about their contact with other gay and lesbian parents. One social work manager talked to me about assessing community contacts:

> It's to do with them being integrated, and having relationships with the wider community, and the child having an experience that is wider than just the household. I'd be looking for a rounded personality, someone who's not only seeking friendships with people who share their own sexual orientation but who also has a family life.

This talk interested me as 'wider community' and 'family' are essentially defined as heterosexual. The manager wants 'someone who's not only seeking friendships with people who share their own sexual orientation', which indicates a fear that lesbians and gay men mix only with their own kind. Heterosexual contact is a requirement. I think that this talk also betrays a fear of homosexuality as challenge to heteronormative expectations; words like 'integrated', 'wider community', 'rounded personality', and so on signify a desire to find potential adopters able to function in a range of community and social settings but, at the same time, a concern that gay or lesbian applicants must not be too challenging of heterosexual ways of life, they must be 'integrated'. The manager's use of the phrase 'family life' clearly makes a distinction between homosexuality and heterosexuality, and associates 'family' with the latter. What this also does is to set up hierarchical notions about who counts as family and as community. Friendships are written off in comparison with 'the wider community' or with 'family life', so that a hierarchy of intimacy is constructed, in which 'one's sexual partner and family of origin are presumed to take precedence over friendships and personal networks' (Budgeon, 2006, para.1.3).

Rarely did I find social workers that asked applicants whether they knew or had contact with other lesbian and gay parents, either as friends, relatives or through gay parenting support groups. Clare said:

Clare: I don't think *[Barbara]* even asked us if we knew other lesbians who had children. I mean, I think we told her that, I think we told her that we had friends…And I don't think she made us think enough about what it was going to be like being lesbian *[adopters]*, and I think it's luck that we knew other people and we had this group *[national support group for gay and lesbian foster carers/adopters]* and all these other things to make us think about it. But if I think about us being in a vacuum, you know, living in a little village somewhere and not knowing anyone else, I think she should have made us think a lot more about what it was going to be like being lesbian parents.

Steve: Oh, I agree...

Clare: And she didn't ask us where we were going to get support as lesbian parents.

Steve: I mean, that's surely crucial?

Clare: And it was us that found out about the *[national support]* group, it was us that found out about the *[local]* support group, she didn't do anything like that. So, I think she was just driven with this thing of getting us through the Panel and that was more than what we were getting out of it.

The point being made by Clare is that lesbian and gay applicants for foster care or adoption need, or appreciate the time, to think about the implications of their sexuality for their becoming parents. She relates this to the question of support and advice, too, making the point that contact with other gay or lesbian parents is crucial. Clare and Nita found and made use of various national/local gay and lesbian foster care/adoption support groups – something that would not be open to, or suit, everyone. But Clare's point is also that these groups provided support, advice and an opportunity to talk about becoming gay or lesbian adopters/foster carers in ways that their social work assessment did not. Clare suggests that Barbara's focus – perhaps inevitably – was on getting the first ever openly lesbian couple through the Adoption Panel, rather than on their particular circumstances as lesbian adopters. That is, Barbara's concerns were about how to represent a lesbian couple in ways that the Panel would find acceptable, and one of these was to present them as having heterosexual contacts and being integrated with the 'wider community'. For example, Nita and Clare were asked to provide an extra referee, 'a heterosexual couple with a child', for the Panel's benefit.

In most cases, respondents suggested that social workers rarely asked them searching questions about how their sexuality related to questions about parenting:

Nita: I don't think the social worker handled the issues to do with our sexuality well. She wanted to be so non-discriminating that she just treated us like she would a heterosexual couple, and on one level that was good because she focused on child care, but we also needed to talk about the specifics of being *lesbian* adopters, and there are many issues we all needed to think through.

Toni and Justina said they were not challenged enough:

Justina: I think the social worker had a fear, really, of challenging us. I don't think through the whole thing I felt challenged. I think she probed but I think she could have probed harder, I think she could have probed deeper.

Toni: Yeah, 'coz there were things we weren't prepared for, really…

Justina: There were assumptions made that, following our very first assessment visit, that everything would be fine.

Steve: Really?

Justina: Yeah, you know, 'You won't have any problems,' and I was thinking, 'How do you know?!'

Toni: Because of what we do I suppose, because of our professional background *[both have worked or are working in community/health/ social services]*. It didn't feel necessarily as thorough as it might have been.

Justina: Toni's just being nice 'coz it's social services! *[laughing]*… I wish they'd been more vigorous really, not because we have anything to hide but I think, in my own mind, that she'd made her mind up when she first met us and that the assessment was just proving her judgement. The second social worker, she restored my faith in social workers because I truly believe she had *[x's]* needs and welfare and everything at heart… But I also think the first social worker was scared and intimidated by us.

Toni: That was a bit her personality anyway, but I do think she was daunted by us being a bit articulate…

Justina: I suppose it really struck me after she said we'd be okay after the first visit and I said to Toni, 'God, how does she know? You know, we could turn out to be axe-murderers!' She had no clue, and how could she say to us we'd have no problem at Panel? We would have had to have said some really horrendous things for her to have not recommended us.

Here, respondents are suggesting that, in attempting to be 'non-discriminatory', social workers actually avoided talking about important issues to do with their sexuality, a point echoed in Brown and Cocker's work (Brown, 1991, 1992; Brown and Cocker, 2008, 2011; Cocker and Brown, 2010). Toni and Justina make the point here (and in Chapter 6) that this has to do with questions of race, class (profession) and gender as much as sexuality, but all respondents argued for greater vigour in social work assessments, acknowledging that there were areas to do with the intersection of sexuality/parenting that they may not, but needed to, have thought about. Thinking about how to engage or interact with schools, health services, community clubs and so on was mentioned by most of my respondents as relevant to their sexuality. Peter, for example, talked about offering to act as a classroom assistant at his adopted son's school. He told me that a teacher responded negatively to this, trying to 'put him off', and he felt that this was about her being uncomfortable with having a gay man in her class. He also mentioned the reactions of some other parents, talking about looks they gave him at the school gates. Nita and Clare, in Chapter 4, talked about being 'up-front' and open with their children's schools, and about a range of positive and negative reactions. But most interviewees made the point that these examples are important differences related to being a gay or lesbian parent that were poorly treated or overlooked in social work assessment.

It is possible to argue that, because the usual categorization of 'foster carer/ adopter' (by implication, 'family' and 'parent') does not include 'gay' or 'lesbian', then social workers are engaged in linguistic reassurance work in order to present gay or lesbian applicants positively. This reassurance work is evident in phrases used in Barbara's assessment of Nita and Clare ('They emphasized that they have not got a problem with boys and they know several boys', 'The couple have contact with several males and have commented that they are all positive, healthy figures', or 'Nita and Clare are not anti-men'), which address a notion of 'the lesbian' as anti-male (Hicks, 2000) for the purposes of the Adoption Panel. Jo and Louise, lesbian foster carers, told me that their social worker asked them extra questions about their 'attitudes towards men' and then wrote that their 'loving relationship is not made obvious and was brought to my attention in a thoughtful and sensitive manner' (Hicks, 1996: 21–2). Mark's stories about his self-identity as a foster carer and adopter also made frequent use of *denial of the relevance of his being gay.* He used phrases like 'the fact that I was gay wasn't an issue', 'I don't really come across, you know, as a gay man', or 'it's not a big part of my life really'. That is not to say that Mark hides his sexuality or does not see its relevance (see Chapter 5), but in relation to his foster care or adoption of children he presents himself – or is involved in dialogues in which he is expected to present himself – as 'a man who happens to be gay'.

This is the self-monitoring aspect of governmentality. Mark's self-presentation or Nita's joke about caving in on questions of gender are about acknowledgement of the production of a gay/lesbian type in dialogue with state expectations and practices. This was also raised in respondents' references to the virtual or 'false' nature of the assessment process, something that just had to be 'got through'. Yet, at the same time, respondents made the point that they wanted their sexuality on the agenda in social work assessments; they did not want it to be the sole focus, but they saw it as an important part. This relates to the production of official state welfare knowledge, but also to the production of self. As Foucault argues, 'so-called sciences', such as psychiatry, medicine and state welfare, are ' "truth games" related to specific techniques that human beings use to understand themselves' (Foucault, 2000d: 224). He makes the point that a technology of the self involves both submission to domination – 'an objectivizing of the subject' – and the effecting of transformation by the subject (Foucault, 2000d: 225). Thus, it is not a case of state social work merely oppressing lesbians and gay men, or of gay and lesbian applicants' lives or stories being twisted or misrepresented by social workers. Instead, a complex set of practices and relations produces a version of the lesbian or gay self as a potential carer of children. Accounts by social workers that I spoke to show that, in some cases, they are keenly aware of, and try to resist, heteronormative practices (Hicks, 1998). I also heard positive stories about social workers from gay and lesbian carers. But, at the same time, social work discourse concerning sexuality constitutes expert knowledge forms/claims and participates in the heteronormative. It is 'a practice of improvisation within a scene of constraint' (Butler, 2004b: 1).

Sex, sexuality, sexual abuse and the Wakefield inquiry

In June 2006, in Wakefield in the north of England, two gay male foster carers were sent to prison for six and five years respectively for sexual offences against four of the children in their care. As a result of this, the Council commissioned an independent inquiry to consider the circumstances of the case (Parrott et al., 2007). I would like to discuss some aspects of the inquiry report for a number of reasons; first, it's crucial not to avoid discussion of the *possibility* of abuse by gay or lesbian carers. The social work assessment process in foster care and adoption is, in some part, about trying to weed out any person who might be unsuitable as a carer of children, and therefore we have to entertain the possibility of unsuitable gay or lesbian applicants. Second, I found in my PhD studies that some social workers claimed to be wary of asking lesbian/gay applicants questions about their sexuality or sexual relations for fear of being seen as 'discriminatory' (Hicks, 1998). This also appears to be a key concern in the Wakefield inquiry with 'a number of staff ... afraid of being thought homophobic', and so not challenging the gay carers in this case about their behaviour or explanations of events (Parrott et al., 2007: 124). Third, in an echo of that very concern, the inquiry opens with a reported statement by the court judge that 'this case is, of course, not about homosexuality', and the report authors stating that the 'fact that the case involves a gay couple is irrelevant' (Parrott et al., 2007: 7). In my view, none of these three issues is as straightforward as they may, at first, appear.

CF and IW, 'the first gay couple in Wakefield who had been open about their sexuality' (Parrott et al., 2007: 48), were approved as foster carers in July 2003. Over about a year and a half, the couple had 18 children placed in their care at different times, for various short-term (including respite) periods. Some of these children are described as having 'learning difficulties', 'behavioural challenges' and 'inappropriate sexualised behaviour' (Parrott et al., 2007: 9). In January 2005, one child made allegations of abuse by the carers which led to a police investigation and their subsequent conviction for various sexual offences, including taking indecent pictures (videos) of, and sexual activity (masturbation, oral sex) with, children.

As with many inquiries into social work practice with children, the report has a with-hindsight tone, and the authors, in a section in chapter 9 called 'So, with the benefit of hindsight...' (Parrott et al., 2007: 123), acknowledge this. This is an important point as the report describes a series of events and – crucially – social welfare workers' reported frustrations or concerns about those events, but makes the point that 'nobody had stopped to take an overall perspective' (Parrott et al., 2007: 124). This is a common problem with reporting in formal inquiries into child care failures, since the benefit of hindsight actually involves the bringing together into one place several incidents for consideration. What inquiries are not good at asking is why and how small, individual events may provoke concerns but do not result in appropriate actions – or, rather, result in actions not deemed appropriate with the benefit of hindsight. The Wakefield inquiry identifies plenty of incidents when workers and managers should have acted differently, but does not really ask why and how it is that they did not. My concern is that this kind of blame-led inquiry, based on a 'with what we know now, why didn't people act?' approach, results in easy explanations, the notion that explanatory narratives actually describe reality, and the idea that better risk assessment procedures will result in the prevention of similar events in the future.

Peter Reder and Sylvia Duncan have critiqued this perspective in their work on child death inquiries. They note that, in a blame/legal framework, stories about incidents are 'reconstructed in terms of individual actions but not understood within their context and in relation to other people' (Reder and Duncan, 2004: 97). This results in reductionist policy recommendations that do not concern themselves with how and why people may or may not communicate and act in practice. Reder and Duncan suggest that practitioners' thinking is actually crucial, since this has to do with people, their actions, their skills and the state of their working environment, described as one in which 'leadership was poor, work demands and pressures high, where there were clear service shortcomings... and where the staff group were fragmented and largely temporary' in the Wakefield case (Parrott et al., 2007: 119). Reder and Duncan's concerns about procedurally led inquiry are important, but in relation to the notion of thinking, we also need to ask some critical questions. The Wakefield inquiry, for example, discusses various aspects of practitioners' thinking regarding gay carers, but it would be naïve to treat these reports as straightforward, since, as explanations, they are also doing work. To use reported 'fear of being thought of as homophobic' (Parrott et al., 2007: 119) as an explanation for why things went wrong is not an innocent or descriptive statement, since it inoculates the author against blame and justifies actions or inactions by locating power with others, a point to which I shall return.

The first key trope of the Wakefield inquiry report that I'd like to focus on is the way in which better detection of risk/abuse is suggested as a solution to identified problems. The Wakefield inquiry says:

> There is insufficient evidence to know whether CF and IW were pae-dophiles who set out to be foster carers in order to have access to children to abuse them; or whether the opportunities fostering offered them to abuse children were greater than their ability to resist such inclinations, perhaps previously latent. During their fostering career, however, there is much in the behaviour pattern of CF and IW which this report describes, to suggest that CF and IW were indeed paedophiles (Parrott et al., 2007: 10)

It is interesting, here, to see that the category of 'the paedophile' is inserted into the report early on. That is, the authors seem to require an identifiable type that poses sexual risk as a form of explanation for events, since they are very careful to assert that homosexuality does not equate with abuse of children. And so 'the paedophile' enters the frame as a type that should have been detected. In addition, the language used – 'inclinations' and 'latent' – suggests an interior being. My argument, here, would be that the arrival of the character type 'the paedophile' works as a potential explanation for events, rather than attention being focused on why and how 'inappropriate sexualised behaviour' (Parrott et al., 2007: 9) – as some of the children's actions are described – and manipulation and actions that raised concerns – as the behaviours of the carers are variously described – were not adequately addressed and contributed to a situation in which sexual abuse took place. Some of the placements with CF and IW, for example, are described as 'highly inappropriate' (Parrott et al., 2007: 86) given the 'type of child for whom [they] had been assessed and approved' (Parrott et al., 2007: 58). But, instead of asking how and why *some* sexual behaviours are deemed 'inappropriate' and others not, and how and why *some* raised concerns whilst others did not, the report tends to focus on failures in risk assessment. That is, whilst discussions of 'the paedophile' are equivocal, the suggestion of an undetected type is inferred.

This failed risk assessment trope also makes appearances in claims that there was a 'lack of a structured approach to seeking and scrutinising information from referees of potential foster carers' (Parrott et al., 2007: 40), and that the social worker's assessment of CF and IW had 'areas of deficit' particularly concerned with 'gender, sex and sexuality', since the worker had been 'trying too hard to focus on their "sameness" ... [that is,] "treating them as just another two people"' (Parrott et al., 2007: 49 and 54):

> Her assessment failed to explore adequately important aspects of the individual psycho-social profiles of CF and IW, their motivations to

foster, their relationship with each other and with others, their sexuality and their attitudes to others' sexuality, and their understanding of emotionally damaged children, experiences of abuse and possible behaviour. None of these gaps was picked up by a supervising team manager or any other peer or senior colleagues. (Parrott et al., 2007: 127)

Here, the report echoes the point, discussed earlier, that assessments of lesbians and gay men – and of anyone, for that matter – that do not ask questions about sex and sexuality are inadequate. For example, on page 49 of the inquiry, Parrott et al. list areas to do with an applicant's sexuality that ought to have been addressed, largely taken from Brown's work (Brown, 1991, 1992). In addition, Appendix 1 reviews my earlier research (Hicks, 1996, 2006b) and suggests that my 'detailed interviews might have provided useful background material for the social worker undertaking the home study in this case, and could have provided useful "homework" for the applicants to stimulate discussion' (Parrott et al., 2007: 156).

However, whilst assessment of good sexual boundaries and an understanding of the need to maintain these is a key part of Brown's arguments, the objections to 'sameness' raised in my work and that of others (including Brown and Cocker, 2008; Cocker and Brown, 2010) relate to the inadequacy of treating gay or lesbian people as though they are heterosexual or, to put this another way, not talking to them about aspects of their lives and potential care of children that relate to being lesbian or gay. Part of the point here is that 'sameness' approaches are actually heteronormative, since they do not recognize or ask about the particularities of being *lesbian or gay* adopters or foster carers, as Nita said. In the Wakefield report, however, criticism of the social worker's 'sameness' approach is not concerned with heteronormative practices but, rather, with the idea that this led to inadequate risk assessment. Thus, they talk about inadequacies, 'irrespective of sexual orientation' (Parrott et al., 2007: 155).

The second trope I'd like to look at is the suggestion that 'social work training...[on] anti-discriminatory and anti-oppressive practice' (Parrott et al., 2007: 124), and a culture of being afraid to speak out against two gay carers because of potential accusations of homophobia, somehow intimidated workers and prevented them raising concerns. There is a suggestion in the report that, because the men were Wakefield's first 'out' gay foster couple, people were afraid to ask questions of their practice. One of the social workers responsible for two of the children placed said:

I think that one of the problems was that the family placement team were very clear that we've got these carers and they are unique...the fact that they were a gay foster couple...we need to do everything to support them, to help them remain foster carers really and that was very clearly coming across even though we were sort of saying, although not stating specifically that we felt the boys were being abused but were saying that we've got numerous concerns about these carers that needed dealing with and...whatever we were saying I felt was not really being listened to one hundred per cent because ultimately they wanted these foster carers to remain foster carers. (Parrott et al., 2007: 74)

This talk is fascinating because it is involved in doing the work of blame allocation – the blame for events lies with the family placement (foster care) team, not with the child care social worker(s). In addition, the social worker suggests that the couple could not be challenged because they were gay, and there is an implication that they were specially treated because of this. The social worker's description of the raising of concerns is crucial, as it indicates the ways in which suspicions about abuse were raised obliquely, if at all. To 'sort of' say something, but not to state it 'specifically', is a key way in which concerns can appear to be clear after the event (for the purposes of an inquiry) but were not at the time. In fact, the only thing that seems clear in this talk – the worker uses the phrase 'very clear/ly' twice – is the suggestion that social workers were not able to raise their concerns due to potential accusations of homophobia. Of course, this is another justificatory technique used after the event – it places the children's social worker in a victim-type role ('I would have spoken out if I could') – but it also locates power with both the gay couple (and, by implication, all gay carers) and the family placement team.

The report itself also uses this kind of explanation, suggesting that CF and IW played on social workers' fears about being called 'prejudiced' in order to deflect inquiries about troubling actions on their part (Parrott et al., 2007: 84). This is repeated in an explanation in which 'the fear of being thought of as homophobic...was just too great' (Parrott et al., 2007: 119). One social worker said, 'you didn't want to be seen discriminating against a same sex couple' (Parrott et al., 2007: 123). But the report authors are also careful to say that this 'explanation' does not fully account for inaction – 'We had a much greater sense of people feeling things and saying nothing. For example, "my blood went cold when I saw the photograph", but "I never for one moment thought they were paedophiles"' (Parrott et al., 2007: 123). Here, again, it is vital to point out that, whilst the fear of being called 'homophobic' is certainly a possible and understandable dynamic for *some* social workers, we should remember that it is also being used as a justificatory device for imputed inaction. To say one is afraid of being called 'homophobic' works to place the self in a powerless/victim-type subject position, in which inaction becomes explainable, and in which the self appears morally good. But this also allows *actually* homophobic notions to be reframed as disallowed concerns; that is, the tone of some of the comments by practitioners in the Wakefield inquiry suggests people who were uncomfortable with the idea of gay men as foster carers, regardless of any concerns about CF and

IW. The authors note this, saying that 'many staff seemed uncomfortable in entering discussion with us about sexuality', and go on to state that some workers' 'understanding, knowledge and experience of people in same-sex relationships, how they communicated ordinarily with them and how they felt about their own and others' sexuality' was questionable. Indeed, some 'seemed unable to discuss sexuality in ways we presumed (rightly or wrongly) they would do with respect to prospective or registered adopters and foster carers whose sexual orientation was heterosexual' (Parrott et al., 2007: 124).

These explanations for events are also doing a lot of work in relation to notions of sexuality and knowledge. The comment 'my blood went cold when I saw the photograph, [but] I never for one moment thought they were paedophiles', for example, returns us again to the notion that a photograph of a child urinating, taken by CF and/or IW, followed by comments by the children that 'CF had taken "loads" of photographs and that there were some photos of them having a wee, having a poo, in the shower and in the bath' (Parrott et al., 2007: 67) is interpreted as appalling, is subject to much formal and informal discussion, is later seen as naïve, then worrying, then 'cute... the sort of photograph that a parent would take of a child' and so on (Parrott et al., 2007: 69–70). That is, whether a particular action or piece of 'evidence' is counted as of concern (much less, 'abuse') is not agreed in any straightforward way, and, without the categorization 'paedophile', the social worker whose 'blood went cold' struggles to turn the artefact into the kind of thing that an 'abuser' would do.

Further, the self-categorization of 'afraid of being called homophobic' also manages to place blame with others, with attitudes towards gay and lesbian people and, by extension, with all gay carers, since it suggests that – without the kind of rampantly anti-homophobic culture that is suggested through social workers' talk – concerns would have been easily raised, addressed and acted upon. I think that the inquiry authors actually feed into this notion by their suggestions that workers were uncomfortable in talking about (homo)sexuality. To say that workers 'seemed unable to discuss sexuality in ways we presumed (rightly or wrongly) they would do with respect to prospective or registered adopters and foster carers whose sexual orientation was heterosexual' (Parrott et al., 2007: 124) *is a 'wrong' presumption* in my view, since the heterosexuality of carers is rarely, if ever, openly discussed. Heteronormative practices mean that most of heterosexuality is assumed or briefly alluded to in discussions about relationships, marriage and (occasionally) sexual expression, but mostly it is *not talked about*, just like race in Chapter 6.

Further evidence of fear of the label 'homophobe' is suggested through talk about 'social work training... ensuring a culture of anti-discriminatory and anti-oppressive practice' leading social workers to have 'blinkered thinking' and being unable to even see, let alone raise, questions about CF and IW (Parrott et al., 2007: 124). The authors state 'staff talked about how the way their social work training – particularly around "non-judgemental attitude", got in the way of their being able to think the unthinkable … One staff member said, "you don't want to reflect negatively on gay couples, especially in the social services".' Yet, at the same time, the authors say they met individuals 'whose beliefs we considered homophobic – particularly about gay men being allowed to become foster carers.' This complicates matters, as what Parrott et al. call 'unexplored homophobia' leads to confusion over prejudice and the fear of 'being seen as prejudiced', so that 'people lost their capacity to discriminate appropriately out of fear of discriminating in the prejudicial sense' (Parrott et al., 2007: 125–6). The authors say they 'found evidence that some of the reluctance to voice concerns about the possibly abusive actions of the carers related to fear of prejudice. This had two aspects: first, that these concerns might really be generated from a personal prejudicial response to their being gay; second, that real suspicions, if voiced, might be reacted to by others as if they were prejudices – including by the carers themselves' (Parrott et al., 2007: 130).

These conclusions are fascinating, as they present a social work culture supposedly dominated by pro-gay attitudes and practices, but one that is, at the same time, full of 'unexplored homophobia'. This suggests that homophobia is a thing undetected or waiting to be expressed, rather than a form of social relations and power. The idea that anti-gay notions are only expressed through overt and obvious homophobia, for example, is very limited since, as we have seen throughout this book so far, ideas about families, gender and sexuality all work through everyday and subtle assertions of heteronormativity. In addition, as Smith has carefully pointed out and was discussed in Chapter 4, ascribing problems or lack of action to homophobia imputes agency to it, as though it were a thing, rather than asking how social relations of ruling within, say, social work organizations are structured by everyday heteronormativity (Smith, 1988, 1990). These are not 'unexplored' or 'repressed' prejudices; they are everyday activities of people and forms of knowledge. For the authors of the inquiry to describe support for gay/lesbian carers or anti-homophobic practice as 'blinkered thinking', for example, is to suggest that all of those who do so cannot entertain the possibility of poor or inappropriate gay carers or the need to ask questions of those carers either in assessment or if practices are of concern.

Whilst there is clearly a tradition of 'non-judgemental thinking' in social work, this ought not to mean the suspension of judgement or analysis *per se*, since it is crucial to acknowledge that all social work involves interpretation, making sense of or *judgement* about others/practices. The notion of being non-judgemental probably expresses an attempt to suggest that social work ought not to judge people negatively on the basis of their sexuality, race, gender, and so on. But the idea of social work without judgement makes no sense, since daily life involves judgement over and over again. How we come to know and talk about sexuality categories, for example, is judgement, and one that results in hierarchical forms of knowledge. To suggest that one cannot question gay or lesbian carers because of a culture of non-judgementalism is to locate the problem within anti-homophobic practice, rather than to ask why and how knowledge about gay foster carers is so limiting and *unspoken.*

If the possibility that two gay carers might be inappropriate or abusive is 'unthinkable' – a strange term, indeed – then the way of knowing about sexuality here seems to offer some kind of reversal in which workers offer ignorance as evidence of a morally good position. Claims that there is a culture of anti-homophobia are used to justify inaction or the dissipating of concerns ('I cannot have known this' or 'I cannot report my concerns'). At the same time, Parrott et al. identify what they describe as homophobic views expressed by individuals, and these seem to centre particularly on the fear of *gay men* caring for children (no doubt, unfortunately, now reaffirmed through the Wakefield case). But this does indicate a work culture that is far from anti-homophobic. Rather, it is mixed, contains practices and ideas that may or may not be described as homophobic, and favours the heteronormative. The authors' use of the word 'fear' is also key here, as it suggests a climate in which workers (who are all written about and discussed as though heterosexual) feel forced into accepting gay foster carers and prevented from asking questions about homosexuality. Whilst it is possible to imagine situations in which no one is able to question homosexuality, my suggestion would be that this is a rather simplistic analysis. Far more salient is the question of 'people feeling things and saying nothing', since this is a common feature of evidence to childcare inquiries and one that is rarely analyzed.

The third trope that stands out for me is that which works to suggest that the inquiry is *not* about homosexuality or the carers being gay. This may seem like an odd position to take in an inquiry *entirely* concerned with questions of sex, sexuality and sexual abuse, but arises out of the wish to make it clear that CF and IW's unsuitability as foster carers ought not to implicate all gay men and lesbians. The report states that it 'is not about the suitability or unsuitability of gay foster carers' and that there 'are many examples in England of successful foster and adoption placements for children with foster carers of different backgrounds, lifestyles and sexual orientations. High quality care is offered to disadvantaged children by many gay carers' (Parrott et al., 2007: 3). This claim is repeated in the court judge's comment that the case 'is not, of course, about homosexuality', the authors' statement that the 'fact that the case involves a gay couple is irrelevant' (Parrott et al., 2007: 7), and:

> There is no conclusion on our part…that there should not be gay or lesbian foster carers in Wakefield or elsewhere…[T]here are many examples

nationally of successful foster caring by people with diverse lifestyles and sexual orientations, in single sex and mixed sex relationships, living alone or with others. There is no reason, we emphasise, for anyone to assume that homosexual foster carers are any more likely to abuse children than heterosexual carers. (Parrott et al., 2007: 130)

Such claims appear necessary within the context of the inquiry in order to avoid accusations of homophobia, to assert general support for gay and lesbian carers and to prevent cooption of the findings by those who wish to oppose all gay parenting. Yet, the question of homosexuality in the inquiry is far from 'irrelevant', since the report deals with 'fear' of accusations of homophobia, the idea that a gay couple cannot be challenged due to a 'non-judgemental/anti-oppressive' culture, homophobic views about gay men as carers, the need to talk to lesbian/gay applicants about their sexuality during assessment, and so on. Further, some of the authors' recommendations hinge on questions of (homo)sexuality, too. For example, they suggest 'awareness training about issues arising from different sexual orientations' and 'learning from the experiences of gay foster carers and the children placed with them' (Parrott et al., 2007: 142 and 144). Yet, as Mallon has argued, '[s]ocial work educators, as well as practitioners, often assume that competence with gay and lesbian groups can be achieved through short-term, and often "one-shot," workshops or gay and lesbian guest speakers' (Mallon, 2006: 71–2).

In addition, this is a policy-led recommendation, which – whilst it may go some way to opening up discussion about gay or lesbian carers – does little to question the everyday forms of homophobia described in the talk by social workers. Further, awareness about 'different sexual orientations' usually means a focus on lesbian, gay and bisexual people – the 'different', here, implies different from heterosexuals – and so this does little to ask questions about heteronormative practices and much to position bisexual, gay and lesbian people as 'other' (and, in social work terms, only ever clients 'out there') to be known about. This is an epistemological question, then, as much as it could be said to be an ethical one, since it revolves around the limited notion that to 'know' gay, bisexual or lesbian people and their 'lifestyles' better is to solve the question of 'homophobia'.

How, for example, would a greater 'awareness' of (homo)sexuality have helped most of the social workers to question or challenge CF and IW's actions or talk, and how would this have helped them to raise their concerns and get these acted upon in dialogue with various other social workers, managers and professionals? In addition, a requirement to attend sexuality 'awareness' training might actually reinforce the notion of a politically-correct/pro-gay culture, which is already used by some of the social workers to justify inaction, to reassert homophobic ideas and to claim ignorance of events or the possibility that discriminatory ideas might have contributed

to the failures in this case. Of course, there are lots of other recommendations in the Wakefield inquiry, many of which are about inadequate social
work structures, resources and practices, and it is important to say this in
order to avoid the notion that the recommendations hinge entirely on the
question of gay carers and homosexuality. Yet, in taking the usual procedurally led focus on outcomes, the inquiry does little to ask more difficult
questions about how notions about sexuality arise in and through social
working. Indeed, the inquiry asserts particular notions of sexuality and
sexual hierarchy itself.

Intervening in heteronormative relations

Lisa Adkins has raised questions about 'neo-liberal modes of regulation
where the voluntary governance of the self increasingly defines "good"
citizenship' (Adkins, 2002: 8). I have highlighted some examples of these
regulatory forms as they occur within state sanctioned child welfare: the
requirement to reassure concerns about gender roles, the avoidance of talk
about sex or sexuality, the infertility test where 'coming to terms with loss' is
expected, the need for evidence of integration with the heterosexual world.
One of the problems with the voluntarist account of the self, such as that
suggested by Giddens (1991, 1992), is 'an overemphasis on the possibilities
of a self-fashioning of identity' (Adkins, 2002: 43). The sexual self produced
through social work assessment, for example, is not a freely fashioned one
on the part of gay or lesbian applicants. Rather, it results from interaction
with state welfare workers and institutional imperatives:

> Whatever sexuality might mean for the individual, it functions as a
> social code, normative framework, principle of social organisation or
> simply put, a way of defining, regulating, and organizing bodies, selves,
> and populations which produce identities, solidarities, and relations of
> domination. (Seidman, 1997: 212)

This applies to social workers as much as it does to gay and lesbian applicants, as one social worker pointed out:

> I had to try to work out what I thought the Panel would ask me about this
> lesbian couple, and it would have been pointless me taking a report to the
> Panel unless I was happy that I'd done so. Basically, you have to represent
> applicants' thoughts and feelings in a way that suits the Panel.

Although chains of blame are at work here – gay and lesbian applicants may
blame social workers; social workers may blame managers or panels; panels
may blame politicians or councillors, and so on – there is a sense in which
gay and lesbian potential parents must be compared with, and live up to, a

heteronormative ideal. Whilst likeness has been a key trope in gay and lesbian parents' narratives about themselves and their children, here likeness has to do with heterosexuality: how *alike* are gay/lesbian and heterosexual parents/carers? Yet – just as with the questions about white norms expressed by black carers in Chapter 6 – gay and lesbian foster care/adoption applicants do not always want to be thought of as *just like* heterosexuals:

> I am not arguing – as I feel many social workers are trapped into trying to prove when presenting carers to panels – that lesbian and gay carers are the same as, or 'as good as' heterosexual carers. Lesbian and gay carers are a different and particular resource for agencies and for some children some lesbian or gay carers may be 'better' or more helpful to them than being placed in a traditional family with heterosexual parents. In some respects we may offer quite similar things to many heterosexual carers, but many of us will offer something quite different. (McDermott, 2002: 2)

Janet McDermott's argument embraces 'difference' because she rejects the notion that lesbian/gay carers/parents must always be compared with heteronormative ideals, but it is also interesting that she acknowledges that social workers, too, are 'trapped' into doing this. In that sense, there are two traps here: to be compared with, and so likened to, heterosexuality; or to be fixed in a place of 'difference'. These traps, in part, relate to questions of institutional relations, since state welfare systems create a problem/disorder – the 'problem of lesbian/gay parents' – which must be disciplined into a version that meets required 'good parent'/risk-avoidant standards. Another way to put this would be to say that heteronormative values and practices are *breached* – as ethnomethodologists would say – when gay/lesbian applicants enter into state child welfare systems, such as foster care and adoption. For, as Howell reminds us, despite 'signs of some degree of liberalising the criteria for becoming adoptive parents, the norm, however, remains a highly conservative stereotypical model of the married couple with a settled way of life and established economy' (Howell, 2006: 155).

My argument would be that norms or relations of ruling are not easily shifted and, further, that they are defended through institutional practices. It is possible to argue, for example, that neo-liberal politics of diversity actually dilute lesbian/gay challenges to institutional norms and reinforce new forms of sexual exclusion. Smith's discussion of lesbian parents' rights 'victories' in Californian legislature, for example, makes just this point, when she shows how the supposed equal treatment of lesbian mothers under child care law actually results in punitive measures against 'poor mothers on welfare' (A.M. Smith, 2009: 843). She describes cases where lesbian couples with children split up, resulting in relationships, not otherwise formally recognized by the state, suddenly being treated as 'equal' for the purposes of pursuing child support claims: 'The postwelfare law is ingenious enough to be exclusionary where the benefits of marriage are concerned while at the same time being broadly inclusive when it comes time to assign support obligations' (A.M. Smith, 2009: 844). Smith argues that this has much to do with shrinking of the welfare state and enforcement of punitive measures against single, female parents with limited resources, rather than a commitment to equal treatment of lesbian/gay parents under the law.

We need to ask similar questions about the forms of relationality, sexuality, gender, race, and so on that are excluded from the frame by social welfare institutions when acceptable versions of the lesbian/gay parent are produced. The processes by which the 'good' gay/lesbian foster carer or adopter is produced and defined, for example, work through technologies of exclusion, as this chapter has argued, and they trap applicants and social workers into making arguments for the maintenance of ideas – gender role, heterosexual networks, standard ideas about family support, avoidance of questions about sex, the infertility imperative – that are actually very limiting ways to think about relational forms. And, although many of these ideas are represented and talked about in psychological, personal and interior forms, they are actually social practices that aim to secure the reproduction of conventional practices of gender, race, sexuality and intimacy.

8
Intimacy

> She knows a woman in her forties who has never married and lives alone. Her life is full of work, good friends, and family, all kinds of passions and forms of self-knowledge. But it's like there's no frame to announce that her life has begun. She knows this is ridiculous, but she swims against a constant undertow.
>
> (Stewart, 2007: 46)

Much of this book has asked about the ways in which new forms of intimacy and relationships are created by gay and lesbian parents. How are bonds, likenesses, connections, belonging, and so on, forged when living on the edge of dominant notions of kin, family and parent/child links? Kathleen Stewart's story about the lone, 40-something woman serves as a reminder, here, that a 'liveable life' (Butler, 2004a: xv) is one that is more easily recognized within discourses about heterosexuality, coupledom and family life. This does not mean that Stewart's character is defined by lack – she creates a life of connections, passions and identity – but it is as though she must be constantly reminded that she is unusual. As Foucault has noted:

> it is quite true that since some of the relationships in society are protected forms of family life, an effect of this is that the variations which are not protected are, at the same time, often much richer, more interesting and creative than the others. But, of course, they are much more fragile and vulnerable. (Foucault, 2000c: 172)

The notion of intimacy itself is a complex one, since, whilst it is often taken to refer to private, couple-based and/or sexual contacts (the idea of 'being intimate' with someone), there are epistemological, social and political aspects to it. Jamieson, for example, reminds us that intimacy is about *'shared detailed knowledge'* (Jamieson, 1998: 8), and states:

> Practices of intimacy refer to practices which cumulatively and in combination create a sense of intimacy between people. These practices

include giving and receiving privileged access to personal resources including time (spending time together but particularly certain types of time: e.g., 'undivided', 'quality' and 'on demand' access to time), knowledge and material things; developing relationship-specific (whether dyadic or collectively developed small group relationships) shared knowledge and understandings, including knowledge of each other and a sense of shared history; performing or receiving practical acts of care; expressing positive affect, care, affection and love. (Jamieson, 2009: 2)

Morgan, too, adds that, in addition to physical and emotional intimacy, intimates 'have particular knowledge of each other' (Morgan, 2009a: 2), and that there are significant examples of intimacy 'which do not include, and may sometimes even reject, any strong sense of family' (Morgan, 2009b: 3). Carol Smart argues that 'the term "personal life" can invoke the social... This is because the very possibility of personal life is predicated upon a degree of self-reflection and also connectedness with others' (Smart, 2007: 28). Thus, to claim intimacy is to reference knowledge and social connection, and it is to enact these at the same time. To be intimate – to claim to have intimacy – seems to suggest superior forms of knowledge, since ideas about knowledge are 'embedded in kinship practices' (Strathern, 2005: 69).

Povinelli's work on the 'intimate event' is highly relevant here, as she talks about notions of normative love being formed at the intersection of two discourses. The first of these she calls the 'autological subject', meaning talk and practices that suggest the possibilities for self-making and creation of new intimate forms. The second is the 'genealogical society', which refers to social constraints on these forms (Povinelli, 2006: 4). Thus, intimacy is 'neither free nor constrained' (Povinelli, 2006: 100). So, gay and lesbian foster care and adoption do not confirm blood or marriage-like ties, but they do create legal bonds. They may challenge heteronormative versions of kin but, at the same time, require kin work in order to create likeness or belonging, as Michelle, Liz, Sarah and Mary argued (Chapter 2). Mary suggested that an 'extraordinary' situation (adoption of children by single lesbian parents) was made 'ordinary' in various ways by them. This is, in part, because subjectivity is forged out of existing discourses about family, connection or kin, but it is also because a feeling of not belonging – or to be seen as someone without intimate connection – is so difficult. This is the tightening of Schneider's 'genealogical grid' (Schneider, 1984: 55), the notion that having genealogy or intimacy becomes the basis for legitimate persons.

Borneman's research (discussed in Chapter 2) reminds us that expected kin relations can be bent out of shape, and his example of the adoption of one gay man by another (Harald and Dieter) is an interesting real life example of what Foucault imagined:

Foucault: We live in a relational world that institutions have considerably impoverished. Society and the institutions which frame it have limited the possibility of relationships because a rich relational world would be very complex to manage. We should fight against the impoverishment of the relational fabric. We should secure recognition for relations of provisional coexistence, adoption...

[G.B.] Interviewer: Of children.

Foucault: Or – why not? – of one adult by another. Why shouldn't I adopt a friend who's ten years younger than I am? And even if he's ten years older? Rather than arguing that rights are fundamental and natural to the individual, we should try to imagine and create a new relational right that permits all possible types of relations to exist and not be prevented, blocked, or annulled by impoverished relational institutions (Foucault, 2000e: 158).

Whilst it is important to acknowledge that much of modern kinship has been stretched out of shape through dissolution of the nature/culture divide (Strathern, 1992) via practices such as assisted reproductive technologies, surrogacy, adoption, step-families, and so on, at the same time there are still strong normativities. Thompson's research on reproductive technologies, for example, identifies 'deeply rooted and familiar ways of forming and claiming kin' (Thompson, 2005: 177) within practices that, at the same time, extend and even deconstruct standard kinship. So, bending of kinship terms and ideas is constrained because this involves formation of subjectivity – or subjectivation – within dominant forms of connection. Adoptees, for example, are frequently expected, even admonished, to seek their 'real' birth family, or this notion is maintained through open adoption and contact with relatives, and much adoption practice seeks to reiterate the standard family.

 This means that normativities do not disappear through practices like gay and lesbian adoption and foster care. As I have argued in Chapters 5, 6 and 7, standard ideas about gender, race and sexuality are produced and used in relation to defining the 'good/acceptable' carer of children. Social workers and gay/lesbian applicants talk in terms of being trapped by expected notions about gender role models, cultural forms, support networks, or ideas about infertility. Black and white lesbians and gay men talk about silences in relation to questions of race and sexuality. Narratives by gay men and lesbians who care for children also draw upon both creative and traditional ways of talking about connections, likeness, belonging and so on. Further, there is a danger in some representations and narratives of the 'same-sex adoptive couple', the white, dyadic homosexual form (perhaps with a transnationally adopted child), becoming a new normativity. That is, a form that most resembles the standard family is promoted over others, such as single adopters, multi-parent families, or extended foster care households. And it is a form that speaks for contemporary notions of diversity politics, one in which the politics of race, nation, gender and sexuality are actually silenced or privatized. The very phrase 'same-sex couple', for example, is an interesting one that nevertheless performs exclusions – it reinforces coupled relations and it allows the words 'bisexual', 'gay', 'lesbian' or 'queer' to remain unspoken.

The idea of the intimate

Morgan has made the point that what is defined as an intimate relationship is one that is highly valued and held in hierarchical contrast to others such as acquaintances (Morgan, 2009a). The relational aspect of this notion – what Plummer calls the *'intersubjective, interactive, interrelated, relational, dialogic, interpersonal, mutual, reciprocal'* (Plummer, 2003: 87) – means that intimacy is not just about 'individually crafted biographies' (Smart, 2007: 29), it has to do with the expression and recognition of social relationships. It also has to do with how relationships are understood and spoken about, so that the very idea of intimacy has a powerful effect upon how people imagine their relationships ought to be and it is a concept used to take up a valued, because connected, subjectivity. To be intimate suggests not only superior forms of connectivity, but also the idea of being a knowing person.

Some authors have also pointed out that certain forms of intimacy are valued over others. Intimacy may be linked to 'domestic space, to kinship, to the couple form, to property, or to the nation' (Berlant and Warner, 1998: 558), which means that many aspects of lesbian, gay or queer lives are displaced from intimate space. Of course, it is for this reason that lesbian, gay and queer people question exclusive intimate forms and argue instead for new, less hierarchical notions, a 'post-traditional intimacy' (Budgeon, 2006, para. 4.12). But, whilst there are practices that open up new spaces of intimacy, Gross' arguments that 'debts to tradition' remain and that the standard, heterosexual family is still dominant are important (Gross, 2005: 306).

Giddens' notion of a 'generic restructuring of intimacy' into the 'pure relationship' (Giddens, 1992: 58), a freely chosen and mutually satisfying bond based on autonomous and democratic relations, sounds idealistic. Several authors offer critiques of Giddens, which centre on his ignorance of social and gendered inequalities (Evans, 2003; Jackson and Scott, 2010; Jamieson, 1998, 1999; Plummer, 2005; Taylor, 2009) and the possibility that his story may just reinforce the idea that, unless we are all in mutually satisfying and egalitarian couple relationships, we are lacking, disconnected, miserable or demonstrating 'fear of intimacy/commitment' (Heaphy, 2007; Jackson and Scott, 1997; Jamieson, 1999; Kipnis, 2003). Giddens' work contributes to a notion of modern intimacy that 'presumes that the majority of [our] needs can and should be met by one person alone' (Kipnis, 2003: 71–2), and it also presents overly optimistic and generalized accounts of lesbian and gay relationships as prime examples. Whilst this may be echoed in some theorists' work on gay intimacies (Stacey, 2005), others have pointed out that most gay and lesbian relationships are far more complicated and fallible than notions of the 'pure' allow (Carrington, 1999; Gross, 2005; Heaphy et al., 2004; Jamieson, 1998). They may draw upon traditional or dominant ideas about connection, they may prioritize couple relations above all others, and there are those who have argued that parenthood represents a properly mature and superior phase of gay life.

In addition, the levels or forms of reflexivity required by the 'pure relationship' are premised on the notion of opportunity and choice. Giddens says the 'pure relationship' is 'not anchored in external conditions of social or economic life – it is, as it were, free-floating' (Giddens, 1991: 89). This reflexive, intimate self is one based on 'a vision of a mobile relation to identity' (Adkins, 2002: 86), which imputes '*lack* of mobility' to some (Adkins, 2002: 99). In Chapter 6, black people, for example, talk about their fixing in place *as a culture* or even *as a damaged or deficient culture* by social welfare practices and professionals, which denies them much sense of mobility in relation to identity. Further, Giddens' notion of modern intimacy doesn't seem to allow much space for questions of parenting (and other non-coupled relations), as its focus on the self and self-fashioning ignores relational ethics and practices of care.

Yet, at the same time, notions of 'invention', 'reinvention', 'choice', 'creation' and the 'do-it-yourself' family have spoken to, or are used by, lesbian and gay parents (Benkov, 1994; Mallon, 2004; Martin, 1993; McDermott, 2004; Stacey, 1996; Weeks et al., 2001), since they wish to acknowledge the work that goes into creating bonds that are otherwise unrecognized or misrecognized within heteronormative relations. Mary, Liz, Sarah and Michelle's talk of the 'triple whammy' effect of trying to create new intimacies and parent/child relations as single, lesbian adopters highlights the ways in which they feel they are not given the same recognition that heterosexual, coupled and biologically linked ones are. Indeed, it is possible to argue that gay and lesbian foster care and adoption, of any variety, asks questions about dominant ideas of parenting/family. It also challenges notions about the categories 'lesbian' and 'gay', since these do not normally include notions of parenting/fostering/adopting, a point that helps to explain not only why there is some general suspicion of, and opposition to, gay parenting but also why some lesbian, gay, bisexual and trans people are opposed to this, too.

This has to do with shifts in the possibilities of self, identity and category. That is, the possibility of becoming a gay parent, a lesbian adopter, and so on is a fairly recent story (Plummer, 1995, 2003; Weeks et al., 2001), and many gay parents tell stories of impossibility/regret shifting to realization. But these shifts have been slow to impact on the wider trans/lesbian/bisexual/gay communities. They have also been slow to impact upon social welfare law and practice, with legislation in the UK, for example, actually taking some time to catch up with the practices of gay/lesbian foster care/adoption that have been going on for a while. This is also slowly making an impact on social welfare practice, with some foster care and adoption agencies attempting to work more fairly with gay and lesbian applicants (Mallon and Betts, 2005; Manchester City Council, 2007; Romaine, 2003), but – as we saw in Chapter 7 – with heteronormative views and techniques still in place.

The claiming of intimate connections, or of 'family' as we saw in Chapter 3, happens within discourse – narrative, practices, images – but, for this to make wider sense, there is some use of recognizable forms. Lesbian and gay families are subject to deviant positioning, and so this is questioned in a variety of ways. For example, the book *Love Makes a Family* (Kaeser and Gillespie, 1999) makes use of diversity politics in order to represent subjects as just one of a range of contemporary family forms. Yet, at the same time, wider hierarchies of relational forms are at work, and there is also a danger, through diversity politics, of fixing 'the gay family' as a particular type. The book uses the 'normal, everyday family' trope, yet reports on, and attempts to challenge, practices of exclusion that position gay families as other, dangerous or deficient. The images themselves work to make the gay family visible and to present a positive view, but their artfulness is, at least in part, made up of recognizable devices of staging, format and so on. The ever-present story of 'I always wanted to be a parent but never thought that I would', another im/possibility account that features in *Love Makes a Family*, is a prime example of the employment of recognizable tropes. It references notions of the natural and of standard family stories in order to gain acceptance.

At the same time, these stories also draw on notions of chosen or elective kin to mark out some difference. But, as many theorists have pointed out, we need to remember that the notion of choice is itself a story, and a rather limited one (Allan, 1989; Jamieson, 1998; Mason, 2008; Pahl and Spencer, 2004; Smart, 2007; Spencer and Pahl, 2006; Taylor, 2009). Gay and lesbian people's talk about 'chosen family' or 'friends as family' is important as it does carve out a place for new intimacies other than those based on blood/marriage-like ties, but it is noticeable that these notions employ the language of choice and/or family. That is, recognizable forms of the mobile/reflexive consumer and of expected relational types are used to account for what might otherwise be denigrated connections. The intimate becomes associated with consumer capital (Illouz, 2007) and 'a range of economic, racial, gender, and national privileges' (Freeman, 2007: 304) that allow for the very idea of choice are assumed. Further, as Jacqui Gabb suggests, the notion that all lesbians and gay men form an elective community of friends is in danger of becoming a new imperative that denies the centrality of the couple in many lives, and makes those who do not have chosen families feel wanting (Gabb, 2001b, 2008). Sara Ahmed adds that this imperative suggests simplistic notions of assimilation/transgression, but these are 'not choices that are available to individuals, but are effects of how subjects can and cannot inhabit social norms and ideals' (Ahmed, 2004: 153).

Weston's discussion of chosen families is important, here, as it is vital to remember that she makes use of the concept of 'choice', not to refer to merely choosing friends as family but, rather, as a choice to reject standard forms of kinship. She says, 'families we choose do not rest directly upon a genealogical referent' (Weston, 1991: 193) and that they are 'defined through contrast with biological or blood family' (Weston, 1991: 211). This is about an intervention into the politics of family, and it is one that can be 'radically innovative and thoroughly assimilationist' at the same time (Weston, 1998: 64), since 'the claim that chosen families are "real" families effectively highlights the indeterminate and ultimately contextually defined meaning of "family" as a category' (Weston, 1998: 79). The idea of lesbian/gay/queer families as freely chosen is a 'persistent misreading', Weston says (Weston, 1998: 85), since choices are constrained and also because diversity in family forms has been around for a very long time. 'Choice' can also privatize these issues so that questions of political challenge or anti-heteronormativity are lost.

As I have argued in Chapter 7, the notion of choice in relation to gay and lesbian foster care or adoption applicants doesn't really make much sense, as here the constraining forms of welfare governmentality take hold. Assessment practices present a version of the lesbian or gay person, in written form to a panel of experts, which is not, in any way, a straightforward description of that applicant. To use Smith's phrase, it is a 'virtual reality' (Smith, 1990b: 74), one that serves the purposes of the welfare organization. Indeed, broader notions of intimacy (including the idea of the elective family) have little space within social welfare ruling relations so that, for example, networks based on friendship rather than blood are treated as unusual. This seems particularly ironic in the context of foster care and adoption services, which are about the creation of intimate ties *not* based upon blood.

I have made extensive use of narratives about everyday life by gay and lesbian parents in this book because I wanted to avoid over-generalized, either/or statements, of the 'they're all either assimilative/conservative or challenging/radical' type. I have suggested that lesbian and gay parents' narratives make use of recognizable forms, such as stories about routines, housework and other mundane labours, in order to appear like an everyday, normal family, yet, at the same time, these sit alongside explicit acknowledgement of the *work* that goes into producing connection and a sense of the ordinary. Nita and Clare's account (in Chapter 4), for example, demonstrates a self-conscious incorporation of the relevance of sexuality into their daily lives, whether this be through the overt rejection of standard, heterosexually-derived gender roles, an 'up-front'-ness about being lesbian adopters, or the making relevant of their lesbianism within contexts such as children's schools, health services and so on. I referred to the idea of a *background category presence* here, meaning that – for most gay and lesbian parents – sexuality is always relevant to social scenes even when it remains unspoken. This is because gay parents often have to anticipate situations where their sexuality might be overlooked or misrepresented (in school work on 'the family', for example), and they do not wish their children to carry the responsibility of either discussing their parents' sexuality or shielding their parents from possible discrimination.

Gay parents live with mundane homophobia, and their reports of this are often very ordinary. Remember Sarah's account of homophobia at her adopted children's school (in Chapter 4)? As Sacks has argued, 'people report … the *ordinariness* of what happened' (Sacks, 1995, vol. 2: 216) so that, as a person, they are not taken to be extraordinary or misguided. This may be because homophobic ideas are fairly quotidian to most gay and lesbian people, and it may also be that my respondents expected me – a gay researcher, someone that many of them knew to have been a former foster carer – to recognize the ordinariness of such events. In addition, being a gay/lesbian parent with adopted or fostered children is to be subject to exclusive, dominant discourses in an everyday way. Smith's ruling relations of the everyday – that is, 'a complex of organized practices, including government, law, business and financial management, professional organization, and educational institutions as well as the discourses in texts that interpenetrate the multiple sites of power' (Smith, 1987: 3) – turns family life into an objectified and standardized form against which others are measured. For this reason, Nita and Clare talk about being 'up-front' in order to intervene into those ruling relations, to make lesbian and adoptive connections present, to bring a background category into the foreground. Similarly, in Róisín Ryan-Flood's study, lesbian mothers 'self-confidently and unapologetically' disclosed their sexuality so that 'they neutralised other people's responses' (Ryan-Flood, 2009: 105). Yet, there are many situations in which this may not be possible or where it even becomes dangerous.

I have argued that gender and race are part of the relational, since ideas about these often work by reference to notions of intimacy (concerns about gender role modelling; questions about likeness; race being more or less remarkable in certain settings). Concern about gender roles within gay and lesbian families is key to social welfare practice, and social workers, as well as gay or lesbian foster care/adoption applicants, are required to answer to this. At the same time, respondents have shown that they question some of these ideas through challenge. They ask awkward questions or they enact gender in different ways. Parenting is read through gendered ideas, so gay men, for example, raise concern for some who do not allow the category of 'parent/carer' to include either 'gay' or 'man'. Gay male parents are acutely conscious of this and of ideas about them as improperly gendered beings – remember William's 'shame' about his young son playing in high heels? Others, such as Mark, emphasize the *maleness* of their parenting, but play down being gay, as though acknowledgement of being a gay parent in some situations spoils an otherwise respected, if minority, identity. Some embrace gender dissidence (Peter's 'but why can't we both be "Mummy"?') but, at the same time, are highly conscious of the views of others and of not wanting to place their child in a difficult situation. Gender performance is a central part of the ways in which subjectivity is taken up and, whilst this does not mean that it must be taken up in expected ways, finding a place within discourses about family, relationships or connections is made much more difficult by dis-identification with those expectations.

Black respondents, similarly, have talked about ways in which they may be excluded from certain groups/communities via suggestions that they are *not like* the majority or do not belong. Louise's example of being made to feel different within a local, majority white community relates to ways in which belonging is racialized. Others have talked about the ways in which a black self is constructed as an identity or 'culture' which must be passed on to children in much the same way that a gender role is imagined to be. This turning of questions of race into an interior self is then linked to fears about the passing on of a damaged racial self, as examples from Toni (the 'transracially adopted/damaged' self), Justina (the 'culturally and deficient other') and Nita and Clare (the 'insufficiently authentically cultured') show. Ideas about the proper passing on of the gendered and racialized/cultured self have to do with the maintenance of dominant ideas and heteronormativity: it is the heterosexual couple that is imagined to pass these on without problem in most cases.

Intimacy is also about the creation of differences, so that intimate contact with others is a part of the way in which racial difference is upheld. 'You see on some faces', as Louise says. Notions of race and culture are made via intimate contact, so that ideas about, for example, a cultural self are produced through contrast and in dialogue with powerful norms. Intimacy, too, is created via racist ideas so that notions about family/nation/

community are dependent upon racial exclusions. As Back and Shamser Sinha say, 'a racist discourse of automatic belonging operates alongside and sometimes within claims about inclusiveness and even ... "diversity" ' (Back and Sinha, 2010: 1).

In part, my argument has been that neo-liberal versions of state welfare, premised on notions of 'diversity culture', actually obscure dominant and heteronormative values. In addition, they may actually protect homophobic ideas (as in the case of the Sexual Orientation Regulations 2007 or the Wakefield inquiry into sexual abuse by gay carers). Within foster care and adoption agencies, ideas about infertility, gender roles and the standard family or network are all forms of ruling relations that gay and lesbian applicants are expected to address and conform to at some level. Of course, respondents express their opposition to these ideas and challenge them through irony, jokes, questions, acting differently, and so on. But still, these ways of thinking – these knowledge forms – are powerful technologies for the production of ideas about family, care, gender, sexuality, race and the like. And they create hierarchy:

> why, when there are so many people, [does] only one plot count ... as 'life' (first comes love, then ...)? Those who don't or can't find their way in that story – the queers, the single, the something else – can become so easily unimaginable, even often to themselves. (Berlant, 1998: 286)

Perhaps this explains, in part, why the narratives of gay parenting that I have considered do draw upon standard plots ('love makes a family'), since to become an imaginable self requires finding a place within discourse. As Butler argues, 'the very terms by which we give an account, by which we make ourselves intelligible to ourselves and to others, are not of our making. They are social in character, and they establish social norms' (Butler, 2005: 21). Lauren Berlant argues that a public, 'collective intimacy through which official mass nationality stays familiar' operates alongside a 'privatized "normal" nation of heterosexual, reproductive family values' (Berlant, 2005: 179). To ask questions about such normative family representations is to be seen to be trespassing upon 'private' space, where notions of private life are associated with the heterosexual familiar and with the idea of the individualized, unfettered self. Yet, as Rose has suggested, our 'personalities, subjectivities, and "relationships" are not private matters, if this implies that they are not the objects of power. On the contrary, they are intensively governed' (Rose, 1999: 1).

This is a crucial point, since it is possible, when thinking about the production of stories, narratives, images and ideas about gay parents, to forget that performance requires a scene and an audience. As Kessler and McKenna put it, 'most of the work is done for the displayer by the perceiver' (1985: 136). This is one of the reasons that I have tried to concentrate upon the ordinary daily scene of lesbian and gay parents' lives, since arguments that gay families are essentially conservative, essentially radical, essentially egalitarian, essentially challenging of gender norms, essentially ... *anything*, are simplistic, as they do not ask how and why subject positions are taken up in different ways in different contexts, or how they are read by others. One of those contexts, I have suggested, is an ordinary, everyday homophobia (Chapter 4), one that must be negotiated by all members in lesbian/gay households and families. My respondents are acutely aware of this, and have talked about how they resist, challenge and negotiate the heteronormative. In that sense, their lives are neither wholly ordinary nor extraordinary, since being a lesbian or gay parent – making and taking up that kind of subject position – involves both. Stanley reminds us that 'the quotidian – that is, the everyday and seemingly mundane and commonplace – is at one and the same time both ordinary and extraordinary' (Stanley, 2010: 2).

Queer genealogies?

> In many ways the concept of performativity is set, in principle, against a conception of lineage or generational connection. Indeed, the thrust of the argument is precisely opposed to those who might insist upon the importance of such concerns. For the notion of performativity insists that any apparent continuity across time and space be treated suspiciously, that it be, analytically speaking, punctuated and fragmented, understood as a fragile accomplishment achieved through processes of citation and repetition. (Bell, 2007: 29)

Vikki Bell's point about performativity is relevant to my arguments since she highlights that, as a concept, it can be used to foreground the ways in which the connected or the relational must be claimed, enacted or practised. This contrasts with assumed, automatic connections related to ideas of traditional blood-kinship. To make a connection, to make an intimate relation, requires reiteration or display, a point that helps to question notions of automatic continuities. Although it is also important to remember that even blood and marriage-like ties have to be enacted and reiterated in order to matter, it's just that these processes are less obvious or self-conscious than with other relational practices.

This is one of the reasons that I have made use of sociological theories drawn from ethnomethodology, institutional ethnography, discourse, queer and feminist theories, since all of these, in different ways, see the social as enacted and turn their analytic attention to people's situated, everyday practices. These forms of sociology concern themselves with social interaction, with ascribed meanings, and with the material practices and effects that are a part of any discourse. Thus, my focus has been on the relational, rather than the individual. In part, this is because social meanings are produced through interaction, within a particular time and space, but it is also because the social categories I have considered have both enabling and disciplinary effects. To produce the self in terms of gender, race, culture, sexuality, connection, kinship, family, and so on, is to produce categories of knowledge.

In an interview, 'Friendship as a Way of Life,' Foucault asked a challenging question, 'What relations, through homosexuality, can be established, invented, multiplied, and modulated?' (Foucault, 2000a: 135). He asked, in relation to gay men, how it was possible to 'be together... [not] necessarily in the form of a couple... What is it to be "naked" among men, outside of institutional relations, family, profession, and obligatory camaraderie?' (Foucault, 2000a: 136). Foucault referred to 'friendship' as summing up the creativity that is inevitably a part of gay relations, but also what causes disturbance; that is, 'affection, tenderness, friendship, fidelity, camaraderie, and companionship, things that our rather sanitized society can't allow a place for without fearing the formation of new alliances and the tying together of unforeseen lines of force' (Foucault, 2000a: 136).

My book has highlighted questions of 'recognition' as a problem. This is a dilemma that other theorists have analyzed (Butler, 2004b; Fraser and Honneth, 2003; McNay, 2008) since, to seek recognition by the state and others, is to enter into the terms of dominant ways of living; that is, the state recognizes only certain, limited relational forms. To be recognized involves some acceptance of state-approved ways of life, yet to be un/misrecognized hurts. Gillespie's argument about representations in *Love Makes a Family* (Kaeser and Gillespie, 1999) sums up recognition's limits:

> But in the name of getting equal rights in this country [USA], it is probably 'better' to just portray the more traditional gay/lesbian families and not focus on for example a family that is involved in a group marriage or multiple partners, etc. (Gillespie, personal communication – feedback on my work, 2009).

Yet, as Janet Jakobsen and Ann Pellegrini say, 'Why should some consensual ways of doing intimacy and family get the stamp of state approval and others not?' (Jakobsen and Pellegrini, 2004: 142). Foucault made the point that, 'if what we want to do is to create a new way of life [*mode de vie*], then the question of individual rights is not pertinent' (Foucault, 2000e: 158), and 'state approval' is not necessarily the goal for many trans, bisexual, queer, lesbian or gay parents. Yet, it has also been interesting, in this book, to examine stories about foster care and adoption, since these necessarily involve entry into relations with, and approval by, state welfare representatives. Chapter 7 details state recognition and it discontents, and my participants talk about many situations in which they are misrecognized.

I'd like to return, finally, to some examples in which the queering of genealogical ideas is a possibility, since my argument is that many of my research participants have raised concerns about the limitations of what Riggs calls relationships based upon 'possessive investments' (Riggs, 2006b: 91; 2010: 121). Riggs' argument criticizes both the racial privilege of 'normative whiteness informing queer rights' (Riggs, 2006b: 94) and asks for an understanding of families 'constituted in ways other than through a logic of possession' (Riggs, 2010: 122). He reminds us, for example, that 'children are centrally involved in the creation of the category "parent" – it is only through relationships with children that adults come to define themselves as parents' (Riggs, 2010: 126), and he raises points about the politics of adoption which, as other authors also argue, invoke necessary questions about privilege, racial dynamics, poverty and class (Eng, 2010; Lehr, 1999; Puar, 2007; Roberts, 2002).

Nevertheless, the tendency to propose new relational forms as more radical/queer than others is not a solution, here, since, as Foucault said, as 'soon as a program is presented, it becomes a law, and there's a prohibition against inventing' (Foucault, 2000a: 139). Perhaps a more challenging, and difficult, approach is to draw from ideas about ambivalence (Pidduck, 2009), questioning possessive investments (Riggs, 2006b, 2010), notions of subjectivation (Faubion, 2001) and poststructural accounts of kinship (Eng, 2003, 2010), to ask whether queer genealogies are possible. Gay, lesbian and queer parents and their children make use of kinship claims, but they are conscious of the *work* involved in such formations, and of the possibilities for un/misrecognition. This relationship to kinship is anguished, and has many gaps and ambivalences, yet it is the acknowledgement of these ambivalences that might allow for less hierarchical notions of subjectivity/connection. To become a subject, to take up subjectivity, necessitates taking up a place within discourses with limited, constraining possibilities. People want to belong, or they want to be a subject that is seen to belong, and yet all forms of belonging, at some level, are exclusive.

Any objections to the genealogical grid, however, may be written off as 'mistakes and aberrations of a well-intentioned system', or through 'situating the intimate event beside a contrasting evil' (Povinelli, 2006: 198–9). This implies that questions of privilege and propriety must be considered, since the taking up of some positions, particularly those to do with family, nation, recognition and even being 'ordinary', may rely upon disavowal of others, achieved through the technologies of race, culture, gender and sexuality. Or, subjects may own the voices or perspectives of others, speaking for them, as Aves' article about Mina, Marisa and Judy did (Aves, 1998). To think about the poststructural is to pay close attention to claims and assertions about meaning within texts, narratives and pictures, but also to ask how ideas about family, kinship or relationality work through representation and exclusion, since 'the distinctions we make are not necessarily given by the world around us, but are instead produced by the symbolizing systems we learn' (Belsey, 2002: 7).

As Eng (2010) argues, to have more than one mother ('carer') has to be allowed, so that children's links with two lesbian mums, with a birth mother and a foster mother, with a gay dad, with a donor dad, with those outside of the family, and so on, become possibilities, and so that relational practices be expanded beyond hierarchical, impoverished and limiting genealogies. This might open up space, neither solely public nor private, domestic nor political, in which those in sexual relationships and those who are not, those in couples and those in other relationships, those who are connected and those who are not, those who choose to care for children and those who choose not to, are not compared for the purposes of maintaining superior ways of living. Perhaps this book, too, might contribute to a less fixed or disciplinary account of lesbian and gay parenting, since it offers a sociological concern with complexity, the everyday, ambivalence and the possibilities contained within desire.

References

Adkins, Lisa (2002) *Revisions: Gender and Sexuality in Late Modernity* (Buckingham: Open University Press).

Agigian, Amy (2004) *Baby Steps: How Lesbian Alternative Insemination is Changing the World* (Middletown, CT: Wesleyan University Press).

Ahmed, Sara (2004) *The Cultural Politics of Emotion* (Edinburgh: Edinburgh University Press).

Alderson, Lynn and Crane, Elizabeth (2004) 'Assessing Lesbians and Gay Men: A Lesbian Social Worker's Perspective', *PinkParents Magazine* (UK), 14, 33–4.

Allan, Graham A. (1979) *A Sociology of Friendship & Kinship* (London: George Allen & Unwin).

Allan, Graham (1989) *Friendship: Developing a Sociological Perspective* (Hemel Hempstead: Harvester Wheatsheaf).

Allen, Mike and Burrell, Nancy (1996) 'Comparing the Impact of Homosexual and Heterosexual Parents on Children: Meta-Analysis of Existing Research', *Journal of Homosexuality*, 32:2, 19–35.

Almack, Kathryn (2007) 'Out and About: Negotiating the Layers of Being Out in the Process of Disclosure of Lesbian Parenthood', *Sociological Research Online*, 12:1, http://www.socresonline.org.uk/12/1/almack.html [accessed 1 April 2011].

Almack, Kathryn (2008a) 'Display Work: Lesbian Parent Couples and Their Families of Origin Negotiating New Kin Relationships', *Sociology*, 42:6, 1183–99.

Almack, Kathryn (2008b) 'Women Parenting Together: A Reflexive Account of the Ways in Which the Researcher's Identity and Experiences May Impact Upon the Processes of Doing Research', *Sociological Research Online*, 13:1, http://www.socresonline.org.uk/13/1/4.html [accessed 1 April 2011].

Almond, Brenda (2006) *The Fragmenting Family* (Oxford: Clarendon Press).

Anderssen, Norman, Christine Amie and Erring André Ytterøy (2002) 'Outcomes for Children with Lesbian or Gay Parents: A Review of Studies from 1978 to 2000', *Scandinavian Journal of Psychology*, 43, 335–51.

Armstrong, Rebecca, Ed Caesar and Kate Hilpern (2007) 'Gay Adoption: True Stories', *The Independent* (UK), 25 January, http://www.independent.co.uk/news/uk/this-britain/gay-adoption-true-stories-852722.html [accessed 1 April 2011].

Atkinson, Paul (1997) 'Narrative Turn or Blind Alley?' *Qualitative Health Research*, 7:3, 325–44.

Averett, Paige, Blace Nalavany and Scott Ryan (2009) 'An Evaluation of Gay/Lesbian and Heterosexual Adoption', *Adoption Quarterly*, 12:3/4, 129–51.

Aves, Corinne (1998) 'Assessment for Adoption: The Child's Perspective', *Journal of Social Work Practice*, 12:1, 31–8.

Back, Les (1996) *New Ethnicities and Urban Culture: Racisms and Multiculture in Young Lives* (London: University College London (UCL) Press).

Back, Les (2007) *The Art of Listening* (Oxford: Berg).

Back, Les and Sinha, Shamser (2010) *Racism's Social Weight*, Forum of Concerned Citizens of Europe [website no longer available 1 April 2011].

Bailey, J. Michael, David Borrow, Marilyn Wolfe and Sarah Mikach (1995) 'Sexual Orientation of Adult Sons of Gay Fathers', *Developmental Psychology*, 31:1, 124–9.

Baker, Paul (2008) *Sexed Texts: Language, Gender & Sexuality* (London: Equinox Publishing).

Ball, Carlos A. and Pea, Janice Farrell (1998) 'Warring with Wardle: Morality, Social Science, and Gay and Lesbian Parents', *University of Illinois Law Review*, 2, 253–339.

Baraitser, Lisa (2009) *Maternal Encounters: The Ethics of Interruption* (London: Routledge).

Barnard, Ian (2003) *Queer Race: Cultural Interventions in the Racial Politics of Queer Theory* (New York: Peter Lang).

Barrett, Helen and Tasker, Fiona (2001) 'Growing Up with a Gay Parent: Views of 101 Gay Fathers on Their Sons' and Daughters' Experiences', *Educational & Child Psychology*, 18:1, 62–77.

Beck-Gernsheim, Elisabeth (2002) *Reinventing the Family: In Search of New Lifestyles* (Cambridge: Polity Press).

Bell, David and Binnie, Jon (2000) *The Sexual Citizen: Queer Politics and Beyond* (Cambridge: Polity Press).

Bell, Vikki (2007) *Culture and Performance: The Challenges of Ethics, Politics and Feminist Theory* (Oxford: Berg).

Belsey, Catherine (2002) *Poststructuralism: A Very Short Introduction* (Oxford: Oxford University Press).

Benkov, Laura (1994) *Reinventing the Family: The Emerging Story of Lesbian & Gay Parents* (New York: Crown).

Benson, Adam L., Louise B. Silverstein and Carl F. Auerbach (2005) 'From the Margins to the Center: Gay Fathers Reconstruct the Fathering Role', *Journal of GLBT Family Studies*, 1:3, 1–29.

Beresford, Sarah (1994) 'Lesbians in Residence and Parental Responsibility Cases', *Family Law*, November, 643–5.

Berlant, Lauren (1998) 'Intimacy: A Special Issue', *Critical Inquiry*, 24:2, 281–8.

Berlant, Lauren (2005) *The Queen of America Goes to Washington City: Essays on Sex and Citizenship* (Durham, NC: Duke University Press).

Berlant, Lauren and Warner, Michael (1995) 'What Does Queer Theory Teach Us about X?' *PMLA*, 110:1, 343–9.

Berlant, Lauren and Warner, Michael (1998) 'Sex in Public', *Critical Inquiry*, 24:2, 547–66.

Bersani, Leo (1995) *Homos* (Cambridge: Harvard University Press).

Bhabha, Homi K. (2004 [1994]) *The Location of Culture* (London: Routledge).

Bhatt, Chetan (1997) *Liberation and Purity: Race, New Religious Movements and the Ethics of Postmodernity* (London: University College London (UCL) Press).

Biblarz, Timothy J. and Stacey, Judith (2010) 'How Does the Gender of Parents Matter?' *Journal of Marriage & Family*, 72, 3–22.

Bigner, Jerry J. and Bozett, Frederick W. (1990) 'Parenting by Gay Fathers', in F.W. Bozett and M.B. Sussman (eds.) *Homosexuality and Family Relations* (New York: Harrington Park Press): 155–75.

Binnie, Jon (2004) *The Globalization of Sexuality* (London: Sage).

Blankenhorn, David (1995) *Fatherless America: Confronting Our Most Urgent Social Problem* (New York: Basic Books).

Borneman, John (2001) 'Caring and Being Cared For: Displacing Marriage, Kinship, Gender, and Sexuality', in J.D. Faubion (ed.) *The Ethics of Kinship: Ethnographic Inquiries* (Lanham, MD: Rowman & Littlefield): 29–46.

Borshay, Deann (dir) (2000) *First Person Plural* (San Francisco: National Asian American Telecommunications Association).

Bos, Henny M.W., Nanette K. Gartrell, Heidi Peyser and Frank van Balen (2008a) 'The USA National Longitudinal Lesbian Family Study (NLLFS): Homophobia, Psychological Adjustment, and Protective Factors', *Journal of Lesbian Studies*, 12:4, 455–71.

Bos, Henny M.W., Nanette K. Gartrell, Frank van Balen, Heidi Peyser and Theo G.M. Sandfort (2008b) 'Children in Planned Lesbian Families: A Cross-Cultural Comparison Between the United States and the Netherlands', *American Journal of Orthopsychiatry*, 78:2, 211–19.

Bozett, Frederick W. (1987) 'Gay Fathers', in F.W. Bozett (ed.) *Gay and Lesbian Parents* (New York: Praeger): 3–22.

Bozett, Frederick W. (1989) 'Gay Fathers: A Review of the Literature', in F.W. Bozett (ed.) *Homosexuality and the Family* (New York; Harrington Park Press): 137–62.

Brenkman, John (2002a) 'Politics, Mortal and Natal: An Arendtian Rejoinder', *Narrative*, 10:2, 186–92.

Brenkman, John (2002b) 'Queer Post-Politics', *Narrative*, 10:2, 174–80.

Brewaeys, Anne, I. Ponjaert-Kristoffersen, A.C. Van Steirteghem and P. Devroey (1993) 'Children from Anonymous Donors: An Inquiry into Homosexual and Heterosexual Parents' Attitudes', *Journal of Psychomatic Obstetrics & Gynaecology*, 14, 23–35.

Brewaeys, Anne, I. Ponjaert, E.V. Van Hall and Susan Golombok (1997) 'Donor Insemination: Child Development and Family Functioning in Lesbian Mother Families', *Human Reproduction*, 12:6, 1349–59.

Brinamen, Charles F. (2000) 'On Becoming Fathers: Issues Facing Gay Men Choosing to Parent', *Dissertation Abstracts International*, 61:5-B, 2794.

British Agencies for Adoption and Fostering (1991) *Form F: Information on Prospective Substitute Parent(s)* (London: BAAF).

British Association for Adoption and Fostering (2005) *Form F,* revised edn (London: BAAF).

British Association for Adoption and Fostering (2009) *Press Release: Statement from BAAF on Today's Front Page of the Daily Mail* (London: BAAF).

Brodzinsky, David M. (2011) 'Adoption by Lesbians and Gay Men: A National Survey of Adoption Agency Policies and Practices', in D.M. Brodzinsky and A. Pertman (eds.) *Adoption by Lesbians and Gay Men: A New Dimension in Family Diversity* (New York: Oxford University Press), forthcoming.

Brodzinsky, David M., Charlotte J. Patterson and Mahnoush Vaziri (2002) 'Adoption Agency Perspectives on Lesbian and Gay Prospective Parents: A National Study', *Adoption Quarterly*, 5:3, 5–23.

Brodzinsky, David M., Robert-Jay Green and Katie Katuzny (2011) 'Adoption by Lesbians and Gay Men: What We Know, Need to Know, and Ought to Do', in D.M. Brodzinsky and A. Pertman (eds.) *Adoption by Lesbians and Gay Men: A New Dimension in Family Diversity* (New York: Oxford University Press), forthcoming.

Brodzinsky, David M. and Staff of the Evan B. Donaldson Adoption Institute (2003) *Adoption by Lesbians and Gays: A National Survey of Adoption Agency Policies, Practices, and Attitudes* (New York: Evan B. Donaldson Adoption Institute), http://www.adoptioninstitute.org/whowe/Gay%20and%20Lesbian%20Adoption1.html [accessed 1 April 2011].

Bronski, Michael (2001) 'Queer as Your Folks: A New Study Says Gay Parents Create Gay Kids. How Will This Research be Used by Conservatives – and Liberals?' *The Boston Phoenix*, 2–9 August. http://www.bostonphoenix.com/boston/news_features/top/features/documents/01743257.htm [accessed 1 April 2011].

Brooks, Devon and Goldberg, Sheryl (2001) 'Gay and Lesbian Adoptive and Foster Care Placements: Can They Meet the Needs of Waiting Children?' *Social Work*, 46:2, 147– 56.

Brown, Helen Cosis (1991) 'Competent Child-Focused Practice: Working with Lesbian and Gay Carers', *Adoption & Fostering*, 15:2, 11–17.

Brown, Helen Cosis (1992) 'Gender, Sex and Sexuality in the Assessment of Prospective Carers', *Adoption & Fostering*, 16:2, 30–4.

Brown, Helen Cosis (1998) *Social Work and Sexuality: Working with Lesbians and Gay Men* (Basingstoke: Macmillan).

Brown, Helen Cosis (2008) 'Social Work and Sexuality, Working with Lesbians and Gay Men: What Remains the Same and What is Different?' *Practice*, 20:4, 265–75.

Brown, Helen Cosis (2011) 'The Assessment of Lesbian and Gay Prospective Foster Carers: Twenty Years of Practice and What Has Changed?', in P. Dunk-West and T. Hafford-Letchfield (eds.) *Sexual Identities and Sexuality in Social Work: Research and Reflections from Women in the Field* (Farnham: Ashgate): 105–20.

Brown, Helen Cosis and Cocker, Christine (2008) 'Lesbian and Gay Fostering and Adoption: Out of the Closet and Into the Mainstream?' *Adoption & Fostering*, 32:4, 19–30.

Brown, Helen Cosis and Cocker, Christine (2011) *Social Work with Lesbians and Gay Men* (London: Sage).

Brown, Helen Cosis and Kershaw, Sheila (2008) 'The Legal Context for Social Work with Lesbians and Gay Men in the UK: Updating the Educational Context', *Social Work Education*, 27:2, 122–30.

Brown, Suzanne, Susan Smalling, Victor Groza and Scott Ryan (2009) 'The Experiences of Gay Men and Lesbians in Becoming and Being Adoptive Parents', *Adoption Quarterly*, 12:3/4, 229–46.

Brown, Wendy (2009) 'Whose Secularism? Whose Equality? For a Return to a Critique of the Family', Keynote address at the Feminist Theory Workshop, Duke University, Women's Studies. http://www.youtube.com/watch?v=sqCP5AJVk_A [accessed 1 April 2011].

Bruhm, Steven and Hurley, Natasha (2004) 'Curiouser: On the Queerness of Children', in S. Bruhm and N. Hurley (eds.) *Curiouser: On the Queerness of Children* (Minneapolis, MN: University of Minnesota Press): ix–xxxviii.

Budgeon, Shelley (2006) 'Friendship and Formations of Sociality in Late Modernity: The Challenge of "Post Traditional Intimacy"', *Sociological Research Online*, 11:3, http://www.socresonline.org.uk/11/3/budgeon.html [accessed 1 April 2011].

Butler, Judith (1990) *Gender Trouble: Feminism and the Subversion of Identity* (New York: Routledge).

Butler, Judith (1993) *Bodies That Matter: On the Discursive Limits of 'Sex'* (New York: Routledge).

Butler, Judith (2004a) *Precarious Life: The Powers of Mourning and Violence* (London: Verso).

Butler, Judith (2004b) *Undoing Gender* (New York: Routledge).

Butler, Judith (2005) *Giving An Account of Oneself* (New York: Fordham University Press).

Cabinet Office (2010) *The Coalition: Our Programme for Government* (London: Cabinet Office).

Calhoun, Cheshire (2000) *Feminism, the Family, and the Politics of the Closet: Lesbian & Gay Displacement* (Oxford: Oxford University Press).

Cameron, Paul (1999) 'Homosexual Parents: Testing "Common Sense" – A Literature Review Emphasizing the Golombok and Tasker Longitudinal Study of Lesbians' Children', *Psychological Reports*, 85, 282–322.

Card, Claudia (1996) 'Against Marriage and Motherhood', *Hypatia*, 11:3, 1–23.

Carlomusto, Jean (dir.) (1997) *To Catch a Glimpse*, http://www.jeancarlomusto.com [accessed 1 April 2011].

Carlomusto, Jean (dir.) (1999) *Shatzi is Dying*, http://www.jeancarlomusto.com [accessed 1 April 2011].

Carrington, Christopher (1999) *No Place Like Home: Relationships and Family Life Among Lesbians and Gay Men* (Chicago, IL: University of Chicago Press).

Carsten, Janet (2000a) 'Introduction: Cultures of Relatedness', in J. Carsten (ed.) *Cultures of Relatedness: New Approaches to the Study of Kinship* (Cambridge: Cambridge University Press): 1–36.

Carsten, Janet (2000b) '"Knowing Where You've Come From": Ruptures and Continuities of Time and Kinship in Narratives of Adoption Reunions', *Journal of the Royal Anthropological Institute*, 6, 687–703.

Carsten, Janet (2004) *After Kinship* (Cambridge: Cambridge University Press).

Chambers, Deborah (2001) *Representing the Family* (London: Sage).

Chan, Raymond W., Risa C. Brooks, Barbara Raboy and Charlotte J. Patterson (1998) 'Division of Labor Among Lesbian and Heterosexual Parents: Associations with Children's Adjustment', *Journal of Family Psychology*, 12:3, 402–19.

Charles, Nickie, Charlotte A. Davies and Chris Harris (2008) *Families in Transition: Social Change, Family Formation and Kin Relationships* (Bristol: Policy Press).

Christian Institute (2002) *News Release: Charity Launches "Adoption Card" to Protect against Gay Adoption*, Newcastle-upon-Tyne, The Christian Institute, http://www.christian.org.uk/pressreleases/2002/october_15_2002.htm [accessed 1 April 2011].

Christie, Alastair (ed.) (2001) *Men and Social Work: Theories and Practices* (Basingstoke: Palgrave Macmillan).

Clarke, Victoria (2000) '"Stereotype, Attack and Stigmatize Those Who Disagree": Employing Scientific Rhetoric in Debates about Lesbian and Gay Parenting', *Feminism & Psychology*, 10:1, 152–9.

Clarke, Victoria (2001) 'What About the Children? Arguments Against Lesbian and Gay Parenting', *Women's Studies International Forum*, 24:5, 555–70.

Clarke, Victoria (2002) 'Resistance and Normalization in the Construction of Lesbian and Gay Families: A Discursive Analysis', in A. Coyle and C. Kitzinger (eds.) *Lesbian & Gay Psychology: New Perspectives* (Oxford: Blackwell): 98–116.

Clarke, Victoria, Celia Kitzinger and Jonathan Potter (2004) '"Kids Are Just Cruel Anyway": Lesbian and Gay Parents' Talk about Homophobic Bullying', *British Journal of Social Psychology*, 43, 531–50.

Cocker, Christine (2011) 'Sexuality before Ability? The Assessment of Lesbians as Adopters', in P. Dunk-West and T. Hafford-Letchfield (eds.) *Sexual Identities and Sexuality in Social Work: Research and Reflections from Women in the Field* (Farnham: Ashgate): 141–62.

Cocker, Christine and Brown, Helen Cosis (2010) 'Sex, Sexuality and Relationships: Developing Confidence and Discernment When Assessing Lesbian and Gay Prospective Adopters', *Adoption & Fostering*, 34:1, 20–32.

Cocker, Christine and Hafford-Letchfield, Trish (2010) 'Out and Proud? Social Work's Relationship with Lesbian and Gay Equality', *British Journal of Social Work*, 40:6, 1996–2008.

Complaint Investigation Report (1995) from Principal Officer [local authority] re. Nita and Clare [anonymized].

Connell, R.W. (1995) *Masculinities* (Cambridge: Polity Press).

Connell, R.W. (2002) *Gender* (Cambridge: Polity Press).

Cooper, Davina and Herman, Didi (1991) 'Getting "the Family Right": Legislating Heterosexuality in Britain, 1986–1991', *Canadian Journal of Family Law*, 10, 41–78.

Crowl, Alicia, Soyeon Ahn and Jean Baker (2008) 'A Meta-Analysis of Developmental Outcomes for Children of Same-Sex and Heterosexual Parents', *Journal of GLBT Family Studies*, 4:3, 385–407.

Dalton, Susan E. (2001) 'Protecting Our Parent-Child Relationships: Understanding the Strengths and Weaknesses of Second-Parent Adoption', in M. Bernstein and R. Reimann (eds.) *Queer Families, Queer Politics: Challenging Culture and the State* (New York: Columbia University Press): 201–20

Dalton, Susan E. and Bielby, Denise D. (2000) ' "That's Our Kind of Constellation": Lesbian Mothers Negotiate Institutionalized Understandings of Gender within the Family', *Gender & Society*, 14:1, 36–61.

Dean, Mitchell (2010 [1999]) *Governmentality: Power and Rule in Modern Society*, 2nd edn (Los Angeles: Sage).

de Jongh, Nicholas (1992) *Not In Front of the Audience: Homosexuality On Stage* (London: Routledge).

Delaney, Shelagh (2000 [1959]) *A Taste of Honey* (London: Methuen).

Delphy, Christine and Leonard, Diana (1992) *Familiar Exploitation: A New Analysis of Marriage in Contemporary Western Societies* (Cambridge: Polity Press).

de Montigny, Gerald A.J. (1995) *Social Working: An Ethnography of Front-Line Practice* (Toronto: University of Toronto Press).

de Montigny, Gerald (2007) 'Ethnomethodology for Social Work', *Qualitative Social Work*, 6:1, 95–120.

Dennis, Norman and Erdos, George (1992) *Families Without Fatherhood* (London: Institute of Economic Affairs (IEA) Health and Welfare Unit).

Denzin, Norman K. (1990) 'Harold and Agnes: A Feminist Narrative Undoing', *Sociological Theory*, 8:2, 198–216.

Denzin, Norman K. (1991) 'Back to Harold and Agnes', *Sociological Theory*, 9:2, 280–5.

Department for Communities and Local Government (2007) *Getting Equal: Proposals to Outlaw Sexual Orientation Discrimination in the Provision of Goods and Services – Government Response to Consultation* (Wetherby: Communities and Local Government Publications), http://www.communities.gov.uk/archived/publications/corporate/gettingequaloutlaw?view=Standard [accessed 1 April 2011].

Department of Health (1990) *Foster Placement (Guidance and Regulations) Consultation Paper No. 16* (London: Her Majesty's Stationery Office).

Department of Health (1991) *The Children Act 1989 Guidance and Regulations: Volume 3, Family Placements* (London: Her Majesty's Stationery Office).

di Leonardo, Micaela (1987) 'The Female World of Cards and Holidays: Women, Families, and the Work of Kinship', *Signs*, 12, 440–52.

Donzelot, Jacques (1997 [1977]) *The Policing of Families* (Baltimore: Johns Hopkins University Press).

Dorow, Sara K. (2006) *Transnational Adoption: A Cultural Economy of Race, Gender, and Kinship* (New York: New York University Press).

Doucet, Andrea (2006) *Do Men Mother? Fathering, Care, and Domestic Responsibility* (Toronto: University of Toronto Press).

Doughty, Steve (2009) 'Slurred by the Adoption Nazis: Critics of Gay Parenting are Branded "Retarded Homophobes"', *Mail Online (UK)*, http://www.dailymail.co.uk/news/article-1181380/Slurred-adoption-Nazis-Critics-gay-parenting-branded-retarded-homophobes.html (last updated 14 May 2009) [accessed 1 April 2011].

Downing, Jordan, Hanna Richardson, Lori Kinkler and Abbie Goldberg (2009) 'Making the Decision: Factors Influencing Gay Men's Choice of an Adoption Path', *Adoption Quarterly*, 12:3/4, 247–71.

Downs, A. Chris and James, Steven E. (2006) 'Gay, Lesbian, and Bisexual Foster Parents: Strengths and Challenges for the Child Welfare System', *Child Welfare*, 85:2, 281–98.

Duggan, Lisa (1995 [1994]) 'Queering the State', in L. Duggan and N.D. Hunter *Sex Wars: Sexual Dissent and Political Culture* (New York: Routledge): 179–93.

Duggan, Lisa (2003) *The Twilight of Equality? Neoliberalism, Cultural Politics, and the Attack on Democracy* (Boston, MA: Beacon Press).

Dyer, Richard (1997) *White* (London: Routledge).

Edelman, Lee (2002) 'Post-Partum', *Narrative*, 10:2, 181–5.

Edelman, Lee (2004) *No Future: Queer Theory and the Death Drive* (Durham, NC: Duke University Press).

Edelman, Lee (2006) 'Antagonism, Negativity, and the Subject of Queer Theory', *PMLA*, 121:3, 821–3.

Edelman, Lee (2007) 'Ever After: History, Negativity, and the Social', *South Atlantic Quarterly*, 106:3, 469–76.

Edwards, Jeanette (2000) *Born and Bred: Idioms of Kinship and New Reproductive Technologies in England* (Oxford: Oxford University Press).

Eglin, Peter and Hester, Stephen (2003) *The Montreal Massacre: A Story of Membership Categorization Analysis* (Waterloo: Wilfrid Laurier University Press).

Eng, David L. (2003) 'Two Mothers: Transnational Adoption and Queer Diasporas', *Social Text*, 21:3, 1–37.

Eng, David L. (2010) *The Feeling of Kinship: Queer Liberalism and the Racialization of Intimacy* (Durham, NC: Duke University Press).

Epstein, Steven (1987) 'Gay Politics, Ethnic Identity: The Limits of Social Constructionism', *Socialist Review*, 93/94, 9–54.

Equality and Human Rights Commission (2010) *When Is Sexual Orientation Discrimination Lawful? (Guidance: Equality Act 2010)*, http://www.equalityhumanrights.com/advice-and-guidance/your-rights/sexual-orientation/when-is-sexual-orientation-discrimination-lawful/ [accessed 1 April 2011].

Erich, Stephen, Heather Kanenberg, Kim Case, Theresa Allen and Takis Bogdanos (2009b) 'An Empirical Analysis of Factors Affecting Adolescent Attachment in Adoptive Families with Homosexual and Straight Parents', *Children & Youth Services Review*, 31, 398–404.

Erich, Stephen, Patrick Leung and Peter Kindle (2005) 'A Comparative Analysis of Adoptive Family Functioning with Gay, Lesbian, and Heterosexual Parents and Their Children', *Journal of GLBT Family Studies*, 1:4, 43–60.

Erich, Stephen, Sharon K. Hall, Heather Kanenberg and Kim Case (2009a) 'Early and Late Stage Adolescence: Adopted Adolescents' Attachment to Their Heterosexual and Lesbian/Gay Parents', *Adoption Quarterly*, 12:3/4, 152–70.

Evans, Mary (2003) *Love: An Unromantic Discussion* (Cambridge: Polity Press).

Fairclough, Anna (2008) 'Growing Up with a Lesbian or Gay Parent: Young People's Perspectives', *Health & Social Care in the Community*, 16:5, 521–8.

Family Diversity Projects (2004–8) *Love Makes a Family* (Amherst: Family Diversity Projects), http://www.familydiv.org/lovemakesafamily.php [accessed 1 April 2011].

Fanthome, Lynne (2007) 'Imagining the Queer and the Child', paper presented at the Lee Edelman Symposium "Queer@Kings", Kings College, London, 1 June.

Farr, Rachel H., Stephen L. Forssell and Charlotte J. Patterson (2010a) 'Gay, Lesbian, and Heterosexual Adoptive Parents: Couple and Relationship Issues', *Journal of GLBT Family Studies*, 6:2, 199–213.

Farr, Rachel H., Stephen L. Forssell and Charlotte J. Patterson (2010b) 'Parenting and Child Development in Adoptive Families: Does Parental Sexual Orientation Matter?' *Applied Developmental Science*, 14:3, 164–78.

Faubion, James D. (2001) 'Introduction: Toward an Anthropology of the Ethics of Kinship', in J.D. Faubion (ed.) *The Ethics of Kinship: Ethnographic Inquiries* (Lanham, MD: Rowman & Littlefield): 1–28.

Featherstone, Brid and Green, Lorraine (2009) 'Judith Butler', in M. Gray and S.A Webb (eds.) *Social Work Theories and Methods* (London: Sage): 53–62.

Featherstone, Katie, Paul Atkinson, Aditya Bharadwaj and Angus Clarke (2006) *Risky Relations: Family, Kinship and the New Genetics* (Oxford: Berg).

Fedewa, Alicia L. and Clark, Teresa P. (2009) 'Parent Practices and Home-School Partnerships: A Differential Effect for Children with Same-Sex Coupled Parents?' *Journal of GLBT Family Studies*, 5, 312–39.

Ferguson, Roderick A. (2004) *Aberrations in Black: Toward a Queer of Color Critique* (Minneapolis, MN: University of Minnesota Press).

Finch, Janet (1989) *Family Obligations and Social Change* (Cambridge: Polity Press).

Finch, Janet (2007) 'Displaying Families', *Sociology*, 41:1, 65–81.

Finch, Janet and Mason, Jennifer (1993) *Negotiating Family Responsibilities* (London: Routledge).

Finch, Janet and Mason, Jennifer (2000) *Passing On: Kinship and Inheritance in England* (London: Routledge).

Flaks, David K., Ilda Ficher, Frank Masterpasqua and Gregory Joseph (1995) 'Lesbians Choosing Motherhood: A Comparative Study of Lesbian and Heterosexual Parents and Their Children', *Developmental Psychology*, 31:1, 105–14.

'Florence, Maurice' [Foucault, Michel] (2000) 'Foucault', in J.D. Faubion (ed.) *Essential Works of Foucault 1954–1984, Volume 2: Aesthetics, Method & Epistemology* (London: Penguin): 459–63.

Folgerø, Tor (2008) 'Queer Nuclear Families? Reproducing and Transgressing Heteronormativity', *Journal of Homosexuality*, 54:1, 124–49.

Foucault, Michel (1981 [1970]) 'The Order of Discourse', in R. Young (ed.) *Untying the Text: A Poststructuralist Reader* (Boston, MA: Routledge & Kegan Paul): 48–78.

Foucault, Michel (1990 [1976]) *The History of Sexuality, Volume 1: An Introduction* (London: Penguin).

Foucault, Michel (1991a [1975]) *Discipline and Punish: The Birth of the Prison* (Harmondsworth: Penguin).

Foucault, Michel (1991b [1978]) 'Governmentality', in G. Burchell, C. Gordon and P. Miller (eds.) *The Foucault Effect: Studies in Governmentality* (London: Harvester Wheatsheaf): 87–104.

Foucault, Michel (2000a [1981]) 'Friendship as a Way of Life', in P. Rabinow (ed.) *Essential Works of Foucault 1954–1984, Volume 1: Ethics, Subjectivity & Truth* (London: Penguin): 135–40.

Foucault, Michel (2000b [1971]) 'Nietzsche, Genealogy, History', in J.D. Faubion (ed.) *Essential Works of Foucault 1954–1984, Volume 2: Aesthetics, Method & Epistemology* (London: Penguin): 369–91.

Foucault, Michel (2000c [1981]) 'Sex, Power, and the Politics of Identity', in P. Rabinow (ed.) *Essential Works of Foucault 1954–1984, Volume 1: Ethics, Subjectivity & Truth* (London: Penguin): 163–73.

Foucault, Michel (2000d [1981]) 'Technologies of the Self', in P. Rabinow (ed.) *Essential Works of Foucault 1954–1984, Volume 1: Ethics, Subjectivity & Truth* (London: Penguin): 223–51.

Foucault, Michel (2000e [1981]) 'The Social Triumph of the Sexual Will', in P. Rabinow (ed.) *Essential Works of Foucault 1954–1984, Volume 1: Ethics, Subjectivity & Truth* (London: Penguin): 157–62.

Foucault, Michel (2002 [1969]) *The Archaeology of Knowledge* (London: Routledge).

Foucault, Michel (2006 [2003]) *Psychiatric Power: Lectures at the Collège de France, 1973–74* (Basingstoke: Palgrave Macmillan).

Francis, David and Hester, Stephen (2004) *An Invitation to Ethnomethodology: Language, Society and Interaction* (London: Sage).

Franklin, Sarah and McKinnon, Susan (2000) 'New Directions in Kinship Study: A Core Concept Revisited', *Current Anthropology*, 41:2, 275–9.

Fraser, Nancy and Honneth, Axel (2003) *Redistribution or Recognition? A Political–Philosophical Exchange* (London: Verso).

Freeman, Elizabeth (2007) 'Queer Belongings: Kinship Theory and Queer Theory', in G.E. Haggerty and M. McGarry (eds.) *A Companion to Lesbian, Gay, Bisexual, Transgender, and Queer Studies* (Malden: Blackwell): 295–314.

Fung, Richard (dir.) (1990) *My Mother's Place*, http://richardfung.ca/ [accessed 1 April 2011].

Fung, Richard (dir.) (2000) *Sea in the Blood*, Fungus Productions, http://richardfung.ca/ [accessed 1 April 2011].

Gabb, Jacqui (2001a) 'Desirous Subjects and Parental Identities: Constructing a Radical Discourse on (Lesbian) Family Sexuality', *Sexualities*, 4:3, 333–52.

Gabb, Jacqui (2001b) 'Querying the Discourses of Love: An Analysis of Contemporary Patterns of Love and the Stratification of Intimacy within Lesbian Families', *The European Journal of Women's Studies*, 8:3, 313–28.

Gabb, Jacqui (2004) 'Critical Differentials: Querying the Incongruities Within Research on Lesbian Parent Families', *Sexualities*, 7:2, 167–82.

Gabb, Jacqui (2005a) 'Lesbian Motherhood: Strategies of Familial-linguistic Management in Lesbian Parent Families', *Sociology*, 39:4, 585–603.

Gabb, Jacqui (2005b) 'Locating Lesbian Parent Families: Everyday Negotiations of Lesbian Motherhood in Britain', *Gender, Place and Culture*, 12:4, 419–32.

Gabb, Jacqui (2008) *Researching Intimacy in Families* (Basingstoke: Palgrave Macmillan).

Garfinkel, Harold (1984 [1967]) *Studies in Ethnomethodology* (Cambridge: Polity Press).

Gartrell, Nanette, Amalia Deck, Carla Rodas, Heidi Peyser and Amy Banks (2005) 'The National Lesbian Family Study: 4. Interviews With the 10-Year-Old Children', *American Journal of Orthopsychiatry*, 75:4, 518–24.

Gartrell, Nanette, Amy Banks, Jean Hamilton, Nancy Reed, Holly Bishop and Carla Rodas (1999) 'The National Lesbian Family Study: 2. Interviews With Mothers of Toddlers', *American Journal of Orthopsychiatry*, 69:3, 362–9.

Gartrell, Nanette, Amy Banks, Nancy Reed, Jean Hamilton, Carla Rodas and Amalia Deck (2000) 'The National Lesbian Family Study: 3. Interviews With Mothers of Five-Year Olds', *American Journal of Orthopsychiatry*, 70:4, 542–8.

Gartrell, Nanette and Bos, Henny (2010) 'US National Longitudinal Lesbian Family Study: Psychological Adjustment of 17-Year-Old Adolescents', *Pediatrics*, 126:1, 1–9.

Gartrell, Nanette, Carla Rodas, Amalia Deck, Heidi Peyser and Amy Banks (2006) 'The USA National Lesbian Family Study: Interviews With Mothers of 10-Year-Olds', *Feminism & Psychology*, 16:2, 175–92.

Gartrell, Nanette, Heidi Peyser and Henny Bos (2011) 'Planned Lesbian Families: A Review of the US National Longitudinal Lesbian Family Study', in D.M. Brodzinsky and A. Pertman (eds.) *Adoption by Lesbians and Gay Men: A New Dimension in Family Diversity* (New York: Oxford University Press), forthcoming.

Gartrell, Nanette, Henny M.W. Bos and Naomi G. Goldberg (2010) 'Adolescents of the U.S. National Longitudinal Lesbian Family Study: Sexual Orientation, Sexual Behavior, and Sexual Risk Exposure', *Archives of Sexual Behavior*, published online 6 November.

Gartrell, Nanette, Jean Hamilton, Any Banks, Dee Mosbacher, Nancy Reed, Caroline H. Sparks and Holly Bishop (1996) 'The National Lesbian Family Study: 1. Interviews With Prospective Mothers', *American Journal of Orthopsychiatry*, 66:2, 272–81.

Gates, Gary J., M.V. Lee Badgett, Jennifer Ehrle Macomber and Kate Chambers (2007) *Adoption and Foster Care by Gay and Lesbian Parents in the United States* (Los Angeles: The Williams Institute (UCLA School of Law)/Washington, Urban Institute). http://www.urban.org/publications/411437.html [accessed 1 April 2011].

Germon, Jennifer (2009) *Gender: A Genealogy of an Idea* (New York: Palgrave Macmillan).

Gianino, Mark (2008) 'Adaptation and Transformation: The Transition to Adoptive Parenthood for Gay Male Couples', *Journal of GLBT Family Studies*, 4:2, 205–43.

Giddens, Anthony (1991) *Modernity and Self-Identity: Self and Society in the Late Modern Age* (Cambridge: Polity Press).

Giddens, Anthony (1992) *The Transformation of Intimacy: Sexuality, Love and Eroticism in Modern Societies* (Cambridge: Polity Press).

Giddens, Anthony (1999) 'Reith Lectures 1999: Runaway World – Lecture 4: Family', London, BBC, http://www.bbc.co.uk/radio4/reith1999/lecture4.shtml [accessed 1 April 2011].

Gillespie, Peggy (1999) 'Preface', in G. Kaeser and P. Gillespie (eds.) *Love Makes a Family: Portraits of Lesbian, Gay, Bisexual, and Transgender Parents and Their Families* (Amherst, MA: University of Massachusetts Press): xi–xvi.

Gillis, John R. (1997 [1996]) *A World of Their Own Making: Myth, Ritual, and the Quest for Family Values* (Cambridge: Harvard University Press).

Goffman, Erving (1979 [1976]) *Gender Advertisements* (London: Macmillan).

Goffman, Erving (1990a [1963]) *Stigma: Notes on the Management of Spoiled Identity* (London: Penguin).

Goffman, Erving (1990b [1959]) *The Presentation of Self in Everyday Life* (London: Penguin).

Goldberg, Abbie E. (2007) '(How) Does It Make a Difference? Perspectives of Adults with Lesbian, Gay, and Bisexual Parents', *American Journal of Orthopsychiatry*, 77:4, 550–62.

Goldberg, Abbie E. (2010a) *Lesbian and Gay Parents and Their Children: Research on the Family Life Cycle* (Washington: American Psychological Association).

Goldberg, Abbie E. (2010b) 'Studying Complex Families in Context', *Journal of Marriage & Family*, 72, 29–34.

Goldberg, Abbie E., Downing, Jordan B. and Sauck, Christine C. (2008) 'Perceptions of Children's Parental Preferences in Lesbian Two-Mother Households', *Journal of Marriage & the Family*, 70, 419–34.

Golombok, Susan, Ann Spencer and Michael Rutter (1983) 'Children in Lesbian and Single-Parent Households: Psychosexual and Psychiatric Appraisal', *Journal of Child Psychology & Psychiatry*, 24:4, 551–72.

Golombok, Susan, Beth Perry, Amanda Burston, Jean Golding, Clare Murray, Julie Mooney-Somers and Madeleine Stevens (2003) 'Children with Lesbian Parents: A Community Study', *Developmental Psychology*, 39:1, 20–33.

Golombok, Susan, Fiona Tasker and Clare Murray (1997) 'Children Raised in Fatherless Families from Infancy: Family Relationships and the Socioemotional Development of Children of Lesbian and Single Heterosexual Mothers', *Journal of Child Psychology & Psychiatry*, 38:7, 783–91.

Golombok, Susan and Tasker, Fiona (1994) 'Children in Lesbian and Gay Families: Theories and Evidence', *Annual Review of Sex Research*, 5, 73–100.

Golombok, Susan and Tasker, Fiona (1996) 'Do Parents Influence the Sexual Orientation of Their Children? Findings from a Longitudinal Study of Lesbian Families', *Developmental Psychology*, 32:1, 3–11.

Gouldner, Alvin W. (1973) *For Sociology: Renewal and Critique in Sociology Today* (London: Allen Lane).

Gouldner, Alvin W. (1975) 'Sociology and the Everyday Life', in L.A. Coser (ed.) *The Idea of Social Structure: Papers in Honor of Robert K. Merton* (New York: Harcourt Brace Jovanovich): 417–32.

Green, G. Dorsey and Bozett, Frederick W. (1991) 'Lesbian Mothers and Gay Fathers', in J.C. Gonsiorek and J.D. Weinrich (eds.) *Homosexuality: Research Implications for Public Policy* (Newbury Park: Sage): 197–214.

Green, Jesse (1999) *The Velveteen Father: An Unexpected Journey to Parenthood* (New York: Ballantine Books).

Green, Richard (1978) 'Sexual Identity of 37 Children Raised by Homosexual or Transsexual Parents', *American Journal of Psychiatry*, 135:6, 692–7.

Green, Richard (1982) 'The Best Interests of the Child with a Lesbian Mother', *Bulletin of the American Academy of Psychiatry and the Law*, 10:1, 7–15.

Green, Richard (1998) 'Transsexuals' Children', *International Journal of Transgenderism*, 2:4, http://www.wpath.org/journal/www.iiav.nl/ezines/web/IJT/97-03/numbers/symposion/ijtc0601.htm [accessed 1 April 2011].

Gross, Martine (2006) 'Biparental and Multiparental Lesbian and Gay Families in France', *Lesbian & Gay Psychology Review*, 7:1, 36–47.

Gross, Neil (2005) 'The Detraditionalization of Intimacy Reconsidered', *Sociological Theory*, 23:3, 286–311.

Gubrium, Jaber F. and Holstein, James A. (1990) *What is Family?* (Mountain View, CA: Mayfield).

Halberstam, Judith (2005) *In a Queer Time and Place: Transgender Bodies, Subcultural Lives* (New York: New York University Press).

Halberstam, Judith (2006) 'The Politics of Negativity in Recent Queer Theory', *PMLA*, 121:3, 823–5.

Halberstam, Judith (2007) 'Forgetting Family: Queer Alternatives to Oedipal Relations', in G.E. Haggerty and M. McGarry (eds.) *A Companion to Lesbian, Gay, Bisexual, Transgender, and Queer Studies* (Malden, MA: Blackwell Publishing): 315–24.

Hall, Christopher, Stef Slembrouck and Srikant Sarangi (2006) *Language Practices in Social Work: Categorisation and Accountability in Child Welfare* (London: Routledge).

Hall, Sandra J. (2010) 'Gauging the Gatekeepers: How Do Adoption Workers Assess the Suitability of Gay, Lesbian, or Bisexual Prospective Parents?' *Journal of GLBT Family Studies*, 6, 265–93.

Hall, Stuart and Back, Les (2009) 'In Conversation: At Home and Not At Home', *Cultural Studies*, 23:4, 658–87.

Halperin, David M. (1995) *Saint Foucault: Towards a Gay Hagiography* (New York: Oxford University Press).

Halperin, David M. (1998) 'Forgetting Foucault: Acts, Identities, and the History of Sexuality', *Representations*, 63, 93–120.

Halperin, David M. (2002) *How to Do the History of Homosexuality* (Chicago, IL: University of Chicago Press).

Halperin, David M. (2009) 'Why Gay Shame Now?' in D.M. Halperin and V. Traub (eds.) *Gay Shame* (Chicago, IL: University of Chicago Press): 41–6.

Hanscombe, Gillian E. and Forster, Jackie (1982 [1981]) *Rocking the Cradle: Lesbian Mothers – A Challenge in Family Living* (London: Sheba Feminist Publishers).

Haraway, Donna J. (1997) *Modest_Witness@Second_Millennium. FemaleMan©_Meets_ OncoMouse™: Feminism and Technoscience* (New York: Routledge).

Haraway, Donna J. (2004) *The Haraway Reader* (New York: Routledge).

Harris, John (2003) *The Social Work Business* (London: Routledge).

Hayden, Corinne P. (1995) 'Gender, Genetics, and Generation: Reformulating Biology in Lesbian Kinship', *Cultural Anthropology*, 10:1, 41–63.

Heaphy, Brian (2007) *Late Modernity and Social Change: Reconstructing Social and Personal Life* (London: Routledge).

Heaphy, Brian, Catherine Donovan and Jeffrey Weeks (2004) 'A Different Affair? Openness and Nonmonogamy in Same Sex Relationships', in J. Duncombe, K. Harrison, G. Allan and D. Marsden (eds.) *The State of Affairs: Explorations in Infidelity and Commitment* (London: Lawrence Erlbaum Associates): 167–86.

Hequembourg, Amy (2007) *Lesbian Motherhood: Stories of Becoming* (New York: Harrington Park Press).

Hicks, Stephen (1996) 'The "Last Resort"?: Lesbian and Gay Experiences of the Social Work Assessment Process in Fostering and Adoption', *Practice*, 8:2, 15–24.

Hicks, Stephen (1998) *Familiar Fears: The Assessment of Lesbian and Gay Fostering and Adoption Applicants* (University of Lancaster (UK), Department of Applied Social Science, PhD thesis), http://usir.salford.ac.uk/2354/ [accessed 1 April 2011].

Hicks, Stephen (2000) ' "Good Lesbian, Bad Lesbian ...": Regulating Heterosexuality in Fostering and Adoption Assessments', *Child & Family Social Work*, 5:2, 157–68.

Hicks, Stephen (2005) 'Queer Genealogies: Tales of Conformity and Rebellion Amongst Lesbian and Gay Foster Carer and Adopters', *Qualitative Social Work*, 4:3, 293–308.

Hicks, Stephen (2006a) 'Empty Spaces, New Possibilities', *Lesbian & Gay Psychology Review*, 7:1, 84–98.

Hicks, Stephen (2006b) 'Genealogy's Desire: Practices of Kinship Amongst Lesbian and Gay Foster-Carers and Adopters', *British Journal of Social Work*, 36:5, 761–76.

Hicks, Stephen (2006c) 'Maternal Men – Perverts and Deviants? Making Sense of Gay Men as Foster Carers and Adopters', *Journal of GLBT Family Studies*, 2:1, 93–114.

Hicks, Stephen (2008a) 'Gender Role Models ... Who Needs 'em?!', *Qualitative Social Work*, 7:1, 43–59.

Hicks, Stephen (2008b) 'Thinking Through Sexuality', *Journal of Social Work*, 8:1, 65–82.

Hicks, Stephen (2009a [2005]) 'Sexuality', in R. Adams, L. Dominelli and M. Payne (eds.) *Practising Social Work in a Complex World*, 2nd edn (Basingstoke: Palgrave Macmillan): 70–84.

Hicks, Stephen (2009b) 'Sexuality and the "Relations of Ruling": Using Institutional Ethnography to Research Lesbian and Gay Foster Care and Adoption', *Social Work & Society*, 7:2, http://www.socwork.net/2009/2/articles/hicks [accessed 1 April 2011].

Hicks, Stephen and McDermott, Janet (1999a) 'Editorial Essay', in S. Hicks and J. McDermott (eds.) *Lesbian & Gay Fostering & Adoption: Extraordinary Yet Ordinary* (London: Jessica Kingsley): 147–98.

Hicks, Stephen and McDermott, Janet (eds.) (1999b) *Lesbian & Gay Fostering & Adoption: Extraordinary Yet Ordinary* (London: Jessica Kingsley).

Hill, Marjorie (1987) 'Child-Rearing Attitudes of Black Lesbian Mothers', in Boston Lesbian Psychologies Collective (ed.) *Lesbian Psychologies: Explorations and Challenges* (Urbana, IL: University of Illinois Press): 215–26.

Hill, Nicola (2009) *The Pink Guide to Adoption for Lesbians and Gay Men* (London: British Association for Adoption and Fostering (BAAF)).

Hirsch, Marianne (1997) *Family Frames: Photography, Narrative and Post-memory* (Cambridge: Harvard University Press).

Hitchens, Donna and Price, Barbara (1978/9) 'Trial Strategy in Lesbian Mother Custody Cases: The Use of Expert Testimony', *Golden Gate University Law Review*, 9, 451–79.

HM Government (2007) *Building on Progress: Families* (London: Prime Minister's Strategy Unit).

Hoeffer, Beverly (1981) 'Children's Acquisition of Sex-Role Behavior in Lesbian-Mother Families', *American Journal of Orthopsychiatry*, 51:3, 536–44.

Hollway, Wendy (2006) *The Capacity to Care: Gender and Ethical Subjectivity* (London: Routledge).

Holstein, James A. and Gubrium, Jaber (1994) 'Constructing Family: Descriptive Practice and Domestic Order', in T.R. Sarbin and J.I. Kitsuse (eds.) *Constructing the Social* (London: Sage): 232–50.

Holstein, James A. and Gubrium, Jaber (1999) 'What is Family? Further Thoughts on a Social Constructionist Approach', *Marriage & Family Review*, 28:3/4, 3–20.

Home Office (1998) *Supporting Families: A Consultation Document* (London: The Stationery Office).

Howard, Jeanne (2006) *Expanding Resources for Children: Is Adoption by Gays and Lesbians Part of the Answer for Boys and Girls Who Need Homes?* (New York: Evan B. Donaldson Adoption Institute), http://www.adoptioninstitute.org/policy/2006_ Expanding_Resources_for_Children.php [accessed 1 April 2011].

Howard, Jeanne and Freundlich, Madelyn (2008) *Expanding Resources for Waiting Children II: Eliminating Legal and Practice Barriers to Gay and Lesbian Adoption from Foster Care* (New York: Evan B. Donaldson Adoption Institute), http://www. adoptioninstitute.org/policy/2008_09_expand_resources.php [accessed 1 April 2011].

Howell, Signe (2006) *The Kinning of Foreigners: Transnational Adoption in a Global Perspective* (New York: Berghahn Books).

Hubbard, Phil (2000) 'Desire/Disgust: Mapping the Moral Contours of Heterosexuality', *Progress in Human Geography*, 24:2, 191–217.

Hubbard, Phil (2002) 'Maintaining Family Values? Cleansing the Streets of Sex Advertising', *Area*, 34:4, 353–60.

Hunter, Nan D. and Polikoff, Nancy D. (1976) 'Custody Rights of Lesbian Mothers: Legal Theory and Litigation Strategy', *Buffalo Law Review*, 25, 691–733.

Hurst, Greg (2007) 'Catholics Get Time to Adjust to Gay Rights', *The Times* (UK), 25 January, 24.

Hutchby, Ian and Wooffitt, Robin (2008) *Conversation Analysis*, 2nd edn (Cambridge: Polity Press).

Illouz, Eva (2007) *Cold Intimacies: The Making of Emotional Capitalism* (Cambridge: Polity Press).

Jackson, Stevi (1999) *Heterosexuality in Question* (London: Sage).

Jackson, Stevi (2006) 'Gender, Sexuality and Heterosexuality: The Complexity (and Limits) of Heteronormativity', *Feminist Theory*, 7:1, 105–21.

Jackson, Stevi and Scott, Sue (1997) 'Gut Reactions to Matters of the Heart', *The Sociological Review*, 45:4, 551–75.

Jackson, Stevi and Scott, Sue (2010) *Theorizing Sexuality* (Maidenhead: Open University Press).

Jakobsen, Janet R. and Pellegrini, Ann (2004) *Love the Sin: Sexual Regulation and the Limits of Religious Tolerance* (Boston, MA: Beacon Press).

Jamieson, Lynn (1998) *Intimacy: Personal Relationships in Modern Societies* (Cambridge: Polity Press).

Jamieson, Lynn (1999) 'Intimacy Transformed: A Critical Look at the "Pure Relationship"', *Sociology*, 33:3, 477–94.

Jamieson, Lynn (2009) 'Intimacy', paper presented to BSA Families and Relationships Study Group Colloquium, "Rethinking Concepts: Families, Intimacies and Personal Relationships", 6 November, London.

Jennings, Kevin (2000) *Testimonial letter on behalf of Gay, Lesbian and Straight Education Network (New York)* (Amherst: Family Diversity Projects), http://www.familydiv.org/lovemakesafamily.php [accessed 1 April 2011].

Jeyasingham, Dharman (2008) 'Knowledge/Ignorance and the Construction of Sexuality in Social Work Education', *Social Work Education*, 27:2, 138–51.

Jones, A. Billy S. (1986) 'A Father's Need; A Parent's Desire', in J. Beam (ed.) *In the Life: A Black Gay Anthology* (Boston, MA: Alyson): 143–51.

Jones, Chris and Hackett, Simon (2010) 'The Role of "Family Practices" and "Displays of Family" in the Creation of Adoptive Kinship', *British Journal of Social Work*, advance access published online 22 February.

Kaeser, Gigi (photographs) and Gillespie, Peggy (ed.) (1999) *Love Makes a Family: Portraits of Lesbian, Gay, Bisexual, & Transgender Parents and their Families* (Amherst, MA: University of Massachusetts Press).

Kane, Emily W. (2006) '"No Way My Boys Are Going to Be Like That!": Parents' Responses to Children's Gender Nonconformity', *Gender & Society*, 20:2, 149–76.

Kemp, Philip (1998) Sleeve notes to British Film Institute DVD release of Richardson (1961).

Kessler, Suzanne J. and McKenna, Wendy (1985 [1978]) *Gender: An Ethnomethodological Approach* (Chicago, IL: University of Chicago Press).

King, Michael B. (1991) 'Homosexuality and Parenthood', *British Medical Journal*, 303, 295–7.

King, Michael B. (1995) 'Parents Who Are Gay or Lesbian', in P. Reder and C. Lucey (eds.) *Assessment of Parenting: Psychiatric and Psychological Contributions* (London: Routledge): 204–18.

Kinsman, Gary (1995) 'The Textual Practices of Sexual Rule: Sexual Policing and Gay Men', in M. Campbell and A. Manicom (eds.) *Knowledge, Experience and Ruling Relations: Studies in the Social Organization of Knowledge* (Toronto: University of Toronto Press): 80–95.

Kipnis, Laura (2003) *Against Love: A Polemic* (New York: Vintage Books).

Kirkpatrick, Martha (1987) 'Clinical Implications of Lesbian Mother Studies', *Journal of Homosexuality*, 14:1/2, 201–11.

Kirkpatrick, Martha, Catherine Smith and Ron Roy (1981) 'Lesbian Mothers and Their Children: A Comparative Survey', *American Journal of Orthopsychiatry*, 51:3, 545–51.

Kirton, Derek (2000) *'Race', Ethnicity & Adoption* (Buckingham: Open University Press).

Klasky-Csupo/Nickelodeon (1997) (production) *Rugrats*, episode 67, 'Mother's Day'.

Kweskin, Sally L. and Cook, Alicia S. (1982) 'Heterosexual and Homosexual Mothers' Self-Described Sex-Role Behavior and Ideal Sex-Role Behavior in Children', *Sex Roles*, 8:9, 967–75.

Lawler, Steph (2000) *Mothering the Self: Mothers, Daughters, Subjects* (London: Routledge).

Lehr, Valerie (1999) *Queer Family Values: Debunking the Myth of the Nuclear Family* (Philadelphia, PA: Temple University Press).

Lesnik-Oberstein, Karín (2008) *On Having an Own Child: Reproductive Technologies and the Cultural Construction of Childhood* (London: Karnac Books).

Lesnik-Oberstein, Karín and Thomson, Stephen (2002) 'What is Queer Theory Doing With the Child?' *Parallax*, 8:1, 35–46.

Lev, Arlene Istar (2010) 'How Queer! – The Development of Gender Identity and Sexual Orientation in LGBTQ-Headed Families', *Family Process*, 49:3, 268–90.

Levine, Martin P. (1998) *Gay Macho: The Life & Death of the Homosexual Clone* (ed. M.S. Kimmel) (New York: New York University Press).

Lewin, Ellen (1993) *Lesbian Mothers: Accounts of Gender in American Culture* (Ithaca, NY: Cornell University Press).

Lewin, Ellen (2009) *Gay Fatherhood: Narratives of Family and Citizenship in America* (Chicago, IL: University of Chicago Press).

Lewis, Jane (2003) 'Family Breakdown, Individualism and the Issue of the Relationship between Family Law and Behaviour in Post-War Britain', in S. Cunningham-Burley and L. Jamieson (eds.) *Families and the State: Changing Relationships* (Basingstoke: Palgrave Macmillan): 69–87.

Lloyd, Moya (2007) *Judith Butler: From Norms to Politics* (Cambridge: Polity Press).

Lorde, Audre (1996 [1980/1984/1988]) *The Audre Lorde Compendium: Essays, Speeches and Journals* (London: Pandora).

Lukes, Steven (2005) *Power: A Radical View*, 2nd edn (Basingstoke: Palgrave Macmillan).

MacCallum, Fiona and Golombok, Susan (2004) 'Children Raised in Fatherless Families from Infancy: A Follow-Up of Children of Lesbian and Single Heterosexual Mothers at Early Adolescence', *Journal of Child Psychology & Psychiatry*, 45:8, 1407–19.

Maldonado, Lisa (2000) *Testimonial letter on behalf of American Civil Liberties Union (San Francisco)* (Amherst, MA: Family Diversity Projects), http://www.familydiv.org/lovemakesafamily.php [accessed 1 April 2011].

Mallon, Gerald P. (2000) 'Gay Men and Lesbians as Adoptive Parents', *Journal of Gay & Lesbian Social Services*, 11:4, 1–22.

Mallon, Gerald P. (2004) *Gay Men Choosing Parenthood* (New York: Columbia University Press).

Mallon, Gerald P. (2006) *Lesbian and Gay Foster and Adoptive Parents: Recruiting, Assessing, and Supporting an Untapped Resource for Children and Youth* (Arlington, VA: Child Welfare League of America (CWLA) Press).

Mallon, Gerald P. (2007) 'Assessing Lesbian and Gay Prospective Foster and Adoptive Families: A Focus on the Home Study Process', *Child Welfare*, 86:2, 67–86.

Mallon, Gerald P. (2008) 'Social Work Practice With LGBT Parents', in G.P. Mallon (ed.) *Social Work Practice With Lesbian, Gay, Bisexual, and Transgender People*, 2nd edn (New York: Routledge): 269–312.

Mallon, Gerald P. (2011) 'Lesbian and Gay Prospective Foster and Adoptive Families: The Homestudy Assessment Process', in D.M. Brodzinsky and A. Pertman (eds.) *Adoption by Lesbians and Gay Men: A New Dimension in Family Diversity* (New York: Oxford University Press), forthcoming.

Mallon, Gerald P. and Betts, Bridget (2005) *Recruiting, Assessing and Supporting Lesbian and Gay Carers and Adopters* (London: British Association for Adoption and Fostering (BAAF)).

Mamo, Laura (2007) *Queering Reproduction: Achieving Pregnancy in the Age of Technoscience* (Durham, NC: Duke University Press).

Manchester City Council – Children's Services (2007 [2004]) *Practice Guidance on Assessing Gay and Lesbian Foster Care and Adoption Applicants* (Manchester: Manchester City Council (UK)), [written by Stephen Hicks with Debbie Greaves, with contributions from Jill Hellings and Viv Lyons].

Margolin, Leslie (1997) *Under the Cover of Kindness: The Invention of Social Work* (Charlottesville, VA: University Press of Virginia).

Marisa and Judy (1999a) 'Assessment for Adoption: The Prospective Adopters' Perspective', unpublished paper submitted to *Journal of Social Work Practice*.

Marisa and Judy (1999b) Letter to the editors of *Journal of Social Work Practice*.

Martin, April (1993) *The Lesbian and Gay Parenting Handbook: Creating and Raising our Families* (New York: HarperCollins).

Martin, April (1999) 'Afterword', in G. Kaeser and P. Gillespie (eds.) *Love Makes a Family: Portraits of Lesbian, Gay, Bisexual, and Transgender Parents and Their Families* (Amherst, MA: University of Massachusetts Press): 251–2.

Martin, Del and Lyon, Phyllis (1972) *Lesbian/Woman* (New York: Bantam).

Mary, Liz and Michelle and Sarah (2004) 'SLAPPERS: A Little Bit Special and a Little Bit Ordinary', *PinkParents Magazine* (UK), 14, 40.

Mason, Jennifer (2008) 'Tangible Affinities and the Real Life Fascination of Kinship', *Sociology*, 42:1, 29–45.

Matthews, John D. and Cramer, Elizabeth P. (2006) 'Envisaging the Adoption Process to Strengthen Gay- and Lesbian-Headed Families: Recommendations for Adoption Professionals', *Child Welfare*, 85:2, 317–40.

McDermott, Janet (2002) 'Supporting Lesbian and Gay Carers and Their Children in Long Term Placements', paper presented to the British Association for Adoption & Fostering (BAAF) Medical Group Seminar, 8 October.

McDermott, Janet (2004) 'Jigsaws, Tapestries and Sticking Like Glue', *PinkParents Magazine* (UK), 14, 6–8.

McGarry, Kevin (2003) *Fatherhood for Gay Men: An Emotional and Practical Guide to Becoming a Gay Dad* (New York: Harrington Park Press).

McNay, Lois (2008) *Against Recognition* (Cambridge: Polity Press).

McNeill, Kevin F., Beth M. Rienzi and Augustine Kposowa (1998) 'Families and Parenting: A Comparison of Lesbian and Heterosexual Mothers', *Psychological Reports*, 82, 59–62.

Melvin, Murray (1998) Spoken commentary on British Film Institute DVD release of Richardson (1961).

Millbank, Jenni (2003) 'From Here to Maternity: A Review of the Research on Lesbian and Gay Families', *Australian Journal of Social Issues*, 38:4, 541–600.

Miller, Daniel (2007) 'What is a Relationship? Is Kinship Negotiated Experience?', *Ethnos*, 72:4, 535–54.

Miller, Peter and Rose, Nikolas (2008) *Governing the Present: Administering Economic, Social and Personal Life* (Cambridge: Polity Press).

Mills, C. Wright (2000 [1959]) *The Sociological Imagination*, 40th anniversary edn (Oxford: Oxford University Press).

Mink, Gwendolyn (1998) *Welfare's End* (Ithaca, NY: Cornell University Press).

Modell, Judith S. (1994) *Kinship with Strangers: Adoption and Interpretations of Kinship in American Culture* (Berkeley, CA: University of California Press).

Modell, Judith S. (2002) *A Sealed and Secret Kinship: The Culture and Practices in American Adoption* (New York: Berghahn Books).

Mooney-Somers, Julie and Golombok, Susan (2000) 'Children of Lesbian Mothers: From the 1970s to the New Millennium', *Sexual & Relationship Therapy*, 15:2, 121–6.

Moore, Mignon R. (2008) 'Gendered Power Relations Among Women: A Study of Household Decision Making in Black, Lesbian Stepfamilies', *American Sociological Review*, 73:2, 335–56.

Morgan, David H.J. (1975) *Social Theory and the Family* (London: Routledge & Kegan Paul).

Morgan, David H.J. (1985) *The Family, Politics and Social Theory* (London: Routledge & Kegan Paul).

Morgan, David H.J. (1996) *Family Connections: An Introduction to Family Studies* (Cambridge: Polity Press).

Morgan, David H.J. (1999) 'Risk and Family Practices: Accounting for Change and Fluidity in Family Life', in E.B. Silva and C. Smart (eds.) *The New Family?* (London: Sage): 13–30.

Morgan, David H.J. (2009a) *Acquaintances: The Space Between Intimates and Strangers* (Maidenhead: Open University Press).

Morgan, David H.J. (2009b) 'Rethinking "Family Practices": Intimacy, Personal Life and Other Possible Alternatives', paper presented to BSA Families and Relationships Study Group Colloquium, "Rethinking Concepts: Families, Intimacies and Personal Relationships", 6 November, London.

Morgan, David H.J. (2011) *Rethinking Family Practices* (Basingstoke: Palgrave Macmillan).

Morgan, Patricia (1995) *Farewell to the Family? Public Policy and Family Breakdown in Britain and the USA* (London: Institute of Economic Affairs (IEA) Health and Welfare Unit).

Morgan, Patricia (2000) *Marriage-Lite: The Rise of Cohabitation and Its Consequences* (London: Civitas – Institute for the Study of Civil Society).

Morgan, Patricia (2002) *Children as Trophies? Examining the Evidence on Same-Sex Parenting* (Newcastle-upon-Tyne: Christian Institute), http://www.christian.org.uk/resources/publications/marriage-the-family/ [accessed 1 April 2011].

Mulé, Nick J. (2008) 'Demarcating Gender and Sexual Diversity on the Structural Landscape of Social Work', *Critical Social Work*, 9:1, http://www.uwindsor.ca/criticalsocialwork/demarcating-gender-and-sexual-diversity-on-the-structural-landscape-of-social-work [accessed 1 April 2011].

Muñoz, José Esteban (2006) 'Thinking Beyond Antirelationality and Antiutopianism in Queer Critique', *PMLA*, 121:3, 825–6.

Murray, Heather (2010) *Not In This Family: Gays and the Meaning of Kinship in Postwar North America* (Philadelphia, PA: University of Pennsylvania Press).

Myers, Steve and Milner, Judith (2007) *Sexual Issues in Social Work* (Bristol: Policy Press).

Nardi, Peter M. (1999) *Gay Men's Friendships: Invincible Communities* (Chicago, IL: University of Chicago Press).

Nash, Catherine (2008) *Of Irish Descent: Origin Stories, Genealogy, and the Politics of Belonging* (Syracuse: Syracuse University Press).

Nelson, Fiona (1996) *Lesbian Motherhood: An Exploration of Canadian Lesbian Families* (Toronto: University of Toronto Press).

Nilan, Pam (1994) 'Gender as Positioned Identity Maintenance in Everyday Discourse', *Social Semiotics*, 4:1/2, 139–62.

Nita and Clare (1994) letter to local authority 'Complaints and Compliments – Office of the Chief Executive and Policy Co-ordinator' [anonymized].

O'Brien, Carol-Anne (1999) 'Contested Territory: Sexualities and Social Work', in A.S. Chambon, A. Irving and L. Epstein (eds.) *Reading Foucault for Social Work* (New York: Columbia University Press): 131–55.

Oparah, Julia Chinyere, Sun Yung Shin and Jane Jeong Trenka (2006) 'Introduction', in J.J. Trenka, J.C. Oparah and Y.S. Sun (eds.) *Outsiders Within: Writing on Transracial Adoption* (Cambridge: South End Press): 1–15.

Pahl, Ray and Spencer, Liz (2004) 'Personal Communities: Not Simply Families of "Fate" or "Choice"', *Current Sociology*, 52:2, 199–221.

Park, Shelley M. (2006) 'Adoptive Maternal Bodies: A Queer Paradigm for Rethinking Mothering?', *Hypatia*, 21:2, 201–26.

Park, Yoosun (2005) 'Culture as Deficit: A Critical Discourse Analysis of the Concept of Culture in Contemporary Social Work Discourse', *Journal of Sociology & Social Welfare*, 32:3, 11–33.

Parks, Cheryl A. (1998) 'Lesbian Parenthood: A Review of the Literature', *American Journal of Orthopsychiatry*, 68:3, 376–89.

Parmar, Pratibha (dir) (1989) *Fostering and Adoption by Lesbian and Gay Parents*, short film for UK Channel 4 TV 'Out on Tuesday' series.

Parrott, Brian, Annie MacIver and June Thoburn (2007) *Independent Inquiry Report into the Circumstances of Child Sexual Abuse by Two Foster Carers in Wakefield* (Wakefield: Wakefield Council).

Parsons, Talcott (1956a) 'Family Structure and the Socialization of the Child', in T. Parsons and R.F. Bales, in collaboration with J. Olds, M. Zelditch, Jr. and P.E. Slater (eds.) *Family: Socialization and Interaction Process* (London: Routledge & Kegan Paul): 35–131.

Parsons, Talcott (1956b) 'The American Family: Its Relations to Personality and to the Social Structure', in T. Parsons and R.F. Bales, in collaboration with J. Olds, M. Zelditch, Jr. and P.E. Slater (eds.) *Family: Socialization and Interaction Process* (London: Routledge & Kegan Paul): 3–33.

Patrick, Dennis (2006) 'The Story of a Gay Foster Parent', *Child Welfare*, 85:2, 123–32.

Patterson, Charlotte J. (1992) 'Children of Lesbian and Gay Parents', *Child Development*, 63, 1025–42.

Patterson, Charlotte J. (1995) 'Families of the Lesbian Baby Boom: Parents' Division of Labor and Children's Adjustment', *Developmental Psychology*, 31:1, 115–23.

Patterson, Charlotte J. (2009) 'Lesbian and Gay Parents and Their Children: A Social Science Perspective', in D.A. Hope (ed.) *Contemporary Perspectives on Lesbian, Gay, and Bisexual Identities* (New York: Springer): 141–82.

Patterson, Charlotte J. and Wainwright, Jennifer L. (2011) 'Adolescents with Same-Sex Parents: Findings from the National Longitudinal Study of Adolescent Health', in D.M. Brodzinsky and A. Pertman (eds.) *Adoption by Lesbians and Gay Men: A New Dimension in Family Diversity* (New York: Oxford University Press), forthcoming.

Peel, Elizabeth (2001) 'Mundane Heterosexism: Understanding Incidents of the Everyday', *Women's Studies International Forum*, 24:5, 541–54.

Perlesz, Amaryll, Rhonda Brown, Jo Lindsay, Ruth McNair, David deVaus and Marian Pitts (2006a) 'Family in Transition: Parents, Children and Grandparents in Lesbian Families Give Meaning to "Doing Family"', *Journal of Family Therapy*, 28, 175–99.

Perlesz, Amaryll, Rhonda Brown, Ruth McNair, Jo Lindsay, Marian Pitts and David deVaus (2006b) 'Full Spaces, Full Lives: Response to Commentary by Stephen Hicks', *Lesbian & Gay Psychology Review*, 7:2, 231–3.

Perlesz, Amaryll, Rhonda Brown, Ruth McNair, Jo Lindsay, Marian Pitts and David deVaus (2006c) 'Lesbian Family Disclosure: Authenticity and Safety within Private and Public Domains', *Lesbian & Gay Psychology Review*, 7:1, 54–65.

Pertman, Adam and Howard, Jeanne (2011) 'Adoption by Gay and Lesbian Parents', in D.M. Brodzinsky and A. Pertman (eds.) *Adoption by Lesbians and Gay Men: A New Dimension in Family Diversity* (New York: Oxford University Press), forthcoming.

Phillips, Melanie (1999) *The Sex-Change Society: Feminised Britain and the Neutered Male* (London: The Social Market Foundation).

Philp, Mark (1979) 'Notes on the Form of Knowledge in Social Work', *Sociological Review*, 27:1, 83–111.

Pidduck, Julianne (2009) 'Queer Kinship and Ambivalence: Video Autoethnographies by Jean Carlomusto and Richard Fung', *GLQ*, 15:3, 441–68.

Plummer, Ken (1995) *Telling Sexual Stories: Power, Change and Social Worlds* (London: Routledge).

Plummer, Ken (2003) *Intimate Citizenship: Private Decisions and Public Dialogues* (Seattle, WA: University of Washington Press).

Plummer, Ken (2005) 'Intimate Citizenship in an Unjust World', in M. Romero and E. Margolis (eds.) *The Blackwell Companion to Social Inequalities* (Oxford: Wiley Blackwell): 75–99.

Pollner, Melvin (1987) *Mundane Reason: Reality in Everyday and Sociological Discourse* (Cambridge: Cambridge University Press).

Popenhoe, David (1996) *Life Without Father* (New York: Free Press).

Potter, Jonathan (1996) *Representing Reality: Discourse, Rhetoric and Social Construction* (London: Sage).

Povinelli, Elizabeth (2002a) 'Notes on Gridlock: Genealogy, Intimacy, Sexuality', *Public Culture*, 14:1, 215–38.

Povinelli, Elizabeth A. (2002b) *The Cunning of Recognition: Indigenous Alterities and the Making of Australian Multiculturalism* (Durham, NC: Duke University Press).

Povinelli, Elizabeth A. (2005) 'What's Love Got to Do With It? The Race of Freedom and the Drag of Descent', *Social Analysis*, 49:2, 173–81.

Povinelli, Elizabeth A. (2006) *The Empire of Love: Toward a Theory of Intimacy, Genealogy, and Carnality* (Durham, NC: Duke University Press).

Pratt, Minnie Bruce (1990) *Crime Against Nature* (Ithaca, NY: Firebrand Books).

Pratt, Minnie Bruce (1999) 'Foreword: Family Album', in G. Kaeser and P. Gillespie (eds.) *Love Makes a Family: Portraits of Lesbian, Gay, Bisexual, and Transgender Parents and Their Families* (Amherst, MA: University of Massachusetts Press): ix–x.

Pringle, Keith (1995) *Men, Masculinities and Social Welfare* (London: University College London (UCL) Press).

Puar, Jasbir K. (2007) *Terrorist Assemblages: Homonationalism in Queer Times* (Durham, NC: Duke University Press).

Rawls, Anne Warfield (2002) 'Editor's Introduction', in H. Garfinkel *Ethnomethodology's Program: Working Out Durkheim's Aphorism* (Lanham, MD: Rowman and Littlefield): 1–64.

Rawls, Anne Warfield, Albert J. Meehan, Catherine Johnson Pettinari, Edward D. Mays and Lynetta Mosby (1997) 'The Application of Interactional Analysis to an Applied Study of Social Work', *Applied Behavioral Science Review*, 5:1, 113–39.

Redding, Richard E. (2008) 'It's Really About Sex: Same-Sex Marriage, Lesbigay Parenting, and the Psychology of Disgust', *Duke Journal of Gender Law & Policy*, 15:127, 127–93.

Reder, Peter and Duncan, Sylvia (2004) 'Making the Most of the Victoria Climbié Inquiry Report', *Child Abuse Review*, 13, 95–114.

Reece, Helen (1996) 'Subverting the Stigmatization Argument', *Journal of Law & Society*, 23:4, 484–505.

Reilly, Thom (1996) 'Gay and Lesbian Adoptions: A Theoretical Examination of Policy-Making and Organizational Decision Making', *Journal of Sociology & Social Welfare*, 23:4, 99–115.

Rhodes, Penny J. (1992) *'Racial Matching' in Fostering: The Challenge to Social Work Practice* (Aldershot: Avebury).

Richardson, Diane (2005) 'Desiring Sameness? The Rise of a Neoliberal Politics of Normalisation', *Antipode*, 37:3, 515–35.

Richardson, Tony (dir.) (1961) *A Taste of Honey*, Woodfall Film Productions. [DVD 1998, Metro Goldwyn Mayer/British Film Institute, BFIVD513].

Ricketts, Wendell (1992 [1991]) *Lesbians and Gay Men as Foster Parents* (Portland: National Child Welfare Resource Center for Management and Administration, University of Southern Maine).

Ricketts, Wendell and Achtenberg, Roberta (1987) 'The Adoptive and Foster Gay and Lesbian Parent', in F.W. Bozett (ed.) *Gay and Lesbian Parents* (New York: Praeger): 89–111.

Ricketts, Wendell and Achtenberg, Roberta (1990) 'Adoption and Foster Parenting for Lesbians and Gay Men: Creating New Traditions in Family', *Marriage & Family Review*, 14:3/4, 83–118.

Riggs, Damien W. (2004a) 'Resisting Heterosexism in Foster Carer Training: Valuing Queer Approaches to Adult Learning and Relationality', *Canadian Online Journal of Queer Studies in Education*, 1:1, http://jqstudies.library.utoronto.ca/index.php/jqstudies/article/view/3271 [accessed 1 April 2011].

Riggs, Damien W. (2004b) 'The Psychologisation of Foster Care: Implications for Lesbian and Gay Parenting', *PsyPag Quarterly*, 51, 34–43.

Riggs, Damien W. (2006a) 'Developmentalism and the Rhetoric of *Best Interests of the Child*: Challenging Heteronormative Constructions of Families and Parenting in Foster Care', *Journal of GLBT Family Studies*, 2:2, 57–73.

Riggs, Damien W. (2006b) *Priscilla, (White) Queen of the Desert: Queer Rights/Race Privilege* (New York: Peter Lang).

Riggs, Damien W. (2006c) 'What's Love Got to Do With It? Ambivalence and the National Imaginary', *International Journal of Critical Psychology*, 16, 32–52.

Riggs, Damien W. (2007a) *Becoming Parent: Lesbians, Gay Men, and Family* (Teneriffe: Post Pressed).

Riggs, Damien W. (2007b) 'On Being Acceptable: State Sanction, Race Privilege and Lesbian and Gay Parents', *Reconstruction: Studies in Contemporary Culture*, 7:1, http://reconstruction.eserver.org/071/riggs.shtml [accessed 1 April 2011].

Riggs, Damien W. (2007c) 'Reassessing the Foster-Care System: Examining the Impact of Heterosexism on Lesbian and Gay Applicants', *Hypatia*, 22:1, 132–48.

Riggs, Damien (2008) 'How Do Bodies Matter? Understanding Embodied Racialised Subjectivities', *darkmatter*, 2, http://www.darkmatter101.org/site/2008/02/23/how-do-bodies-matter-understanding-embodied-racialised-subjectivities/ [accessed 1 April 2011].

Riggs, Damien W. (2009) 'Race Privilege and its Role in the "Disappearance" of Birth Families and Adoptive Children in Debates over Adoption by Non-heterosexual

People in Australia', in D. Cuthbert and C. Spark (eds.) *Other People's Children: Adoption in Australia* (Melbourne: Australian Scholarly): 161–75.

Riggs, Damien W. (2010) *What About the Children! Masculinities, Sexualities and Hegemony* (Newcastle-upon-Tyne: Cambridge Scholars).

Riggs, Damien W. (2011) 'Australian Lesbian and Gay Foster Carers Negotiating the Child Protection System: Strengths and Challenges', *Sexuality Research & Social Policy*, 8, forthcoming.

Riggs, Damien W. and Augoustinos, Martha (2009) 'Institutional Stressors and Individual Strengths: Policy and Practice Directions for Working with Australian Lesbian and Gay Foster Carers', *Practice: Social Work in Action*, 21:2, 77–90.

Riggs, Damien W. and Due, Clemence (2010a) 'Gay Men, Race Privilege and Surrogacy in India', *Outskirts: Feminisms Along the Edge*, 22, http://www.chloe.uwa.edu.au/outskirts/archive/volume22/riggs [accessed 1 April 2011].

Riggs, Damien W. and Due, Clemence (2010b) 'The Management of Accusations of Racism in *Celebrity Big Brother*', *Discourse & Society*, 21:3, 257–71.

Roberts, Dorothy (2002) *Shattered Bonds: The Color of Child Welfare* (New York: Basic Books).

Romaine, Mary (2003) *Assessing Lesbian and Gay Foster Carers and Adopters (Practice Note 44)* (London: British Association for Adoption & Fostering (BAAF)).

Rose, Nikolas (1999) *Governing the Soul: The Shaping of the Private Self*, 2nd edn (London: Free Association Books).

Roseneil, Sasha and Budgeon, Shelley (2004) 'Cultures of Intimacy and Care Beyond "the Family": Personal Life and Social Change in the Early 21st Century', *Current Sociology*, 52:2, 135–59.

Rosky, Clifford J. (2009) 'Like Father, Like Son: Homosexuality, Parenthood, and the Gender of Homophobia', *Yale Journal of Law & Feminism*, 20, 257–355.

Ross, Lori E., Rachel Epstein, Scott Anderson and Allison Eady (2009) 'Policy, Practice, and Personal Narratives: Experiences of LGBTQ People with Adoption in Ontario, Canada', *Adoption Quarterly*, 12:3/4, 272–93.

Rubin, Gayle (1975) 'The Traffic in Women: Notes on the "Political Economy" of Sex', in Reiter, R.R. (ed.) *Toward an Anthropology of Women* (New York: Monthly Review Press): 157–210.

Rubin, Gayle (1993 [1984]) 'Thinking Sex: Notes for a Radical Theory of the Politics of Sexuality', in H. Abelove, M.A. Barale and D.M. Halperin (eds.) *The Lesbian and Gay Studies Reader* (New York: Routledge): 3–44.

Rubin, Gayle (2009) 'A Little Humility', in D.M. Halperin and V. Traub (eds.) *Gay Shame* (Chicago, IL: University of Chicago Press): 369–73.

Russett, Cynthia (2011) 'American Adoption: A Brief History', in D.M. Brodzinsky and A. Pertman (eds.) *Adoption by Lesbians and Gay Men: A New Dimension in Family Diversity* (New York: Oxford University Press), forthcoming.

Ryan, Scott D. (2000) 'Examining Social Workers' Placement Recommendations of Children with Gay and Lesbian Adoptive Parents', *Families in Society*, 81:5, 517–28.

Ryan, Scott D. (2007) 'Parent–Child Interaction Styles Between Gay and Lesbian Parents and Their Adopted Children', *Journal of GLBT Family Studies*, 3:2/3, 105–32.

Ryan, Scott and Brown, Suzanne (2011) 'Gay and Lesbian Adoptive Parents: Stressors and Strengths', in D.M. Brodzinsky and A. Pertman (eds.) *Adoption by Lesbians and Gay Men: A New Dimension in Family Diversity* (New York: Oxford University Press), forthcoming.

Ryan, Scott D. and Cash, Scottye (2004) 'Adoptive Families Headed by Gay or Lesbian Parents: A Threat...or Hidden Resource?' *Journal of Law & Public Policy*, 15:3, 443–66.

Ryan, Scott D., Sue Pearlmutter and Victor Groza (2004) 'Coming Out of the Closet: Opening Agencies to Gay and Lesbian Adoptive Parents', *Social Work*, 49:1, 85–95.

Ryan, Scott and Whitlock, Courtney (2007) 'Becoming Parents: Lesbian Mothers' Adoption Experience', *Journal of Gay & Lesbian Social Services*, 19:2, 1–23.

Ryan-Flood, Róisín (2009) *Lesbian Motherhood: Gender, Families and Sexual Citizenship* (Basingstoke: Palgrave Macmillan).

Ryburn, Murray (1991) 'The Myth of Assessment', *Adoption & Fostering*, 15:1, 20–7.

Sacks, Harvey (1995 [1989 and various earlier dates]) *Lectures on Conversation, Volumes 1 and 2* (edited by G. Jefferson) (Oxford: Blackwell).

Saffron, Lisa (2004) 'Panel Without a Clue', *PinkParents Magazine* (UK), 14, 20–1.

Savage, Dan (1998) 'The Baby', *New York Times Magazine*, 15 November, 95.

Savage, Dan (2000) *The Kid: What Happened After My Boyfriend and I Decided to Go Get Pregnant* (London: Fusion Press).

Schacher, Stephanie Jill, Carl F. Auerbach and Louise Bordeaux Silverstein (2005) 'Gay Fathers Expanding the Possibilities for Us All', *Journal of GLBT Family Studies*, 1:3, 31–52.

Schegloff, Emanuel A., Gail Jefferson and Harvey Sacks (1977) 'The Preference for Self-Correction in the Organisation of Repair in Conversation', *Language*, 53, 361–82.

Schneider, David M. (1980 [1968]) *American Kinship: A Cultural Account*, 2nd edn (Chicago, IL: University of Chicago Press).

Schneider, David M. (1984) *A Critique of the Study of Kinship* (Ann Arbor, MI: University of Michigan Press).

Sedgwick, Eve Kosofsky (1994a [1990]) *Epistemology of the Closet* (London: Penguin).

Sedgwick, Eve Kosofsky (1994b) *Tendencies* (London: Routledge).

Sedgwick, Eve Kosofsky (2003) *Touching Feeling: Affect, Pedagogy, Performativity* (Durham, NC: Duke University Press).

Segal, Lynne (ed.) (1983) *What is to be Done about the Family?* (Harmondsworth: Penguin).

Seidman, Steven (1997) *Difference Troubles: Queering Social Theory and Sexual Politics* (Cambridge: Cambridge University Press).

Sgambati, Vince (2009) 'What's Race Got to Do With It?', *Journal of GLBT Family Studies*, 5:4, 366–73.

Sharma, Arvind (1993) 'Homosexuality and Hinduism', in A. Swidler (ed.) *Homosexuality and World Religions* (Valley Forge, PA: Trinity Press): 47–80.

Shelley-Sireci, Lynn M. and Ciano-Boyce, Claudia (2002) 'Becoming Lesbian Adoptive Parents: An Exploratory Study of Lesbian Adoptive, Lesbian Birth, and Heterosexual Adoptive Parents', *Adoption Quarterly*, 6:1, 33–43.

Silvera, Makeda (1995) 'Confronting the "I" in the Eye: Black Mother, Black Daughters', in K. Arnup (ed.) *Lesbian Parenting: Living With Pride and Prejudice* (Charlottetown: Gynergy Books): 311–20.

Simpson, Bob (1994) 'Bringing the "Unclear" Family into Focus: Divorce and Remarriage in Contemporary Britain', *Man* (New Series), 29:4, 831–51.

Skeates, Jane and Jabri, Dorian (eds.) (1988) *Fostering and Adoption by Lesbians and Gay Men* (London: London Strategic Policy Unit).

Smart, Carol (2007) *Personal Life: New Directions in Sociological Thinking* (Cambridge: Polity Press).

Smart, Carol (2009) 'Relationality and Socio-Cultural Theories of Family Life', paper presented to BSA Families and Relationships Study Group Colloquium, "Rethinking Concepts: Families, Intimacies and Personal Relationships", 6 November, London.

Smith, Anna Marie (1994) *New Right Discourse on Race and Sexuality: Britain, 1968–1990* (Cambridge: Cambridge University Press).

Smith, Anna Marie (2007) *Welfare Reform and Sexual Regulation* (Cambridge: Cambridge University Press).

Smith, Anna Marie (2009) 'Reproductive Technology, Family Law, and the Postwelfare State: The California Same-Sex Parents' Rights "Victories" of 2005', *Signs*, 34:4, 827–50.

Smith, Dorothy E. (1987) *The Everyday World as Problematic: A Feminist Sociology* (Boston, MA: Northeastern University Press).

Smith, Dorothy E. (1990a) *Texts, Facts, and Femininity: Exploring the Relations of Ruling* (London: Routledge).

Smith, Dorothy E. (1990b) *The Conceptual Practices of Power: A Feminist Sociology of Knowledge* (Toronto: University of Toronto Press).

Smith, Dorothy E. (1999) *Writing the Social: Critique, Theory, and Investigations* (Toronto: University of Toronto Press).

Smith, Dorothy E. (2005) *Institutional Ethnography: A Sociology for People* (Lanham, MD: Rowman & Littlefield).

Smith, Dorothy E. (2006) 'George Smith, Political Activist as Ethnographer and Sociology for People', in C. Frampton, G. Kinsman, A.K. Thompson and K. Tilleczek (eds.) *Sociology for Changing the World: Social Movements/Social Research* (Black Point: Fernwood): 18–26.

Smith, Dorothy E. (2009) 'Categories are not Enough', *Gender & Society*, 23:1, 76–80.

Smith, George W. (1988) 'Policing the Gay Community: An Inquiry into Textually-mediated Social Relations', *International Journal of the Sociology of Law*, 16, 163–83.

Smith, George W. (1990) 'Political Activist as Ethnographer', *Social Problems*, 37:4, 629–48.

Social Services Department [anonymized] (1994) Letter from Assistant Director (Children's Services) and Chair of the Permanence Panel.

Somerville, Jennifer (2000) *Feminism and the Family: Politics and Society in the UK and USA* (Basingstoke: Macmillan).

Sourbut, Elizabeth (1996) 'Gynogenesis: A Lesbian Appropriation of Reproductive Technologies', in N. Lykke and R. Braidotti (eds.) *Between Monsters, Goddesses and Cyborgs: Feminist Confrontations with Science, Medicine and Cyberspace* (London: Zed Books): 227–41.

Speer, Susan A. (2005) *Gender Talk: Feminism, Discourse and Conversation Analysis* (London: Routledge).

Spencer, Liz and Pahl, Ray (2006) *Rethinking Friendship: Hidden Solidarities Today* (Princeton, NJ: Princeton University Press).

Spivey, Christina A. (2006) 'Adoption by Same-Sex Couples: The Relationship between Adoption Worker and Social Work Student Sex-Role Beliefs and Attitudes', *Journal of GLBT Family Studies*, 2:2, 29–56.

Stacey, Judith (1996) *In the Name of the Family: Rethinking Family Values in the Postmodern Age* (Boston, MA: Beacon Press).

Stacey, Judith (2004) 'Cruising to Familyland: Gay Hypergamy and Rainbow Kinship', *Current Sociology*, 52:2, 181–97.

Stacey, Judith (2005) 'The Families of Man: Gay Male Intimacy and Kinship in a Global Metropolis', *Signs*, 30:3, 1911–35.

Stacey, Judith (2006) 'Gay Parenthood and the Decline of Paternity as We Knew It', *Sexualities*, 9:1, 27–55.

Stacey, Judith and Biblarz, Timothy J. (2001) '(How) Does the Sexual Orientation of Parents Matter?', *American Sociological Review*, 66:2, 159–83.

Stack, Carol (1997 [1974]) *All Our Kin: Strategies for Survival in a Black Community* (New York: Basic Books).

Stanley, Liz (1992) *The Auto/biographical I: The Theory and Practice of Feminist Auto/biography* (Manchester: Manchester University Press).

Stanley, Liz (2002 [1984]) 'Should "Sex" Really be "Gender" – or "Gender" Really be "Sex"?', in S. Jackson and S. Scott (eds.) *Gender: A Sociological Reader* (London: Routledge): 31–41.

Stanley, Liz (2010) 'On Small and Big Stories of the Quotidian: The Commonplace and the Extraordinary in Narrative Inquiry', in D. Robinson, P. Fisher, T. Yeado-Lee, S.J. Robinson and P. Woodcock (eds.) *Narrative, Memory and Ordinary Lives* (Huddersfield: Huddersfield University Press): 1–24. http://www2.hud.ac.uk/hhs/nme/books/2010/index.php [accessed 1 April 2011].

Stanley, Liz and Wise, Sue (1993 [1983]) *Breaking Out Again: Feminist Ontology & Epistemology* (London: Routledge).

Steckel, Ailsa (1987) 'Psychosocial Development of Children of Lesbian Mothers', in F.W. Bozett (ed.) *Gay and Lesbian Parents* (New York: Praeger): 75–85.

Stewart, Kathleen (2007) *Ordinary Affects* (Durham: Duke University Press).

Stockton, Kathryn Bond (2002) 'Eve's Queer Child', in S.M. Barber and D.L. Clark (eds.) *Regarding Sedgwick: Essays on Queer Culture and Critical Theory* (New York: Routledge): 181–99.

Stockton, Kathryn Bond (2004) 'Growing Sideways, or Versions of the Queer Child: The Ghost, the Homosexual, the Freudian, the Innocent, and the Interval of Animal', in S. Bruhm and N. Hurley (eds.) *Curiouser: On the Queerness of Children* (Minneapolis, MN: University of Minnesota Press): 277–315.

Stockton, Kathryn Bond (2009) *The Queer Child, or Growing Sideways in the Twentieth Century* (Durham, NC: Duke University Press).

Stone, Linda (2006 [1997]) *Kinship & Gender: An Introduction,* 3rd edn (Boulder, CO: Westview Press).

Strah, David with Susanna Margolis and Kris Timken (photographs) (2003) *Gay Dads: A Celebration of Fatherhood* (New York: Jeremy P. Tarcher/Penguin).

Strathern, Marilyn (1992) *After Nature: English Kinship in the Late Twentieth Century* (Cambridge: Cambridge University Press).

Strathern, Marilyn (1993) 'Review of: Weston, Kath, *Families We Choose: Lesbians, Gays, Kinship*', *Man* (new series), 28:1, 195–6.

Strathern, Marilyn (1996) 'Cutting the Network', *Journal of the Royal Anthropological Institute* (new series), 2:3, 517–35.

Strathern, Marilyn (2005) *Kinship, Law and the Unexpected: Relatives Are Always a Surprise* (Cambridge: Cambridge University Press).

Strong, Thomas (2002) 'Kinship Between Judith Butler and Anthropology? A Review Essay', *Ethnos*, 67:3, 401–18.

Sukthankar, Ashwini (1999) 'Editor's Note', in A. Sukthankar (ed.) *Facing the Mirror: Lesbian Writing from India* (New Delhi: Penguin Books): xi.

Suleri, Sara (1992) *The Rhetoric of English India* (Chicago, IL: University of Chicago Press).

Sullivan, Ann (1995) 'Policy Issues in Gay and Lesbian Adoption', *Adoption & Fostering*, 19:4, 21–5.

Sullivan, Maureen (2004) *The Family of Woman: Lesbian Mothers, their Children, and the Undoing of Gender* (Berkeley, CA: University of California Press).

Sullivan, Richard and Harrington, Margaret (2009) 'The Politics and Ethics of Same-Sex Adoption', *Journal of GLBT Family Studies*, 5, 235–46.

Symons, Johnny (dir) (2002) *Daddy & Papa*, New Day Films. [DVD 2006, Persistent Films].

Tan, Tony Xing and Baggerly, Jennifer (2009) 'Behavioral Adjustment of Adopted Chinese Girls in Single-Mother, Lesbian-Couple, and Heterosexual-Couple Households', *Adoption Quarterly*, 12:3/4, 171–86.

Tasker, Fiona (1999) 'Children in Lesbian-led Families: A Review', *Clinical Child Psychology & Psychiatry*, 4:2, 153–66.

Tasker, Fiona (2002) 'Lesbian and Gay Parenting', in A. Coyle and C. Kitzinger (eds.) *Lesbian & Gay Psychology: New Perspectives* (Oxford: Blackwell): 81–97.

Tasker, Fiona (2005) 'Lesbian Mothers, Gay Fathers, and Their Children: A Review', *Journal of Developmental & Behavioral Pediatrics*, 26:3, 224–40.

Tasker, Fiona (2010) 'Same-Sex Parenting and Child Development: Reviewing the Contribution of Parental Gender', *Journal of Marriage & Family*, 72, 35–40.

Tasker, Fiona L. and Golombok, Susan (1991) 'Children Raised by Lesbian Mothers: The Empirical Evidence', *Family Law*, 21, 184–7.

Tasker, Fiona and Golombok, Susan (1995) 'Adults Raised as Children in Lesbian Families', *American Journal of Orthopsychiatry*, 65:2, 203–15.

Tasker, Fiona L. and Golombok, Susan (1997) *Growing Up in a Lesbian Family: Effects on Child Development* (New York: The Guilford Press).

Taylor, Yvette (2009) *Lesbian and Gay Parenting: Securing Social and Educational Capital* (Basingstoke: Palgrave Macmillan).

Thadani, Giti (1996) *Sakhiyani: Lesbian Desire in Ancient and Modern India* (London: Cassell).

Thompson, Charis (2005) *Making Parents: The Ontological Choreography of Reproductive Technologies* (Cambridge: The Massachusetts Institute of Technology (MIT) Press).

Thompson, Julie M. (2002) *Mommy Queerest: Contemporary Rhetorics of Lesbian Maternal Identity* (Amherst, MA: University of Massachusetts Press).

Thompson, Neil (1997 [1993]) *Anti-Discriminatory Practice*, 2nd edn (Basingstoke: Macmillan).

Tobias, Sarah (2005) 'Several Steps Behind: Gay and Lesbian Adoption', in S. Haslanger and C. Witt (eds.) *Adoption Matters: Philosophical and Feminist Essays* (Ithaca, NY: Cornell University Press): 95–111.

Trenka, Jane Jeong (2009) 'Transnational Adoption and the "Financialization of Everything"', *Conducive Magazine*, August/September, http://www.conducivemag.com/2009/08/transnational-adoption-and-the-"financialization-of-everything"/ [accessed 1 April 2011].

Turner, William B. (2000) *A Genealogy of Queer Theory* (Philadelphia, PA: Temple University Press).

Vaid, Urvashi (1995) *Virtual Equality: The Mainstreaming of Gay and Lesbian Liberation* (New York: Anchor Books).

Van Gelderen, Loes, Nanette Gartrell, Henny Bos and Jo Hermanns (2009) 'Stigmatization and Resilience in Adolescent Children of Lesbian Mothers', *Journal of GLBT Family Studies*, 5, 268–79.

Wardle, Lynn D. (1997) 'The Potential Impact of Homosexual Parenting on Children', *University of Illinois Law Review*, 3, 833–920.

Ware, Vron and Back, Les (2002) *Out of Whiteness: Color, Politics, and Culture* (Chicago, IL: University of Chicago Press).

Warner, Michael (1993) 'Introduction', in M. Warner (ed.) *Fear of a Queer Planet: Queer Politics and Social Theory* (Minneapolis, MN: University of Minnesota Press): vii–xxxi.

Warner, Michael (1999) *The Trouble with Normal: Sex, Politics, and the Ethics of Queer Life* (Cambridge: Harvard University Press).

Weeks, Jeffrey (2007) *The World We Have Won: The Remaking of Erotic and Intimate Life* (London: Routledge).

Weeks, Jeffrey (2008) 'Regulation, Resistance, Recognition', *Sexualities*, 11:6, 787–92.

Weeks, Jeffrey, Brian Heaphy and Catherine Donovan (2001) *Same Sex Intimacies: Families of Choice and other Life Experiments* (London: Routledge).

West, Candace and Fenstermaker, Sarah (2002) 'Accountability in Action: The Accomplishment of Gender, Race and Class in a Meeting of the University of California Board of Regents', *Discourse & Society*, 13:4, 537–63.

West, Candace and Zimmerman, Don H. (2002 [1987]) 'Doing Gender', in S. Fenstermaker and C. West (eds.) *Doing Gender, Doing Difference: Inequality, Power, and Institutional Change* (New York: Routledge): 3–23.

Weston, Kath (1991) *Families We Choose: Lesbians, Gays, Kinship* (New York: Columbia University Press).

Weston, Kath (1998) *Long Slow Burn: Sexuality and Social Science* (New York: Routledge).

Weston, Kath (1999) 'Introduction: Capturing More Than the Moment: Lesbian/ Gay Families in the Making', in G. Kaeser and P. Gillespie (eds.) *Love Makes a Family: Portraits of Lesbian, Gay, Bisexual, and Transgender Parents and Their Families* (Amherst, MA: University of Massachusetts Press): 3–10.

Wetherell, Margaret (1998) 'Positioning and Interpretative Repertoires: Conversation Analysis and Post-Structuralism in Dialogue', *Discourse & Society*, 9:3, 387–412.

White, Vicky (2006) *The State of Feminist Social Work* (London: Routledge).

Williams, Val (1994) *Who's Looking at the Family?* (London: Barbican Art Gallery).

Winnubst, Shannon (2006) *Queering Freedom* (Bloomington, IN: Indiana University Press).

Wise, Sue and Stanley, Liz (2004) 'Beyond Marriage: "The Less said about Love and Life-Long Continuance Together the Better"', *Feminism & Psychology*, 14:2, 332–43.

Wolpert, Ellen (2006) *Testimonial letter on behalf of Cambridge (MA) Community Partnerships for Children* (Amherst, MA: Family Diversity Projects), http://www.familydiv.org/lovemakesafamily.php [accessed 1 April 2011].

Woodford, Michael R., Katharine Sheets, Kristin Scherrer, Roxanne d'Eon-Blemings, Ingrid Tenkate and Blair Adams (2010) 'Lesbian Adoptive Couples: Responding to Shifting Identities and Social Relationships', *Affilia*, 25:3, 278–90.

Yngvesson, Barbara (2010) *Belonging in an Adopted World: Race, Identity, and Transnational Adoption* (Chicago, IL: University of Chicago Press).

Young, Michael and Willmott, Peter (2007 [1957]) *Family and Kinship in East London* (London: Penguin).

Zimmerman, Don H. (1992) 'They Were All Doing Gender, But They Weren't All Passing: Comment on Rogers', *Gender & Society*, 6:2, 192–8.

Zimmerman, Don H. and Pollner, Melvin (1973 [1970]) 'The Everyday World as a Phenomenon', in J. Douglas (ed.) *Understanding Everyday Life: Toward the Reconstruction of Sociological Knowledge* (London: Routledge & Kegan Paul): 80–103.

Index